S0-BFD-381

THE FABRIC OF THEOLOGY

The Fabric of Theology

A Prolegomenon to Evangelical Theology

Richard Lints

Reproduced by permission of
Wm. B. Eerdmans Publishing Co.

Wipf and Stock Publishers
150 West Broadway • Eugene OR 97401

1999

Copyright © 1993 by Wm. B. Eerdmans Publishing Co.
255 Jefferson Ave. S.E., Grand Rapids, Mich. 49503
All rights reserved

Reprinted by *Wipf and Stock Publishers* 1999
150 West Broadway • Eugene OR 97401

Previously Published by Eerdman's Publishing Co., 1993.

Unless otherwise noted, Scripture references in this work are taken from the HOLY
BIBLE: NEW INTERNATIONAL VERSION. Copyright © 1973, 1978, 1984 by
the International Bible Society. Used by permission of Zondervan Bible Publishers.

To Ann, my best friend,
whose entire fabric is woven
with grace and kindness.

Contents

PART II
Theology: Past and Present

PART III
Theology: Frameworks and Visions

Acknowledgments

THE WRITING of books is most often a labor of love. The writing of this book has been no exception. However, I also realize that many others have contributed selflessly to this project. I would like to extend to them heartfelt thanks (and recognition) for their time, efforts, and good judgment (especially where it prevailed over my initial thinking).

My sincere gratitude goes to the Association of Theological Schools and the Pew Foundation for a generous grant that made possible much of the research for this book. The trustees and the administration of Gordon-Conwell Theological Seminary also granted me a sabbatical year to write the book. That year was spent in the delightful surroundings of Duke Divinity School, the full resources of which were extended to me by the dean, Dennis Campbell.

My deepest personal gratitude goes to George Marsden, who served as a consultant to my project for the ATS/Pew grant. He was a source of much encouragement and critical insight and a wonderful conversation partner during the year in Raleigh/Durham. His constant, interested questions improved the manuscript all along the way. (Unfortunately the same cannot be said for his work on my golf game.) Paul Helm also served as a consultant to the project and faithfully read the manuscript and offered very helpful comments. These two individuals bear much responsibility for whatever is good in this manuscript. They are to be absolved of any responsibility for that which is lacking, however; that can be attributed to my stubbornness in not having listened when I probably ought to have.

Many others have contributed to the conversation out of which this book came. My colleagues at Gordon-Conwell continue to challenge me to think more carefully and biblically. In particular, the faculty involved with and the discussion arising from the biblical-theological forum at Gordon-Conwell on issues relating to this project have proven especially influential in my own thinking. From sister institutions, Richard Gaffin, John Feinberg, and Mark Noll have also read parts of the manuscript and were extremely helpful. Robert Neville and Gabriel Fackre interacted formally with a key chapter during one of our lively Boston Theological Society meetings and they are much to be thanked. Jon Pott at Eerdmans and Tim Straayer, my editor there, have played a significant role in making this manuscript far clearer and far more readable than it was when it first arrived on their desks.

I have taught much of this material in classes, and, as I suspect is normal, the ideas contained herein were most carefully scrutinized in that context. It is a joy to teach at Gordon-Conwell with students as bright and committed as those that have passed through my courses. My Byington research assistants over the past couple of years (Craig Troxel, Judi Hornibrook, Dale Westervelt, Joel Scandrett, and Kurt Peterson) have helped in diverse ways toward the completion of the book. Special thanks go to Jamie Hutchinson, who persevered through an independent study on this material and whose comments were unfailingly helpful and insightful.

Finally, a very great debt of gratitude is owed my family. They have spent countless hours without Dad while he stared at the computer, and they have gone countless places with Dad in search of yet one more piece of the research puzzle. My wife, Ann, has remained kind, gentle, and patient with a husband who too often has said it is almost finished. She has also graciously interacted with much of the material in this manuscript and helped to keep my focus on what was important. Katie, Sarah, and Lucas continued to remind me that what I was writing about was indeed ultimately important, though they did not fail to remind me that turning off the computer occasionally was also very important. The book is much more a testimony to their perseverance than to mine.

PART I

THEOLOGY:
TEXTS AND CONTEXTS

CHAPTER 1

Preliminaries to Prolegomena

Truth thoroughly digested is essential to the growth of Christian character in the individual and in the church. All knowledge of God has its influence upon character, but most of all the knowledge of spiritual facts in their relations.

Augustus Hopkins Strong[1]

INTRODUCTION

CHILDREN'S books often reflect the concerns of the broader culture in which they are composed. My wife came across a children's book in our local public library recently and thought it interesting enough to bring home. Its plot seemed relatively intricate for the intended audience of three- and four-year-olds. When my wife read the book to our children, they were constantly asking her to slow down. They seemed intrigued with the complexity of the story and bombarded her with questions about it. The moral of the story concerned the relationship between truth-telling and peer pressure. What made the story especially compelling in our children's eyes was the fact that it did not conclude with an easy moral victory. In the end, the little boy who had remained faithful to the truth did not receive accolades for having done so.

---

1. Strong, *Systematic Theology: A Compendium and Commonplace-Book Designed for the Use of Theological Students* (Rochester, N.Y.: E. R. Andrews, 1886), pp. 9-10.

My wife and I reflected together on how different this seemed from most of the children's literature our evangelical subculture produces. It provided a thoughtful and complex narrative that led our children to think about fundamental moral issues in complex ways and in fact challenged their character. It stood in stark contrast to so much of the current crop of shallow evangelical children's literature (and music) that seems aimed at entertaining children but not changing them in any way. Psalty simply sings a song and the problems (moral and otherwise) go away. A popular evangelical children's Bible is written in the format of a comic strip complete with easy answers to tough questions. And so on and on.

This is not a book about children's literature. It is a book about theology — a topic not in vogue in society at large or in evangelical circles. But like current children's literature, current theology gives evidence of a central moral vacuum created by a dearth of serious and sustained reflection. Christian character cannot be created without a kind of thinking that strains the soul. Children who are raised on literature uninformed by a theology of suffering will be that much more likely to develop into morally shallow and unreflectively selfish adults. Adults who are not driven by a theological vision will be driven by a vision of expediency. Many cultural analysts are arguing that expedience has become a dominating value among today's evangelicals.[2]

Evangelicals pride themselves on their commitment to the proclamation of truth — the truth of the gospel. Given that fact, it may seem ironic that evangelicalism is now characterized more by cultural accommodation than by resistance to cultural trends that have relativized the very concept of truth. Theory and practice have been divorced, and evangelicals, along with society at large, have chosen to stand on the "practical" side of the chasm between them. The problem is that without bridges to theoretical grounding, they have no sure means by which to determine the "rightness" of any given practice. They have declared certain behaviors, such as abortion, to be immoral, but such declarations are often divorced from a theology of life and so simply serve as red

2. See, for example, Os Guinness, *The American Hour: A Time of Reckoning and the Once and Future Role of Faith* (New York: Free Press, 1993); James Davison Hunter, *American Evangelicalism: Conservative Religion and the Quandary of Modernity* (New Brunswick, N.J.: Rutgers University Press, 1983); Martin Marty, "The Revival of Evangelicalism and Southern Religion," in *Varieties of Southern Evangelicalism*, ed. David Edwin Harrell, Jr. (Macon: Mercer University Press, 1981), pp. 17-21; and Ken Myers, *All God's Children and Blue Suede Shoes: Christianity and Popular Culture* (Westchester, Ill.: Crossway Books, 1989).

flags, effectively distinguishing the evangelical camp from others but not really connecting to anything else in their lives. Too often evangelicals view morality in terms of the great controversies of the day rather than in terms of connections to older and more substantive notions of virtue and character.

Theology ought to possess a pride of place in evangelicalism, but, like serious biblical study, it has on the whole been relegated to the backwaters of a few theological seminaries. The study of God is increasingly being replaced by a fascination with the self. Like their archenemy Rudolf Bultmann, evangelicals have begun to embrace "relevance" as a fundamental criterion of truth.

Ken Myers has argued eloquently that evangelicalism has responded to modern culture by creating a look-alike culture.[3] It has sought to mimic the cultural forms of modern American society in an effort to share in its overwhelming popularity. Christian soap operas, Christian exercise videos, and Christian heavy metal music have all been created in the hope of grabbing some of the unquestioned success of their secular counterparts. Few evangelicals have grappled with the toll that this cultural accommodation takes on the message of the gospel. They have all but jettisoned such key themes as suffering, humility, meekness, courage, and truth from their thought.

It is not my intent in this book to describe the interface between modern popular culture and serious theology, but I am concerned about the profound influence that modern culture has on the practice and reception of serious theology in our evangelical subculture. I do not argue that theology must be fundamentally revamped to meet the needs of modernity; rather, I argue (1) that modernity is a force with which we must reckon and (2) that we cannot construct theology without a profound recognition of this fact.

Further, I should point out that I do not intend this book to serve as a philosophical justification of the theological project. A concern for the conceptual evidence in favor of maintaining belief in God in an age of unbelief is interesting and important in its own right, but that is not what I will be talking about in these pages. Nor is it my primary concern to offer a defense of the place of theology in the academy or even in the education of the church today. It is vital that we understand the relationship between theology and the other disciplines, but this is not my

---

3. See chaps. 1, 9, and 10 of Myers's *All God's Children and Blue Suede Shoes.*

focus here. Nor does the principal focus of this book fall on the actual doing of theology, although that endeavor is of critical import for the purposes of this study. My principal aim in this work is simply to describe the theological project. In an age in which theology has come into disrepute, this will appear to some a hopeless cause, but, hopeless or not, the task must be confronted. We must seek to create again eyes that would see, ears that would hear, and minds that would think. In a culture that lacks a sustained and serious desire for reflection, the call to think theologically will undoubtedly fall on many deaf ears. However, in the face of the looming cultural crisis, it is my hope that it will also reach a few that are receptive.

How ought we to reconstruct the capacity for theological thinking? People think in pictures today. Images dominate the mental landscape. Even the movement from one image to another occurs along lines established in large measure by cultural habit rather than by way of any natural connections between the images. We have all had the experience of being reintroduced to images of specific events and places when we hear a special song. The connection between the song and the events is seldom causal in any way: the lyrics and music do not provide an "interpretation" of the events. The relation between them is arbitrary; that song just happened to be playing when we were originally immersed in the events. In this sort of context, connecting mental images by way of reasonable and logical thinking, let alone theological thinking, will appear to beg important questions. The argument that thinking and reflecting on the work and words of God ought to be the means by which we bring coherence to the disparate mental images of the modern person is open to the criticism that it assumes the truth of the conclusion we are attempting to establish — namely, that truth is best established by thinking and reflecting. The project will not appear "reasonable" to many modern evangelicals because this is not the manner in which they normally connect up the images of their own lives. They live on the practical side of the chasm, and such values as coherence and reasonableness are not preeminently important to them.

In a day when lives are assiduously disjointed, it may seem to make little sense to "argue" for the unity of theology with the rest of the educational curriculum of the university or even for the importance of its role in Christian education in the church. With lives so compartmentalized, how can knowledge be unified and coherent? Indeed, the rampant pluralism of modernity has made it virtually impossible to "argue" in any traditional sense. We cannot assume either a common rationality or a coherence to the vast amounts of information that constantly bombard us. It would not be going too far to say that the epistemology of the typical modern person is essentially schizophrenic. Knowledge does not fit together. A modern cultural critic characterizes this phenomenon in terms of the "repaganization" of the world — our tendency to interpret life through the fragmented imagistic world of TV.[4] What hope does theology have in such a context?

[My goal in this book is to draw a simple picture — a picture of theology. I want to provide an alternative to the fragmented picture of modernity, a picture marked by coherence and organic unity, a picture of theology as a whole piece of fabric rather than a patchwork quilt. I seek to provide an image that challenges the reigning paradigms of thought and life. Actually, I seek to provide a theological *vision* more than a theological *image,* a vision that can facilitate the reinterpretation of life, of how we think, act, and live.]

To achieve that goal, I will offer some methodological suggestions about how we might think anew about the reigning images of theology and thereby recapture a theological way of thinking about the world. Technically speaking, this is a work in "theological method" — a phrase that identifies its place in the world of the subspecialties of theology proper. But since people rarely think of theology as a discipline in a coherent sense any longer,[I would prefer to characterize the central aim of this work not as a curricular defense of some subspecialty within the theological curriculum but rather as an attempt to sketch a picture which suggests that a theological way of thinking about the world is both possible in the modern world and absolutely vital to the proclamation of the gospel.]

Along the way, I offer a number of case studies to illustrate essential points. People think in terms of stories, and I have tried to connect theology up to stories — fundamentally the story of God, but also stories from people in the past. I have also attempted to understand the battleground on which the theological vision competes — the modern world and its alleged successor, postmodernism. The cultural crisis looming on the horizon of Western civilization is captured well by postmodern

---

4. See Camille Paglia, *Sexual Personae: Art and Decadence from Nefertiti to Emily Dickinson* (New York: Random House, 1989). See also Neil Postman, *Amusing Ourselves to Death: Public Discourse in the Age of Show Business* (New York: Viking Press, 1985).

thinkers, and perhaps if we enter into dialogue with them, we evangelicals may catch something of the crisis and be awakened from our theological slumbers. This should help to account for large sections of this
book that one might not expect to appear in a treatise on "theological
method." Given the age in which we live, such material seems to me
justifiable.

The issues examined in this book are preliminary to the actual
framing of the theological vision. Methodological questions have to be
answered before turning to the larger task. What is theology after all?
What is a theological vision? How do theology and culture relate? How
does the construction of dogma relate to the biblical text? Where does
one's religious tradition fit in? What principles of organization (e.g.,
historical, philosophical, cultural) ought to be used in theology? How
might one go about finding principles to determine which principles
ought to be employed (the metamethodological question)? These and a
host of other knotty questions are the proper purview of a work on
theological method, and in this book I attempt to speak to them.

One question — actually a pair of interrelated questions — sum-
marizes this central concern: What is a theological vision, and how does
one construct such a vision? It may seem strange to think of a theological
vision as something that is constructed. Is it not the case that God has
revealed himself in the Scriptures, and is theology not therefore simply
a matter of reading the truth about God off the pages of Scripture? To
some extent, the answer to both questions is Yes, but to proceed no
further than that in response to these complex questions is to engage in
[the "fundamentalist fallacy" — the conviction that God reveals himself
outside of a cultural setting to communicate timeless truths to people
who themselves are not influenced by their own cultural setting.]

It is my firm conviction that people are deeply influenced in how
they think and how they express their thoughts by the culture they
inhabit. This significantly complicates the task of discovering and communicating the entire counsel of God. And the task is further complicated by the reality of sin in all our lives, influencing how we think and
also how we communicate our thoughts.

If God has in fact revealed himself, then this revelation should
be normative for our thinking about God. If God has also given some
indication about the purposes of history, then this revelation should be
normative for our thinking about the world and our place in it. To
frame a theological vision is simply to attempt to capture in a careful

and deliberate manner this "way of thinking" about God, the world, and ourselves. A theological vision seeks to capture the entire counsel of God as revealed in the Scriptures and to communicate it in a conceptuality that is native to the theologian's own age. A theological vision invites one to commit to a peculiar "way of thinking," and this involves discovering as well as recovering the revelation of God and then understanding how that revelation affects the way one thinks and lives. When we realize that everyone has some "way of thinking" about God, the world, and humanity, we ought to realize that everyone has a theological vision. But a question remains for evangelicals arriving at this point: How do we construct a theological vision carefully, deliberately, and biblically?

Answering this question is made a little more difficult by the fact that evangelicals have not typically written books on theological method. On the whole, evangelicals simply write theology. They do not think much about what it means to write theologically or to think in terms of methodological constraints. The few major evangelical theologies written during the past fifty years have typically included nothing more than a short section on theological prolegomena, and these have characteristically served more to mask the underlying complexity of the methodological questions of the age than to deal with it.[5] Nor has the difficulty of communicating methodologically in a subculture that does not think methodologically been much noticed.

In Chapter 2, I take a closer look at why evangelicals have tended not to ask questions about theological method, and I offer a brief historical diagnosis of this void. It is imperative to understand the void as part of a larger disinclination on the part of evangelicals to think theologically. It is important that evangelicals comprehend the intellectual and cultural context that informs their own vision of the world, for unless they do so, they will simply continue to make the same mistakes they have made in the past.

Peter Berger has argued that every culture accepts certain beliefs and behaviors as normal and reasonable and then proceeds to judge all

---

5. Some important works have omitted any reference to theological method at all. See, for example, G. C. Berkouwer, *Studies in Dogmatics*, 14 vols. (Grand Rapids: William B. Eerdmans, 1952-1961); Louis Berkhof, *Systematic Theology*, 2 vols. (Grand Rapids: William B. Eerdmans, 1938); and Donald Bloesch, *Essentials of Evangelical Theology* (San Francisco: Harper & Row, 1978).

other proposed belief and action in light of these established standards, which he calls "plausibility structures."[6] If we are going to discuss an evangelical theological method and an evangelical theological vision, it is essential that we identify the plausibility structures unique to evangelical culture. There are a number of ways to uncover these structures. For example, the fact that many evangelicals view God as an agent of the transformation of the self and understand their relationship with God largely in terms of "self-esteem" gives us insight into certain aspects of their plausibility structures and hence into their vision of reality. It is important that we take such matters into account before we attempt to offer an alternative theological vision (or at least alternative aspects of the evangelical theological vision).

My pointed interest in evangelicalism may seem strangely out of place in a work devoted to theological method. Does one not believe and behave in response to methodological constraints simply because they are biblical or true or cogent or reasonable — rather than because they are specifically evangelical? If Berger is right, the answer is No. People believe and behave out of a particular context, and we have to understand that context before we can understand the methodological issues at hand. Chapter 2 is devoted to a consideration of the influence of culture and the evangelical subculture on theological method.

This is not to suggest that what follows is primarily a work of cultural analysis, however, either of modernity as a culture or of evangelicalism as a subculture within modernity. But some cultural analysis is necessary because of the interconnection between theology and life. Although culture does not determine one's theological vision (or lack thereof), it does influence that vision, and evangelicals are risking much by failing to take this influence seriously.

In Chapters 3 and 4 I lay out the framework into which a theological vision fits, drawing attention to key assumptions in the construction of both the framework and the vision. In particular, I analyze the path or trajectory through which redemptive revelation moves to reach us in the modern age. All theologians (and everyone is a theologian) have several filters through which they hear the revelation of God. They hear as

---

6. See Peter Berger, Brigitte Berger, and Hansfried Kellner, *The Homeless Mind: Modernization and Consciousness* (Garden City, N.Y.: Doubleday, 1974); and Peter Berger, *A Rumor of Angels: Modern Society and the Rediscovery of the Supernatural* (Garden City, N.Y.: Doubleday, 1969).

participants in their own culture. They hear as individuals in a certain religious tradition and as part of a certain church community. They hear as individuals with certain sets of experiences and certain capacities for reason. The movement of the biblical revelation through these filters is often referred to as the theological trajectory, and it is this trajectory that provides the conceptual parameters within which a theological framework is constructed.

In Chapter 5 I offer several case studies from the history of Christianity to shed some light on the methodological task in a variety of theological, cultural, and historical contexts. These case studies serve not simply as historical explorations but as models and paradigms for an evangelical theological vision. They are meant to highlight significant questions that for a host of reasons have not been raised in our own day and that must be raised if modern evangelicals are to have a coherent theological framework. By way of contrast, in Chapter 6 I analyze postmodern theology in an effort not only to elucidate a significant and contending theological vision in the present era but also in an effort to unearth methodological questions that evangelicals have unfortunately failed to ask even though they are critical for the framing of a contemporary evangelical theological vision.

In the final three chapters, I offer a proposal for the construction of an evangelical theological framework and vision. The proposal is greatly dependent upon the notion of "redemptive history" and its role in holding the Scriptures together organically and theologically. As a result, I take some care to explain this concept of "redemptive history" and its implications for a theological vision. I conclude by exploring several important consequences of this theological vision and their implications for evangelical spirituality.

But before turning more directly to those preliminaries, it is necessary to address a few preliminaries to the preliminaries. What is a theological vision? What is a theological framework? What kinds of concepts are these? How do they apply to a volume on theological prolegomena? Further, what does one assume in having as a goal the construction of a theological framework and the appropriation of a theological vision? What kinds of philosophical assumptions are necessary to get the project off the ground in the first place?

A work on method must start somewhere and assume certain things. Those assumptions ought to be made clear from the outset. I would urge those who disagree either with the way the assumptions are stated or with the assumptions themselves to bear with the work nonetheless. If the assumptions are not to your liking initially, the results might warrant a reconsideration in the end.

As I have already suggested, this work is avowedly evangelical in its intent. I do not apologize for this. But it is my sincere hope that this assertion does not serve to cut off dialogue between evangelicals and nonevangelicals on the topics I discuss in these pages. Part of what follows is criticism of the evangelical perspective — criticism that has been echoed in other quarters of the theological world. Part of what follows is designed to promote discussion by more clearly identifying the questions that an evangelical theological method must address. And another part of what follows is meant to stimulate dialogue with nonevangelicals for the purpose of helping evangelicals to understand themselves and others better.

[Theology is more than just autobiography.[7] Yet each theologian does have an autobiography to relate,]and mine is an evangelical autobiography. This ought not to discredit what I have to say, nor do I presume that what I have to say should assume a special authority simply because it is delivered from that particular vantage point. My hope is that it will warrant a hearing on its own merits.

THE NATURE AND PURPOSE
OF A THEOLOGICAL VISION

Each of us possesses a "way to think about the world."[8] Though individuals may have similar experiences, they may understand those experiences differently. Part of the reason for these differences is that different individuals employ different conceptual frameworks as they seek to understand the nature and character of their experiences. An astrologer may assume that certain victories in war take place because of the relative positioning of the stars. A military strategist may attribute the same

---

7. I differ strongly with John Hick on this point. In his vision of world theology *God Has Many Names* (London: Macmillan, 1980), especially the first two chapters, Hick offers a description of his own spiritual pilgrimage that is supposed to demonstrate how theological beliefs arise simply and solely because of biographical considerations.

8. Here and subsequently, I use the term *world* to refer to all that exists, including myself and God. No intended metaphysical assumptions are implied in the use of the term.

victories to the superiority of the winning forces and strategic planning. An Old Testament prophet assumed that victory in war came solely by the hand of God. The same events are "explained" in three different ways.

Are we to conclude that the experiences of these three individuals can "rightly" be understood in any of these three ways? Or is one of the "explanations" true and the others false? Does it matter how the experiences are "explained"? How are we to adjudicate among competing "ways to think about the world" if a given set of experiences is cited as evidence in favor of each? In order to get at these questions, we will have to pay some attention to the concept of a "way to think about the world." From this general discussion, we will draw some important conclusions regarding our specific concern about a "theological way to think about the world" or what might be called a "theological framework."

We might picture a person's perspective on his or her experiences as something like a map or matrix on which certain experiences and actions are placed and arranged. The significance of any given experience would in part be a function of where it was placed on the map. And the shape and character of the map would influence to a great extent where any particular experience or action would be placed on it. An individual hearing certain words or seeing certain things would grant them a significance determined on the basis of the role they played on the map, on the basis of the relationships to other words or experiences. These new experiences might "fit together" or they might be "in conflict," but in any event it would be the matrix that would inform the individual about what it means for experiences and actions to "fit together" and to be in "conflict." The matrix itself helps to place one's experiences in a certain order and helps one to understand them in a certain way.

Bob overhears his wife talking on the telephone about a meeting the following morning in an undisclosed location with a person whose name he does not recognize. He attaches no great significance to the matter and moves on to deal with something else. Sam overhears his wife engaged in a similar conversation and immediately assumes that she is having an adulterous affair. Both men have heard exactly the same conversation, and yet they understand it very differently because they are mapping their respective experiences on different matrices.

The matrix is neither identical with nor separate from the experiences and actions. Yet the matrix is absolutely essential for understanding the experiences and actions. We cannot make any neat and tidy distinction between the matrix and the experience, though we can describe a conceptual relationship between them.[9] The map is not some neutral entity simply waiting to be filled up with experiences. The matrix is actually liable to change as it incorporates certain kinds of experiences. It may also change in response to sociological factors — political forces, economic needs, and so forth. This is to say that the meaning of any given experience is not entirely determined by the matrix even though it is greatly influenced by it. Likewise, the matrix both influences and is influenced by the experiences.

People are aware of their matrices to different degrees. Laura may think long and hard about the matrix she possesses and try with great energy and reflection to change it. Phil might simply accept the reality of his matrix without making any serious effort to alter it in any way. Amy might be wholly unaware that she has a matrix even though she inevitably and consistently acts and believes in accord with it. Those who, like Amy, remain largely ignorant of their matrices will be the group most likely to be controlled by them.

Early fundamentalists argued with great passion and energy that they were solely interested in trying to return to the simple faith of the Bible.[10] However, much of their dispensational eschatology, their peculiar brand of ecclesial independence, and their trenchant warfare on the academy was often more a reflection of their own Americanized matrix than a reflection of the Bible.[11] The doctrine of manifest destiny that has long intrigued Americans is especially adaptable to the speculations of premillennial dispensationalists. The rugged individualism that

---

9. There are connections here to the central concerns expressed by Donald Davidson in his very influential article "On the Very Idea of a Conceptual Scheme," *Proceedings of the American Philosophical Association* (1974): 5-20. Davidson, a prominent Anglo-American philosopher, argues against absolute relativism by suggesting that different conceptual schemes cannot ever be completely incommensurable. His argument in grounded partly in his assertion that we cannot make a valid dualistic distinction between "conceptual schemes" and the content (i.e., experience) that can be poured into them. It is not the case that people have "bare experiences" that they simply drop into their particular conceptual schemes. He concludes that people with divergent conceptual schemes are still able to converse with each other because of common experiences that "overflow" the different conceptual schemes.

10. See chaps. 5-7 of *The American Quest for the Primitive Church*, ed. Richard Hughes (Urbana, Ill.: University of Illinois Press, 1988).

11. For the finest exposition and defense of this thesis, see George Marsden, *Fundamentalism and American Culture: The Shaping of Twentieth Century Evangelicalism, 1870-1925* (New York: Oxford University Press, 1980). I have more to say on this point in Chap. 2.

has long been associated with the American character has led quite naturally to certain varieties of ecclesial independence. And the long-running American distrust of large institutions was easily translated into the fundamentalist distrust of the modern university and the learning associated with it.[12] The Bible was not the only source from which early fundamentalism drew, the express statements of their preachers to the contrary notwithstanding.

[Evidence suggests that most people draw on multiple matrices to organize the way they think about and experience the world. An individual might possess one matrix that organizes relationships with family members, one matrix that organizes relationships with colleagues in the workplace, one matrix that organizes relationships in the church community, and so on. Some of an individual's matrices may be more dominant than others, but I think it safe to say that very few people possess only one map by which to make sense of all of their experiences. Modern culture, with its many discordant demands, affords few people the opportunity to lead so focused a life. As people increasingly perceive the world to be complex, they become more likely to possess multiple matrices and less likely to possess any sort of "meta-matrix," any overarching means by which to organize their various categories of experience. They lead disjointed lives, passing from one matrix to another without making any concerted effort to integrate the whole, to resolve the disparities.[13]

Another metaphor we might use to think about "ways to think about the world" is that of lenses shaped and colored by past experience so as to define (or, in varying degrees, to distort) our view of present experience. Different lenses produce dramatically different perceptions of the world around us. This is a common enough phenomenon. Two people with very different convictions discuss matters of great importance and come away feeling like ships that have passed in the night. Two people look at a landscape, and where one sees overwhelming evidence of the majesty and grandeur of God the Creator, the other sees nothing more than an extended food chain in which one thing eats

---

12. I would emphasize that I am thinking of early fundamentalism in presenting these examples. In a longer and more nuanced treatment of the topic, I would point out that the relative reflectiveness of different conceptual schemes actually extends along a spectrum. I am certainly not suggesting that it would be adequate to speak of just two camps — those who reflect upon their perspective and those who do not.

13. I suspect this might explain in part the relative frequency of the what psychologists call "cognitive dissonance" in modern culture.

another and in turn is eaten by something larger. Each asks of the other, "Can you be looking at the same thing I'm looking at?"

While it is reasonable to suppose that some lenses will provide a more accurate view of the world than others, Christian intuition suggests that in a fallen world, all lenses will distort the view to some extent.[14] Sin obstructs everyone's view of the world to a significant extent, and although it extends a more distorting influence on some views than on others, it remains the case that, this side of paradise, God possesses the only genuinely uncorrupted vantage point.

Since the publication of Thomas Kuhn's landmark work *The Structure of Scientific Revolutions,* philosophers of science have frequently drawn on his use of the term *paradigm* in discussions of ways of looking at the world. Kuhn argued that science normally occurs within the context of established theories or models that provide rules establishing what constitutes acceptable evidence and acceptable interpretation of that evidence. During the period in which a given scientific paradigm is securely dominant, it tells scientists what counts as good evidence and what does not. The paradigm also suggests ways that conflicts between different bodies of evidence are to be explained. But when one model supersedes another (e.g., the Copernican model of celestial mechanics supersedes the Ptolemaic, or the Einsteinian model of physics supersedes the Newtonian), these rules and criteria change. Evidence that had supported one interpretation under the preceding paradigm is interpreted in a very different manner under the new paradigm. All scientific theories tend to be "under-determined" by external evidence, and thus a set of "facts" will not necessarily lead a scientist with absolute necessity toward one theory rather than another. The choice of theories occurs in the context of a paradigm that itself determines how the evidence is to be weighted, evaluated, and understood.

In Kuhn's later work, he placed constraints on his earlier work by suggesting that different paradigms are never mutually exclusive to the extent that they share nothing in common.[15] Certain kinds of evidence normally prove helpful in deciding between two paradigms that address

---

14. The apostle Paul employs this metaphor in 1 Cor. 13:12, where he writes, "Now we see but a poor reflection [as in a mirror]; then we shall see face to face. Now I know in part; then I shall know fully, even as I am fully known" (NIV).

15. See Kuhn, *The Essential Tension* (Chicago: University of Chicago Press, 1977). *The Structure of Scientific Revolutions* was first published in 1962.

the same evidence in similar ways and according to similar rules. And while he grants that phenomena outside the realm of science itself can contribute to paradigm shifts, he argues that the principal force for change remains an accumulation of conflicting evidence that undermines the utility of one paradigm and hence promotes acceptance of another.[16]

Contemporary theologians influenced by European philosophical and literary developments speak in still another way of a "way to think about the world." They use the term *preunderstanding* to refer to the set of conceptual parameters that influence the process of making sense of one's experiences.[17] Two individuals may understand the significance of racial oppression in completely different ways because of the prior commitments each brings to a discussion of the nature of race and oppression. In everyday life, these "preunderstandings" typically remain below the surface; they can be recognized and examined only through significant and serious dialogue with other individuals who share different commitments.[18] The confrontation of divergent views on specific issues will often reveal the underlying disparities in the respective preunderstandings, for it is the collection of preunderstandings that frame both the language about and the experience of the specific issue, whether it is a matter of race, finance, or even loyalty to a sports team.

What does all this have to do with theology? Precisely this: my theological convictions are both an influence on and a function of my "way to think about the world." When I believe in God, my way of thinking about the world is bound to undergo significant change. The

16. The work of Paul Feyerabend points strongly to the extrascientific factors that influence the doing of science. See especially his *Against Method: Outline of an Anarchist Theory of Knowledge* (New York: Schocken Books, 1978). Feyerabend defends an anarchy of scientific methods owing to what he believes is the decisive influence of political and sociological (i.e., nonscientific) factors in scientific revolutions. On this point Feyerabend is putting forth a paradigm for the understanding of paradigms that is itself largely unsupported by the actual practice of science even as Kuhn understands it. For a critical discussion of the post-Kuhnian conceptions of scientific change, see *Criticism and the Growth of Knowledge*, ed. Imre Lakatos and Alan Musgrave (Cambridge: Cambridge University Press, 1970).

17. For a classic characterization of this notion of "preunderstanding," see Hans-Georg Gadamer, *Truth and Method* (New York: Crossroad, 1975), pp. 235-74.

18. This explains in part the fascination that modern theologians have demonstrated with ecumenical dialogue. Evangelicals of certain stripes have also emphasized substantive ecumenical dialogue for precisely these same reasons. One particularly clear example is Robert Wuthnow's *The Struggle for America's Soul: Evangelicals, Liberals, and Secularism* (Grand Rapids: William B. Eerdmans, 1989).

shape of the lens is transformed not simply because a particular belief has been added to the (noetic) stock but also because this belief impinges upon other regions of the noetic structure. In that sense it may be more helpful to think of this belief in God not simply as one belief among many but rather as some kind of "control belief," since it asserts a control over a vast number of other beliefs.[19] A control belief greatly influences what kind of questions I will ask and be interested in asking; it begins to shape my priorities and govern my behavior in certain ways.

It is an oversimplification to suggest that a single belief will function in this manner. It is closer to the mark to suggest that only a group of beliefs will achieve this sort of control. The belief that God exists, for example, is normally accompanied by a host of other beliefs — what that God is like, whether that God can and does communicate, how that God is known, and what that God requires of us. For shorthand purposes, I will call this the "theistic matrix."[20]

I would emphasize at the outset that theistic matrices come in all shapes and sizes and assert a variety of influences depending upon the makeup of the matrix itself. What I think about God will affect in some fashion what I think about myself and the world around me. It will influence what I think is important in life and my understanding of the significance of death. It may even influence what I do in the morning when I get out of bed.

The theistic matrix is one of a number of matrices that most people possess. Some have a vocational matrix that may or may not be connected with their theistic matrix. Some have a leisure-time matrix that may or may not be connected with any other of their matrices. Inevitably there will be some connections between a person's matrices, though the vast majority of these connections may be held at a subconscious level. Steve might not see that his obsessive-compulsive behavior at work is connected with his love of professional wrestling as a leisure-time activity, for example, even though the connection would be quite apparent to any more objective observer.

[The theological implications of the interconnections of matrices are extensive. The Christian gospel calls us not only to a well-formed

---

19. The term "control belief" comes from Nicholas Wolterstorff, *Reason within the Bounds of Religion*, 2d ed. (Grand Rapids: William B. Eerdmans, 1984).

20. Even the atheist can be said to have a theistic matrix, involving basic beliefs about life and death, personal identity, and the character of reality.

theistic matrix but also to make conscious connections between that matrix and the other matrices of our lives. What I believe about God ought to influence how I view my own identity, my vocation, my family, my leisure pursuits, and so on. It is this matrix of matrices that I have been calling the theological vision. It is composed more narrowly of the theistic matrix (what I will be calling a theological framework in later chapters) and more broadly of the interconnections between the theistic matrix and all other matrices in one's noetic structures. Theology involves not just the study of God (the theistic matrix) but also the influence of that study on the rest of one's life. It is possible to distinguish these two levels, but they are never separable in practice.]

Conscious reflection may help bring to the surface the principal beliefs of the theistic matrix. It is the purpose of this study, in part, to think clearly about the formation of those beliefs in the theistic matrix. My driving concern in this volume is to elucidate the process by which the theistic matrix is derived and to illuminate the significance of that matrix for the remaining matrices of a person's noetic structure. In the language of the succeeding chapters, it is to ask how one should construct a theological framework and how a theological vision ought to arise from that framework.

To that end, I raise three fundamental questions in the remainder of this work. In chapters 3 and 4 I ask what factors are involved in the construction of a theistic framework. In chapters 5 and 6 I ask what history can teach us about this formative process. And in chapters 7, 8, and 9 I investigate the principles of constructing a theological framework and ask how a theological vision arises from the framework.

But before we can turn to these questions, we must first give attention to some remaining preliminaries. We have to look more closely (1) at the sorts of philosophical assumptions that inevitably underlie the theistic frameworks that give rise to theological visions and (2) at the cultural assumptions that evangelicals bring with them to the task of thinking theologically in the modern world.

PHILOSOPHICAL ASSUMPTIONS

It is the dubious distinction of those who write about methodological questions in any discipline to appear as if they are supporting the world on the back of an elephant that is itself not supported by anything else.

Methodological foundations will especially appear to be unsupported to those who do not share the foundations. For example, an individual who rejects the authenticity of the Johannine corpus will be inclined to dismiss as unconvincing an argument that relates the farewell discourse in John 14–17 to the inauguration of the new kingdom, on the grounds that the assumption of the reliability of the text is unsupported. It is not clear that there is any way to avoid this problem; after all, one has to start somewhere. This is part of the reason why methodological prescriptions are frequently offered with little defense, as if they have arisen ex nihilo. Assumptions do make a difference, but it is notoriously difficult to spell out the precise difference they make.[21]

A crucial point in methodological discussions is whether the fundamental starting points will bear the weight of the system in an appropriate manner. One way to determine this is to listen to the entire story and then engage in reflection and discussion to determine if the methodological constraints are adequate.

There are two major controlling philosophical assumptions employed in the following work. I am drawing attention to them here not to remove them from the realm of public discussion but, as I suggested above, because a work on method must begin somewhere. These foundations deserve further discussion, but before we can constructively enter into such a discussion, it is imperative that we note what weight they will bear.[22] The two assumptions can be set out as follows:

— *Realism principle:* Individuals normally know the world pretty much as it really is.

— *Bias principle:* Individuals never know the world apart from biases that influence their view of what really is the case.

Theologians have long emphasized the first principle while affirming the second principle in only a very qualified fashion. The reason for

21. Nicholas Wolterstorff has put the matter this way: "It is often said . . . that everyone has a 'set of presuppositions' or a 'perspective on reality' to bring to a theoretical inquiry. That may be true. But saying such things cannot be the end of the matter. It must at best be the beginning" (*Reason within the Bounds of Religion*, p. 22). I could not agree more.

22. These are not intended to be epistemological foundations, and thus I will not enter into the thorny discussion surrounding different perspectives on what a Christian epistemology actually looks like. I am here merely discussing methodological starting points.

this has to do with the nature of disagreement. If truth can be known, then there must be some mechanism to explain why everyone does not agree with that truth. The bias principle normally serves that purpose. It is often suggested that those who disagree with the truth must be affected by personal biases of some sort. Those who see the truth clearly are freer of such biases. The following set of brief illustrations from Protestant and evangelical history should make this point clear.

At the time of the Reformation, the realism principle appeared in the form of the principle of the perspicuity of Scripture, which specifies that the meaning of the biblical text is not hidden from the ordinary layperson.[23] It was the conviction of the Reformers that God has endowed humanity in such a manner that when the Bible is translated into our native tongues, a plain sense of the text will arise naturally in the mind of the reader. The individual does not create that meaning but rather discovers it plainly in the pages of the text.

The Reformers correspondingly used the bias principle to explain what they characterized as the egregious errors perpetrated by the Roman Catholic Church in matters of doctrine. Luther unabashedly claimed that it was the pope's desire for power that led to the practice of indulgences: no clear and plain reading of Scripture led to this heretical practice, he said, but rather a biased reading of the text that merely reinforced the pope's already well-formed convictions and desires.

The realism principle also cropped up during the Enlightenment era in the context of evangelical apologetics. Many Christians, including, notably, Bishop Butler and William Paley, argued that the world clearly manifests signs of being the creation of a divine being. The very complexity and design present in the natural world shouted of the divine origin of the universe to these apologists. They maintained that any individual who approaches the evidence objectively will see the world pretty much as it really is — that is to say, as a divine creation.

In the era of the Enlightenment, the orthodox apologetic project did not receive the academic acceptance that some had thought it might. The "clear and plain" evidences did not seem so clear and plain to everyone, especially to many academics in European universities. How could this be explained? Why did the intellectual community — alleged

---

23. Even given this principle, however, it should be noted that both Luther and Calvin argued that the ordinary layperson still ought to be guided by the educated clergy. I take up this point at greater length in Chap. 5.

guardians of truth — show reckless abandon with the overwhelming evidence presented by the orthodox apologists? How could one possibly deny the order and design in the world when it was there for all to see? The apologists found an answer in an understanding of the noetic effects of sin. They argued that the Enlightenment detractors of the gospel failed to recognize the clear evidence for what it was because they apprehended it with jaundiced eyes. The charge was that these detractors did not *want* to see the evidence, as plain as it might be — that their own personal bias against the truth impaired their ability to see the Creator's handprints in the natural order.[24]

In the twentieth century, evangelical theology has struggled with the issue of contextualization.[25] What is the relationship between the Bible and culture? How do the foundations of doctrine relate to the foundations of knowledge generally? In many ways evangelicalism is several decades behind Protestant liberalism in raising the hermeneutical question of horizons (i.e., the vantage points of individuals involved in conversation). In modern theology the central concern is the relationship between the biblical horizon and the horizon of the interpreter in the twentieth century.

[In that strain of evangelicalism called fundamentalism, theology has always been considered culturally neutral. Fundamentalists have always been fearful of the historicist notion of theology.[26] They have championed biblical authority by claiming there is only one horizon in theology — the biblical text itself. They have argued that dogmas are already revealed throughout the Scriptures and simply have to be trans-

---

24. This doctrine of the noetic effects of sin was especially well developed in the Dutch Reformed tradition, particularly in the thought of Herman Bavinck and Abraham Kuyper. In part this was seen as a reaction against the "evidential apologetics" that had characterized Butler and Paley.

25. Two of the significant volumes in this controversy are Charles Kraft's *Christianity in Culture: A Study in Dynamic Biblical Theologizing in Cross-Cultural Perspective* (Maryknoll, N.Y.: Orbis Books, 1979) and ⌈*Down to Earth: Studies in Christianity and Culture,* ed. John Stott and Robert Coote (Grand Rapids: William B. Eerdmans, 1980).⌉

26. By *historicism* here I mean the argument that all intellectual movements and their expressions (including the message of the Bible) are determined by the particular historical setting out of which they arise. In theological matters, historicists assert that the Bible affirms certain beliefs and practices because of the historical setting in which it was originally written. For a helpful characterization and critique of historicism, see Jeffrey Stout, *The Flight from Authority: Religion, Morality and the Quest for Autonomy* (Notre Dame, Ind.: University of Notre Dame Press, 1981).

lated into the vernacular. They have tended to construct theology by way of careful induction from all the relevant texts (i.e., proof-texting), with little concern for the context of the original passage or differences of meaning between a first-century and a twentieth-century context. It has been their conviction that history does not impede one's ability to know the biblical text pretty much as it really is.

Fundamentalists have also made use of the bias principle in their defense of biblical authority. The early fundamentalist revolt against the rising tide of biblical criticism relied on the charge that theological liberals were reading the Bible through the lenses of a naturalistic world-view that generated an outright denial of such biblical phenomena as miracles and predictive prophecy. As examples they pointed to such theological projects as Bultmann's program of demythologization and Tillich's religious existentialism.

All of this is simply to establish the point that evangelicals have, in a number of ways, employed both the realism principle and the bias principle (though it is not by any means to suggest that they have been unique in doing so). They have not always been explicit about the ways in which they have done so — in fact, they have often denied making use of the bias principle in their own work — but it is hard to read evangelical history without seeing these two fundamental principles integrated into the theological project in one fashion or another.[27] It might be argued that they have misunderstood how the principles ought to be integrated with one another, but I consider it beyond dispute that both principles are present in one fashion or another in their work.

Recent discussion in the evangelical community has centered on the question of the proper relationship between these two fundamental principles.[28] However, the perspective has changed somewhat. Evangelicals are no longer claiming that their opponents are the only parties guilty of employing the bias principle. Even those in the conservative and theologically orthodox tradition are now willing to admit their own biases and to wrestle seriously with their effects. Contemporary discus-

27. I suspect that modern and postmodern theological traditions have likewise employed both the reality and bias principles, though of the two they have more clearly emphasized the bias principle. This is most evident in current liberation theologies, which employ ideological critique as a formal theological principle.

28. Fine examples can be found in two relatively recent collections of essays: *The Use of the Bible in Theology: Evangelical Options*, ed. Robert K. Johnston (Atlanta: John Knox Press, 1985), and Stott and Coote's *Down to Earth*.

sion has focused on a number of questions associated with this admission. Are there historical influences that shape the way even the evangelical tradition has developed its theology from the biblical text? In what sense can modern evangelicals be said to get their epistemological hands on an ancient document such as the Bible in spite of their biases? Does any individual ever completely employ either the realism principle or the bias principle to the exclusion of the other? If every individual is biased to some extent, how is it still possible to know the true message of the Bible with any assurance?

Answers to these thorny questions fall roughly into two categories. Proponents of one of these categories emphasize the realism principle and proponents of the other category emphasize the bias principle. What separates the dialogue between these two camps from earlier evangelical discussions is the fact that both sides recognize the comprehensive nature of the two principles. It is now generally acknowledged in a manner that it was not acknowledged in previous discussions that both principles are operative to some extent in the efforts of everyone engaged in the theological project. Biases are present in every theological program and perspective, the evangelical program and perspective included. Evangelicals cannot escape charges that they are influenced by their own history, by the culture in which they write and teach, and by the personalities from which they draw leadership. An illustration might suffice in making this point clear.

The vitality of religion in America is strikingly different from that in most other industrialized nations of the twentieth century. Church pews are filled with nearly 40 percent of the American population on a weekly basis — roughly double the percentage in nearly every other country in the modern Western world. Many observers of religion remain unconvinced that this is simply a result of the purity of the gospel preached in America or of the genuineness of the faith practiced in our land. Among the many reasons proposed for the remarkable popularity of American religion is its ability to adapt to its surroundings. Nathan Hatch has persuasively argued that American Christianity has been uniquely molded by the American democratic ideal.[29] The development

---

29. See Hatch, "Evangelicalism as a Democratic Movement," in *Evangelicalism and Modern America*, ed. George Marsden (Grand Rapids: William B. Eerdmans, 1984), pp. 71-82, and his recent expansion of the thesis in *The Democratization of American Religion* (New Haven: Yale University Press, 1989).

of the means to communicate effectively to large masses of people, the power and authority of the majority to determine direction, and radical institutional pluralism have all contributed to the Americanization of the original religious vision of our founding fathers and mothers.

The theological vision of the evangelical movement has been created in large measure by popularizers, individuals with no other perceivable gift than the ability to communicate effectively. It is given legitimization by popular vote, usually in the form of large conferences organized by one of our modern "circuit riders." And it survives by the creation of simple slogans — "the Bible alone," "inerrancy vs. infallibility," "the evil of secular humanism," and the like. The movement is often a mirror of our culture rather than a prophetic voice within it. Ironically, this is part of the reason for its resilience in modern America.[30]

The unity of evangelical theology is distinctively colored by its drive toward institutional diversity. Evangelical Methodists often feel closer to evangelical Presbyterians than they do to nonevangelicals in their own denomination. The movement sustains itself by steering clear of the party politics of each individual denomination. But one result of this is that the theology of the movement is often reduced to the lowest common denominator in order that everyone in the movement might be included. Significant differences are often glossed over. Lengthy theological discourses are a good deal less favored by the movement than popular "how-to" manuals defining the essence of Christianity in twenty-five pages or less.

I write this not to offer an outright condemnation of the movement but merely to establish the point that evangelicalism has been deeply influenced by the culture in which it has thrived. Ours is not a simple distillation of the pure gospel.[31] Nor can we lay claim to a Christian

---

30. A small proviso ought to be added here. There are themes within the evangelical movement (e.g., its emphasis on evangelism and family values, its opposition to abortion) that do run counter to the prevailing values of American society. But the point here is that even these resistance themes are communicated in a thoroughly Americanized framework. I treat this idea at greater length in Chap. 2.

31. The search for the reexpression of the primitive gospel is well documented in Joel A. Carpenter's essay "Contending for the Faith Once Delivered: Primitivist Impulses in American Fundamentalism" and Grant Wacker's essay "Playing for Keeps: The Primitivist Impulse in Early Pentecostalism," both in *The American Quest for the Primitive Church*, ed. Richard T. Hughes (Urbana, Ill.: University of Illinois Press, 1988), pp. 99-119 and 196-219, respectively.

America as much as we can to a Americanized Christianity.[32] As evangelical theology approaches the twenty-first century, it must take these trends seriously. It is not feasible any longer to argue that only our opponents are biased in their theologizing. Evangelical theology must not only engage a culture that is largely resistant to its claims of absolute truth but must also recognize the influence which that culture has exercised upon it. Evangelicals must acknowledge the reality of cultural influence and cultural bias even in their own community.

It is easy enough to say that; it is quite another thing to accomplish it. If we grant that culture shapes theology, can we still assert that the truths we believe are absolute or objective in any significant sense? Is relativism our option if we admit the validity of the bias principle in all of theology? Some evangelicals believe that it is. These individuals maintain that the only road theology can take is to become yet more adapted to modern culture than it already is.[33] But this is to exclude entirely the realism principle. If the realism principle is also affirmed, it provides options beyond just relativism and cultural adaptation. Evangelicals profess that the biblical text can be known (realism principle), and this establishes the possibility of constructing theology in such a manner that it can challenge the values of modern culture instead of merely adapting to those values.

[My argument in this book is that an evangelical theology ought to be fully cognizant of both the realism principle and the bias principle. These two philosophical assumptions underlie all theological construction. The abandonment of either one of the principles ensures eventual distortion. Those who deny the existence of their own biases will inevitably come to be dominated by them. Those who completely turn their backs on the reality principle end up absolutizing the biased nature of theology — an absolutization that itself ironically contradicts the essence of the bias claim.] This latter distortion can be seen in the history of the "lives of Jesus" research that was produced by several leading biblical scholars in the religiously liberal universities of nineteenth-century

---

32. For an extended development of this thesis, see Nathan O. Hatch, Mark A. Noll, and George Marsden, *The Search for Christian America* (Westchester, Ill.: Crossway Books, 1983).

33. An example of this perspective can be found in the assumptions of the church growth movement associated with the School of World Mission at Fuller Theological seminary. Some of the theoretical underpinnings for this movement are contained in Charles Kraft's *Christianity in Culture*.

Europe. The rise of historical consciousness in these universities during the past century was accompanied by an absolutizing of the ethos of this historical context in the academic analysis of the biblical material. In attempting to find the "real" Jesus behind the Bible, these scholars revealed far more about nineteenth-century Europeans than they did about the first-century Palestinian figure of Jesus. Not surprisingly, the Jesus of their portraits ended up endorsing religious liberalism of the romantic stripe. The unconditional affirmation of the bias principle by these scholars resulted in a masked but nonetheless unrestrained affirmation of the realism principle — namely, that certain nineteenth-century European academics saw the world as it really was.[34]

Evangelicals were often derided in these same scholarly circles for their precritical approach to the Scriptures. They were accused of not taking the humanity of the Bible seriously. While this oft-heard criticism may have been a gross overgeneralization, it did point to a weakness in the movement. While evangelicals proudly maintained the divine origin of the Bible, they did not as readily recognize the humanity of those who were reading and interpreting the biblical text. Evangelicals were frequently uncritical of the biases and prejudices associated with their own cultural vantage point in the reading of the Bible. They assumed that the biblical text could be interpreted without the interference of these biases and prejudices, which is to say that they often considered their theology to be culturally neutral.

Evangelicals have not been as critically self-conscious as they should have been. They have not understood themselves as well as they have understood their opponents. Part of the task of theology is to reflect on the one who reads the biblical text. Theology is about God, but it is also about those who have been created in God's image and have become distorted images. A genuine biblical theology will strongly affirm that humans (Christian and non-Christian) are inevitably influenced by their own culture, tradition, and experience. Until and unless the evangelical community wrestles more seriously with this fact, they will not overcome the unreflective biases that characterize the evangelical appropriation of the Bible. To that end it is imperative that they understand the peculiar cultural shape of evangelicalism and its impact on the theological framework and vision of the evangelical community.

34. For an elaboration of this phenomenon in modern theology, see David F. Wells, *Search for Salvation* (Downers Grove, Ill.: InterVarsity Press, 1978).

It is also important to keep in mind that the mere presence of a cultural lens does not vitiate the evangelical interpretation of the biblical text. Evangelicals have rightly affirmed the realism principle in approaching redemptive revelation. God's word can be understood and appropriated, and this continuing legacy of the evangelical movement must not be forfeited. My central concern in this work will be to outline an evangelical theology that is at once biblically and culturally sensitive. I offer an extended argument for integrating the realism and the bias principles in theology. I make a call to understand evangelical biases while also affirming the public character of truth and the absolute character of God's truth.

CHAPTER 2

The Face of Evangelicalism and the Task of Evangelical Theology

> When churches abandon or de-emphasize theology, they give up the intellectual tools by which the Christian message can be articulated and defended. In the resulting chaos of religious ideas, the principal criterion left to the community as it seeks to find its way is, quite naturally, that of expediency.

Peter Berger[1]

DEFINING EVANGELICALISM

PART of the process of constructing an evangelical theological framework is understanding the cultural context out of which evangelicals have traditionally thought about theological matters. Evangelicals have been profoundly influenced by their culture and cannot begin to think clearly about a theological framework unless and until they reflect carefully on their own cultural context. Normative prescriptions about the formation of a theological framework will be ineffective without a preliminary account of the cultural lens through which evangelicals view their approach to the theological project. It is imperative not only to

---

1. Berger, *The Noise of Solemn Assemblies* (Garden City, N.Y.: Doubleday, 1961), p. 124.

understand the culture into which the evangelical proclamation of the gospel goes but also the culture out of which the evangelical theological framework is shaped in the first instance.

There are dangers associated with any attempt to locate so poly-morphous a group as contemporary American evangelicals on a cultural map. The sheer diversity of the movement does not augur well for a unified definition. And yet the ready acceptance of the term *evangelical* suggests that many believe they know what it means to be an evangelical even if they cannot put it into words clearly. Thankfully, for our pur-poses, there is a growing literature and a growing consensus regarding the nature of evangelicalism. Its history is becoming well documented and its subgroups are increasingly being identified and analyzed.

[In the clearest prescriptive analysis yet available, George Marsden suggests that there have been two kinds of definitions of evangelicalism — broad conceptual definitions and more narrow institutional definitions.[2] Broader definitions focus on the doctrinal unity among those who count themselves as evangelicals. Under this rubric, evangelicals are people who affirm the final authority of Scripture, the deity of Christ and the sufficiency of his atoning work on the cross, the necessity of a conversion experience, the importance of evangelism and mission, and the call to a sanctified life.]

There are three problems with isolating the movement solely on the basis of these doctrinal commitments. First, this approach fails to account adequately for the significant diversity of the movement. Evan-gelical Methodists are not the same as evangelical Presbyterians, even though they may feel that they share a kindred spirit. Second, the con-ceptual definitions often fail to differentiate evangelicals sufficiently from nonevangelicals. Many groups that prefer not to be identified as evangelicals nonetheless affirm the sorts of doctrinal commitments that are commonly associated with evangelicals.[3]

The third and [the most important problem associated with this approach to defining evangelicalism is that the doctrinal criterion is in fact tangential rather than central to the essence of the movement. Put simply, the evangelical movement is not held together by a confessional or theo-

---

2. See Marsden, "The Evangelical Denomination," in *Evangelicalism and Modern America* (Grand Rapids: William B. Eerdmans, 1984), pp. vii-xix.

3. On the danger of defining evangelicals on the basis of doctrinal commitments, see George Marsden, "Evangelicalism in the Sociological Laboratory," *Reformed Journal*, June 1984, pp. 20-24.

logical framework. Clearly certain theological beliefs are important to evangelicals, but they do not inhere in any larger theological construct that could be accurately identified as "evangelical theology."[4] To focus on the theological beliefs of the movement may be to give the false impression that a common theological framework unites the various sectors of the evangelical movement. In reality, it is a diversity of theological frameworks that more nearly captures the essence of evangelicalism. The movement's unique identity is defined to a considerably greater extent by cultural, institutional, and personal factors than by a narrow set of common doctrinal beliefs. An astute observer of the modern scene has put it this way:

> Where local congregations are hugely successful, they are so as clienteles or constituencies, not as confessional expressions. . . . It is hard to picture a member of the Crystal Cathedral having chosen membership because its pastor and its official status are part of the Reformed Church in America. If a member leaves in disaffection, it will not be because of that reformed tie but because some other minister or some other channel appeals more.[5]

The narrower institutional definitions focus on evangelicalism as a "dynamic movement, with common heritages, common tendencies, an identity, and an organic character."[6] This approach places emphasis on the social structures that hold the movement together and give its constituents a sense of common identity. These definitions also stress the historical origins of the movement in its various cultural contexts.

There are dangers inherent in these types of "social definitions" as well, though they are not insurmountable. The risks normally have to do with specifying the unifying social stances of the movement too precisely. Attempts to define evangelicalism in terms of political conservatism exclude the evangelical "left," for example. Many self-consciously evangelical groups repudiate political conservatism in their calls for justice and peace.[7]

---

4. This is to be contrasted with the traditions that are confessional in their identity, notably the Lutheran, the Reformed, and the Presbyterian branches of Protestantism.

5. Martin Marty, "The Clergy," in *The Professions in American History*, ed. Nathan O. Hatch (Notre Dame, Ind.: University of Notre Dame Press, 1988), p. 85.

6. Marsden, *Evangelicalism and Modern America*, p. x.

7. Such groups, often called "evangelical progressives," include the Sojourners community in Washington, D.C., and Evangelicals for Social Action, and their views appear in such publications as *The Other Side* and *Sojourners* magazine. For helpful com-

Sometimes evangelicals are characterized as anti-scientific. Many outside the movement assume that all evangelicals endorse "scientific creationism" and reject mainstream scientific views in such areas as cosmology and paleontology. This is scarcely the case, however. Evangelicals have shown themselves to be increasingly open to "literary" (as opposed to literalistic) readings of the first chapter of Genesis,[8] and a substantial number reject as folk science the offerings of such proponents of scientific creationism as Henry Morris and the Institute for Creation Research. Suffice it to say that there is no firm consensus within the evangelical community on the issue of the relationship between science and the Bible.

[The lesson to be learned from these examples is that the most accurate definition of evangelicalism will necessarily be vague and somewhat ambiguous. Evangelicals are like a collection of many siblings connected by some loose family resemblances. The differences between them are often as important as the similarities. The unifying strands will almost always admit of exceptions, and when the analysis becomes too fine-grained, it will lose some of its explanatory power.]

THE SECOND GREAT AWAKENING AND THE RISE OF THE EVANGELICAL EMPIRES

Evangelicalism is a loose-knit coalition with a history that has moved in many different directions.[9] Prior to the ascendancy of theological

mentary on this "progressive" element within evangelicalism, see Richard Quebedeaux, *The Young Evangelicals* (New York: Harper & Row, 1974), and James Davison Hunter, "The New Class and the Young Evangelicals," *Review of Religious Research* 22 (December 1980): 155-59.

8. Proponents of "literary" readings maintain that the literary form of Genesis demands that the text be read not as straightforward chronological history (i.e., a journalistic account of creation in six twenty-four-hour days) but rather as providing a theology of creation. Even strong inerrantists such as Meredith Kline (*Kingdom Prologue* [South Hamilton, Mass.: Meredith Kline, 1988] and Henri Blocher (*In the Beginning* [Downers Grove, Ill.: InterVarsity Press, 1986]) have argued against reading Genesis 1 as chronological history.

9. The diversity of American evangelicalism is evident in a number of terms that have been used to characterize it. George Marsden has called it a "denomination"; Timothy Smith has called it a "kaleidoscope"; Randall Balmer has called it a "quilt." For a good overall perspective on the diversity of the movement, see the final chapter of Balmer's study *Mine Eyes Have Seen the Glory* (New York: Oxford University Press, 1989).

liberalism in the nineteenth century, most professing Christians in America were theologically conservative, but this widespread theological conservativism did not provide any sort of significant common identity.[10] Differences among the diverse Protestant groups and denominations that dotted the landscape of America in the seventeenth and eighteenth centuries continued to constitute significant aspects of each group's sense of identity. Prior to the nineteenth century, individuals were much less likely to locate their religious identity in an "evangelical faith" common to the diverse Protestant groups in the land than in the theological distinctives of their own particular tradition. The clear tendency was not to identify oneself as an evangelical (or anything like that sort of designation) but rather as Reformed, Methodist, Episcopal, Baptist, or the like.[11]

This "identity in diversity" began to change with the Second Great Awakening in the early part of the nineteenth century. The outbreak of evangelical revivals in this period coincided with intense evangelistic efforts to reach the frontiers of American society. Cooperation among the many conservative Protestant denominations was required to carry out the effective evangelization of the new frontiers in America. Illustrative of this cooperation is the Plan of Union in 1801, which effectively merged Presbyterian and Congregational evangelistic efforts on the frontier despite their ecclesiastical differences. The emergence of groups such as the Evangelical Alliance and various voluntary societies in the first decades of the nineteenth century constituted evidence that many Americans had begun to think in terms of a "common evangelical faith" in addition to their denominational distinctives.

Independent mission agencies and conferences grew in number, detached from the ecclesiastical control of any specific church or denomination. These "evangelical empires," which were assembled in response to urgent evangelistic needs, were free from external ecclesi-

10. By "theological conservativism," I mean in this context a belief system that affirms supernaturalism, the divine inspiration of the Bible, and the full divinity of Jesus Christ.

11. A possible exception to this generalization can be found in the first generation or two of the Puritan founders of the United States of America, whose identity was founded in a theological unity. But they were able to conceive of themselves in nonsectarian terms only because there was so little theological diversity in their ranks to challenge the vision. This changed quickly enough, as evidenced by the controversy over religious pluralism associated with Roger Williams.

astical control and confessional traditions. Later in the century, revivalists such as Charles Grandison Finney (1820s and 1830s) and Dwight L.
Moody (1850s and 1860s) operated outside of denominations altogether, working to capture support from individuals across many different denominations.

During America's Second Great Awakening in the early years of
the nineteenth century, many conservative revivalists pointedly expressed disdain for all confessional traditions. Many shifted the test of
truth away from one's fidelity to the creeds of the church and measured
it instead by one's personal experience with the Holy Spirit. Finney
expressed a common sentiment when he stated that the notion that the
Westminster Confession of Faith, written in 1642-46, "should in the
nineteenth century be recognized as the standard of the church, or of
an intelligent branch of it, is not only amazing, but I must say that is
highly ridiculous. It is as absurd in theology as it would be in any other
branch of science, and as injurious and stultifying as it is absurd and
ridiculous. It is better to have a living than a dead Pope."[12]

The revivalist located the "living Pope" not in Rome but in the
human heart. The experience of the Holy Spirit became the lens through
which the works and words of God were interpreted.[13] The work of the
Spirit was severed from the confessions and the creeds of the church in
such a manner that an individual led by the Spirit was considered to be
directly and immediately in touch with the meaning of Scripture. The
work of the Spirit was not mediated by the community of past believers.
As Finney himself said, "I found myself utterly unable to accept doctrine
on the ground of authority. . . . I had nowhere to go but directly to the
Bible, and to the philosophy or workings of my own mind. I gradually

---

12. Finney, *Lectures on Revivals of Religion* (Cambridge: Harvard University Press,
1960), p. xii.
13. William G. McLoughlin has noted the implications of focusing on the experience of the Holy Spirit in Finney's thinking: "For all his lawyer-like logic, for all his
comparisons of the Holy Ghost to an advocate arguing before a jury, and carefully
reasoned arguments taken step by step, there was a strong element of mysticism about
Finney" (Introduction to Finney's *Lectures on Revivals of Religion*, p. xxxi). At one point
Finney refers to a person who prayed so fervently that his nose bled. He continually
authorized his beliefs with such phrases as "being led by the Spirit" and "instructed by
God," and he implored others to "watch for the leading of the Spirit and when those
came to follow them without hesitation." For further details on this side of Finney and
the revivalist tradition generally, see William G. McLoughlin, *Modern Revivalism: Charles
Grandison Finney to Billy Graham* (New York: Ronald Press, 1959).

formed a view of my own which appeared to me to be unequivocally taught in the Bible."[14]

A curious effect of this emphasis on the subjective leading of the Spirit was the growth in power of the "popular popes" of evangelicalism. Though highly individualistic in their approach to salvation and populist in their biblical interpretation, populist Bible teachers and preachers served to draw people together into a mass movement largely through the strength of their personal popularity. As Mark Noll puts it, "Evangelical interpretation assigned first place to popular approval."[15] The right of private interpretation that they promoted can be understood as a desire for freedom from the domination of opposing viewpoints. It would seem that the early evangelicals were not so much interested in removing all human authority as they were in choosing human authorities with whom they agreed. And once they found these individuals, they were willing to invest them with a great deal of de facto authority.[16]

A striking result of the rise of the popular leader was the displacement of the theologian from a place of preeminence in the evangelical movement. The new leaders of the movement were popularizers of the gospel message, revivalists, and Bible conference preachers. This tradition persists even today; the theological leadership of the movement is provided by preachers who travel the circuit of popular conservative Bible conferences.[17]

14. Finney, *Memoirs of Rev. Charles G. Finney* (New York: A. S. Barnes, 1876), pp. 42-43.

15. Noll, *Between Faith and Criticism: Evangelicals, Scholarship and the Bible in America* (San Francisco: Harper & Row, 1986), p. 151.

16. The well-documented surge in independent evangelical religious organizations and conferences in the nineteenth and early twentieth centuries is testimony to the willingness of people to grant authority to popular leaders. For general historical treatments of this phenomenon, see Leonard Sweet, "The Evangelical Tradition in America," in *The Evangelical Tradition in America*, ed. Leonard Sweet (Macon: Mercer University Press, 1984), pp. 1-86; George Marsden, *Religion and American Culture* (New York: Harcourt Brace Jovanovich, 1989); and Douglas W. Frank, *Less Than Conquerors: How Evangelicals Entered the Twentieth Century* (Grand Rapids: William B. Eerdmans, 1986).

17. Examples abound, but such individuals as John Stott, Chuck Swindoll, John MacArthur, and John Wimber are clear examples of this continuing trend. A notable exception to this is the enduring legacy of the Oxford don C. S. Lewis, though even in his case it must be admitted that evangelicals have paid far greater attention to his works of children's fantasy and popular apologetics than they have to his technical pieces on literary theory. Even the theologians of the movement — Carl Henry, J. I. Packer, and R. C. Sproul, for example — write for popular audiences. Interestingly, they speak and

Revivalists of the Second Great Awakening such as Finney championed a Bible unencumbered by theological systems and authoritative interpreters. They promoted the idea that each individual has the right to interpret the Bible in his or her own way. [Theological democracy was conceptually linked to political democracy, and they both became entrenched cultural assumptions.] Nathan Hatch argues that a demand for the right of private interpretation in biblical matters began to take hold in Protestant circles as a result of the cultural revolution of the late 1700s and was linked to the rise of the notion of the sovereignty of the people.[18]

It was also during the period of the late 1700s and the early 1800s that reliance on theology as the preeminent means for the interpretation of Scripture began to decline. Christians of all denominations demonstrated an increasing inclination toward subjective interpretation. In connection with this, there was generally less acknowledgment of the authority of church tradition, and in some cases repudiation of it. Earlier Protestant circles associated with individuals as different as Luther, Calvin, Wesley, and Whitefield had all stressed the importance of interacting with past communities of interpretation as one approached the Bible. The first proponents of the shift away from this emphasis in favor of an "inward turn" became manifest in a movement known as the New Lights, revivalist-oriented individuals who reacted strongly against the entrenched Calvinism of New England Puritanism. Central to their movement was the notion that Scripture can be interpreted solely in light of one's own private experience and understanding.[19]

A century earlier, [the Enlightenment had blazed a wide trail through European culture — and introduced a crisis of authority.] The decline of the authority of church tradition in matters of biblical interpretation during the eighteenth century was one evidence of this. In the nineteenth century, the crisis of authority made further inroads yet, extending to the questioning of the biblical revelation itself. Religious thinkers in the universities were consumed with the question of the

---

write as *evangelical* theologians rather than as theologians speaking out of specific faith communions (Henry is a Baptist, Packer an Anglican, and Sproul a Presbyterian).

18. Hatch, "Sola Scriptura and Novus Ordo Seclorum," in *The Bible in America*, ed. Nathan O. Hatch and Mark A. Noll (New York: Oxford University Press, 1982), pp. 59-78.

19. There were groups and individuals who espoused similar sentiments prior to this period (e.g., Quakers, Anne Hutchinson, the Radical Puritans of the seventeenth century), but none of these exerted as much influence as the New Lights.

veracity of divine revelation. Could God actually communicate with his creation, either in the form of deeds (miracles) or words (the Bible)? If God could not communicate, in what sense could the Bible be considered authoritative?

The revivalists of the Second Great Awakening seemed convinced that God could and did communicate with deeds and words. They ardently defended divine revelation but argued (as the secularists had a century earlier) that this revelation was not properly mediated by either tradition or theology: it came directly to each individual through personal experience. As a result, the individual became the arbiter of what the Bible did and did not say. The new evangelical coalition attached little importance to the aid of the past or even the present community of interpreters in matters of biblical interpretation.[20] External authorities were jettisoned and divine authority was internalized — a strategy not

20. This may be owing in part to the adoption of Common Sense epistemology by evangelicals in the nineteenth century. Common Sense epistemology was the common language of all the diverse intellectual movements on American soil in the early decades of the nineteenth century. It both captured and contributed to the American optimism regarding the capacity of the individual to know apart from corrupting influences. (See George Marsden, "Everyone One's Own Interpreter? The Bible, Science and Authority in Mid-Nineteenth-Century America," in *The Bible in America*, pp. 79-100.) Many evangelicals developed their own distinctive understanding of Common Sense Realism, a component of which was a tendency to view sin in purely voluntaristic terms, as having little or no impact upon the mind. Thus they assumed that even individuals infected by sin could nevertheless have fairly direct epistemic access to the facts of Scripture, because sin affects the will but not the mind.

It should be noted that this evangelical permutation of Common Sense Realism was a step away from the more commonly received American version, which was itself a step away from the Scottish original. Common Sense Realism originally arose as an attack against the skepticism of David Hume and the pessimism of other European Enlightenment thinkers. Thomas Reid (the originator of the movement) originally sought to resurrect the natural intuitive conviction that individuals can know the world. While this may have led to an overly optimistic view of a person's capacity to know, it clearly served as a corrective to the opposite error — namely, that humans can never know anything. It is against the European background that Old Princeton must be understood, for example: the Old Princeton theology was meant to serve as a corrective to the extreme skepticism of much of nineteenth-century biblical scholarship. These points provide some useful qualifications to the cautionary notes put forward by David F. Wells in his essay "Charles Hodge," in *Reformed Theology in America*, ed. David F. Wells (Grand Rapids: William B. Eerdmans, 1986), pp. 36-59; Mark Noll in his introduction to *The Princeton Theology, 1812-1921: Scripture, Science, and Theological Method from Archibald Alexander to Benjamin Warfield*, ed. Mark A. Noll (Grand Rapids: Baker Book House, 1983); and George Marsden in *Fundamentalism and American Culture*.

altogether different from that of the Enlightenment. Hatch goes so far
as to suggest that "at one level then, the Enlightenment in America was
not repudiated but popularized" by evangelicals of the early nineteenth
century.[21]

Allied with the belief in the autonomy of the modern interpreter
was a growing disdain for denominational structures. Many evangelicals
focused on the desirability of visible unity in the body of Christ. They
maintained that denominations and theological systems alike created
barriers to this unity, and they endorsed the elimination of denominations altogether. Unity was attainable, they argued, if Christians would
only focus on the fundamentals of the faith. Ironically, while these
evangelicals denounced the diversity of denominations and theological
authorities as divisive, they championed the diversity of autonomous
individual experience as a means to bring coherence to the movement.
And indeed, the potential divisiveness of individual autonomy was held
in check for a time by the power of the individual evangelical empires
and a common commitment to fight the onslaught of modernism.[22]

THE FUNDAMENTALS AND
THE WAR WITH MODERNISM

As the nineteenth century came to a close, the focus slowly began to
change as evangelicals made all other concerns secondary to the need
to combat the enemy of theological liberalism. Independent Christian
colleges and theological journals sprang up in dedication solely to this
battle. Enemy lines were being drawn not between denominations but
within them. Conservative Presbyterians struck alliances with conservative Baptists against liberal foes in both denominations.

In the early decades of this century, when the controversy between
fundamentalism and modernism raged, the central defense of the fundamentalists centered on the exposition of certain key doctrines such as
the virgin birth, the penal substitutionary view of the atonement, the

21. Hatch, "Sola Scriptura and Novus Ordo Seclorum," p. 74.
22. Even without these external pressures, religious individualism is almost always
accompanied by a pressure toward conformity of one sort or another. This is true in
religious as well as secular matters, as we are reminded by Robert Bellah and his collegues
in their fine work *Habits of the Heart: Individualism and Commitment in American Life* (Berkeley
and Los Angeles: University of California Press, 1985).

infallibility and inerrancy of the Bible, and the reality of miracles and the supernatural. Though largely overlooked at the time of publication, *The Fundamentals* became a symbol of identity for the burgeoning evangelical movement of the 1930s and 1940s. This collection of twelve essays by noteworthy conservative Bible teachers, preachers, and scholars was significant because of the united front it painted of the movement. Dispensational premillennialists were allied with Reformed postmillennialists and conservative Baptists. There was one common enemy, theological liberalism, which by its very cultural strength demanded a unified attack. Figures as diverse as Reuben Torrey, B. B. Warfield, and E. Y. Mullins collaborated on this exposition and defense of central orthodox theological beliefs.[23]

To preserve unity in the project, several important doctrinal differences were placed in the background. Political expediency demanded that theological polemics be directed in one direction only — against theological modernism. Disputed social issues such as Darwinism, political socialism, and perfectionism were placed on the back burner in the interests of the common cause. Unity centered in the defense of a set of core dogmas and stress on the urgency of preaching the simple gospel to the whole world.

The Fundamentals were largely ignored by the secular academy, but their symbolic importance for the later evangelical movement was potent nonetheless. They dramatically shaped the vision of the movement in the middle part of this century. But two troubling legacies from this early evangelical apology survived with them: the narrow unity of the early movement led to subsequent fragmentation, and the early distillation of the gospel into a simple core led to the subsequent abandonment of a rich theological vision.

Differences among the original authors, initially suppressed in the name of unity, came home to roost in the later period. The expanding conservative movement never reached agreement on a vast range of points, and fragmentation inevitably ensued. Though evangelical Methodists and Presbyterians felt closer to each other than they did to the liberal elements in their own denominations, their theological unity was

---

23. *The Fundamentals: A Testimony to Truth* (Chicago, 1910-1915). It is also interesting to note that at least two Britons who were not strict inerrantists — James Orr and G. Cambell Morgan — contributed essays to the collection. It is important to keep in mind, though, that they did not write on the doctrine of Scripture.

built on a very narrow foundation. The set of core dogmas upon which they might agree included the deity of Christ, the necessity of a personal conversion experience, the inerrancy of the Bible, and the importance of missions. Though linked with key theological themes of the church throughout its history, this set of core dogmas originated as much in resistance to modernism as it did in ties to the history of the church.[24] The movement gained its theological unity as much from its common enemy as from a common theological heritage. The "fundamentals" served as a simple set of dogmas on which all evangelicals could agree and against which none of the historic theological traditions stood. The evangelical coalition eliminated issues of obvious biblical importance from the list of the fundamentals if conservative Christendom had not yet reached consensus on them — issues such as the nature of Christian sacraments and divine election.

The war with modernism reached a climax in the modernist-fundamentalist debates of the 1920s and the Scopes trial of 1925 in particular.[25] It was in this decade that fundamentalism reached its clearest expression. Paramount was the concern to guard against the naturalism of the modernists and their critical assaults on the integrity of the Bible. Though the quality and tone of the responses differed among the numerous evangelical groups, this apologetic thrust increasingly served to strengthen the bond that united the numerous "evangel-

But are evangelicals simply united by our common enemy, modernism, or now post-modernism?

24. Some have made the interesting argument that evangelicalism is not so much a movement of resistance to post-Enlightenment modernism as it is a capitulation to the Enlightenment. They contend that evangelicalism is essentially a pietist expression of modernism; the pietism dictates a set of emphases different from those of secular modernism, but the basic structures are much the same. See, e.g., David W. Bebbington, *Evangelicalism in Modern Britain: A History from the 1730s to the 1980s* (London: Unwin Hyman, 1989). In a different way, George Marsden traces several Enlightenment features in the history of evangelicalism, especially the appropriation of Common Sense Realism as a philosophical framework; see *The Evangelical Mind and the New School Presbyterian Experience* (New Haven: Yale University Press, 1970).

25. This controversy is helpfully explored in a number of places. For a useful source that isolates and assesses the controversy in terms of contrasting theologies, see Alan P. F. Sell, *Theology in Turmoil: The Roots, Course and Significance of the Conservative Liberal Debate in Modern Theology* (Grand Rapids: Baker Book House, 1986). For a most careful historical treatment of the controversy, see George Marsden, *Fundamentalism and American Culture: The Shaping of Twentieth-Century Evangelicalism, 1870-1925* (New York: Oxford University Press, 1980). For the most perceptive treatment of the issues from the perspective of a fundamentalist actually involved in the debates of the 1920s, see J. Gresham Machen, *Christianity and Liberalism* (New York: Macmillan, 1923).

ical empires." Strange alliances were forged in the heat of battle. For example, the highly educated and deeply Reformed scholar J. Gresham Machen frequently appeared on the platform at the dispensationally oriented and low-brow Winona Bible Conference.[26] Stranger still, the Oxford-educated W. H. Griffith Thomas was involved in the founding of Dallas Theological Seminary, a distinctively dispensationalist institution. "Fundamentalism was a mosaic of divergent and sometimes contradictory traditions and tendencies that could never be totally integrated," says Marsden. "Sometimes its advocates were backward looking and reactionary, at other times they were imaginative innovators. . . . At times they seemed ready to forsake the whole world over a point of doctrine; at other times they appeared heedless of tradition in their zeal to win converts."[27]

James Davison Hunter has argued that four prominent traditions have shaped modern evangelicalism.[28] Of the four, he argues that the Baptist tradition is presently the most prominent. It is characterized by a highly individuated conception of salvation, a conviction about the importance of personal volition in the salvation process, and a vision of faith as highly subjective. In this tradition, church structure tends toward congregationalism. The second major tradition is the Holiness/Pentecostal tradition, which places a strong emphasis on themes of personal piety and the importance of the role of the Holy Spirit in sanctification. Perfectionism occurs in some strands of this tradition, and in others the "baptism of the Holy Spirit" is prominent. A third tradition is the Anabaptist, in which faith is expressed in more objective and rational ways. It tends to be less experiential and more communitarian. It is also characteristically activist in social concerns and dominantly pacifistic. The final tradition he notes is the Reformed/Confessional. In this tradition, faith is expressed in rational terms and practiced in an ascetic manner. It

26. Machen, educated in dignified Southern aristocracy, wrote to his mother that at the Winona Bible conference, "practically every lecture, on whatever subject, was begun by the singing of some of the popular jingles, often accompanied by the blowing of enormous horns and other weird instruments of music" (cited by Ned B. Stonehouse, Jr., in *J. Gresham Machen: A Memoir* [Grand Rapids: William B. Eerdmans, 1954], p. 232).

27. Marsden, *Fundamentalism and American Culture*, p. 43.

28. See Hunter, *American Evangelicalism: Conservative Religion and the Quandary of Modernity* (New Brunswick, N.J.: Rutgers University Press, 1983), pp. 7-9. Robert Webber makes a similar point, though highlighting even greater diversity than Hunter. He suggests that there are fourteen varieties of evangelicalism based on distinctive themes; see *Common Roots: A Call to Evangelical Maturity* (Grand Rapids: Zondervan, 1978).

typically manifests a high degree of concern with education and matters of the intellect.[29]

The relatively broad diversity present in these formative evangelical traditions is significant. The breadth of theological visions was brought into a working unity by distilling the essence of the gospel to a small set of easily understood doctrines. The lowest-common-denominator approach seemed attractive to many because it facilitated the assembly of a much larger army to wage war against theological modernism. The intensifying cultural strength of religious liberalism demanded a concerted effort on the part of the opposing conservative traditions. However, the drive toward unity made strange bedfellows. Dispensationalists stood shoulder to shoulder with nondispensationalists, and ecclesiastical separatists joined hands with their more moderate mainstream brethren. Sharp differences between Reformed and Arminian understandings of salvation no longer seemed to matter much.[30] Baptists and paedo-baptists preached on the same platforms against the evils of modernism.

The net result of this broad evangelical ecumenism was the loss of a theological framework. Theological truth was separated from the fabric in which it inhered. Truth still mattered to evangelicals, but no longer as an expression of the full organic unity of the revelation of God in Scripture. It became a political platform, the assemblage of a disparate collection of dogmas that had been gathered with the intent of avoiding offense to any of the diverse theological traditions represented in the evangelical coalition. The theological task degenerated into the faithful

29. The precise structure of these categories is relatively unimportant for the purposes of this study. It is the broad diversity of theological traditions and frameworks underlying the evangelical theological vision that is significant for our purposes. For different ways to slice the pie, though with roughly the same results, see George Marsden, "The Evangelical Denomination," in *Evangelicalism and Modern America*, pp. vii-xix; Ernest R. Sandeen, *The Roots of Fundamentalism: British and American Millenarianism, 1800-1930* (Chicago: University of Chicago Press, 1970); Robert Handy, *A Christian America* (New York: Oxford University Press, 1971); John Jefferson Davis, *Foundations of Evangelical Theology* (Grand Rapids: Baker Book House, 1984); and Richard Quebedeaux, *The Young Evangelicals.*

30. In the mid-eighteenth century, Jonathan Edwards and opponents clearly saw the incompatibility of these two views of conversion. It was less than a hundred years later that the revivalist Charles Grandison Finney attempted to produce what William G. McLoughlin has characterized as the "spongy modification of Jonathan Edwards's Calvinism in terms of Wesley's Arminianism which is [now] called evangelicalism" (Introduction to Finney's *Lectures on Revivals of Religion*, p. xxviii).

repetition of core dogmas rather than a harvesting of the rich fields of Scripture with the help of the community of interpreters of the past.

In the long battle with modernism that took place from the mid-nineteenth century to the early twentieth century, evangelicals gradually lost their cultural hegemony and retreated to a defensive posture, protecting a small but valued treasure. The more constructive and positive posture that had characterized conservative traditions in earlier ages slipped away.[31] Embattled evangelicals now set themselves to the task of protecting the doctrinal message of Scripture rather than exploring it. What theology they did construct was produced not in conversation with the community of interpreters throughout Christian history but in the context of a preoccupation with their war against modernism. There were, of course, exceptions to this trend, but they remained in the minority.[32]

SOCIAL ENGAGEMENT AND ADAPTATION

As it gradually dawned on the leaders of the fundamentalist movement that they had lost the battle for the soul of the nation in the theological wars of the 1920s, they began to develop two basic responses to the culture in which they now found themselves to be a weaker minority. Some viewed separation (theologically and culturally) as the only viable response. Others insisted on engaging the culture in a more direct fashion. The clash over strategy eventually ruptured the fragile evangelical alliance. Somewhere during the period from 1930 to 1950, the coalition split into fundamentalist and neo-evangelical camps. Once again, the evangelicals were drawing their identity less from an essential theological framework than from a social and cultural strategy.

In the late 1940s, many on the faculty of Fuller Theological Seminary, the newly created neo-evangelical seminary near Los Angeles, sought to create a theological framework akin to that of Old Princeton,

31. I am not seeking to promote the idea of a golden age of conservative and orthodox theological traditions here. Important problems permeated this history as well, among them the problem of theological imperialism. On the myth of an earlier "golden era" in American church history, see Mark A. Noll, Nathan O. Hatch, and George Marsden, *The Search for Christian America* (Westchester, Ill.: Crossway Books, 1983).

32. The clearest exception in the fundamentalist camp was the Princeton scholar J. Gresham Machen, who rooted his theology in the Reformed confessions of the sixteenth and seventeenth centuries. Yet even Machen remained preeminently concerned with the task of fighting modernism rather than the task of retrieving Christian history.

seriously committed to scholarship in defense of Protestant orthodoxy.[33] On the other side of the divide, the fundamentalist Bob Jones University resolutely set itself against engagement of secular scholarship.

The separatist strategy of fundamentalism survived in isolated pockets, but it became progressively clear that the neo-evangelical strategy would become the dominant strand within conservative Protestant circles. Indeed, today it is this strand that sets the agenda for the evangelical movement as a whole.[34]

At the beginning of the twentieth century, conservative Christians expressed concern that American universities had become bastions of secularism and religious liberalism. They believed that, with few exceptions, the academy had become a foe of orthodoxy. In connection with this, many evangelicals began to associate theological reflection with the style and agenda of the secular academy and so began to view it as distasteful. Many determined that it would be best to bypass the university altogether and take the battle directly to the people.[35] This required adaptation to modern mass media in the form of easily remembered slogans and well-packaged presentations of the gospel. *The Fundamentals* was an early illustration of this. Evangelicals increasingly became skilled in the use of mass communication and mass marketing.[36]

Theological liberals adapted to modernity by assuming a passive

33. The "Old Princeton" group of theologians, associated with Princeton Seminary in the nineteenth century, was committed to an intellectual exposition and defense of conservative Presbyterianism. It included such individuals as Charles Hodge, B. B. Warfield, and A. A. Hodge.

34. There is evidence of this in Jerry Falwell's rapprochement with mainstream evangelicals in his book *The Fundamentalist Phenomena: The Resurgence of Conservative Christianity* (Garden City, N.Y.: Doubleday, 1981). It is also evident in the fundamentalist emphasis on television as a prime medium for evangelism: in taking to the airwaves, fundamentalism has unconsciously adapted to one of the fixtures of modern culture and thereby ceased to be isolationist from that culture.

35. During the last quarter of the nineteenth century, evangelicals also sought an answer to the secularization of the academy through the creation of their own institutions of higher learning. This may have appeared to bespeak a commitment to honest intellectual inquiry, but in fact it constituted a retreat into the safe bastions of orthodoxy and a relatively sterile and repetitious presentation of orthodox theology rather than a genuine engagement of the issues. In the end, this strategy simply served to isolate the evangelical movement further from the larger culture and from the past.

36. This is not to say that evangelical scholars produced no work during this period; but, unlike the situation in the liberal camp, scholars in the evangelical camp did not provide the leadership of the movement.

ecumenicity. They treated the growing cultural pluralism with kid gloves. They gave up all claims to the uniqueness of the Christian message in the hope that all the diverse cultural forces might live together in peace. Evangelicals maintained a far less tolerant stance. They insisted that Christianity made exclusive truth claims, and they made these claims the centerpiece of their message. And yet, despite their inflexibility on this level, evangelicals showed themselves to be highly tolerant of modernity on another level. They condensed their message into something that could be easily grasped, claimed for it some uniqueness, and then marketed it as a superior commodity in the marketplace of modernity. In essence, they adapted the proclamation of the gospel to the methods of modern mass marketing. As the founder of a popular evangelism program put it, "There are five great laws of selling or persuading: attention, interest, desire, conviction, and close. It does not matter whether you are selling a refrigerator or persuading men to accept a new idea or philosophy, the same basic laws of persuasion hold true."[37]

In making these changes, evangelicals removed the defense of orthodox dogma from theological reflection and attached it instead to an antimodernist stance, using the most modern of methods in doing so. They pursued their goal of resisting all things modern by adopting a strategy that involved acquiescing at key points to modernity. It is fundamental to my concerns in this book to highlight their resultant retreat from critical theological reflection and their drive toward winning mass acceptance by using the techniques of the market economy. The modern free market has shown itself to be essentially indifferent to truth: on the whole, it showers its rewards not on what is most true but rather on what is most attractively packaged. It is my contention that in attempting to play the tricky game of mass marketing exclusive truth, evangelicals ironically ended up distancing themselves yet further from their theological heritage of devotion to truth.

Evangelicals had traditionally used truth as a criterion in determining the presence of the Holy Spirit, but to this they began to add the criterion of success: God could be found where there was truth (primarily in the Bible) and where evangelistic efforts were successful.[38]

---

37. James Kennedy, *Evangelism Explosion* (Wheaton, Ill.: Tyndale House, 1977), p. 46.

38. Finney was so bold as to assert that "those are the best educated ministers who win the most souls" and "a wise minister will be successful."

Over time, these two criteria were increasingly distanced from each other. The Bible remained the touchstone in matters of doctrine, but in matters of practice, the presence of the Spirit was intuited rather than directly correlated with the framework of the Scriptures. Evangelism was oriented toward the production of results, and fidelity to the biblical record was assigned a secondary importance.[39]

Evangelical revivalists became skilled in producing this success by manipulating parts of the worship service in such a manner that people would inevitably respond. The typical frontier revival service of the nineteenth and early twentieth centuries began with several songs pitched at an emotional level calculated to create a solemn but expectant atmosphere. The music was meant to make the people feel comfortable and render their hearts vulnerable. Very personal and individual prayers came next. Such prayers were never offered in the third person, for this would have given too abstract a tone for the tastes of the simple lay folk in attendance. The climax of the service was the preaching of an evangelistic sermon built around several key stories or illustrations and demanding some immediate response on the part of the audience — usually an altar call at the very end of the sermon. The effectiveness of the sermon was judged by the number of people who came forward.[40]

These services rarely emphasized the Lord's Supper or corporate prayers. The preacher functioned as a story-teller, directing the service to each individual rather than to the gathered community as a whole. The congregation became spectators, churches were built like theaters, and sermons became forms of entertainment.

These "new measures," as they were called, often drew on a very traditional conception of theology, but as a practical matter they established a cultural context in which theology was significantly devalued relative to personal spiritual experience. A complement to the new measures of the Second Great Awakening arrived with the ascendancy of the New School theology, which had been constructed in the long shadow of Jonathan Edwards but was in many ways diametrically op-

39. This point is helpfully developed in an unpublished essay entitled "Old and New School Christianity" by a colleague of mine, T. David Gordon.

40. The parallels with modern televised evangelism are striking, the central difference being that the medium has changed the nature of the response. The altar call has been replaced with appeals to phone in or send money.

posed to Edwards's staunch Calvinism.[41] As it was implemented by such individuals as Lyman Beecher, Nathaniel Taylor, and E. A. Park, the New School theology subverted Edwards's insistence on the exaltation of God and promoted instead a Pelagian reliance on the human will. Though initially distinct from one another, the New School theology and Finney's new measures eventually came together.[42] The New School theology called on people to change their own hearts at once, and the new measures provided the stimulus and the procedures by which they might do so. And although initially many viewed the new measures as theologically neutral, the history of the evangelical revivals of the nineteenth century bears witness to the fact that they had clear theological implications.[43] On the surface, Protestant theological liberalism and the fundamentalist-evangelical coalition of the twentieth century were fierce adversaries, but it is important to note that both had roots in a pragmatic-experiential, low-church, antitradition heritage.

The basic trend is evident in the popular hymnody of the period as well. In contrast to the strictly biblical psalms of Puritan days and the biblical paraphrases and theological themes of the eighteenth century, nineteenth-century hymns and twentieth-century choruses were centered in the feelings and experiences of the believer.[44] The slave spirituals fell into a different category, incorporating both direct biblical

41. The New School theology has also been called the New England or New Haven theology, since it is associated with several theologians at Yale University.

42. William G. McLoughlin has argued that Finney adopted the New School theology at an early stage. He cites as evidence for this assertion Finney's rejection of the traditional Calvinist emphasis on the controlling role played by divine election and the associated deemphasis of the role of the human will in matters of personal salvation. (See McLoughlin's introduction to Finney's *Lectures on Revivals of Religion.*) It is my contention, however, that Finney did not stand in any sort of direct theological lineage. If his theology resembled the New School theology, it did so only coincidentally.

43. In a discussion of Dwight L. Moody, the great evangelical evangelist of the latter half of the nineteenth century, George Marsden notes that "although Moody was not a frankly pragmatic analyst of the techniques of successful evangelism in the way Charles Finney had been, he often tested doctrines for their suitability to evangelism.... Almost everyone noticed . . . that Moody emphasized the love of God. Moreover — a striking omission — he did not preach Hellfire and God's wrath. . . . It appears that he avoided distressing subjects largely because he sensed that because of the mood of the modern age they did not meet his pragmatic test" (*Fundamentalism and American Culture,* p. 35).

44. See Marsden, "Everyone One's Own Interpreter?" p. 85. In this discussion, Marsden is drawing on Sandra S. Sizer's book *Gospel Hymns and Social Religion: The Rhetoric of Nineteenth Century Revivalism* (Philadelphia: Temple University Press, 1978).

themes (often recounting narratives of salvation history) and an emphasis on personal experience.

During the first half of the twentieth century, many evangelicals hoped and worked for a restoration of religion to purer ways.[45] They did not foresee that many of the strategies they adopted to battle modern ways constituted an implicit capitulation to those modern ways on another level. It is to this situation that evangelical theology is now called to speak in a renewed and vigorous way. Evangelicals must learn to be conscious of the forces of modernity in order to develop an ability to speak prophetically to them and, when necessary, against them.

IDENTITY AND INDEPENDENCE

Our present experience underscores the point that evangelicalism has never been a monolithic movement. Diversity persists because the origins of the movement were diverse.[46] Ironically, a growing consensus in one area — concerning the merit of certain forms of social involvement — has led to a deepening fragmentation of the movement in other areas. As evangelicals unite behind a variety of strategies to press forward a social agenda (affirming family values, opposing abortion and gay rights, etc.), their theological diversity is becoming ever more apparent. The family resemblances that provided a framework for an earlier generation to participate in the common tasks of evangelism and to fight a common enemy are now overshadowed by family differences. Intra-evangelical debates now dominate evangelical journals, and the worrisome question

45. Joel Carpenter has argued that "restorationism" was not the sole and most likely not even the dominant motive in the evangelical coalition at the turn of the century. See his "Contending for the Faith Once Delivered: Primitivist Impulses in American Fundamentalism," in *The American Quest for the Primitive Church*, ed. Richard T. Hughes (Urbana, Ill.: University of Illinois Press, 1988), pp. 99-119. Granting that, it still seems to me undeniable that many evangelicals were motivated, at least in part, by a concern to return to the purer, simpler ways of the past.

46. The presumption that the movement is monolithic is a fallacy common to those criticisms of evangelicalism that focus on only one of its many aspects. An important example of the sort of criticism that overlooks this essential diversity is Ernest R. Sandeen's work *The Origins of Fundamentalism: Toward a Historical Interpretation* (Philadelphia: Fortress Press, 1968). Sandeen focuses on millenarianism as the central force within evangelicalism. This is obviously an important element, but it is far from being the only or even the central influence.

of theological boundaries (actually a concern about the *lack* of such boundaries) now preoccupies many evangelical colleges and seminaries.

Having said this, I think it important to stress the point that there are still elements that work to hold the movement together. While the forces that promote unity do not at present appear as strong as the forces that are pulling it apart, they are by no means unimportant. There remains in the movement a central core of doctrines, a network of institutions, and a spirit of individualism that link the various constituent groups.

The core of essential doctrines was initially assembled with the intent of unifying different groups in the battle against modernism, but over time evangelicals have come to emphasize these "essentials of the gospel" so strongly that many view other theological doctrines as peripheral. The set of core dogmas includes all beliefs that evangelicals contend can be established indisputably from Scripture. Other dogmas may be true, but, judged by this standard, they remain "open to interpretation."

Allowing for minor modifications by one group or another, the core evangelical doctrines are the following:

1. *Scripture has final authority.* God has spoken to his people in the pages of Scripture. When Scripture deals with an issue definitively, it is settled once and for all.
2. *God does his saving work in history.* The supernatural has broken into space and time. The miracles and other divine interventions recorded in Scripture actually happened.
3. *Eternal salvation is possible only through the atoning death of Christ.* The forgiveness of sins occurs through and by the means of the sacrificial death of Christ on the cross. Christ died on our behalf and received the punishment that ought justly to be ours.
4. *We receive salvation only through personal faith in Jesus Christ.* We are personally attached to the work of Christ by a trust and commitment to him and by believing in what he has done on our behalf. This entails a personal relationship with God the Son.
5. *Evangelism and missions are critically important.* Believers are to care for those who are lost both here and abroad by communicating the gospel in understandable terms. The proclamation of the gospel is a mandate that falls heavily on every believer's shoulders.
6. *It is important to have a spiritually transformed life.* Our faith must make a difference in how we live. Christians are to be changed people.

Few current evangelical confessions, such as those under which most evangelical colleges and seminaries operate, contain statements on doctrinal matters that mark points of difference between members of the evangelical coalition. Such matters as church governance, the sacraments, and the charismatic gifts are seldom treated in these creeds. It is also significant that in most cases there is no "theological fabric" behind these confessions, no distinctive theological tradition (either Calvinistic or Arminian) underlying the confessions' soteriology, no clear set of interpretive guidelines underlying the doctrine of Scripture.

The single most significant doctrinal controversy for contemporary evangelicalism has involved the inerrancy of Scripture. Is the Bible true in every detail? It is a critical issue because of the role it has played in determining evangelical identity. At present, the truth of the doctrine itself is less important than the question of whether it is essential to evangelicalism. A good case can be made that throughout the ages the church has always affirmed some version of inerrancy, but it is a good deal less clear that this affirmation has ever served as a litmus test for orthodoxy to the extent that it recently has in evangelical circles.[47] Evangelicals were convinced that the challenge to the notion of a written revelation presented in nineteenth-century liberal theological circles demanded a response. It was this apologetic context that brought inerrancy to the forefront of evangelicalism and against this background that the doctrine received its clearest formulation.

The current controversy seems so intractable in large measure because there is no larger theological framework within which to settle the issue. There is neither an effective channel for serious theological dialogue nor an authorized ecclesiastical context in which to make a determination of what constitutes orthodoxy.[48] There are few checks

47. The much-debated proposal of Jack Rogers and Donald McKim (presented in *The Authority and Interpretation of the Bible: An Historical Approach* [New York: Harper & Row, 1979]) that inerrancy was a creation of several nineteenth-century professors at Princeton Seminary is now generally regarded as discredited. See especially John Woodbridge, *Biblical Authority: A Critique of the Rogers and McKim Proposal* (Grand Rapids: Zondervan, 1982). It ought to be said, however, that the doctrine of Scripture has been emphasized during the past century in a significantly different manner than it was during the previous history of the church.

48. John Meuther points out the interesting fact that the two most recent "heresy trials" centering on the doctrine of inerrancy occurred outside of an ecclesiastical context. See "Contemporary Evangelicalism and the Triumph of the New School," *Westminster Theological Journal* 50 (1988): 339-47.

and balances on the discussion because of the nature of evangelicalism as a movement.

Attempts to resolve disputes over boundaries of orthodoxy are terribly awkward for evangelicalism. It is a movement built up of loose coalitions in the first place, and the imposition of standards in that setting runs against the grain of the independence of the diverse elements making up the coalition. Antimodernist elements in the movement want clear boundaries to distinguish evangelicalism from the theological liberalism of modernity. Antifundamentalist elements in the movement want a more serious engagement of the modern world and hence a deemphasis of the boundaries separating evangelicals from the modern world.[49]

The fragmentation that now characterizes evangelicalism is at least partly attributable to the lack of a common theological tradition. The structural reason for this is the proliferation of independent institutions all in one way or another representative of evangelicalism. The evangelical community has always more nearly approached a collection of evangelical empires, each feeling kinship with other evangelical institutions while nonetheless staking out its own respective audiences and strategies. The empires, associated with conferences, seminaries, or individual revivalists, have demonstrated a disinclination to employ the the university as an instrument with which to mold culture. But in choosing to avoid this institution, they have abandoned the customary channel for reflective discussion of theological issues. In a similar fashion, they have also bypassed the traditional guardians of the faith — the church — and in doing this, they have abandoned the traditional champion of orthodoxy. The evangelical empires have focused principally on taking their message directly to the people. Public opinion — in this context, specifically evangelical opinion — became the arbiter of truth. This lay orientation was well suited to the rise during the nineteenth and twentieth centuries of a middle class enamored of the ideals of

49. The inerrancy debate is now often cast in two contrasting lights. Those who passionately defend inerrancy view theological liberalism as the main enemy. Those evangelicals who are critical of inerrancy often view fundamentalism as the principal foe. For a trenchant defense of inerrancy against the inroads of theological liberalism, see Norman Geisler's introduction in *Inerrancy* (Grand Rapids: Zondervan, 1979). For a critical assault on the arguments for inerrancy because of their increasingly fundamentalist overtones, see Jack Rogers, "The Church Doctrine of Biblical Authority," in *Biblical Authority*, ed. Jack Rogers (Waco, Tex.: Word Books, 1978), pp. 15-46.

American democracy. And although this individualism did pose some dangers to the movement, the sense of independence also helped evangelicalism maintain a healthy distance from the corrupting pressures of the antisupernaturalism and moral relativism that were becoming dominant in American culture.

The evangelical movement is now clearly transdenominational.[50] It has no significant conceptual or institutional framework within which to cope with denominational distinctives. The organizational pluralism of the movement overshadows any drive toward cohesive institutional authority. The only real authority in the movement resides with a few individuals who have managed to speak more compellingly than others and thereby exerted a special influence.

From the 1940s onward, Billy Graham has stood out as the premier global representative of American evangelicalism. His evangelistic method has shaped the focus of the movement even for those who have not worked directly with him. There were prominent evangelists before Graham, but he became the first accepted figure of the movement as a whole in the twentieth century. He is now increasingly viewed as its elder statesman and its international ambassador. This is not to say that Graham has been without his detractors in the movement, however. His optimistic assessment of the Soviet Union in the mid 1980s and his unwillingness to work with mainline denominations in the early part of his career were not universally accepted. But even if his authority has never approached papal dimensions, his sense of urgency for the evangelistic task, his open-air methods of mass evangelism, and his sense of theological moderation are now deeply embedded in the movement.

A second central identifying institution for evangelicalism is the National Association of Evangelicals (NAE), which provided the first structure within which leaders in the movement could interact formally with one another. The NAE has helped shape both the ethical and social/cultural agendas of evangelicals. In recent years it has also become a central forum for the expression of differences.

A final institution that ought to be noted is the evangelical periodical *Christianity Today*. Founded in 1956, it quickly became recognized as the voice of the movement. It reflected the movement as much as it

---

50. It can be argued that the movement has always been transdenominational. However, there has been a distinct lessening of individual loyalty to denominational structures over the past several generations.

helped shape it. It provided discussions of issues in a popular and simple style.[51] It has tended toward a conservative political stance (as has the movement as a whole), and it has sought to provide a forum for the interchange of ideas on issues of importance to the movement. As evangelicalism has changed, so has *Christianity Today*.[52]

A number of other independent institutions lie near the center of evangelicalism's identity. These include college and high school ministries (InterVarsity, Campus Crusade, Navigators, Young Life, Youth for Christ, Campus Life), overseas mission boards (North Africa Mission, South America Missions, Greater European Missions), mission conferences (Urbana Conference), institutions of higher education (seminaries such as Fuller, Trinity, Gordon-Conwell, Dallas, and Westminster and colleges such as Wheaton, Westmont, and Gordon), and evangelical publishing houses (Baker, Zondervan, and Eerdmans).

It is this orientation toward transdenominational institutions that now most clearly characterizes the movement. The willingness to identify with such organizations rather than with traditional denominational structures marks out the evangelical temperament. Those willing to be called "evangelicals" locate their identity in these transdenominational contexts. The result is that the structure of the evangelical movement, according to Marsden, "is somewhat like that of the feudal system of the Middle Ages. It is made up of superficially friendly, somewhat competitive empires built up by evangelical leaders competing for the same audience, but all professing allegiance to the same king."[53]

The transdenominational character of the movement has enabled evangelicals to carry out tasks that they never could have in the context of established structures. The undertakings of the vast evangelical mission network constitute a prime example. Closer to my concern in this book is the serious biblical scholarship that has accompanied the evangelical revival of the past forty years. Such scholarship could never have been produced in structures that did not take the Bible seriously or that were not committed to biblical supernaturalism.

51. I would add here that although the writing style of the periodical has remained popular and accessible throughout its history, it consistently met higher intellectual standards in the early years of publication than it has in its more recent history.

52. The Christianity Today Institute, an evangelical "think tank," is an interesting case in point, reflecting the degree to which evangelicalism has become more open to serious academic scholarship and interchange.

53. Marsden, "The Evangelical Denomination," p. xiv.

The institutional diversity of the movement has also fostered some independence of thinking on major theological issues. The essentials of the gospel have been starkly simplified and removed from some of the cultural accretions of earlier traditions. Accommodation to the naturalistic temper of the modern age has been effectively resisted, and the gospel remains in the hands of the layperson.

A THEOLOGICAL PATCHWORK QUILT

It is a curious fact that evangelicals in the midst of a cultural renaissance have not produced much theology that is taken seriously by the larger culture. There are prominent evangelical philosophers, historians, and social scientists in the modern academy, but there is a dearth of theologians. This is curious because there *are* specific theological beliefs at the heart of the evangelical movement. In contrast to adherents of other traditions, Protestants (and evangelicals, importantly, among them) have long stressed the cognitive elements of faith. One must not merely believe; one must believe certain truths. The recognition of central theological propositions has long marked out conservative Protestantism. Why is it, then, that in the recent ascendancy of the evangelical movement there has been no corresponding ascendancy of evangelical theology?

It is likely that some accidental factors have contributed to producing this situation. Academic prominence depends to some extent on the native intelligence of individual scholars. It might be argued that evangelical theology has not attained prominence because the evangelical community has not produced a theologian with the abilities of an Augustine, Calvin, or Edwards.[54] It might also be argued that, unlike other disciplines, evangelical theology cannot be carried on in a neutral manner. Evangelical theologians might find it harder to gain recognition in the secular academy than, say, evangelical historians would, because in the very nature of their work theologians will be identifying themselves as evangelical, whereas evangelical historians need not necessarily

---

54. But it is worth noting in this regard that the evangelical community has managed to produce scholars gifted enough to make their mark on the disciplines of philosophy, history, and the social sciences. These scholars may not rank with Augustine, Calvin, or Edwards in the history of Christendom, but their profound influence in the academy is unmistakable.

do so. However, I suspect that a deeper conceptual reason lies behind this dearth of evangelical theologians. In tracing out this conceptual reason, I hope also to shed light on the evangelical theological task.

As evangelicals awaken from their cultural hibernation and begin to commit themselves anew to the theological task, it is imperative that they analyze some of the cultural biases inherent in evangelicalism that inhibit serious theological reflection and the construction of a deeper theological framework. In saying this, I am not trying to disparage the intrinsic strengths of the movement; I am simply suggesting that evangelicalism, like humanity in general, is affected by the fall and must be willing to take account of its shortcomings seriously. It is no more or less susceptible to enculturation than other parts of Christendom. For this reason, it must seriously engage in cultural reflection, not only relative to its "enemies" but also with regard to the movement itself.

It is becoming increasingly apparent that the evangelical consensus concerning the essential theological beliefs of the gospel has created a false sense of unity for contemporary evangelicalism. It forces evangelical Lutherans to repress aspects of their tradition that are distinctively Lutheran, Presbyterians to repress what is distinctively Presbyterian, Methodists to repress what is distinctively Methodist, and so on. Evangelicals have not yet developed a "principled pluralism" that could accommodate both a commitment to the essentials and a recognition of the theological diversity of the movement. And yet without such a framework, theology will, beyond the essentials, continue to be viewed as peripheral and hence unimportant.

Nor is there any theological fabric holding the evangelical identity together. Evangelicals have set about defending a collection of distinct theological beliefs rather than producing a unified vision of theology. They have assembled not a well-crafted piece of clothing but a loosely stitched patchwork quilt.

The very nature of evangelicalism has precluded the larger, grander project of constructing a theological framework. From its inception, the evangelical theological project has been dominated by forces that have undermined sustained theological reflection in continuity with the community of interpreters of the past. Cultural forces have helped to impede efforts to gather from the rich fields of Scripture those raw materials that are essential to the construction of a theological framework. Instead, evangelicals have favored the shallow repetition of theological slogans. The pragmatic temper of the modern age and the ten-

dency to regard sustained intellectual inquiry as relatively insignificant
are as characteristic of evangelicalism as they are of the culture at large.

Abraham Kuyper noted that at the beginning of the twentieth
century in the Netherlands, theology was no longer being written for
the church but was instead being written for the academy. I dare say that
on this side of the Atlantic, evangelicalism has taken another step down
the road: evangelicals write their theology for the masses with little
regard for either the church or the academy.[55] Many evangelical theologians appear to equate writing for the masses with writing for the
church (or at least their particular constituency considered as a church).
What is missing is a vital and vibrant concern for a theological framework
that will genuinely challenge the church and be profoundly reflective of
the greatness of God rather than the triviality of modern culture. There
are signs of hope on the horizon. The serious and sustained intellectual
inquiries of leading evangelical historians, philosophers, and social scientists justify some confidence for the future of evangelical theology. Consciousness has also been raised about the contextualization of evangelical
theology, and there is a growing awareness among evangelicals that
attempts to ignore this contextualization will limit their potential to
produce theology.

It is not enough simply to ask "What must we believe about God?"
We must be so bold as to ask "How would God have us bring him glory
in our thoughts and actions in the modern world?" We must press on to
develop a richer theological vision and not simply seek to protect certain
theological beliefs. To begin the process of constructing this theological
vision, we have to pay careful attention to the revelation of God. However, we will invariably hear the voice of revelation only after it has
passed through several filters. We will hear it through the filter of modern
culture. We will hear it through the filter of a given religious tradition.
We will hear it through the filter of our own personal experiences and
strength of reason. The biblical revelation proceeds through these filters
along a specific trajectory, and the first step toward constructing a theological framework will be to look carefully and deliberately at the nature
of this trajectory. It is to that task that we turn in Chapter 3.

---

55. There are some significant exceptions to this, however, such as nineteenth-
century theologies associated with Old Princeton, Mercersburg, and H. B. Smith.

The Foundation of Theology

The word of God always comes as adversarius noster, our adversary. It does not simply confirm and strengthen us in what we think we are, and what we wish to be taken for. . . . This is the way, the only way, in which the word draws us into concord and peace with God.

Gerhard Ebeling[1]

EPISTEMOLOGICAL GRACE

THEOLOGY, if it is true, is lived. It is lived in the life of the church, those whom God has called out from a rebellious world. Moreover, it is lived in the midst of the world, not in isolation from it. God has not removed the church from the world of rebellion, nor has he removed the world of rebellion from within the church. The church is constituted of fallen creatures who live in a fallen world, and their theological vision ought continually to remind them of this. The truth that God reveals works redemptively in the hearts of individuals and derivatively in the culture in which those individuals reside.

To lose sight of the intimate connection between theology and redemption is to lose the Christian theological framework. It is to put

1. Ebeling, *Introduction to a Theological Theory of Language* (London: Collins, 1963), p. 17.

57

on the blinders of sin, to block the reality of God's redeeming activity from view. It is to exchange this redemption for a preoccupation with the world and the self. It is to construct a world in which we are magnified and God is relegated to insignificance, in which we render God's incarnational redemption in all its glorious truth secondary to our own self-exaltation.

Culture tends to lose regard for the divine truth in one of two ways. Either the biblical text is banished from the modern situation in the fashion of the radical biblical critics or the biblical text is identified with the modern situation in the style of the health-and-wealth gospel. At both extremes the redemptive truth of God is stripped of its life-giving power. In the former case, theology is replaced by anthropology, and in the latter case, theology is replaced by psychological notions of self-fulfillment. In both cases the authority of God's revelation is suppressed in favor of socially acceptable or desirable mores.

The resolution of these dilemmas lies not merely in allowing the biblical revelation to stand in judgment over these aberrations but also in allowing it to stand in judgment of us. Rudolf Bultmann attempted to demythologize the Christian faith by removing all of the offensive metaphysical beliefs from the Bible. Though it is imperative that we not demythologize the text, it is essential to allow the text to demythologize us, to show us those parts of our sense of identity that are human fabrications. The truth of God is liberating, but it is also painful to creatures who are fallen. It brings grace and judgment at the same time.

In the sense I have been describing, then, theology must first be about a conversation with God. This conversation began at creation and took on tragic dimensions at the fall. It became an uncomfortable conversation, for as God revealed himself, fallen humanity appeared that much more wretched in contrast to his glory. But the conversation continued nevertheless, reaching a redemptive climax in the person and work of Christ. Many refuse to enter into the conversation. They do not want to face up to either the depth of their own sin or the greatness of God's character. The divine speech recorded in the Bible presents a stinging judgment as well as our only hope. The doctrines of sin and redemption are the main hinges of the theological framework that have held Christendom together through the ages, and if we fail to take either of them seriously, the framework cannot stand.

The Christian theological framework is all about understanding this speech of God and appropriating it in the lives of those he has called out. Thus, the theological framework is primarily about listening—listening to God himself. A great danger to the theological framework lies in our desire to do all the talking. Most prominently this occurs when we place boundaries on what we can conceive of God as having said in his Word. For example, it has sometimes been argued that God could not have actually died on a cross, because that is repugnant to the modern mind.[2] But, it must be asked, why is this repugnant to the modern mind? Is it because the doctrines of the incarnation and crucifixion are logically incoherent, or is it because the modern mind rejects the prospect of a salvation that does not depend on human effort? We should not dismiss lightly a concern for logical coherence, but neither should we treat casually the deeply offensive nature of the gospel in the face of human sin.

How are we then to listen in on the divine conversation? The apprehension of the conversation must begin with some awareness of who has initiated the conversation and how it was originally begun. It is God who spoke in the first place and who will speak in the last place. His very voice brings things into being, and it is by the living Word that things are restored to being. The apprehension of the conversation must take this into account. God's voice seems strange to us, different. It has a haunting ring to it. Its redemptive quality is paradoxically wrapped in clothes of judgment. The voice reveals God and it reveals us — only too painfully. Our own fallenness is clothed in the greatness of God. God speaks not that we might put him into a psychological test tube but that *we* might be put into one and thereby restored. As David Wells has aptly said, God "is not a quantity that can be 'mastered' even though he can be known, and though he has revealed himself with clarity, the depth of our understanding of him is measured, not by the speed with which theological knowledge is processed but by the quality of our determination to own his ownership of us through Christ in thought, word and deed."[3]

So the Christian theological framework must take into account the God who is known and who has made himself known. Secondarily, it must take into account the one to whom this knowledge comes. God speaks not in a vacuum but to and through people and in and through

---

2. For a contemporary defense of this claim, see the essays in *The Myth of God Incarnate*, ed. John Hick (London: SCM Press, 1978).

3. Wells, "The Theologian's Craft," in *Doing Theology in Today's World: Essays in Honor of Kenneth S. Kantzer*, ed. Thomas E. McComiskey and John D. Woodbridge (Grand Rapids: Zondervan, 1991), p. 193.

history. The speech of God has entered into time and space. It comes clothed in a cultural history and addresses itself to people across different cultural histories. The language is often eloquent, sometimes earthy, always appropriate.

It is a speech often misunderstood and misinterpreted, because those who listen to the speech come with expectations about it. Hoping it will say one thing, they are often disillusioned that it says another. In quiet (and sometimes not-so-quiet) acts of desperation, they interpret the speech as meaning something that was never intended. They turn the conversation strangely upside down. Many listen but mold the message in order to avoid the force of the rebuke it is meant to deliver. They substitute an all-too-human message for the divine message.[4]

Do we all do this to some degree? Yes. Must it happen all the time? No. We all participate in the fallenness of creation. By nature, we do not desire the things of God. Even in redemption, we continue to resist the "good news" at the fierce urging of the sin that remains within us. It is not merely "someone else" who distorts the truths of God; we have to acknowledge that we do so ourselves. If we want to be able to listen to the conversation with God, we have to be able to see how our own expectations color our understanding of the conversation. The impulses that drive us are not always holy and pure. There is a class of influences, says Abraham Kuyper, that are

> essentially sinful because they result from the injurious effect worked by sin immediately *upon our nature.* The Christian Church confesses this to be the *darkening of the understanding,* which does not mean that we have lost the capacity of thinking logically. . . . No, the darkening of the understanding consists in something else, and would be better understood if we called it the *darkening of our consciousness.* Over against sin stands love, . . . and even in our present sinful conditions the fact is noteworthy, that where this sympathy is active you understand much

---

4. The classic example of this sort of reductionism is Ludwig Feuerbach's masterly reinterpretation of Christianity in the garb of atheistic humanism, *The Essence of Christianity* (1841; reprint, New York: Harper, 1957). It was Feuerbach's intent to do nothing short of changing "the friends of God into the friends of man, believers into thinkers, worshippers into workers, candidates for the other world into students of this world, Christians, who on their own confession are half-animal and half-angel into men — whole men." In the introductory essay to the modern edition of Feuerbach's work, Karl Barth refers to this as the archetypal "anthropologization of religion."

better and more accurately than where this sympathy is wanting. A friend of children understands the child. . . . A lover of animals understands the life of the animal. . . . Without this inclination and desire toward the object of your study, you do not advance an inch. . . . This *estrangement* from the object of our knowledge is the greatest obstacle in the way to our knowledge of it.[5]

Our knowledge of God is impoverished to the extent that he is not always our first love. Our theological vision is impaired to the extent that we indulge our desire for sinful self-glorification.

Is the situation then hopeless? Is there any reason for confidence that we can understand the speech of God? A small measure of hope resides in the conviction that God has not left himself without a witness in our lives. The capacity to know God is not destroyed by sin even if it is greatly distorted. The mind still perceives the witness of God even if that witness is twisted in infinitely diverse ways and to infinitely different degrees. The witness remains. The very fact that we twist the message indicates that we grasp it in some fashion, however remotely.

In a strange manner, the ability to understand the message of God is at once a divine blessing and a divine curse — a blessing in that we are able to perceive at least a remnant of God's glory, and a curse because this glory reminds us of our sin and of our attempts to efface that glory. When we remake God in our own image, we are strangely reminded of the God who has made us in his own image.

As I have already noted, we hear the divine conversation only after it has passed through several filters — our culture, our religious tradition, our personal history, and so on. If we take these filters seriously, we may be able to decrease the distortion with which we hear the conversation. In the words of modern discourse, the biblical text has a trajectory. It is like an arrow shot through different layers, through the various filters that reside within each of us. We do not simply stand objectively at the opposite end of the field, waiting for the arrow to pass through these "subjective" layers. The layers are part of who we are, and when the arrow shoots through the layers, it shoots through us.

It is worth paying careful attention to these layers. In fact, I have devoted most of this chapter and the next to an analysis of them. But

5. Kuyper, *Principles of Sacred Theology,* trans. J. Hendrik DeVries (Grand Rapids: William B. Eerdmans, 1954), pp. 110-11.

before we move on to that, it is important that we focus on the *structure*
of the analysis I have just offered. In calling attention to the filters
through which we hear the conversation with God, I am calling attention
to an emphasis that has for the most part been lost in evangelical discussions of theology. And yet I want to retain the fundamental point of
the evangelical tradition — namely, that theology begins with the speech
of God. The Christian theological framework originates with the text of
Scripture, and the interpreter enters the process only derivatively. Why
is it that the theological framework is constructed with God in view first
and ourselves in view only secondarily? Why is it that evangelicals have
long cherished the approach "from above"?[6]

God has revealed himself in many and various ways to humankind.
The psalmist declares, "The heavens declare the glory of God; the skies
proclaim the work of his hands" (Ps. 19:1). The author of the letter to
the Hebrews suggests that "in the past God spoke to our forefathers
through the prophets at many times and in various ways" (Heb. 1:1), and
the apostle Paul wrote in his letter to the church at Rome that the
Gentiles "show that the requirements of the law are written on their
hearts, their consciences also bearing witness, and their thoughts now
accusing, now even defending them" (Rom. 2:15). God's activity of self-
revelation reached its climax in the person and work and words of Jesus.
Being truly God, Jesus disclosed God as no part of creation could. Being
truly human, Jesus provided a vital conceptual link between the Creator
and the creature. He established in his own person the reality of meaningful communication between God and humankind. He decisively precludes any conceptual disjunction between God's revelation in words,
actions, and persons and our understanding of that revelation. Jesus
speaks words that are truly divine and truly human. Jesus performs
actions that are truly divine and truly human. Jesus is himself, in the
core of his very being, both divine and human. He establishes the truth
of an effective link of communication between the divine and the human.
In the words of Gabriel Fackre, Jesus Christ is the expression of God's
"epistemological grace."[7]

6. It could be argued that modern theology is demarcated from classical orthodox
theology by the fact that the former is done "from below" whereas the latter is done
"from above" — above and below being the places where the fundamental conceptual
boundaries for the theological vision are established.

7. Fackre, *The Christian Story*, vol. 2: *Authority: Scripture in the Church for the World*
(Grand Rapids: William B. Eerdmans, 1987).

Many have questioned the reality of this communicative link between God and his creatures. A complete doctrine of the incarnation offers one way to answer such questions. The premise that Jesus is very God and very man establishes a conceptual framework in which it is reasonable to contend that God can communicate in terms understandable to human beings. This argument can gain further support from the concept of the *imago Dei*. God creates human beings in the divine image.[8] Setting aside the complexities of this concept for the moment, we can at least say that there is a consensus in the biblical tradition that human beings are, in some important sense, divine representatives.[9] The image is something that belongs to the visible world and therefore is representative of God's dominion, holy character, rational actions, and deliberations in the created, visible order. So it is no accident that the apostle Paul refers to Christ as "the image of the invisible God" (Col. 1:15), suggesting that Jesus is the clearest conceptual bridge between God and humankind.[10]

God makes his disclosures to humankind not as ends in themselves but for the purpose of executing his intentions, one of which (but surely not the only one) is to redeem his people. In this case, the revelation of God in its manifold forms points beyond itself to his redeeming activity, accomplished in some measure through his disclosures. God speaks in these different ways, not merely that he might be known in some abstract sense but that the relationship with humankind rent asunder by the tragedy of sin might be restored. Revelation and redemption are inseparably linked.

We can derive two fundamental points from all of this. First, God can be known because his self-revelation is comprehensible to his crea-

---

8. The concept of the *imago Dei* is controversial to the extent that it depends on an analogy, and analogies are inherently imperfect. The controversy arises out of differences of opinion concerning precisely which aspects of the human character are in fact analogous to aspects of the divine character and which aspects are significantly different. The fall was a matter of human beings seeking to be "like God" when in fact they were "only an image."

9. For a helpful treatment of this important issue, see Meredith Kline, *Images of the Spirit* (Grand Rapids: Baker Book House, 1980).

10. Paul goes on to suggest that this is possible because "by him all things were created: things in heaven and on earth, visible and invisible, whether thrones or powers or rulers or authorities; all things were created by him and for him" (Col. 1:16). Jesus is both the creative force through which God creates (this is why creation bears the shape it does) and the conceptual bridge between God and his creation (this is why we are able to understand God).

tures. Our knowledge of God is always partial, but it is nonetheless authentic because it is inseparably linked to the divine disclosure and the fact that we have been created in the image of God. When God speaks, he can be understood by the divine image bearers. The second point is that this knowledge of God is redemptive at its core. The Bible is not primarily a book of doctrines. As Geerhardus Vos suggested, "The Bible is not a dogmatic handbook but a historical book full of dramatic interest."[11] Its dramatic interest lies in the unfolding of God's redemptive purposes in human history. The Bible, in its form and its content, records the dramatic story of God reaching into human history and redeeming a people for himself. The form and content of our theology must reflect this.

The Christian theological framework is not created by a masterful human imagination. In fact, it is not fundamentally a human construct at all. It is, in the first instance, discovered in the divine initiative of God's own self-disclosure. If theology is the science concerning God, it is a science with its roots in God's manifestation of himself. Thus, genuine theology listens before it talks.

This is not to deny that all theology inevitably involves some human additions. We listen with ears that are unavoidably inclined toward biases of some sort. We hear more (and sometimes less) than is actually communicated by God in his word. Nor are we unwilling victims of these distortions; in fact, we actively promote them as expressions of our character in a fallen world. Often we hear what we want to hear.

David Tracy, a modern Roman Catholic theologian, speaks of the need for theologians to be connected to three "publics": the church, the academy, and the culture.[12] A "public" is a realm in which theological conversation takes place. Tracy's point is that theology is a social discipline, hammered out in the context of the "conversation partners" of the discipline. Your thought will be a function of who you are talking to on a regular basis.[13] The evangelical's insistence that theology must be done "from above" is based on the assumption that the primary conversation

11. Vos, *Biblical Theology* (Grand Rapids: William B. Eerdmans, 1948), p. 17.

12. See chap. 1 of Tracy's *The Analogical Imagination: Christian Theology and the Culture of Pluralism* (New York: Crossroad, 1981). I discuss the three publics at greater length in Chap. 4.

13. Given this principle, it is understandable that evangelicals generally talk theology only with other evangelicals. It remains a most curious fact that evangelicals have generally tried to talk apologetics only with other evangelicals, however.

partner in theology is God himself. And so to Tracy's three publics, evangelicals would add a fourth — God himself.

The goal of the Christian theologian is to hear with as few distortions as possible. In the language of modern theology, this is achieved by making as clear a distinction as possible between the horizons of the biblical text and the experience of the interpreter. The better we understand who we are as interpreters, the better we will be able to understand the speech of God in its original context. The better we understand the speech of God in its original context, the better we will be able to understand our own distorting influences.

Is this a hopelessly doomed task from the outset if the former depends on the latter and the latter depends on the former? Can we even hope to know what God says if such knowledge depends on our knowing how the words of God are distorted, and this in turn depends on our having some original understanding of the undistorted meaning of God's words? Certainly human inventiveness offers no hope for breaking out of this vicious circle. But there is hope in the divine initiative. God has not only disclosed himself in the acts and words of Scripture but also reveals himself in the very makeup of the human constitution. The biblical text and our own self-understanding are not different sources of our knowledge of God; rather, the former serves as the fundamental conceptual apparatus for understanding the latter. God impresses upon the hearts of humankind the truth of his disclosure in creation and in the Scriptures. As John Calvin put it, "There is within the human mind, and indeed by natural instinct, an awareness of divinity."[14] This "disposition to believe" is activated in the presence of compelling circumstances, which traditional Protestant theology identifies as the preaching of the gospel and the inner testimony of the Holy Spirit. We repress this knowledge of God only at great peril to ourselves. Ironically, however, any attempt to repress such knowledge contains within itself the germ of understanding God: we cannot repress the knowledge of God without having some minimal understanding of what it is that we are attempting to repress.

The fundamental point here is that the evangelical theological vision begins with God's revelation. It is possible to begin at this point because

---

14. Calvin, *Institutes of the Christian Religion*, Library of Christian Classics, vols. 20-21, trans. Ford Lewis Battles, ed. John T. McNeill (Philadelphia: Westminster Press, 1960), 1.3.1.

we are created to understand God's revelation (even if we do not embrace it). As we come to understand the revelation, we come to understand ourselves anew. And the more we understand ourselves, the more we will understand the revelation of God. There is a fundamental direction to the conversation with God. First he speaks (through the unfolding of the history of redemption recorded in Scripture, which reaches a climax in the person and work of Christ), and then we hear that speech. As we listen to the message, we may understand ourselves anew. The message originates with God and takes seed in our minds and hearts, and only then do we comprehend that God is Lord over redemptive history and that we have a particular role to play in this history.

The Christian theological framework finds its shape most definitively, then, in the initiating revelation of God. It must not underemphasize the expectations that the interpreter brings to that revelation, but neither must it negotiate the fundamental starting point in the construction of the theological framework. God must remain the Lord of history and the Lord of theology. The biblical revelation is the final court of appeals for the theologian.

Theology is the most noble and impassioned of disciplines, as John Murray has noted, "because its province is the whole counsel of God and [it] seeks, as no other discipline, to set forth the riches of God's revelation in the orderly and embracive manner which is its peculiar method and function."[15]

THE USE OF THE BIBLE IN THEOLOGY

The Christian theological framework originates with a question: If God has spoken, what has been said? Knowing the answer to this question depends to some extent on knowing the answer to another question: How were the words spoken? That is to say, context is crucial to meaning.

A given string of words can have very different meanings in different contexts. For example, the sentence "There's a fire" might be a cry for help if I shout it at the top of my lungs in front of a blazing house. Or it might be an expression of relief if I utter it after having struggled for several hours to fix a burner in my gas stove.

---

15. Murray, "Systematic Theology," in *The Collected Writings of John Murray*, vol. 4 (Edinburgh: Banner of Truth Trust, 1982), p. 4.

The matter is further complicated in the case of divine speech by the multitude of styles that God uses. He "speaks" creation into being. He speaks through the prophets. He speaks with miracles. He speaks through the providential ordering of redemptive history. And he speaks climactically in the living Word, Jesus Christ himself.[16]

The theological vision ought to capture something of this richness. It seeks a framework that understands and embraces the varieties of God's speech. Sometimes God speaks as a theological professor (as in much of Paul's epistle to the Romans), but this is the exception rather than the rule. As Richard B. Gaffin, Jr., has put it, "Revelation is not so much divinely given gnosis to provide us with knowledge concerning the nature of God, man, and the world as it is divinely inspired interpretation of God's activity of redeeming men so that they might worship and serve him in the world."[17] God does communicate truth, but he typically does so not in the form of tenseless propositions but in the form of poetry and providence and proverbs. He is a master storyteller, and even more amazing is the fact that he also brings to pass the stories that he tells.

Much of the biblical revelation appears in the form of historical narrative, a recounting of selected events in the past. God tells this story, with its many subplots, in order to shape the way we think about history. Broadly speaking, God is telling us that history moves with purpose and that it moves toward a goal that may not be readily apparent. On the surface, life may seem meaningless, but underneath the very foundations of history, God is bringing all things to their proper consummation.

When the Pharaoh imprisoned Joseph, it seemed like a divine defeat. And yet Scripture reminds its readers (as God reminded Joseph and his brothers) that this was no mere accident of history; it was one chapter in the unfolding of the divine plan. The fact that it was part of the divine plan did not remove culpability from Potiphar's wife or Joseph's brothers. They were fully responsible for their evil actions. Yet

---

16. It is important to keep in mind the relative mystery surrounding much of Jesus' teaching. The oft-repeated phrase "Let those who have ears to hear, hear, and let those who have eyes to see, see" is a powerful reminder of the mystery of the gospel to those who remain deaf and blind to it. It was not until the inbreaking of the Spirit at Pentecost that the disciples themselves seem to have understood the import of the mission and ministry of Jesus.

17. Gaffin, introductory essay in *Redemptive History and Biblical Interpretation: The Shorter Writings of Geerhardus Vos,* ed. Richard B. Gaffin, Jr. (Phillipsburg, Pa.: Presbyterian & Reformed, 1980), p. xvii.

in a strange manner these evil actions furthered the divine plan. Later Joseph was able to say to his brothers, "You intended to harm me, but God intended it for good to accomplish what is now being done, the saving of many lives" (Gen. 50:20). The unfolding of God's redemptive purposes in the events surrounding the life of Joseph did not remove the story from the plane of human history. The Egyptian political and penal system were not separated out from the divine story, nor were the Pharaoh's seemingly arbitrary whims unconnected with God's providential involvement and oversight. God works in and through human history without making it any less human. Biblical history is at once both factual (Joseph's brothers were culpable) and purposeful (God remained faithful to the promises originally delivered to Abraham). Our theological framework ought to reflect this blending of the divine and the human in the unfolding of the biblical revelation.

Evangelical theology showed a weakness in this area that has been caricatured by not a few critics during the past century.[18] The charge is that evangelicals have tended to view the Bible as an ancient theology textbook. They have assumed that the task of the modern evangelical theologian is simply to look in the right places for answers to any given problem — places where God has lectured (or dictated a lecture) on a specific doctrine. The theologian gathers as many passages of Scripture as possible, gleaning the truth from this inductive search and ordering results around several typically modern and evangelical topical headings, such as the doctrine of God, the doctrine of creation, the doctrine of the church, and so on.

The caricature proceeds to suggest that it is a basic evangelical assumption that the larger the body of texts one accumulates, the better will be the resultant theology. If one can find ten Scriptures favoring infant baptism and only two favoring believer's baptism, then the evangelical theologian can conclude with a reasonable degree of certainty that one ought to believe in infant baptism. The criticism is then made that this process turns theology into the counting of biblical noses. Apart from the fact that this is an exaggeration and that few theologians have ever been completely guilty of such excesses, the critique does point to

18. See, e.g., David Tracy, *Blessed Rage for Order: The New Pluralism in Theology* (New York: Seabury Press, 1975), pp. 24-25. Tracy is speaking about Vatican I in his discussion of the "Orthodox Theology" model, but his critique is very much applicable to the evangelical theological vision as well.

a weakness in the way the evangelical community has traditionally moved from the biblical text to theology proper.[19] Like many caricatures, this one contains an element of truth.

The element of truth is that evangelical theology has given evidence of an inclination to abstract "doctrines" from the original context of the Scriptures, a predilection for what is typically called proof-texting. The assumption underlying this activity is that creedal beliefs ought to be determined by a simple enumeration of texts. The upshot is that evangelicals tend to focus more on using these doctrines as a litmus test for evangelical identity than they do on attempts to integrate the doctrines with behavior. It is as if they make one set of forays into the Bible to establish key doctrines and then make a subsequent set of forays to establish principles of Christian behavior. They tend to show little regard for the complexity of either the movement from the biblical text to doctrine or the movement from doctrine to life. What little expositional preaching there is in the evangelical movement too often proceeds without concern for the theological implications of the text. Evangelicals have exhibited a much greater interest in finding the simple practical principles of the biblical stories than in undertaking the laborious and difficult task of understanding the theological framework of the text, seeing how this framework fits into the overall vision of the biblical history, and then determining how it moves through history into our own culture and situation.

The evangelical theological framework ought to be intimately draped in life, in culture, in behavior, and in history in its original context. The Bible is not a simple collection of dogmas for belief that can be neatly separated from a simple collection of moral principles ready-made for application to our day-to-day concerns. The Bible makes no simple distinction between doctrine and morals or between theology and life, and neither must those who use it to construct an evangelical theological framework.

The evangelical tradition desperately needs to reorient its principles of theological construction. They must resist an inclination to divorce doctrine from the overarching flow of history in the Scriptures.

---

19. I have greatly simplified a complex issue here in the interest of briefly describing a general weakness. I do not mean to give the impression that I think evangelicals have shown no interest in such matters as the harmonization of conflicting texts or the linkages between different doctrines in their construction of theology.

They must abandon the unfortunate distinction between doctrine and life and the tendency to presume that such a distinction exists in the biblical text itself. They must seek to understand the entirety of life — both how they think and how they act — in the larger framework of God's purposes in history. Until they understand those purposes (as they are revealed in and through the redemptive telling and shaping of the historical story of Scripture), they will not be able to know what to believe or how to act in the modern world as obedient disciples to the fullness of God's revelation.

STAGES OF REORIENTATION

The first stage in this reorientation process is the realization that the crafting of the theological framework involves the entire counsel of God. One must not be content to understand merely the component parts of this counsel (much less just parts of the parts); one must also pay attention to the whole. The complex unity of a great painting is such that all the parts gain their significance from the whole and from their relationships to one another; every part of the canvas sheds light on every other part. The art of interpreting the Scriptures must likewise engage this fundamental principle.

The entire canon of Scripture (often referred to as the "canonical context") serves as the foundation from which the rest of the theological framework is constructed. The theological framework must be drawn from the entire biblical record, even those parts that disturb us at the outset.[20] Theology is built up from the full sweep of redemptive history recorded in the Scriptures. "The various passages drawn from the whole compass of Scripture and woven into the texture of Systematic Theology," says John Murray, "are not to be cited as mere proof texts or wrested from the scriptural and historical contexts to which they belong, but, understood in a way appropriate to the place they occupy in this unfolding process, and applied with that particular relevance to the topic under consideration."[21]

20. Given the principle that righteousness disturbs unrighteousness, it could be argued that the passages that disturb us the most ought to play a central role in our theological vision.

21. Murray, "Systematic Theology," p. 4. What Murray here calls "Systematic Theology" is the same as what I have been referring to as "theological vision."

A second significant stage in the reorientation process is the realization that God's revelation is progressive. He does not deliver it in a static fashion, as if he were offering a classroom lecture. Hence, it would be wrong to conceive of theology as merely a matter of recounting such a lecture in note form. God's revelation unfolds over time. The disciples comprehended much more of that message after Pentecost than they did before Pentecost. In a far clearer fashion than Moses, Joshua saw the fulfillment of the promise of God concerning the land that "flowed with milk and honey." It is one of the central themes in the biblical revelation that testimony to the sovereign lordship of God over all creation increases over time. This increase in the clarity with which the witness of God is manifest on earth is a matter of great consequence for our construction of theology.

In the beginning, Adam and Eve enjoyed perfect clarity in their comprehension of the purposes and presence of God. The creatures and the Creator understood each other. But the fall destroyed this clarity, and Adam and Eve immediately sought to cover their nakedness, to find shelter from God, to hide from him. God had not become any less visible to them; rather, they sought to remove his presence from their sight. In an action with obvious theological import, Adam and Eve were banished from the Garden. Their return was prevented by the flaming sword, an indication that the presence of God had become a place of dread for the fallen couple. Human dissoluteness reached its nadir in the person of Lamech.[22] Lamech usurped the place of God when he took revenge for his wounds by killing another, and his pride culminated in the claim that "if Cain is avenged seven times, then Lamech seventy-seven times" (Gen. 4:24).[23]

God does not leave himself without a witness on the earth, however. He raised up Noah as a remnant to be a faithful witness. Mocked and scorned by his neighbors, Noah nonetheless testified of his God in the

22. It is significant that Lamech is the seventh generation after the fall, seven being traditionally associated with perfection in the biblical record. The genealogical concern of the author of the account in Genesis points to the "perfectly fallen" character of Lamech, which is more than justified given the account of his wicked actions.

23. Lamech underscores his own effrontery with the reference to Cain. The account of the first murder establishes the point that vengeance properly belongs to God alone, and yet Lamech takes pride in having taken it into his own hands. In fact, he asserts that his action is of far greater importance than that of Cain (sevenfold vs. seventy-sevenfold).

building of the ark. The witness of the remnant increases with the promise given to Abraham that his descendants would be as numerous as the stars in the heavens. It was a witness that increased contrary to reasonable expectations. Abraham and Sarah bore a child in their old age and this son served as a living reminder of the presence and promise of God. The witness of God increased as the Jews were brought out of the land of Egypt and populated the land of Canaan. Though taken into exile twice, the Jews nonetheless extended the witness of God into all nations.[24] While in the land of Canaan, the Jews increased in number greatly but were reminded that this numerical increase was not itself a sign of the presence of God — any more than their numerical decrease during the two exiles was a sign of the waning of God's presence. Countless stories in the Old Testament remind the reader that there always remained within the nation of Israel a remnant that truly believed and testified to the power of God. Indeed, God's presence seemed to be strongest when the situation seemed hopeless.[25] The presence of God unfolds in ways that are unexpected and ironic to human eyes, but it continues to unfold steadily nonetheless.

This unfolding of the redemptive plan of God reached a climax in the coming of Jesus as a baby. With his arrival, there was a manifold increase in the witness of God. God had become human for human eyes to see and human ears to hear. And yet in a paradoxical way, Jesus reminded his audiences that only those with eyes to see will see and only those with ears to hear will hear.

The disciples waited expectantly for the final flowering of the kingdom of God as Jesus entered triumphantly into Jerusalem at the time of the Passover feast. They expected him to gain ascendancy and be crowned a king finally in the land of Israel. With the advantage of hindsight (and the epistles), it is clear that they misunderstood the nature of Christ's kingship. Contrary to further expectations, the witness of God was made manifest in defeat, the death on the cross. But in his humiliation, Christ was exalted. He became a king not simply of the Jewish people but of every nation and every people. Following the defeat of the cross, the witness increased still further. At Pentecost, the Spirit

24. This was a partial fulfillment of the promise to Abraham that through his descendants all the nations would be blessed (cf. Gen. 12:3 and Gal. 3:8).

25. The story of Jonah and the large fish and Daniel in the lions' den are apt illustrations of this.

descended and the church extended beyond all known ethnic barriers. Both Jew and Gentile now began to serve as vessels testifying to the lordship of God over all the earth.

Much of contemporary experience can be interpreted as evidence that God could not possibly be in control. But the Christian nonetheless maintains the hope that God is not only in control but is actually using the present circumstances to further the divine plan of redemption. Though it seems to many today that the number of those who still testify to Christ's lordship is relatively low, we are confident that at the end of time, "at the name of Jesus every knee should bow, in heaven and on earth and under the earth, and every tongue confess that Jesus Christ is Lord, to the glory of God the Father" (Phil. 2:10-11). The consummation of history will result in the final and perfect witness to the glory of God.

Salvation occurs in this context. People are not saved simply to be removed from the punishment of hell. Redemption occurs in order that lives might be a living testimony to the glory of God. We are saved in order to serve as faithful representatives of his lordship over all the earth. The unfolding of this redemptive history in the lives of believers continues into the present day, and we cannot understand salvation unless we understand the redemptive history into which it fits. This history lies at the very core of the biblical revelation.

A third stage in the reorientation process arises from the second stage. As we find the history of the redemptive plan of God unfolding in the pages of Scripture, we must remember that the story is being told in a number of different genres. Scripture is not entirely a historical narrative any more than it is entirely a series of dogmatic treatises. It contains both, but it extends beyond them as well. For a host of reasons, different literary styles are employed in God's written revelation. A theological framework must seek to account for both the diversity of styles and the purposes for which these styles are employed.

In order to listen to the speech of God appropriately, we must take care to note the differences in the text as it unfolds. Some of these differences are related to genre. Some are related to the diversity of human authors through whom God has chosen to work. The biblical authors did not step out of their own distinctive personalities or historical contexts when they wrote. Each wrote with goals and purposes in mind. Some of the New Testament letters were written with specific churches and situations in mind. Others were written with more general audiences and purposes in view. Some of the biblical authors used terms in unique ways that can be fully appreciated only in the fuller context of their entire corpus. Much of the diversity within the text can be accounted for on the basis of diverse pastoral concerns, theological motives, and styles peculiar to different historical epochs.[26] God works perfectly through these human vessels, but it must not be forgotten that he does work *through them*.

A fourth stage is a corollary of the third. For all the complexity and diversity of the various styles and differences among the human authors, it must be remembered that the unity of God underlies this diversity. God holds redemptive history together. God is the guarantor of the purposefulness of that history. God does not speak, as it were, out of two sides of his mouth. Hence, our theological framework should reflect the unity of the revelation of God, which is itself a reflection of the unity of divine activity in history. God works through many human vessels and speaks in many different genres, but it is the same God who is working and speaking in each instance.

THE STRANGE UNITY OF TWO AUTHORS

Biblical unity is not always readily apparent to our human eyes. God works in ironic ways. His ways are not our ways, and the wisdom of the world considers the gospel foolishness. In order to discern the unity of the text, we must be less concerned with the constraints of human wisdom than with the revelation of the text itself. The fundamental framework of our theological vision must arise from the fundamental framework of the Scriptures. The Scriptures are not an accumulation of ambiguously related particulars (though some people are inclined to view it that way) that remain unorganized until we apply the structuring principles of some extrabiblical prolegomenon or system. The Scriptures hold together because they have been delivered by a single divine author. Our reading of the text ought to be guided by the inherent unity of the biblical text, and we ought to construct our theological framework in keeping with this kind of reading of the text.

26. See D. A. Carson, "Unity and Diversity in the New Testament: The Possibility of Systematic Theology," in *Scripture and Truth*, ed. D. A. Carson and John Woodbridge (Grand Rapids: Zondervan, 1983), pp. 65-95; and O. Palmer Robertson, "The Outlook for Biblical Theology," in *Toward a Theology for the Future*, ed. David F. Wells and Clark Pinnock (Wheaton, Ill.: Creation House, 1971), pp. 65-91.

Focusing on the unity of the biblical text will help to improve our understanding of the meaning of any given biblical passage. We will necessarily lose some of the meaning if we concentrate only on uncovering the human author's original intention in writing the passage. The great nineteenth-century Oxford scholar Benjamin Jowett insisted that "Scripture has one meaning — the meaning which it had in the mind of the Prophet or Evangelist who first uttered or wrote it, to the hearers or readers who first received it."[27] Jowett maintained that the most primitive meaning of a text is its only valid meaning and that the historical-critical method is the only key that can unlock it. As a matter of practical fact, this method makes our interpretation of the text dependent solely on our assumptions about the human authorship of the text. But this is only part of the story. Certainly evangelicals can share with Jowett a concern for the original authorial intention in Scripture, but they must take care not to lose sight of the other half of the dual authorship or they will surely lose sight of the meaning.

Biblical interpretation in the evangelical tradition has often proceeded with the assumption that the divine author guarantees the reliability of the human author's words.[28] Evangelicals have affirmed that the vantage point of the divine author is accurately communicated through the intentions of the human author. They have also warned that any affirmation of a "manifold sense" (i.e., more than one meaning) would render the science of hermeneutics impossible because the flight from the one meaning of the actual text in its historical context could take any direction whatsoever. If meaning is not ruled by the particular text, they have argued, then it cannot be ruled at all.

But is this so? If meaning is to be tied to authorial intention, then that meaning cannot simply be identified with the intention of the human author. We can derive our best assessment of the authorial intention of the human author from the entire context of his writing. The same should be the case with respect to the divine intention — that is to say, we can derive our best assessment of God's authorial intention from the context of the canon as a whole. Displaying unusual acumen for a systematic

27. Jowett, quoted by David Steinmetz in "The Superiority of Pre-critical Exegesis," *Theology Today* 37 (April 1980): 27.

28. See, e.g., chap. 6 of Clark Pinnock's *Biblical Revelation* (Chicago: Moody Press, 1971); and Louis Berkhof, *Principles of Biblical Interpretation* (Grand Rapids: Baker Book House, 1950), pp. 57-60.

theologian commenting on the field of biblical hermeneutics, J. I. Packer puts the matter as follows:

> If, as in one sense is invariably the case, God's meaning and message through each passage, when set in its total biblical context, exceeds what the human writer had in mind, that further meaning is only an extension and development of his, a drawing out of implications and an establishing of relationships between his words and other, perhaps later, biblical declarations in a way that the writer himself, in the nature of the case, could not do. Think, for example, how messianic prophecy is declared to have been fulfilled in the New Testament, or how the sacrificial system of Leviticus is explained as typical in Hebrews. The point here is that the *sensus plenior* which texts acquire in their wider biblical context remains an extrapolation on the grammatico-historical plane, not a new projection onto the plane of allegory. And, though God may have more to say to us from each text than its human author had in mind, God's meaning is never less than his.[29]

The interpretive process will change if we affirm a dual authorship of the text, if we tie the meaning of the Scriptures not only to the original context of the human author but also to the historical-redemptive context of the divine author. We must understand the human authors in their proper historical context, and this original context may suggest limits on possible interpretations of the divine intent. But there are additional limitations beyond this: if we look only at the historical context of the human author, we might not see links to later (or even earlier) passages — links that become important when we take the context of the divine author into account and admit the entirety of the canon as one of the interpretive keys for understanding any particular biblical text.

In saying this, I am by no means endorsing the sort of allegorical interpretation of biblical texts that presumes to uncover hidden or spiritual meanings that are only accidentally related to the plain meaning of the text. To countenance such an approach would be to open the door to an endless variety of exotic readings of the text. Suppose an interpreter of the Psalms were to begin with the assumption that the number of letters in a psalm has a special significance, for example. On finding that

29. Packer, "Biblical Authority, Hermeneutics, and Inerrancy," in *Jerusalem and Athens: Critical Discussions on the Theology and Apologetics of Cornelius Van Til*, ed. E. R. Geehan (Nutley, N.J.: Presbyterian & Reformed, 1971), pp. 147-48.

a given psalm contains 666 letters, the interpreter might then suspect that the psalm contains secret clues to the identity of the anti-Christ. I believe that all such speculations are fruitless — because I believe that God discloses no meaning in the biblical text that is *unrelated* to the plain meaning of the text. But this is not to say that the meaning of the text is limited to that plain meaning. God may disclose meaning "through and over time." Thus, the redemptive foreshadowings of the Old Testament take on a new significance in the light of New Testament events. These linkages are important because the divine author is providentially involved in the authorship of the *whole* biblical text and in the providential ordering of the history to which the biblical text witnesses.

The "organic unity" of Scripture should free us to read each text in the context of the entire whole and the whole in the light of each particular text. It is wrong to suggest that either the divine authorship overwhelms the humanity of the text or that the reality of the human authorship precludes us from seeing unity in the overall text placed there by the divine author.

REDEMPTIVE HISTORY AND THE PROGRESS OF THEOLOGY

As readers of the Bible in its finished form, we are able to see its unity-in-diversity more completely and clearly than was possible for any who lived during the biblical times themselves. Like the disciples at Pentecost, we see the resurrection of Jesus more clearly than those in the pre-resurrection community had. As redemptive history unfolded with increasing testimony to the glory of God, so the interpretation of that history unfolded with greater clarity. A post-resurrection theological framework should capture more of the richness of God's redemptive work than was possible before the resurrection.

In his farewell discourse (John 14–17), Jesus told his disciples that after he had left them, the Father would send the Spirit, and the Spirit would guide them into all truth by reminding them of all he had said to them (John 14:25-31). He did not say that the Spirit would bring new knowledge but rather a new understanding of what he had already spoken. As a result of the work of the Spirit, the disciples would be empowered, said Jesus. But to what end would they be empowered? Jesus told the disciples that they would be his "*witnesses* in Jerusalem, and in all Judea and

Samaria, and to the ends of the earth" (Acts 1:8). The power of the Spirit is the power of understanding and testifying clearly to the risen Lord across all ethnic boundaries. This constituted a significant enrichment of the disciples' theological framework prior to the resurrection. It should lead to a significant enrichment of our theological framework as well.

Our interpretation of the Bible ought to take into account the progress present in the ongoing unfolding of the redemptive plan of God through marked stages. It ought also to take into account the unity of the redemptive plan ensured by the divine authorship and governance of that plan.

The Christian theological framework ought to be shaped by this ongoing concern for unity-in-diversity. The structural unity-in-diversity of the theological framework does not originate with the reader or with any system imposed on the text but with the unity-in-diversity of the divine and human authors of the biblical text. There is unity because there is one divine author. There is diversity because the divine plan (story) unfolds in and through history. The evangelical theological framework ought to mirror the organic unity of the Scriptures as well as the actual development present in the biblical history. As Richard B. Gaffin, Jr., has noted, the biblical "process is not heterogeneous, involving ongoing self-correction. Nor does it have anything to do with an evolutionary movement from what is erroneous and defective to what is relatively more true and perfect. . . . The movement of the revelation process is from what is germinal and provisional to what is complete and final."[30] Development is evident in the biblical text, but it is divinely guided and inspired. The great irony of the Christian religion is that God has acted in and through the pages of human history. The Creator redeems the creature by humbling himself even to the point of death on a cross. This is foolishness to the unbelieving world, but it is the sole source of hope for the disciple of Christ.

CONCLUDING COMMENTS

This enigma helps to define the theological framework in a number of important ways. First, it is important to recognize that the Christian

---

30. Gaffin, "Systematic and Biblical Theology," *Westminster Theological Journal* 38 (1975-76): 289.

theological framework finds its uniqueness in its fundamental commitment not only to the redemption brought by Christ but also to the redemptive revelation of which Christ is the climax. The final authority for the theological framework resides not in our experience of the redemptive work of God but in his interpretation of that redemptive experience. Theology in its form and substance as well as its function in the church must be determined by God's authoritative Word.

Second, the revelation of redemption must be seen in its entirety. The theologian must not lose sight of either the beginning or the end of this process. God's redemptive history moves with a purpose, and the consummation of that history is fundamental to the proper interpretation of each of its individual episodes. This serves to underscore the point that the Christian theological framework must be grounded in the *entire* canon of Scripture. Theology must not lose sight of the whole as it looks at the parts. This is true not only with respect to the content of theology but also with respect to its form. Too frequently the evangelical theological framework has lacked a sense of movement toward a consummation. It has tended to emphasize specific doctrines rather than the entire "doctrinal package."

Third, though an emphasis on the unity of the canon ought clearly to be fundamental in our construction of the theological framework, we must also remember the diversity present within this canon. The biblical revelation was written over a period of a millennium and a half. Many human authors participated in the project, each with a unique personal history and perspective. The diversity of perspective and variety of purpose manifest in the different writings that constitute the biblical canon make one more fully aware of the complexity of the redemption offered through that canon. In this sense, theology must be regarded as a historical discipline. It must concern itself with the progression of revelation that is recorded in Scripture. The textual evidence in support of a particular doctrine cannot stand in isolation from its historical context. In constructing the theological framework, we must be sensitive to the historical flow in the "evidence." Theologians seeking a final, timeless representation of the character of God, man, and the world have too frequently been inclined to read all biblical texts in the same manner, to overlook the fact that the historical context of Isaiah is different from, say, the historical context of John's Revelation. We must be careful to distinguish between such contexts as we interpret texts with the purpose of shaping a theological framework.

The diversity present in the historical character of revelation is also present in the synchronic diversity of perspective. Just as there are many strands in history that can help us to understand the redemption in Christ, so there are many strands in the context of the post-Pentecost experience (Paul, Peter, John, etc.) that can help us to understand the complexity of the redemption we have in Christ.[31] Furthermore, within each of these perspectives we can find several different styles of speech that are used to capture the richness of this redemption. For example, Paul speaks of redemption using the language of the marketplace (redemption), the law courts (justification), the family (adoption), and the Old Testament cultus (sacrifice). Our theological framework ought to give some indication of the complexity of this salvation that is indicated by the many metaphors that are used to characterize it.

A subpoint needs emphasis here: the progressive nature of revelation must be treated with all seriousness, but appeals to the progressive character in order to exclude inconvenient or socially unpalatable components of the biblical revelation ought to be seen as illegitimate. We seek the progress from perfect seed to perfect tree, not the progress from bad to good or from wrong to right.

A fourth and final point concerns the situation of the contemporary theologian in relation to the divine author of the biblical text. We must remember that all theology should be framed within the context of doxology. Reflections on the revelation of God should be wrapped in praise and adoration of God. The entire doctrinal endeavor must be understood in the context of knowing and worshiping God. Theology must not only serve our minds (though it must not do less than this) but must also be grounded in a heart prepared by God. As the great Dutch theologian Abraham Kuyper remarked nearly a century ago, "without the sense of God in the heart no one shall ever attain unto a knowledge of God, and without love, or, if you please, a holy sympathy for God, that knowledge shall never be rich in content."[32] A disinterested theological vision may capture the mind but it will only impoverish the soul. Evangelical theology ought never to lose sight of the author and finisher of our faith.

---

31. Richard Gaffin helpfully emphasizes this point in "Systematic Theology and Biblical Theology," *Westminster Theological Journal* 38 (1975-1976): 284-88.
32. Kuyper, *Principles of Sacred Theology*, p. 112.

CHAPTER 4

The Trajectory of Theology

My personal self-understanding and personal experiences of faith [contra Bultmann] must not only be seen as exegetical aids, but also as possible sources of error.

Oscar Cullmann[1]

INTRODUCTION

THEOLOGY is not simply a list of dogmas to be believed; it encompasses a framework for thinking about the world and a vision for living in it. It seeks to capture the minds and hearts of believers so that they might think Christianly and act Christianly. Theology is the most noble and impassioned of disciplines, and if confined to the classroom, it will shrivel and die.

Theology must be lived in the life of the church, in the lives of those whom God has called out from a rebellious world. It must be lived in the midst of the world, not in isolation from it. The church is composed of fallen creatures who live in a fallen world and whose theological vision is inevitably influenced by the profound impact of sin on their hearts and minds. Yet the fundamental hope of Christians is the hope that the Holy Spirit brings in the power of God's word to transform their minds and hearts in accord with God's purposes. An emphasis on God's

1. Cullman, *Salvation in History* (New York: Harper & Row, 1967), p. 298.

81

epistemological grace expressed in Spirit and Word is a fundamental element of the evangelical theological vision.

The Scriptures in their fullness are the divine witness to and interpretation of God's redemptive activity in history. God both speaks and acts to save his people, but he does not remove them from either their culture or their history. God saves his people *in* history, not *from* history. Awareness of this fact should force the theological vision to take into account the "filters" of that history: tradition, culture, and reason.

The biblical revelation stands in an authoritative position relative to these filters, but inevitably they influence the interpretation of that authority. The filters do not determine by themselves the nature of the authority, but they do exert a certain influence on the directions in which that authority moves in the life of the believer. The goal of theology is consciously to bring the biblical revelation into a position of judgment on all of life, including the filters, and thereby to bring the cleansing power of God's redemption into all of life.

It is imperative that the theological framework make manifest those parts of our identity that are human fabrications, aspects about which we think more highly or more disparagingly than we ought. The truth of God is liberating, but it is also painful to creatures who are fallen. It brings grace and judgment at the same time.

Theology must first be about a conversation with God. The Christian must be reminded that the conversation is often a monologue: God speaks and we listen. It is not always that way, but it moves in that direction most fundamentally. The Christian theological framework is primarily about listening — listening to God. One of the great dangers we face in doing theology is our desire to do all the talking. As I have already suggested, we most often capitulate to this temptation by placing alien conceptual boundaries on what God can and has said in the Word. In the terminology of this chapter, we concede a disproportionate influence to our filters in our efforts to understand the biblical revelation. We force the message of redemption into a cultural package that distorts its actual intentions. Or we attempt to view the gospel solely from the perspective of a tradition that has little living connection to the redemptive work of Christ on the cross. Or we place rational restrictions on the very notion of God instead of allowing God to define the notions of rationality.

How ought we then to listen in on this divine speech and engage in the theological conversation? We must begin by recognizing who has initiated the conversation and how it was originally spoken. It is God who spoke in the first place and will speak in the last place. His very voice brings things into being, and it is by the living Word that things are restored to being.

Having recognized the source of the conversation, we must then take into account those with whom he speaks. God does not speak in a vacuum but to and through people and in and through history. The speech of God has entered into time and space. It comes clothed in a cultural history and is addressed to people across different cultural histories, and for this reason (among others), it is often misunderstood and misinterpreted. All who listen to the speech do so with certain expectations. Hoping or expecting that God will say one thing, they are often disillusioned when he says something else. They listen with ears that do not hear and they look with eyes that do not see. Like Nicodemus, they are looking for the natural birth while Jesus speaks of the spiritual birth. Or, like the Pharisees in John 8, they understand their lineage in ethnic terms rather than in theological terms.

Nicodemus and the Pharisees stood in a tradition, were conditioned by a culture, and applied certain principles of rationality to their conversations with Jesus. We do the same today. It is part of the theologian's task to bring the people of God to an awareness of their historical, cultural, and rational filters so that they will not be ruled by them.

So, in our efforts to listen to the conversation with God, we must begin by throwing light on the expectations that color our understanding of the conversation. Next we must seek to understand the impact that these expectations have had on our appropriation of the redemptive work of God. And finally, we must strive to understand how to communicate our Lord's message in our unique circumstances with as few distortions as is humanly possible.

THE USE OF TRADITION IN THEOLOGY

The message of Scripture is transmitted from generation to generation in a variety of ways. It is handed down through a set of practices, a body of beliefs, and a cultural ethos. The theological use of the term *tradition* signifies the means of passing on the message of the Scriptures from generation to generation. In this sense, every theologian and every believer stand within a theological tradition. This tradition may be vast and varied (as in the case of Roman Catholicism) or it may be fairly narrow and uniform (as in the case of dispensational premillennialism). Theologians inevitably stand within several theological traditions. In fact, a variety of historical sources influence all believers in their understanding of the gospel. One individual might feel a certain kinship to both Luther and Calvin, for instance, while another might find fruitful suggestions for the forging of a contemporary theological vision in the work of Augustine and Aquinas. In order to proceed, we will have to take a closer look at what constitutes a tradition and what influence a tradition ought properly to exert on the shaping of the evangelical theological framework.

The term *tradition* has picked up a considerable variety of connotations in everyday usage, and these have extended to its use in theological contexts. People have different views about the value of the past. Some speak dismissively of "dead traditionalism" while others much prefer the "traditional" to the merely "faddish." These fundamental differences of perspective have serious implications for the theological employment of this concept. How does the past relate to the present? How does the past relate to the original Scriptures? What authority (if any) do past theological statements have for the modern theologian? What does the reformation of tradition amount to in the Protestant churches? These and a host of other knotty issues point to the difficulty of getting a precise handle on the nature of tradition. I make no presumption of being able to resolve all of these issues, but I do think that we can take a valuable step toward reducing the confusion by clarifying how it is that we will be using the term.

In the discussion that follows, *tradition* will signify the faith transmitted by the community of interpreters that has preceded us. This body of faith includes the creedal statements that have formalized vital theological convictions of successive generations. It includes the set of behavioral principles (written and unwritten) that have been considered central to the interpretation of the gospel through the ages. It undoubtedly includes some awareness of what, in various contexts, the community of interpreters has judged to be heretical. In sum, I will be using the term *tradition* to refer to the entire collected expressions of biblical interpretation (written and unwritten) to which particular past communities have committed themselves and by which they have sought to transmit their faith to subsequent generations.

Of course this definition of *tradition* leaves room for certain ambiguities. During the development of a tadpole into a frog, there is a time when the entity is clearly a tadpole and a time when it is clearly a frog, but there is also a period during which one would be hard pressed to say which of the two it is. Similarly, most traditions are clearly defined by certain perspectives and clearly differentiated from other perspectives, but between this clear center and its opposition there is often a gray area in which the differences are not so obvious.

Initially the boundaries of the Protestant tradition seemed clear enough in the minds of the Reformers (at least after 1522). The council of Trent (1540-1544) affirmed that the Protestants were no longer Roman Catholics, and in significant ways the Protestant tradition was defined in terms of a pointed rejection of certain Roman Catholic beliefs and practices, such as the institution of the papacy, the sale of indulgences, and most importantly the Roman Catholic doctrine of justification. Still, there remained areas in which there was not so clear a distinction between the Protestant and Roman Catholic tradition — matters such as the two natures of Christ, the doctrine of the Trinity, and so forth. Moreover, the Protestant front was by no means monolithic itself. Differences between one Reformer and the next over such issues as the Lord's Supper and baptism precluded the development of a single uniform Protestant tradition.[2] My point here is that every tradition possesses a core and a periphery and also that we can quite properly speak of different traditions within a tradition.

As we proceed to work out how tradition is related to the construction of a modern theological vision, we will do well to keep the essential diversity of tradition in mind. It might be reassuring to imagine that the modern Christian community has emerged from and continues to interact with a single tradition, but this would be to ignore much that is at the heart of our Christian past. This is especially the case with respect to the modern evangelical movement, which has emerged from a considerable variety of historical movements.[3]

2. I do not mean to suggest here that sixteenth-century Roman Catholicism was free of such diversity. In fact, there were a number of influential communities of interpretation within the Church holding markedly different views. Their significant diversity has simply been masked by the fact that they all remained under the one institutional umbrella of the Roman Catholic Church while the Protestants did not.

3. For further elaboration of this point, see chap. 2 of James Davison Hunter's *American Evangelicalism: Conservative Religion and the Quandary of Modernity* (New Brunswick, N.J.: Rutgers University Press, 1983).

What role should we accord to tradition in the construction of a theological framework, then? The validity of any particular theological conviction ought finally and ultimately to be judged by its fidelity to the Scriptures rather than its fidelity to any given tradition. And yet, entering into a conversation with the past as well as the present communities of interpretation can help us to make a determination of what constitutes fidelity to the Scriptures. Modern theologians will undoubtedly be inclined to pay closer attention to more recent voices in the community of interpreters, but they should not assume that our own time is the sole stronghold for wisdom in such matters. We would be arrogant to assume that nineteen centuries of the Christian community have nothing significant to say to us today.

Having said this, it is also important to affirm that each new generation of believers must defend the fundamental principles of the faith anew. These principles must be "owned" in the contemporary context. The convictions of one's theological ancestors held merely on trust will not in the final analysis be held sincerely at all. They may be prescribed in the mind, but they will not become inscribed on the heart. In part this is so because the cultural context changes from one era to the next, each new context posing new questions and asking the old questions in new ways. If the faith is not defended anew in the face of the difficulties that arise in each new cultural setting, it will die. It cannot simply remain parasitic on the faith of generations past.

The Distant Past

One of the central underlying difficulties for the modern community of interpreters is the way in which we moderns have divorced ourselves from the distant past. As Allan Bloom has poignantly reminded us, it is difficult to convince modern students of the importance of anything that occurred prior to 1970.[4] Focusing on the wonders of modern technology, many assume that everything of real historical significance has occurred in the modern era. Few experience nostalgia for anything further back than the middle part of the twentieth century. And though the modern era affords us more leisure time than the people of any previous period in history have known, it has also created an environment in which we

---

4. See Bloom, *The Closing of the American Mind: Education and the Crisis of Reason* (New York: Simon & Schuster, 1987).

are far less likely to invest that leisure time in reflection generally or in attempts to recover the insights of the past specifically. Furthermore, the effects of the cultural phenomena that distract us from a reflective appreciation of tradition are compounded by two forces in the religious culture that are specifically opposed to the appropriation of tradition. One is the liberal desire to be freed from tradition in order to pursue new interpretations, and the other is the evangelical desire to return to the spirit of the primitive church antecedent to all tradition. The former yearns to be freed from the past in order to move into the future; the latter yearns to be freed from the past in order to move yet further into the past.

Antitraditionalism

During the past two centuries, university theologians have expressed ongoing concern about the role of tradition in the shaping of theology.[5] Their anxiety is associated with the ascendancy of the idea of "progress" during this period.[6] The greater a culture's interest in progress, the greater will be the conceptual distance it perceives between past and present. Part of the modern anxiety can be explained by the speed with which modern science has advanced — apparently at a pace far outstripping the "progress" of civilized religion in the West. The dawn of the new science in the seventeenth and eighteenth centuries, the emergence of the industrial revolution in the nineteenth century, and the rise of the technological revolution in the twentieth century have all contributed to this sense of alienation from the past. The ethos of Western civilization suggested to many that science left unhindered by religion and the church would solve the fundamental problems of humanity.

Many theologians perceived a theological chasm opening up at the dawn of the nineteenth century. Citing what they believe to be an essential conflict between old language and new knowledge that emerged at this time, liberal theologians often give the impression that modern

5. John Henry Newman's *Essay on the Development of Christian Doctrine* (1845) is often seen as a watershed in discussions of this type. Newman experienced an evangelical conversion early in life but later moved toward a high Anglo-Catholic view of church tradition, converted to Roman Catholicism, and was appointed a cardinal.

6. See Christopher Lasch, *The True and Only Heaven: Progress and Its Critics* (New York: W. W. Norton, 1991). For a helpful historical overview, see Robert Nisbet, *The History of the Idea of Progress* (New York: Basic Books, 1980).

Christendom began then.[7] They contend that the impressive advances in scientific knowledge over the past two centuries pose intractable problems for the simple reiteration of older confessions and beliefs. At the outset they argued that the repristination of earlier traditions was no longer a possibility because of a conflict between the conceptual schemes of the modern and premodern eras, between the scientific and prescientific eras. God became simply the God of the gaps — gaps in our knowledge of the world that science had not yet filled in but would do so in good time if left free and unhindered. Belief in religious miracle was replaced by belief in scientific miracle. The three-tiered universe of traditional Christianity (heaven above, hell below, and the earth in between) was abandoned in favor of the new single-tiered universe of modern science, a universe shaped entirely by natural forces. Bultmann captured the modern spirit well when he said that traditional supernaturalistic Christian belief "is impossible in this age of the electric light and the wireless."

Liberal Protestants began to discuss not the authority of tradition but rather how the confessional tradition got started in the first place. Freed of the constraints of an authoritative Bible and an authoritative church, they sought to explain the development of doctrine in the history of the church in naturalistic terms, focusing on political, social, and economic factors.[8]

---

7. Evangelical theologians often imply that Christendom ended then. In this light, it is curious that evangelicals are not more conscious of the pre-nineteenth-century traditions that form a large part of their own theological heritage. One recent interpretation of this fact is intriguing: Nathan Hatch charts the course of the emphasis on the call for a primitive return to the Scriptures (i.e., interpretation without recourse to tradition) and argues that in the American setting it came first from theological liberals who were seeking to free themselves from the entrenched conservative Calvinism of New England. In an earlier period, the Socinians had argued against traditional Protestants with appeals to the text of Scripture as distinct from the dogma of tradition. Hatch concludes from the American context that the impulse to free oneself from tradition is essentially a liberalizing tendency — i.e., a movement away from the biblical text. If he is correct, then it is ironically the case that insofar as this remains an essential thrust within evangelicalism, the movement will increasingly move away from the biblical text. See Hatch, *The Democratization of American Christianity* (New Haven: Yale University Press, 1989).

8. For some fine Protestant historical treatments of this issue, see Jaroslav Pelikan, *Historical Theology: Continuity and Change in Christian Doctrine* (New York: Corpus, 1971), and Owen Chadwick, *From Bossuet to Newman: The Idea of Doctrinal Development* (London: Cambridge University Press, 1957).

This interest jelled with the crisis created in the nineteenth century by biblical scholars who suggested that the church in its many and varied expressions had actually corrupted the true teaching of the Scriptures. The celebrated German theologian Friedrich Schleiermacher argued that the pure teaching of Jesus had been corrupted by Greek philosophy and Roman legalism, resulting in the tradition that is now called orthodoxy. His thesis was taken up and developed by two of his disciples, August Neander and Adolf Harnack. These two impressive historians attempted to show that the essential teaching of the New Testament had been thoroughly corrupted by the orthodox tradition as that tradition was manifested in the creeds of the early ecumenical councils. The crisis reached a crescendo of sorts with the work of the radical German biblical scholar F. C. Baur. Baur discovered that certain epistles in the New Testament actually contained elements of doctrine and discipline remarkably similar to the later orthodox tradition. He showed that several of Paul's letters assumed the existence of a fixed church order, for example. And elsewhere in the New Testament, there were already signs of "doctrine" or "right belief" playing a central role in defining the early church community. In essence, Baur argued, the New Testament itself contained an early form of Catholicism (orthodoxy). Baur's radical suggestion, however, was not to offer this finding as evidence in support of the fidelity of later orthodoxy to the biblical witness but rather to see it as confirming that "tradition" had already seeped into the New Testament itself and thereby corrupted the simple message of Jesus. He argued that the Bible informs us more about the faith of the early church than about the real historical Jesus. In reaching this radical conclusion, Baur launched a furious search among other scholars to determine which of the recorded words of Jesus could be considered free from the interpretation of the apostles, free from any corrupting traditions.[9] That search in modified form continues today.

The yearning to find the "core" teaching of Jesus motivates the biblical criticism that lies behind many of the contemporary liberation theologies. Convinced that the orthodox traditions have long corrupted the liberating message of Jesus, these theologians argue that the inter-

---

9. Against this general line of argument, Gerald Bray has offered a fine exposition of the bridges between the teaching of the New Testament and the teaching of the early creeds. See his *Creeds, Councils and Christ* (Downers Grove, Ill.: InterVarsity Press, 1984).

pretive key that unlocks this message is the Exodus event of the Old Testament.[10] The political and economic liberation of the people of Israel manifested the true intentions of God, they say, and thus serves to interpret the mission of Jesus. Jesus came to show the downtrodden freedom from oppression (defined in political, economic, or social terms). In this sense, they are suggesting that Jesus' ministry did not have a primarily theological purpose (i.e., a purpose associated with the relationship between Creator and creature); rather, his primary concern was with socio-political and economic matters, with seeking to restore just and equitable relationships in social structures.

In this context, the ideological critique of religious tradition plays a central role. The contention is that Christian tradition illustrates the prejudices of the past more than it illumines the ancient texts that were the objects of study in these earlier periods. History tells one more about who was more powerful than who was accurate. [The victors wrote the history books and hence defined "orthodoxy."[11] In contrast to traditional histories of the early church, contemporary radical theologies suggest that the important history in Christendom is the history of heresy, because the dissident and the downtrodden are more likely to be uncorrupted by the power structures in any given culture and hence they are more likely to be closer to the "truth."] This, they say, is the thrust of

10. On this, see especially part 4 of the classic theological text of the liberation theology movement by [Gustavo Gutiérrez, *A Theology of Liberation*] (Maryknoll, N.Y.: Orbis Books, 1973).

11. Among biblical scholars this thesis has been most ardently defended by Walter Bauer in *Rechtglaubigkeit und Ketzerei im ältesten Christentum* (Tübingen: Mohr-Siebeck, 1934; ET *Orthodoxy and Heresy in Earliest Christianity*, ed. Robert A. Kraft and Gerhard Krodel [Philadelphia: Fortress Press, 1971]). Bauer argued that the early church was marked by widespread doctrinal pluralism that was eventually suppressed by the rise of Catholic orthodoxy. He believed not merely that there were doctrinal differences between the early church and Jesus (as liberals suggested in the nineteenth century) but that doctrinal diversity was at the heart of the tradition of the early church. Bauer's views have been picked up and defended most ably by Helmut Koester in "Gnomai Diaphorai: The Origin and Nature of Diversification in the History of Early Christianity," in *Trajectories through Early Christianity*, ed. James M. Robinson and Helmut Koester (Philadelphia: Fortress Press, 1971), pp. 114-57. An excellent corrective to this line of argument can be found in I. Howard Marshall's essay "Orthodoxy and Heresy in Earlier Christianity," *Themelios* 2 (1976-1977): 5-14. For bibliographic data relating to the continuing influence of Bauer's work, see Daniel J. Harrington, "The Reception of Walter Bauer's *Orthodoxy and Heresy in Earliest Christianity* during the Last Decade," *Harvard Theological Review* 77 (1980): 289-98.

the message of the Exodus event in the Old Testament and the life of Jesus in the New Testament.

Antitraditional Traditionalism

[Evangelicals have a much different concern for tradition. While they have all too frequently followed the liberal's search to find the "real Jesus" free from tradition and dogma, they have not typically cast the search in terms of justice and liberation from oppression. Their search has more typically begun with isolating the words of Jesus — placing them in red letters in their Bibles, for instance. And they have proceeded to dwell on the "practical parts" of the New Testament, avoiding any dogmatic pronouncements of the apostles.]

It is ironic, then, that evangelicals should so often be accused by the larger theological community of having a Roman Catholic view of tradition (as enunciated at the Council of Trent in response to Martin Luther). It is a common perception of modern theologians that the evangelical movement relies on its confessions as infallible interpreters of the Scriptures. I would like to suggest that this criticism is misplaced, however. In fact, the more fundamental "sin" — and, indeed, the enduring legacy — of contemporary evangelicalism is that the movement has not taken tradition seriously enough. "No creed but the Bible" is the victory slogan inherited by much of modern evangelicalism from its eighteenth- and nineteenth-century ancestors. Originally this cry echoed American individualism, and it gave expression to the conviction that the past community of interpreters was irrelevant to the modern task of interpreting the Bible. Though times have changed over the past century, this underlying conviction has not. Evangelicals have further removed the core teaching of Jesus from the theological fabric of the apostolic witness of the New Testament and later theological tradition because of their standing in modern culture. Theological conservatives have become a "cognitive minority" in the West, and this change of status is partially responsible for their desire to be acceptable to the mainstream once more, to regain lost ground. And so they have made an effort to downplay many of the offensive parts of the evangelical tradition, to package the gospel so that it is attractive to the "unchurched." As David F. Wells recently put it, ["The wider evangelical movement has lost the stomach for any kind of confession which violates the etiquette required in the presence of the pluralism and relativity which our modernity has spawned."[12] This is evident in three important characteristics of the evangelical movement: its use of inductive methods of Bible study, its parachurch orientation, and its ahistorical devotional piety.[13]

The Private Bible

In many evangelical churches the Bible is studied primarily with the aid of inductive Bible study materials, by which I mean materials that focus principally on the issue of what the text has to say to the individual approaching it.[14] Implicit in the approach of such materials is the assumption that the biblical text is essentially accessible to the average person who is willing to spend a little time with it.

In some ways this might seem a reaffirmation of the Reformers' belief in the right of private interpretation. They maintained that each individual has a right and a responsibility to interpret the text. Martin Luther viewed the task of translating the Bible into the vernacular as a critical aspect of bringing this goal to fruition. If all people could read the Bible in their own native tongue, he believed, then all might be freed from the interpretive dictates of the papacy and thereby enabled to fulfill their responsibility to interpret the biblical text properly.

The charge quickly came from Rome that if the Bible was placed in the hands of every layperson, a thousand different interpretations would arise, and a thousand different churches would result. Rome was, on this matter, prophetic. Without an infallible interpreter, each in-

---

12. Wells, in an unpublished paper entitled "Theology in Culture: The Fragmenting Vision." I would underscore the point that I am talking here about general trends within evangelicalism. I do not mean to suggest that there are no strands within evangelicalism that stress the importance of tradition. Indeed, one need only consult the rather substantial literature chronicling evangelicals on the "Canterbury Trail" for evidence of such strands. See, e.g., Robert Webber, *Evangelicals on the Canterbury Trail* (Waco, Tex.: Word Books, 1985). But my essential argument here still stands: with minor exceptions, the evangelical movement as a whole has given ample evidence of its disregard for tradition.

13. As I have argued earlier, evangelicalism cannot be primarily identified with a single theological vision. As a result it must be remembered that although these three marks of evangelicalism are characteristic of the movement in its popular expression, the theological identity of the movement is also closely connected with these popular social structures.

14. I am indebted to my colleague T. David Gordon for the following line of argument. This is most clearly spelled out in a unpublished paper of his entitled "The Hidden Assumptions of Small Group Bible Study."

dividual felt free to interpret the text as he or she saw fit — and this consequence did run counter to the Reformers' principle that the Bible is properly interpreted by itself. That is to say, the Reformers held that the proper context for the interpretation of the text is not the subjective interaction between a particular passage and a particular person but rather the interaction of a given passage with the whole of Scripture itself, the essential unity of which is established by its divine origin. And determinations of this sort, they believed, are most effectively accomplished by the corporate study of the Scriptures. The question we should be seeking to answer is not "What does this text say to me?" but "What does this particular biblical text mean, and how does it fit into the entirety of the biblical record?"

The inductive Bible study approach may encourage individuals to read the Bible as they never have before, but it will also encourage them to read the text according to their own subjective interests.[15] The Bible becomes captive to the whims of the individual freed from external constraints, and in such a situation the individual can imagine the text to say whatever he or she wants it to say. If our central concern in approaching the text is how it makes us feel or what it seems to be saying to us, then the church is doomed to having as many interpretations of the text as there are interpreters. In banishing all mediators between the Bible and ourselves, we have let the Scriptures be ensnared in a web of subjectivism. Having rejected the aid of the community of interpreters throughout the history of Christendom, we have not succeeded in returning to the primitive gospel; we have simply managed to plunge ourselves back to the biases of our own individual situations.

The Parachurch Church

A second force retarding the evangelical community's appropriation of tradition is its lack of any cohesive tradition that it can call its own. We have already seen that the evangelical community is actually several different communities bound together by social and cultural factors. There may be a small doctrinal core that the evangelical coalition holds in common, but surrounding this is a vast theological diversity that prohibits the movement from constructing essential links with any particular tradition (or set of traditions).

15. This same point is argued briefly by Elliot Johnson in the first chapter of his *Expository Hermeneutics* (Grand Rapids: Zondervan, 1990).

The evangelical movement is largely transdenominational. An evangelical Presbyterian often feels closer to an evangelical Methodist than to a liberal Presbyterian. The effect of this is that evangelical Presbyterians and Methodists typically locate their identity less in the Presbyterian or Methodist heritage than in the nebulous theological heritage of evangelicalism — a heritage that is neither Presbyterian nor Methodist, no more Baptist than paedo-baptist, no more charismatic than noncharismatic, no more dispensational than nondispensational. This parachurch orientation of the movement effectively cuts it off from many theological traditions — traditions in which issues such as soteriology, the sacraments, ongoing revelation, and the covenant have a central importance. Where there is no "church," there will be little "tradition" to nurture the group.

It is sometimes claimed that theology divides communities and that appeals to theological traditions perpetuate this divisiveness. In the powerful desire for unity that drives the evangelical vision, theological distinctives are viewed as roadblocks. This is obviously true at one level. A Reformed Baptist and a free-will Baptist may discover that their underlying disagreement regarding the initiative of God in salvation is as significant as their agreement about the nature of baptism. Downplaying their disagreement will undoubtedly help them to move toward unity — but how genuine or significant can this unity be?

Evangelicals have retained a remarkable courage in the face of pressures to compromise on theological distinctives surrounding the person and work of Christ. Against the tide of contemporary theology, they have continued to profess the full divinity and full humanity of Christ. This has not earned the movement any accolades in the contemporary academy or done much to bolster the unity of the church universal. But regardless, evangelicals have continued to insist, with the apostle Paul, that "even if we or an angel from heaven" — or, I might add, a theological professor from a major university — "should preach a gospel other than the one we preached to you, let him be eternally condemned!" (Gal. 1:8).

We must not underrate the importance of this stand. The evangelical insistence that the gospel must not be compromised is commendable. But given this perspective, why should we then be content to condense the gospel into a set of five (or ten) core dogmas? Should we not think of the gospel in terms of the whole counsel of God? If the gospel begins with the entire Trinity, should we not consider the person and work of the Father *and* the Son *and* the Spirit to be essential to the gospel? If the gospel is enacted in the actual historical situations of real people, should we not consider the nature of human freedom, the visible signs of the gospel, and the earthly form of the gospel community to be essential to the gospel?

The gospel cannot be contained in a set of five core dogmas any more than an individual can be accurately described in terms of five core characteristics. A person is the sum of all his or her parts (and possibly more), and this is no less true of the gospel. Ought the evangelical community to relegate to insignificance those parts of the gospel about which there is disagreement? On some points of difference with the liberal theological community, the evangelical world has resoundingly answered in the negative. Issues of the person and work of Christ are one area in which they brook no compromise.[Why, then, should the evangelical community fear theological differences within its own ranks?

A truncated theological vision will enrich no one. It will further the sanctification of neither the mind nor the soul. Only the truth of God in its entirety, empowered by the Holy Spirit, brings this sanctification.]

The evangelical insistence on adherence to a small core of theological distinctives serves to detach these distinctives from traditions that might further the appropriation of the entire counsel of God. The evangelical coalition has many different sources. The diversity of theologies represented in the coalition is but one obvious evidence of this. And there is scant hope that all these differences can be resolved this side of paradise. Nevertheless, we have a sacred obligation to take truth seriously, and so we have an obligation to undertake the risks associated with the discussion of divergent theological visions. Theological discussion ought to remain high on the agenda of the evangelical — not with a view merely to repeating our five core dogmas or because of the value of such discussion as an end in itself but because grappling with our differences might actually drive us closer to the truth. It is truth we are after, and we must not despair of achieving it or try to ignore the biases that prevent us from achieving it.

Temporal Piety

A third and final factor contributing to the evangelical community's difficulty with tradition is the ahistorical character of its devotional piety. The classics of evangelical devotional literature stretch back no further than 1952, with the publication of C. S. Lewis's *Mere Christianity*. Evangelicals have removed themselves from the encouraging admonitions of Christian writers from centuries past. They have convinced themselves that every important thing has happened in the present century and every important book (excepting the Bible, of course) has been written in their own lifetime.

Certainly the twentieth century is different in many ways from the centuries that preceded it. The rise of modern technologies has altered modern life in unmistakable ways. The cultural advancement of secularism has transformed the ways we live and think. But it seems to me that this is all the more reason we should seek out nourishment from those who managed to live free from these extraordinary pressures. The past offers us a wealth of fresh perspectives and hence the means by which we can better understand our own biases and interpret our own perspective. If we refuse to learn from the past, we will at the very least be doomed to repeat its errors.[16]

Throughout redemptive history, God himself has reminded his people of their history. How often in the pages of the Old Testament do we hear the refrain "I am the LORD your God who brought you out of Egypt, out of the land of slavery"? The power of its memory held Israel together as a community. The heroes of the faith mentioned in Hebrews 11 were meant to inspire the recipients of that letter to run the good race and to persevere. Thinking historically may also deliver us from what C. S. Lewis aptly called "chronological snobbery" — the conceit that we are necessarily wiser than our forebears.

Christians are never safe from the temptation to link the gospel in some fashion with the cultural values of their own time. Reflecting on the historical origins of such values and ideals may help us to identify some of the formative cultural elements that have shaped and/or distorted our understanding of God and his revelation and thus may help us begin to distinguish between what is normative for all time and what is time-bound.

---

16. This is spelled out with clarity by Mark Noll, Nathan Hatch, and George Marsden in *The Search for Christian America* (Westchester, Ill.: Crossway Books, 1983). See especially chap. 7, "The Clean Sea-breeze of the Centuries: Learning to Think Historically."

The Mean between Two Extremes

Having considered some of the elements of evangelicalism that militate against our appropriation of tradition, can we now locate some elements that might help us to engage in this task? We must begin by distancing ourselves from common but counterproductive ways of thinking about tradition — the extremes of characterizing it as either worthless or infallible. Obviously we will find no motivation to appropriate tradition if we presume that it has nothing to offer us, but neither will we as evangelicals tolerate the suggestion that tradition bears as much unquestionable authority as Scripture. Yet if we can grant tradition a value that lies somewhere between these two extremes — if we can acknowledge that the diverse traditions represented in the evangelical coalition do have something of value to offer one another — then we may be encouraged to enter into a conversation with these traditions that will be beneficial in our efforts to construct a theological tradition.

I believe we might best begin by reappropriating our own individual traditions within the evangelical coalition. Calvinists could look to the writings of Augustine and Calvin and Edwards, Methodists could look to the work of Wesley and Arminius, and so on. This would immediately serve to move us out of the stuffy confines of our own time, to establish links to categories of thought that are not in captivity to modernity, to open us up to the possibility that theological wisdom can actually be found in ages other than our own.

There are risks involved for an evangelical theological vision that takes it own traditions seriously. The primary risk is the realization that there is no single evangelical tradition. If Calvinists reappropriate their tradition and Methodists reappropriate theirs, they will run the risk of offending one another and other evangelicals who will refuse to identify with the features of those traditions that seem alien to their own. The process would emphasize the reality that there is no single theological vision that can be called "*the* evangelical theological vision." But there could be benefits to confronting this reality. The evangelical community could begin to wrestle more openly with whether and how the multiple theological visions relate to the entire counsel of God revealed in Scripture. The members of the coalition might be encouraged to delve more openly into a consideration of the lines of development from the Scriptures to theological traditions other than their own and to make more reasoned and enlightened assessments of the relative adequacy of the different theological visions represented in these traditions.

Let me be open on this point: [I am making here a plea for a principled pluralism — based not on the assumption that there is an underlying pluralism of theologies present in the Scriptures or in the mind of God but rather on a recognition of the reality of individual biases in appropriating the unifying theology of the Scriptures.] We cannot find our way to truth unless we are willing to recognize our own biases. We can make this task easier by exposing ourselves to the thought of those who do not share these biases. Consensus among theologians ought not to be a criterion of adequacy in theology, nor ought the lack of consensus to be a criterion of inadequacy. The church of the first five centuries may teach us very significant lessons in this regard. The creeds in which the early church grounded its identity originated with the creeds that actually appear in the pages of the New Testament. The first Christian confession is assumed to have been something as simple as the phrase "Jesus Christ is Lord," found in a prominent position in Philippians 2:11. It was an early means of getting at the core message of Christ. This early confession may have helped to hold the infant church together in a small way, and yet it would be preposterous to suggest (as some do) that it was this brief phrase alone that served the purpose.[17]

Philippians 2:5-11 looks much like an early Christian hymn that Paul took over and used for his distinctive purposes. This early confession arises in a doxological context that by its very nature is consumed with the revelation of God himself. Notice the theology of the entire hymn. It contains parallel statements about the "form" of Christ being both divine and human. In the Revised Standard Version reading of 2:6, there is the phrase "in the form of God," and in 2:7 there is the phrase "taking the form of a servant" quickly modified by the phrases "being born in the likeness of men" and "being found in human form." In the climax of the hymn, there is an affirmation of the cross as the fulfillment of the redemptive mission of Jesus that culminates in the consummation of all of history with the affirmation of Christ's lordship. This is a summary of the entire theological framework presented in the Scriptures. It links together the entire counsel of God, and, though brief, it amounts to more than simply a truncated set of core theological dogmas.

17. If, as most believe, the letter to the Philippians dates from the early 50s, the confession found here most likely came to prominence in the latter part of the 40s.

As the gospel quickly spread as a result of the missionary efforts of the apostles, there developed a theological framework with a readily grasped form. It helped to define the very mission of the church. It served as a mechanism by which converts were introduced into the church and by which the faithful were empowered to resist the pagan religions that surrounded them. Paul makes reference to it in Romans 6:17 (RSV) when he mentions "the standard of teaching" to which the earlier believers in Rome had apparently been committed and that undergirded the practice of their faith. In his letter to the church at Galatia, Paul uses the phrases "hearing with faith" (3:2, RSV) and "the [gospel] we preached to you" (1:8) in some significant sense to refer to the body of teaching that held the church together and from which the church at Galatia had strayed. The context in which these phrases are used suggests that they refer to the teaching related to being justified by the substitutionary and sacrificial death of Christ. And yet much more is implicit. Paul makes a lengthy argument in the third chapter of Galatians about the relationship of the law and the gospel and the relationship of the Old Testament to the New Testament, and this also serves as part of the context for the gospel "digest."

In Paul's second letter to Timothy, he uses the phrase "the pattern of sound teaching" (1:13), which he elsewhere describes as a treasure. Timothy obviously had some sense of what this phrase referred to; we may presume that in part at least it referred to a digestible package of beliefs expounding the revelation of the message of salvation in and through Christ. But there is also a lengthy exposition of the nature and functions of the church in this letter that cannot easily be separated from the "message of salvation."

The author of the letter to the Hebrews suggests that the teaching about Melchizedek is milk — baby food — and believers should be interested in moving on to more solid food — that is to say, more substantial teaching. If the story of Melchizedek is considered baby food in this context, we must surely conclude that the author is equating solid food with the entire counsel of God.

As the church moved beyond the apostolic era, specialists began to appropriate the New Testament Scriptures in much the same manner that the apostles had appropriated the Old Testament Scriptures. Because the early church was so substantially lay oriented, it had a special need for broadly accessible summaries of the teaching of the apostles. The Scriptures retained supreme authority, but early on the confessions became popular in liturgical settings and as tools to facilitate the dissemination of the gospel. Nevertheless, it was always understood that these confessions were meant to be used only as aids in understanding the entire counsel of God, not as substitutes for it. This distinguishes them sharply from the "four easy steps" or "five simple beliefs" of modern evangelicalism.]

It is important to realize, too, that these early creeds originated in the practicing worship of the early church. Theology arose in the first instance from doxology. Scripture played a central role for the early church and was summarized for use in worship. These digests turned into early creeds, and these early creeds gave the church identity during periods of great upheaval. The definitions were enlarged as the church confronted greater opposition to its teaching and a call for greater clarity regarding the implications of the gospel in the context of the early Greco-Roman communities.

The early creeds attempted to lay the parameters for proper belief and worship in the early church and yet they did not resolve all the questions being asked (as is evident from the subsequent credal clarifications in the Nicene Creed, the Athanasian Creed, the Creed of Constantinople, etc.). The early creeds clearly expressed the conviction that Jesus was fully God and fully man, but prior to the Council of Chalcedon in the fifth century there was no consensus as to how this should be conceptualized. Left unclear were questions surrounding the precise philosophical and conceptual framework of issues such as the interaction between the divine and human natures of Jesus. The church did not stop asking the philosophical questions or fully resolve the tensions between the Eastern and Western branches of the church on this question even at Chalcedon. Even so, the early church was able to forge a significant consensus on matters to which the biblical text did speak — namely, the full divinity and full humanity of Jesus. This principled pluralism resulted in a unifying theological framework even if it did not resolve all the questions being asked.

As we look back on this early tradition, several significant issues come to the fore. The early creeds were attempts to isolate and codify those parts of the church consensus that were embedded within the Scriptures, but these attempts were made in the midst of a complex of philosophical, social, political, economic, and theological factors. We can with good reason ask a number of difficult questions about how these factors affected doctrinal development in the early church (as in any age). What cultural influences were involved? Why were certain philosophical compromises made? What particular arguments from Scripture were made? It is important that we understand and affirm the fact that such nontheological factors did significantly affect the theological development of the early church, and yet in doing so we must take care not to overlook the essentially theological character of this development — a character sorely lacking by comparison in our own age. The early church era was by no means an age of pure theology, but it was an age in which theological issues were of paramount importance.

We should not leave this consideration of the reappropriation of tradition without taking note also of the contribution that the theological framework of a particular tradition can make with respect to worship and right living. As Benjamin B. Warfield asserted, "Doctrinal development turns on the progressively growing fitness of the system of doctrine to produce its practical fruits."[18] The best theology has an intensely personal nature. Doctrine must not only serve life but speak to life. Tradition cannot help but bring theology to life by reminding each new era of its own calling before God. The church in ages past understood in ways foreign to modern minds that all of life is lived in the presence of God. The modern church would be well served by a reminder that the secular character of modern life is a modern invention and a modern heresy. The clean sea-breeze of the centuries just might help to refresh our memories on that point.

The natural world

THE USE OF CULTURE IN THEOLOGY

We turn now to the question of how the theological framework is affected by and interacts with contemporary culture.

It may be a slight exaggeration to suggest that the evangelical community exhibits the same kind of methodological anarchy as the larger theological community. It would probably be nearer the truth to say that evangelicals are divided in their loyalty to any of a variety of positions ranging between two basic methodological strategies associated with the pressing concern for the contextualization of the gospel.[19] According to

18. Warfield, "The Idea of Systematic Theology," in *Studies in Theology* (New York: Oxford University Press, 1932), p. 86.

19. By "contextualization of the gospel" I mean the manner in which the expression of the biblical message is shaped in and by the native conceptuality of a given culture.

David Wells, "In the one understanding of contextualization, the revelatory trajectory moves only from authoritative Word into contemporary culture; in the other, the trajectory moves both from text to context and from context to text."[20] Theologians in the evangelical tradition invariably lean toward one or the other of these basic understandings. And while the choice may not be as stark as it first appears, the underlying tendencies are significant enough to warrant further analysis. To get at this sticky issue, it might be helpful to isolate the two extremes and examine the ways in which evangelicals are inclined toward one or the other.

Let us consider first the extreme that starts from the assumption that "the revelatory trajectory moves only from authoritative Word into contemporary culture." This is to assume that the biblical message is in some important sense free of cultural influence both in its origin and in its contemporary expression. Those evangelicals most closely aligned with the fundamentalist movement have tended to view theology as transcultural or culturally neutral. Always fearful of the historicist notion of theology, these evangelicals have typically championed biblical authority by claiming that there is only one horizon in theology — the biblical text itself. They have assumed that the meaning of the biblical text can be readily transferred into the contemporary situation without distortion or cultural influences. Today we need simply open the pages of Scripture in a modern translation and read it in the light of our native "common sense" in order to understand it correctly. In 1826, Alexander Campbell expressed the sentiment in this manner: "I have endeavored to read the scriptures as though no one had read them before me, and I am as much on my guard against reading them to-day, through the medium of my own views yesterday, or a week ago, as I am against being influenced by any foreign name, authority, or system whatever."[21]

The other extreme, which starts with the assumption that "the trajectory moves both from text to context and from context to text," suggests that the meaning of the biblical message is actually determined by the constraints of the contemporary culture, that the Scriptures can have no other meaning than that which is permitted by the conceptuality of the present-day situation. The "horizon" of the text is narrowly de-

20. Wells, "The Nature and Function of Theology," in *The Use of the Bible in Theology*, p. 195.

21. Campbell, quoted by Nathan Hatch in *The Democratization of American Christianity*, p. 229.

fined by the prevailing "horizon" of the modern world. This takes different forms, from the imposition of the categories of Heidegger's phenomenology on the biblical text in the theology of Rudolf Bultmann to the lenses of self-fulfillment through which the Scriptures are interpreted in the new psychological theology of Robert Schuller.

Most evangelical discussion has taken place not at the extremes but somewhere on the spectrum between them. Recently, most evangelicals have been willing to admit that the cultural lens must play some role in the construction of an adequate theological framework. And very few have been willing to abandon, at least overtly, the primacy of Scripture in the formation of a theological vision. Despite this general move to the center, however, there remain sharp and important differences among evangelicals on matters of contextualization. The critical dispute is focused on the *degree* to which culture ought to be formative in the construction of an evangelical theological framework and the appropriation of a theological vision. Before we proceed, then, we would do well to take a closer look at the nature of the culture that is exerting this influence.

The Power and Ambiguity of Culture

As with *tradition,* we will do well to preclude some confusion at the outset by defining what we will understand the term *culture* to mean in the context of this discussion. I can think of few better preliminary definitions than that offered by Lesslie Newbigin in a recent volume:

> By the word *culture* we have to understand the sum total of ways of living developed by a group of human beings and handed on from generation to generation. Central to culture is language. The language of a people provides the means by which they express their way of perceiving things and of coping with them. Around that center one would have to group their visual and musical arts, their technologies, their law, and their social and political organization. And one must also include in culture, and as fundamental to any culture, a set of beliefs, experiences, and practices that seek to grasp and express the ultimate nature of things, that which gives shape and meaning to life, that which claims final loyalty. I am speaking, obviously, about religion.[22]

---

22. Newbigin, *Foolishness to the Greeks: The Gospel and Western Culture* (Grand Rapids: William B. Eerdmans, 1986), p. 3.

Culture, then, is not merely the external world, nor ought it to be narrowly associated with the public institutions in a society. It encompasses the way people think about the world, the way in which they speak about the world, and the way in which they live within that world. It is the web of the total human experience in the world. Culture is at once outside of and within humans.

It is easy to think of culture in the abstract, as if it were some entity far removed from the concrete life of ordinary people. However, culture is nothing more than the constant and curious conversation that goes on between every one of us and the environment in which we reside — we ourselves being part of that environment. In this sense, we are shaped by culture as much as culture is shaped by us. In the words of the contemporary sociologist of religion Peter Berger,

> Society is a dialectic phenomenon in that it is a human product, . . . that yet acts back upon its producer. Society is a product of man. There can be no social reality apart from man. Yet it may also be stated that man is a product of society. Every individual biography is an episode within the history of society, which both precedes and survives it. Society was there before the individual was born and it will be there after he has died. What is more, it is within society, and as a result of social processes, that the individual becomes a person, that he attains and holds onto an identity, and that he carries out the various projects that constitute his life. Man cannot exist apart from society. The two statements that society is the product of man and that man is the product of society, are not contradictory.[23]

Each person's identity is wrapped up with the whole cultural web and as a result moves in many different directions. It may be appropriate to speak of a person's identity as being the result of the conversation with culture. Each of our voices is part of that conversation and, in a certain sense, a part of what we hear in the conversation. And there are countless other voices in the conversation as well that influence both our understanding of ourselves and of the world outside. This in turn influences how we listen and what we actually hear in the ongoing conversation. This "identity circle" continues endlessly.

---

23. Berger, *The Sacred Canopy: Elements of a Sociological Theory of Religion* (Garden City, N.Y.: Doubleday, 1967), p. 3. *Society* here means the same thing as what I am referring to as "culture."

We will not be able to trust a simple analysis of people or cultures to provide an adequate account of the reality of the situation. People are complex, and the cultural contexts in which they find themselves are similarly complex. Any given culture may be characterized by certain dominant themes, but it would be most odd if there were not some internal resistance to those trends within the culture. Analyses invariably show culture to be a sort of amalgam between high culture (the dominant themes) and low culture (resistance to the dominant themes).

The complexity increases when we try to take proper account of the relationship between God and culture. God creates cultures in the first instance and God will consummate them in the final instance. God interacts with culture in and through the providential guidance of history and also stands in judgment over every culture. Each culture, in its own peculiar way, pronounces its opposition to the purposes of God — and, ironically, in the midst of its opposition it also facilitates the accomplishment of the purposes of God. As both a product and a producer of humankind, culture is never neutral with respect to the Creator. Neither should we suspect that the conversations of any culture take place in complete isolation from God. He remains the Lord of history, his presence bringing hope to culture and judgment to those movements in culture that seek to denigrate his lordship.

As individuals, we neither escape this judgment nor ought we to lose sight of the hope. Part of our own identity circle is the conversation centered in our interaction with God. How and what we hear as we listen to the speech of God (what has traditionally been called the "Word of God") is inevitably influenced by a variety of other "conversations" in which we are engaged in our lifetime. Some of these conversations help us to understand the important conversation with God, and some thwart our understanding of that conversation.

Our conversations inevitably involve a subjective element. We enter into these conversations as individuals, and what we "hear" and how we "talk" is influenced by our personal appropriation of the web of experiences and institutions that make up culture. It is impossible to remove the subjective character of these conversations (e.g., by attempting to read the Bible without any regard for one's own character), nor should it be thought a worthy goal to attempt to do so.

Certain impulses drive and shape each of our characters. Collectively, these arise from and in turn shape the culture in which we reside. In a world in which sin is a dominant impulse, we must take seriously the critique of culture and consequently of each individual (including ourselves). This is no simple task, given the manifold varieties of sin.

Part of this process is understanding the role that God plays in the conversation — not only the manner in which we hear what he has to say but also the nature of who it is that is speaking to us. The theologian's hope lies not in an ability to remove our cultural blinders so that we might see God but in the power of God to break through our cultural blinders and thereby enable us to see ourselves more clearly by the radiance of his glory. Strategically, this begins with conversion, but it continues most forcefully as we immerse ourselves in God's story, as we begin to think in the categories of God's revelation. This process reaches fruition when we adopt a prophetic stance within our culture. This entails understanding our culture and speaking to it in a language that is both intelligible to it and critical of it,[24] a process that is bound to be painful, for it will inevitably remind us of our own depravity.

Modern Culture

What are the dominant trends within modern culture? This is not an easy question to answer, nor should we expect it to be so. Perhaps it would be best to begin with some preliminary reflections on premodern cultures in order to develop a vantage point.

Premodern societies tended to more rural than urban; populations were typically diffused through many smaller, isolated pockets. There was relatively little technological sophistication and little division of labor. Social relationships in these cultures tended to be more personal, intimate, and essential. The institutions of kinship and family were at the core of individual and social experience. A simpler social structure and worldview promoted greater social solidarity. Political hegemony

---

24. Modern hermeneutical theory moves in just the opposite direction. Proponents of such theory argue that because we stand within the "language game" of a postindustrial modern society, we are captive to the working assumptions of that culture and are unable to assume a "precritical" stance in relationship to the conceptual framework of the Scriptures. The result is that modern culture stands prophetically against the divine revelation rather than the other way around. This sort of argument shows up in the ideological critique of the Bible contained in much feminist literary theory. See, e.g., Rosemary Radford Ruether, *Sexism and God-Talk: Toward a Feminist Theology* (Boston: Beacon Press, 1983), and Elisabeth Schüssler Fiorenza, *In Memory of Her: A Feminist Theological Reconstruction of Christian Origins* (New York: Crossroads, 1983).

was maintained by an elite whose authority was based on traditional sanctions. Broadly speaking, premodern cultures were less pluralistic religiously, politically, and socially than their modern counterparts.

The movement toward modernity constitutes a rejection in some fashion of many of the characteristics of premodern cultures.

Modernization is typically understood to be a process of institutional change associated with technologically engendered economic growth. Modern culture has focused on profit as the chief means to motivate labor and ensure the distribution of goods and services. This has produced a high degree of institutional specialization and segmentation of the workforce.

The increasing role of technology also is characteristic of emergent modern cultures. A science-based technology provides modern cultures with their principal source of images of life and its possibilities. Technology has become the dominant metaphysical reality of modern culture and its principal source of eschatological hope.

Modern social relationships tend to be impersonal and arbitrary. Populations are concentrated in urban areas, the structure of which is essentially depersonalizing. The primary mode of social organization in all spheres of modern life is bureaucratic: human thought and activity is organized and administered chiefly in keeping with the principles of "bureaucratic rationalism."

Modern culture brings social and cultural worlds of vastly different origins and character into contact with one another on a regular basis. Political power in such contexts tends to move away from a central stronghold and into the hands of the populace, a shift that is facilitated and accelerated by the rise of the mass media.

The worldview of modernity is on the whole rational and secular. Dismissive of traditional sanctions, moderns tend to be open to innovation and experimentation. The mass media blare forth these tentative values, endowing them with an aura of normativity and acceptability by dint of sheer repetition. Traditional guardians of transcendence and normativity such as religion tend to be secularized and trivialized by the mass media. Unsure of how to deal with the holy, modernity typically seeks to turn it into a commodity so that it might be harnessed for such patently profane purposes as the accumulation of economic profit.

Harvey Cox, a theological trend follower par excellence, has suggested that modernity is nowhere better evidenced than in a major commercial airport:

The sovereign nation state is here, as the invisible voices announce departures to the great capitals of the globe — Cairo, London, Jakarta, Lagos, in modulated affectless tones. If we are on an international flight we clutch our passports and visas, paper reminders that however much we would like to be citizens of the modern world, it is a national government that decides whether we leave and where we can enter.

Science and technology gleam here. Numbers, the favored language of *scientia* in our relentless quantified era, claim an equal stature with words. It is flight four thirteen, leaving at two twenty from gate thirty-two on corridor three. *Techne* is here too, though the shattering roar of the great jet engines is muffled by the carefully engineered insulation in the walls. The sky, the rain, the wind are tamed, held at bay by weatherproof windowpanes. Everywhere the machine shimmers: the sleek, shiny planes; the ingenious devices for moving thousands of people along endless corridors, from one level to another, in and out of planes; the quietly mysterious computer screens that summon up one's name and flight plan out of a vast electronic cerebrum. Science does not need to flaunt itself at an airport. It pervades everything.

Here also System, Standard Procedure, Rational method, and Regular Mode of Operation rule. The smiles of the uniformed attendants behind the counters, scrupulously marked for appropriate function, serve to smooth the transaction without inviting intimacy. Television screens carry an endless blinking parade of arrivals and departures carefully arranged for rapid recognition. Newsstands, gift counters, coffee shops, and washrooms are placed as though some prescient deity knew exactly when and where they would be needed. The spaces between people are defined entirely by function. Who is going where, on what airline, at what time? When we meet our fellow voyagers depends on what stage of the thoughtfully segmented boarding process we are in. Conversation, if any, is pleasant and shallow. Everyone shares the feeling that this experience should be made as temporary as possible.

And money talks, discreetly. Here at the Big Airport the whole world is literally within our reach. In the space of a few hours we can be on any continent, savor snow or desert, sample chapatis or tacos or pasta, view mosques or pavilions or temples. It is a prospect that would have made Magellan or Marco Polo or even Ali Baba giddy. We have only to pay; preferably not with currency notes but with the little plastic pearl of great price that allows us to plug into a universal treasury of merit and enjoy momentary satisfaction at the cost of some vague future day of reckoning. Nor does capitalism, communism, or socialism matter much here. Whether the money is charged as rubles or pesos or dollars or francs is irrelevant. It is money, any money that makes these magic carpets fly.

And religion? Where is God? At Logan airport in Boston there is a niche thoughtfully set aside for the divine. Squeezed into a side corridor, not far from where lost luggage can be sought, the footsore traveler can say a prayer to Our Lady of the Airways. The chapel is its improbable setting. There is a priest assigned to Our Lady of the Airways. Masses occur, occasionally funerals, sometimes even weddings. Unkind rumor has it that being assigned there is a kind of mild punishment imposed on a cleric who has come to the Chancery's attention once too often. Surely no Ricci or DeNobile bearing the gospel almost single-handed to China or India, no Adoniram Judson wading ashore in pagan Burma ever faced as unpromising a field as someone who is sent to make God's ways known here in the Big Airport, the modern world in miniature.[25]

Cox captures well the beast we call modern culture. It is at once impersonal and compelling, foreboding and attractive. Its power lies in its elemental complexity. It reduces God to a matter of personal preference, allowing him to play nothing but a perfunctory role in society. It glories in its own technological prowess and offers the hope of a bright new tomorrow served up with unprecedented efficiency and convenience.

The modern workplace tends to be largely impersonal, detaching people in their work environment from the roles they play in the context of families, churches, and neighborhoods. The recent influx of women into the workplace has made the effects of this dislocation even more profound. People cannot count on long-term relationships with others in the workplace, because the average person now changes his or her "career path" half a dozen times before retirement. Instability in relationships is heightened further by the increased mobility that modern

---

25. Cox, *Religion in the Secular City: Towards a Postmodern Theology* (New York: Simon & Schuster, 1984), pp. 184-85. Peter Berger has also used the metaphor of the airplane in his analysis of modernity, suggesting that the ability to fly over vast reaches of the world gives us an impression of our own god-likeness with respect to those on the ground below. Modern technology provides us with a vast array of choices that were simply not available in the premodern world, and we equate this increase in choice with an increase in power. See Berger, *The Heretical Imperative* (Garden City, N.Y.: Doubleday, 1979), pp. 1-2.

technology affords. Greater job status typically brings greater mobility, which undercuts stable relationships, which causes many to look to their jobs for satisfaction, which leads them to work harder, which results in promotions and greater job status, which brings still greater mobility, which brings still greater instability in relationships, and so on and on in an endless cycle.

Modernity tends to relegate traditional religious belief to the private sphere. One might well experience the significance of God in one's personal life, but it is not considered appropriate to let such experiences intrude on one's public behavior.[26] Many have come to view God as a silent conversation partner amid the noise of modern culture. Sunday morning provides a respite from the rat race, a quiet interlude between the important segments of a person's life — the Monday-through-Friday job and the weekend recreation.

Populist Culture and Popular Dissent

And yet this is only part of the story for modern citizens of the United States. As Nathan Hatch has persuasively argued, there is a significant thread running through the history of American culture that is absent from many other Western developed nations: an enduring (and unique) stress on the individual.[27] The individual is the hero of American culture, while public institutions are viewed with great distrust.

The benefits of this emphasis are well known. Fired with a vision of the rights of the individual, revolutionaries threw off the tyranny of the European aristocracies in favor of political democracy. They made education the right of every child in the land (or at least every child of a parent who was accorded the right to vote) and produced unprecedented levels of literacy. They parted ways with European class structure as economic rewards for individual initiative eventuated in the rise of a substantial middle class.

The story of individualism has a curious side to it. At significant points in American history, popular dissent became a moving force in culture. However, within a generation of these eruptions of dissent, it

26. For further discussion of these themes, specifically with respect to their impact on the evangelical community, see Hunter, *American Evangelicalism*.

27. See especially chap. 8 of Hatch's book *The Democratization of American Christianity*.

would become institutionalized. Then there would be dissent against the new status quo — in effect, a popular desire to return to the conditions that the previous generation had protested against. Change became the only constant in public causes. This pattern of populist dissent → establishment → populist dissent (PEP) — has greatly speeded up in the present age with the rise of modern telecommunications. Fads now spring up, spread widely, and die out faster than they ever did before.

In religious matters, we see this sort of thing happening in both conservative and liberal contexts. The desire to free oneself from the authority of tradition (and the social institutions that sustain it) first showed up on American soil when theological liberals attempted to free themselves from the entrenched Congregational orthodoxy of New England of the late eighteenth and early nineteenth centuries. The conservative and revivalist movements of the early nineteenth century responded in kind to the growing establishment of the mainline denominations (Presbyterian, Congregational, and Episcopal). This then gave rise to the populist backlash against the conservatives at the turn of the twentieth century. And the cycle goes on.

It is not hard to trace this influence within evangelical circles even today. The PEP pattern occurs much more quickly today in evangelical circles because of the deep attachment to the central cultural force of television. Part of the evangelical strength in the early days of the movement was its contention that it was swimming against the tide of culture (an image that was attractive to many Americans). By the mid-1970s it had become increasingly apparent that the evangelical empire had become sufficiently well established that it could no longer be considered a cultural outsider in any significant sense. The tide had turned. As evangelicalism was swept away in the wave of its own popularity, it increasingly took on the role of the cultural villain. Public skepticism about the movement was amplified by the exploits of a number of prominent television evangelists during this period. They played a role similar to that of the evangelical revivalists of the nineteenth century: instead of standing against the tide of culture, they became prime representatives of the culture's worst characteristics — greed and immorality.

This points to an underlying problem of being prophetic in modern American culture. Part of the power of the prophetic voice lies in its distance from the mainstream values of the culture. And yet the underlying value of popular dissent in America soon tends to transform these distant voices into mainstream voices. And in becoming mainstream, the voice inevitably loses its prophetic character.

Clearly it is no simple matter for us to deal sensitively with the issue of our culture as we construct a theological vision. This much is clear, however: we will not succeed by underestimating either the power of modern culture or the power of God to communicate to modern culture.

Theological Responsibilities

The primary cultural task of the theologian is to clothe the entire counsel of God in a conceptuality that is intelligible to the modern community. The goal is to facilitate the communication of the gospel in a language that modern people will understand and be able to apply to their lives.[28] This obviously requires significant acquaintance with the entire counsel of God. Suffice it to say here that we must begin with redemptive-historical exegesis and then proceed to translate that framework into a conceptuality that informs the reality of our social structures and applies to the dominant patterns of contemporary life.[29]

The modern theologian must be able to speak the language of the modern world; it will not be sufficient simply to repeat phrases from earlier generations. This means that the modern theologian must be cognizant of the power of language and the connotations that accompany words in the modern world. Contemporary images and metaphors are loaded, and we have to examine their baggage carefully before we put them to use in our theology. It is a fundamental challenge facing contemporary theology to educate a church that is largely ignorant of the Scriptures and therefore largely ignorant of the controlling biblical images and metaphors that have informed theology in ages past. The translation of the redemptive historical message of the Scriptures into the vernacular of modern culture will be meaningless unless and until the

---

28. I am setting aside at this point questions related to the task of convincing the modern person of the truthfulness of the message, since for the most part these lie outside the scope of this chapter.

29. For a slightly different way of putting this concern, see David F. Wells, "An American Evangelical Theology: The Painful Transition from *Theoria* to *Praxis*," in *Evangelicalism and Modern America*, ed. George Marsden (Grand Rapids: William B. Eerdmans, 1984), pp. 83-93.

church itself is educated in the vernacular of the Scriptures. We have to go back before we can go forward.[30]

Contemporary theologians must also seek to challenge the contemporary mind to think more critically about its own culturally accepted values. An evangelical theological vision must strive to bring the entire counsel of God into the modern world in order that the modern world might be transformed. This is the intended goal of contextualizing the redemptive message of the Scriptures.

This assumes that it is possible to communicate across cultures and that it is possible for a culture to receive truth from outside itself without ceasing to operate. The acknowledgment that culture influences our apprehension of the biblical message does not betray relativist assumptions. There is such a thing as cross-cultural communication (and cross-temporal communication); indeed, such communication serves as the basis for civil discourse in the modern world and for rational decision-making in the human community. It is possible to talk with and understand persons from outside one's own culture, whether that means talking with someone down the street or across the globe. The process is more difficult as the differences between the cultures increase, certainly, but it remains possible nonetheless. To deny that this is the case would be to affirm the absolute isolation of cultures. And if everyone is a product and producer of culture, then in some sense every individual represents a different culture, so if communication is not possible across cultures, we would have to conclude that no two individuals could ever genuinely communicate with each other. Ordinary experience and basic intuition would certainly seem to suggest that this is not the case.

The reason is simple enough. The relativist claim that culture prescribes the boundaries of understanding for every individual within that culture is itself a claim that transcends these cultural boundaries. In making a claim that appears perfectly universal, the relativist is making at least one statement that can be communicated across cultures. On this reading, "the relativity claim dies from its own knife wounds."[31] And so

---

30. We have to understand such biblical concepts as "redemption," "salvation," and "re-creation" in their original context before we can use them to inform our own context. In subsequent chapters, I will suggest that it is a far better strategy to transport these images and metaphors into modern culture and modern language through education rather than simply to translate them into wholly new terms in our culture.

31. Gabriel Fackre, "The Use of Scripture in My Work in Systematics," in *The Use of the Bible in Theology,* p. 211. Alvin Plantinga refers to this fallacy as the problem of

we affirm that it is possible for cultures to communicate beyond their barriers. However complicated the process might be, it is not hopeless. In assembling their theological vision, evangelicals must not lose sight of either this hope or this complexity.

Our final and fundamental hope rests in the conviction that God himself communicates across cultures, principally across the cultural chasm that lies between himself and us. As Gabriel Fackre has suggested, "We are not so locked into our ecclesial or cultural positions that its truth cannot make itself known to us — the Word addresses the hearer — even to the extent that a contemporary perspective from which a text is viewed can be challenged, modified and even overturned by the text."[32]

The theological foundations for affirming the ability of the biblical message to penetrate the modern culture begin with an affirmation of the relational continuity between God and humanity. We are created in his image with the ability to communicate with him and with each other. The relational discontinuity created by the fall does not destroy our ability to communicate but in fact still assumes it. Our perversion of the moral law and our abuse of the creation mandates assume our ability to understand in some sense the God from whom we have strayed: at the very least we understand him to the extent that we are able to communicate our hatred of him. As the relationship is restored by the cross of Christ, the task is to recover a sense of urgency to communicate our love of God and to proclaim his Word to a world that is still lost and dying.

The world is in desperate need of the gospel. It is this fundamental conviction that lies behind our efforts to communicate it to the modern culture. This gospel restores life and hope — not as the world views life and hope but rather on the terms established by God. In God's creation, life consists not in gaining material possessions but in union with Christ. In this creation, hope resides not in our ability to bring earthly peace but rather in God's ability to bring history to its proper consummation.

The movement of history toward its proper consummation entails that the entire counsel of God accomplishes its purpose in each generation and in each culture. The trajectory of the divine revelation in this sense moves from the original divine disclosures through human history toward the end of time: it moves *through* cultures, not above or beyond them.

"self-referential incoherence"; for a different application of this principle, see the first chapter of *Does God Have a Nature?* (Milwaukee: Marquette University Press, 1978).

32. Fackre, "The Use of Scripture in My Work in Systematics," p. 211.

Divine revelation does not occur in the interaction between the Bible and my experience within culture. The meaning of revelation can be ascertained with the aid of the conversation that takes place between the Bible and my experience within a particular culture, but it is the biblical revelation that possesses the unique authority to challenge and transform my culture-bound experience.[33] The revelatory trajectory does not move from text to context and back again to the text. Neither does the interpreter stand at the midpoint of this interchange determining what God's word for our time actually is. The cognitive horizon of the interpreter must be prescribed and thereby challenged by the meaning of the biblical revelation.

In denying the validity of the "revelatory circle," I am not denying the validity of the "hermeneutical circle." In the latter, we discover the meaning of the text as we come to understand our own cultural pre-dispositions and the impact that these have on our interpretation of the Scriptures. There is interaction between text and context in this sense. There is also a recognition in the hermeneutical circle that the biblical text is an ancient text written out of cultures quite different from our own. This establishes the importance of understanding not only modern culture but also the culture in which the original revelation occurred. We have to take the difference between these two horizons seriously if we are to construct our theological framework properly in the modern culture.

As we turn exegesis into doctrine, we have a very real need to be aware of our cultural predispositions as interpreters. We may be tempted by these cultural predispositions to select only certain parts of Scripture in our attempts to determine its overall meaning, for example, and proceed to construct a theology that is partially distorted by these pa-rameters.[34] Interpreters must be willing to place themselves under the

---

33. C. René Padilla helpfully discusses this point but then goes on to say — somewhat misleadingly in my judgment — that "to be valid and appropriate, [theology] must reflect the merging of the horizons of the historical situation and the horizons of the text" ("Hermeneutics and Culture — A Theological Perspective," in *Down to Earth: Studies in Christianity and Culture*, ed. John R. W. Stott and Robert Coote [Grand Rapids: William B. Eerdmans, 1980], p. 73). It is my contention that the horizons ought not to be fused but rather that the horizon of the historical situation ought to be transformed by the horizon of the text.

34. Though I disagree with some of his examples, I do think William Dyrness offers a helpful discussion of this problem in his article "How Does the Bible Function in the Christian Life?" in *The Use of the Bible in Theology*, pp. 159-74.

authority of the whole of the Scriptures. The anxiety created by reading a discomfiting passage is often a healthy sign: it suggests that a corrupting cultural predisposition is being revealed for what it is. It is in the willingness to work to overcome these types of predispositions skillfully and prayerfully that the community's theological framework will most nearly reach its intended goal.

Another part of the intended goal of constructing a theological framework is the demythologization of modern culture. The myths of modern culture are exposed and unmasked for what they are only in the light of divine revelation. This debunking of the values of modern culture includes uncovering the accretions to biblical faith within the community of believers as well as the perversions perpetuated as truth within the larger culture. The end result is that the community is to be freed not from the demands of the gospel but from the distortions of modern culture. As Lesslie Newbigin suggests,

> The missionary encounter of the gospel with the modern world will, like every true missionary encounter, call for radical conversion. This will be not only a conversion of the will and of the feelings but a conversion of the mind . . . that leads to a new vision of how things are and, not at once but gradually, to the development of a new plausibility structure in which the most real of all realities is the living God whose character is "rendered" for us in the pages of Scripture.[35]

Finally, if we who stand within the context of the modern world are to understand the cultural lens correctly, we will have to open ourselves up to the judgment that the Word brings. This must be true of evangelicals especially. The "radical conversion" of which Newbigin speaks must happen not only to modern culture but to each one of us. Personal accountability to the Word is a matter of the utmost urgency in our day. Furthermore, we must not seek to be obedient only in matters of the private sphere; we must seek to be accountable in every aspect of our lives in all their complexity. The proper goal of the theological vision is a change that encompasses the will, the feelings, and the mind. In this regard, the evangelical theological vision calls for repentance and faith because this is what God himself calls for. Anything less would amount to a cultural vision masquerading as the truth.

35. Newbigin, *Foolishness to the Greeks,* p. 64.

THE USE OF REASON IN THEOLOGY

The anti-intellectual strain within American Christianity in general and evangelicalism in particular is a common theme in recent discussions of Christianity and culture.[36] We need not go into that here, however. Our interest is to establish a framework for the proper use of reason in constructing a theological vision.

The use of the term *reason*, like that of *tradition* and *culture*, is not without some ambiguity in modern discussions. Some view it is as a device used to supersede the authority of divine revelation. Some view it as the only means to establish unbiased truth. Some view it as simply one way to get from a premise to a conclusion. I will be using the concept in a broad sense to refer to a person's ability to deal with beliefs relative to evidence.[37] My goal is to explore the nature of the human ability to reason and to provide some clarification of the nature of evidence. Then I will apply this understanding of reason and evidence to the role they play in the construction of a theological framework and the application of a theological vision.[38]

Native and Cultural Rationality

The following discussion depends in large measure upon two central insights — (1) that mechanisms of belief formation provide a noetic foundation for each of us and (2) that a culture's "plausibility structure" plays a key role in determining the acceptability of any individual's religious beliefs. Put simply, these two claims suggest that some elements of "reason" are part of the very constitution of our beings as creatures of God and other elements of "reason" depend on the culture we inhabit.

36. Richard Hofstadter's *Anti-Intellectualism in American Life* (New York: Alfred A. Knopf, 1963) is a classic study in this regard. For more recent studies tracing this strand within American evangelicalism, see George Marsden, "The Collapse of American Evangelical Academia," in *Faith and Rationality: Reason and Belief in God*, ed. Alvin Plantinga and Nicholas Wolterstorff (Notre Dame, Ind.: University of Notre Dame Press, 1983), pp. 219-64; and Hunter, *American Evangelicalism.*

37. At first glance, this may appear to be too narrow a use of the term, but I believe that this is the meaning it most generally receives in the context of the modern discussion. I will proceed to provide some further framework to account for the narrowness of the definition.

38. Some of what follows has been adapted from my article "Irresistibility, Epistemic Warrant and Religious Belief," *Religious Studies* 25 (December 1989): 425-33.

We can refer to these elements of reason as "native rationality" and "cultural rationality," respectively. Native rationality is typically the concern of professional philosophers, while cultural rationality is more typically the concern of anthropologists and other social scientists. I believe that these two types of rationality are closely related to one another, though they are by no means identical. In order to maintain the distinction between the two, I will be using the terms *rational* and *rational warrant* when referring to native rationality, and the terms *plausible* and *plausibility structures* when referring to cultural rationality.

Native rationality involves mechanisms within each of us that work naturally to produce beliefs. Because of our status as created beings, we all share a basic human constitution that incorporates certain universal epistemic faculties, and to some degree these faculties operate similarly in all of us. This basic human constitution consists not in an assemblage of innate ideas but rather in certain native structures of belief. There is no consensus in the human community concerning the precise number or character of these native structures of belief, but it is part and parcel of being human that we believe in the reality of the external world, the existence of other human beings, and perhaps in a basic distinction between right and wrong as well.

Beyond the limits of our native structures of belief, we are all subject to cultural influences that further define the sorts of things we consider it plausible to believe. Contemporary sociologists tell us that these plausibility structures are an essential part of the fabric of a culture, defining acceptable ranges of beliefs for both individuals and institutions.[39] If they are correct, we will have to reject the assumption that reason is some antiseptic tool that can function simply in terms of itself. We will have to deal with the fact that social structures implant in us, as in members of other cultures, certain intellectual needs and rational

---

39. Peter Berger has done pioneering work in this area. See especially Berger, *A Rumor of Angels: Modern Society and the Rediscovery of the Supernatural* (Garden City, N.Y.: Doubleday, 1969), and Berger et al., *The Homeless Mind: Modernization and Consciousness* (New York: Random House, 1974). I characterize Berger as a pioneer because, unlike many of his sociological predecessors (Marx especially), Berger is not committed to the conviction that culture *determines* rationality. If rationality is determined by culture, then rationality is relative to every particular culture. As Berger has said in a later work, the purpose of his early work *A Rumor of Angels* was to "relativize the relativizers." I largely agree with Berger, and in what follows I use "cultural rationality" to refer to the influences (though not *determinative* influences) that a culture exerts on the use of reason.

norms. The norms implanted by the social structures of modern culture would necessarily be tied to secular modes of thinking and behavior.

The gospel, in its fundamental thrust, swims against the tide of modern culture in many ways. Secular thought rejects its supernaturalism as implausible and dismisses many of its moral demands as quaint or repugnant. Part of the task of the evangelical theologian is to lay bare the fundamental assumptions of a culture — assumptions that characteristically go unnoticed by that culture — and relate these to the principles of rationality that undergird the gospel. The conflict and the confrontation intrinsic to this strategy cannot be ignored.

In attempting to construct a modern theological framework, we must come to grips with the character of this confrontation. We have to recognize that no one operates in a cultural vacuum and that "cultural reason" has a powerful impact on the way people think about reality. As Peter Berger has suggested, the average middle-class American who was confronted with a vision of a demon would be more apt to call a psychiatrist than an exorcist.[40] This is owing to the cultural conditioning that person has received from modern technological society. The possibility that demons might exist is virtually excluded by the intellectual framework dominant in the culture that has socialized and educated this person. It is an interpretation of reality considered implausible by the major social institutions that surround this individual every day.

This is not to say that the individual would be wrong to interpret the experience in terms of demons. The mere fact that a culture has determined that it is not normal to believe in demons does not mean that there are no such beings. Though modern secular society rejects belief in demons, it remains an open question whether it is correct in having done so. It would be difficult to sustain the assertion that modern culture cannot err in its fundamental convictions. For one thing, conflicts are inevitable in any culture as notoriously ambiguous as our own. More fundamentally, we know that all cultures change over time, and yet if a culture was always correct, any change in its convictions would be irrational.

In any event, we can at least say that the intellectual reaction of any individual to an experience such as a demonic vision will be far more intelligible if we consider it in its proper cultural context. One way or another, the backdrop of our culture's plausibility structures will help to

---

40. Berger, *The Heretical Imperative*, pp. 9-11.

explain our intellectual activities. As we seek to construct and defend a theological framework, we must take into account this backdrop and the influence it exerts on the modern mind. Evangelicals must accept the reality of a "cultural rationality." This is not to say that we have to accept the *authority* of modern culture's plausibility structures; but in order to communicate effectively to others, we will have to recognize where they stand with respect to the message we mean to bring — what they will consider plausible without argument because their culture has established those beliefs as plausible, and what will need special explanation or defense.

Our task of determining another person's plausibility structures is somewhat simplified, however, by the fact that we can depend on certain areas of universal agreement that derive from the fact that we all belong to what we might refer to as the "culture of createdness." And in this culture God is the fundamental author of plausibility structures. Inasmuch as we are all created in the image of God, we all possess a noetic structure that operates according to divine prescriptions. God has created us in such a way that when we are confronted by the imminent danger of, say, a speeding car at an intersection, we believe that walking into the intersection will put us at great risk of injury. This is a "natural" belief formation. There are many beliefs about the external world of this sort. Regardless of what our culture (or the epistemologists of our culture) may tell us about the plausibility of believing in speeding cars, it will nonetheless remain rational to believe in speeding cars when we see one nearing an intersection we are about to cross.

In other words, there seem to be some fixed warrants to a person's beliefs. And the best way of accounting for these is by way of the creative act of God that brought our noetic constitution into being. It is reasonable to suppose that if God creates us, then he creates us to interact intellectually with the rest of the created order in certain prescribed fashions. This is what I have been referring to as "native rationality."

In thinking about the nature of rationality, it is imperative to keep these two central insights in mind — that people are creatures of God with a native rationality and that they are also inhabitants of a particular culture that influences what they assume to be rationally acceptable. The following account is intended as a pointer toward a proper epistemic framework that is sensitive to both of these insights. My concern here is to analyze both the role of cultural expectations and motives and the role of the divinely made human constitution in the process of acquiring beliefs.

The central problem is to clarify the proper role of evidence relative to a cultural context. Why are certain kinds of evidence in favor of a conclusion acceptable while other kinds are not? When modern culture suggests that it is plausible to believe in ethical relativism while one's natural noetic constitution resists this conclusion, is one conclusion reasonable and the other not? How might one decide? Is there a platform that stands above the assessment of evidence by which that assessment can itself be judged adequate? Or is the nature of the intellectual project itself ill-conceived in these terms?

It is my contention that at least some beliefs are irresistible in the sense that we do not decide to believe them. If God instills beliefs in people irrespective of culture, then those beliefs will override any conflicting evidence that a culture may offer. In particular, if our belief in God is, in some instances, irresistible, then that belief may not be in need of any evidence whatsoever. It will be a commendable belief simply because it is irresistible. However, the framework will be incomplete until it can be shown that there are other instances in which evidences are entirely appropriate as a means of making one's belief in God commendable.[41]

For purposes of simplicity and clarity, I will focus on one particular belief—the belief that there is a God in whom alone there is salvation. However, the framework that will emerge from this discussion will be sufficiently general to be straightforwardly extendable to other beliefs without much alteration.

Irresistible Beliefs

It has been widely argued in philosophical circles that our beliefs in general are not under our direct voluntary control.[42] We cannot simply by a decision of the will (however construed) decide what to believe or what to refrain from believing in many ordinary instances of believing.

41. This is somewhat contrary to the Calvinist epistemology suggested by Alvin Plantinga, Nicholas Wolterstorff, and others. See Plantinga, "Reason and Belief in God"; and Wolterstorff, "Can Belief in God Be Rational If It Has No Foundations?" in *Faith and Rationality*, pp. 135-86.

42. The clearest statement to this effect that I have encountered is in an unpublished paper by William Alston entitled "Concepts of Justification." See also Bernard Williams, "Deciding to Believe," in *Problems of the Self* (Cambridge: Cambridge University Press 1973), pp. 136-51.

This is to say that doxastic voluntarism now seems a dubious doctrine at best, regardless of how emphatic Descartes and other traditional epistemologists seemed to be in supporting it.

It is customary to speak about beliefs being "warranted" for a person when those beliefs are worthy parts of his or her noetic structure. Accordingly, to say "Belief p is warranted" is to say something epistemically commendatory about a person acquiring the belief in question. The person has followed proper procedures in coming to acquire that belief. And conversely, to say that a belief is unwarranted is merely to say something epistemically derogatory about the belief formation process. Proper procedures have not been followed.

Another way to say this is to speak of the intellectual obligation a person has to acquire rational beliefs.[43] This kind of "epistemic warrant" has to do with our *manner of believing* — that is, with how we have arrived at our belief. Have we tried our best to believe only what is true and avoid what is false? Have we followed "rational procedure" in arriving at our beliefs, or have we arrived at them in a purely accidental or arbitrary fashion?

Sarah might believe that it is going to be a sunny day tomorrow because she wants to go swimming. She might also know that various weather reports are often a more reliable indicator of tomorrow's weather patterns. Normally the desire for a belief to be true is not adequate reason to warrant a person in coming to hold that belief. The link between the desire for a sunny day and the reality of the sunny day is purely accidental. And if Sarah's belief that it was going to be a sunny day tomorrow were based entirely on her desire to go swimming tomorrow, it would be normal to say that her belief about tomorrow was not warranted. However, if she came to believe that it was going to be a sunny day tomorrow because she had meticulously studied weather reports that had previously been reliable, it would be normal to say that her belief about tomorrow is warranted. The difference in the two cases is the origin of Sarah's belief and therefore the manner in which she acquired her belief. In the first instance, we say that the belief is acquired in an arbitrary fashion, and in the second, we say that the belief is acquired according to proper procedure.

"Epistemic commendation" may also refer to the positive status of

---

43. See chap. 1 of Roderick Chisholm's *Theory of Knowledge*, 2d ed. (Englewood Cliffs, N.J.: Prentice Hall, 1973).

a belief relative to some body of evidence (however this is defined) or its approximation to truth. This construal has to do with the *belief itself in relation to the evidence*. Is the belief based on the requisite amount and kind of evidence? Is the belief rationally supported? Fred believes in the existence of Bigfoot on the basis of certain unexplained footprints and alleged visual sightings. But it is debatable whether this evidence is adequate to support his belief. The evidence could be explained in ways that Fred has not considered. In this case, we say that Fred's belief is unwarranted because it is not based upon sufficient evidence.

On both construals of "epistemic warrant" (rational procedure and a rational relation to evidence), I am warranted in believing something if I fulfill certain obligations — either the obligation to try my best to believe what is true or the obligation to believe only what is properly connected to the evidence (whatever that evidence might be).[44]

Leaving aside disputes about how these obligations ought best to be construed, I want to suggest that there are significant instances in the life of a believer when his or her belief in God (and probably other beliefs relating to the divine revelation) may actually be irresistible. And in such cases, whatever obligations may have applied in other contexts no longer apply. They are overridden because of the nature of the case.

An illustration from another normative context ought to clarify this. In most cultures it is believed that one always ought to keep one's promises. Morally speaking, if one promises to do x, then one has an obligation to do x. We allow for exceptions to this obligation, however. If circumstances should prevent one from doing x, then we conclude that it is permissible for him not to do x. If Jim promises to meet Sally on Saturday morning, then Jim has an obligation to meet Sally on Saturday morning. Suppose, however, that Jim is in a car accident on Saturday morning on his way to meet Sally. Further suppose that the accident is caused by a drunken driver and Jim is completely without fault in the accident. Jim is taken to the hospital near death, incapable of voluntary movement. In this case it would be appropriate to say that Jim's obligation to meet Sally has been overridden. It is morally permis-

---

44. Chisholm refers to this obligation when he says, "We may assume that every person is subject to a purely intellectual requirement — that of trying his best to bring it about that for every proposition h that he considers, he accepts h if and only if h is true" (*Theory of Knowledge*, p. 14).

sible for him to "break his promise." It is my contention that the proper use of reason is analogous to this in certain respects, that the dynamics of belief admit of certain exceptions to our common understanding of epistemic warrant.

If God creates us, it would be reasonable to suppose that there will be a natural correlation between our beliefs and the rest of the created order around us. And further, might it not be the case that God has so created us so that we come to possess a set of irresistible beliefs largely for our benefit? If I see and hear bolts of lightning crashing in around the house I am currently occupying, it is generally not within my power to refrain from believing that there is a tremendous storm outside. On the basis of this "irresistible" belief much good is accomplished — namely, I do not decide to walk outside during this storm and place myself in great danger.

In this light it seems right to suggest that there are instances of perceptual believing (i.e., beliefs of ordinary perception — beliefs formed on the basis of seeing, hearing, tasting, smelling, and touching) when we are not free to believe whatever we would like. Suppose, for example, that I have an obligation (or believe myself to have an obligation) to avoid believing anything false and therefore conclude that in my reading I should stick to trustworthy periodicals and stay away from gossip magazines. This resolve would give me some control over the sorts of materials I would be exposed to, but it would not give me control over the sorts of beliefs that might arise from my reading the materials that I have chosen to accept. Any beliefs that arise when I scan the pages of a trustworthy periodical will in a certain sense be "forced upon me." It is possible that I would never come to hold a belief "p" regarding page 302 in volume 2 of a trustworthy periodical if I never in fact glanced at page 302. However, given certain actions in certain conditions (i.e., that I look at page 302 in normal lighting conditions with good eyesight), it is impossible that I will not come to hold belief "p" regarding page 302 in volume 2 of the trustworthy periodical (even if I do not know it to be page 302 in volume 2). The belief may simply be that there is an object in front of me, or it may be more complicated, such as "there is an object in front of me with black letters written on it in an orderly fashion." Whatever this belief might be, it is clear that it is causally contingent on which actions I perform, but, given the actions that I do perform, there is no such causal contingency left over. This is to say that the antecedent conditions *determine* the belief in this case. For this reason, the belief is irresistible.[45] I am not *free* with respect to this belief. Its irresistibility, then, commends it as a worthy (i.e., rational) epistemic candidate. Whatever intellectual obligations may apply in the case, they are overridden by the nature of the case.

Extending the examples cited above, might it not be the case that belief in God occurs as a result of an initial irresistible impulse? Many theologians through the centuries have suggested that there is an innate human capacity that, when properly stimulated by the Holy Spirit, moves us to believe in God.[46] Were it not for the fact that this innate human capacity has been suppressed by sin, we would believe in God with the same kind of spontaneity that we believe in the external world around us. The difficulty we have with believing in God is part of the unnatural condition brought about by our willful rebellion against God. Our natural condition is to live in affirmation of God's existence and lordship. The Holy Spirit stimulates this natural capacity in some, and the result is spontaneous and irresistible belief in God. Might we not expect this scenario to be the case if God is both the Creator and Redeemer? According to the apostle Paul, "Since the creation of the world God's invisible qualities — his eternal power and divine nature — have been clearly seen, being understood from what has been made, so that men are without excuse" (Rom. 1:20). His use of the metaphor of sight points to a connection between belief in God and what I have referred to as perceptual believing. The verse suggests a certain inevitability about our belief in God because it is so "clearly seen." The natural mechanisms in every person are such that in certain circumstances (i.e., living in God's creation) the belief in God occurs irresistibly. But people rebel against the demands placed on their lives as a result of this belief in God. Part of this rebellion is the active suppression of belief in God, as the apostle goes on to explain in the remainder of the chapter.

Paul appears to be making this argument for two reasons. He wants first to establish that no one is able to claim ignorance in regard to a knowledge of God. The Jew and the Gentile alike are equally culpable

45. I am using "not free" and "irresistible" in a roughly synonymous fashion, since both are descriptive in this context of particular actions performed by an agent.

46. Most notable among these theologians is John Calvin, who argues to this effect forcefully in Book 1, Chap. 2 of his *Institutes of the Christian Religion*. Herman Bavinck likewise speaks of the work of the Spirit as the "spontaneous testimony . . . which *forces itself upon us* from every side" (*The Doctrine of God*, trans. William Hendriksen [Grand Rapids: William B. Eerdmans, 1951], p. 79; italics mine).

because they are both constructed in such a manner that they "clearly see" God in and through his creation. The belief is so evident that it is "forced upon them" in equal measure. And owing to the rebellion of both against God, he has given them over to the lusts of their hearts — which is to say that he has allowed them to revel in their own distortions of reality. There are now cultural conditions of rationality that run counter to the way God has created them. The expectations of pagan culture are now such that it has become culturally acceptable to deny the existence of God and his lordship. In this instance the social structures created by man are themselves instruments by which irresistible beliefs become implausible.

This argument rests on the conviction that our natural inclinations toward some beliefs are influenced by certain expectations and motives. This might be easier to understand if we keep in mind the fact that the irresistibility of the beliefs we are discussing extends to the entire process of acquiring beliefs. Some beliefs we acquire irresistibly, but others we acquire for certain conscious motives (culturally accepted mores), and these latter beliefs might be said to come under some kind of voluntary control. For example, a committed British Tory might choose to read only those articles that she knows favor Tory candidates and policies. She might refuse to read any article critical of the Thatcher revolution and thus sustain only those beliefs that are favorably disposed to the Tory party. Her own motives, under a voluntary control, would then have influenced which beliefs she had come to hold, and in this sense that part of her noetic structure could be characterized as "resistible," and she could rightly be held responsible for it.

As gestalt psychology has made clear, motives influence beliefs. The perception of the external world is not a simple game of mapping an "experience of X" onto "X" in the real world and thereby coming up with a true belief. My perception of a traffic accident may differ greatly from that of the person standing beside me, because our different motives and expectations influence the act of perception. To the limited extent that I have control over these motives and expectations, I may be said to have indirect voluntary control over the beliefs that arise from my act of perception. A full-blown Christian epistemology would argue that cultural motives can (and do) actually interfere with belief in God because of the effects of sin on our motives. This is implied by the first part of Paul's argument. Rebellion against God results in a set of distorted beliefs about the world, and Jew and Gentile are equally culpable for these distorted beliefs. However, this is not the end of the story.

The second part of Paul's argument is that God is merciful and brings redemption to his people. Part of the redemptive process is the gracious restoration of belief in God. God "strangely warms" the heart and thereby brings us back to the natural and instinctive affirmation of his existence and lordship. This affirmation is not owing to inclinations of the fallen human heart but rather to the restoration of the heart that prompts an unconditional acceptance of the overwhelming presence of God. The renewed belief in God is irresistible for much the same reasons that belief in God was originally irresistible and our belief in the external world remains so. We are created to acquire these beliefs naturally in the requisite circumstances, and we cannot live without affirming them.[47]

The philosophical reason for this is that some beliefs are not influenced by expectation and motivation. Some beliefs force themselves on us in a manner not influenced by any other factors. Is it not reasonable to suppose that though many beliefs (maybe even most) are under some sort of indirect voluntary control, there still remain some beliefs that are not under any kind of voluntary control? Paul believed it was, and his account can easily be extended to include other kinds of belief.

I have in mind here very simple perceptual beliefs. The perception that I have by touch of the hardness and softness of bodies, of their extension, figure, and motion would be included here.[48] One might also include beliefs about current conscious mental states ("I seem to be having a headache now") and the simple past ("I remember having cereal for breakfast").

There is an irresistible character to many of our rock-bottom commonsense perceptual beliefs about the external world. I am not at all suggesting that these beliefs are infallible or that we might not change

47. It is important to recall that the reason for the belief that God exists is not connected in this instance with the evidence that he is our Creator and that he has created us in such a manner. This "evidence" is the *result* of our belief, not the cause of it. It may offer a "retroactive" explanation of the belief in God, but it does not constitute an "evidential base" for that belief.

48. I do not want to affirm the Lockean notion that the mind is a blank tablet imprinted by impressions. Surely it is the case that beliefs will be a function of the complexity of mental faculties and environmental conditioning. What appears as an orderly message to an American may appear as a mere scribble to a Korean. Nonetheless there remains an irresistibility in the acquisition of beliefs for both — even though the irresistibility results in different beliefs.

our minds about them on subsequent reflection. I am simply trying to establish the point that we do not have much choice in accepting a realistic account of perception. The external world exists whether we like it or not. And God exists whether we like it or not.

Various attempts to provide arguments for our belief in the external world have all proven to be failures. In the end, they all assume the conclusion that they seek to prove. The account I have just given is similar. It depends on the premise that there is an inherent implausibility to skepticism regarding belief in the external world. Any argument that the external world does not really exist is unconvincing because we know that the conclusion is false. But it is my assertion that it is a fundamental part of our constitution to believe this.

It has not been my intent to try to ground belief in the external world or God on some further basic set of beliefs; rather, I have tried to explain why these beliefs seem warranted in the first instance. Our belief in the external world (or, more correctly, particular beliefs about particular parts of the external world) is warranted not because of some more foundational belief but because it is (often) irresistible — because it is natural to believe in the external world. The analogy between perceptual beliefs and belief in God seems striking at this point. The traditional attempts to prove God's existence typically depend on the intrinsic acceptability of their conclusion (viz., God exists) for their apparent rational appeal. The irresistibility of belief in God in many instances suggests that, like simple perceptual judgments, this belief is indeed warranted — but not warranted on the basis of other beliefs in one's noetic system.

A fundamental difference between belief in God and belief in the external world is that sin has greatly eroded the former while the latter has remained largely intact in the modern world.[49] Modern cultural norms offer much greater resistance to belief in God than to belief in the external world. In many ways modern culture has come to expect a posture of unbelief with respect to God. If my account is correct, this is entirely predictable. But we may still ask how this affects the project of constructing an evangelical theological framework.

---

49. There are individuals who continue to deny the reality of the external world, but these remain a very small minority. It is also important to affirm that cultural bias does negatively affect our understanding of the external world, though usually not to the extent that we deny its existence.

Skepticism and Doubt

The ability to question belief in God (and in many instances abandon that belief) characterizes the post-Enlightenment West, and it might seem strange in modern culture to foreclose on that question by arguing for the "irresistibility" of belief about God. Skeptics (i.e., those who do not accept belief in the existence of a God who is the sole provider of salvation) want to know why they should think that a person's "epistemic faculties" are working properly in acquiring this irresistible belief in God. Might it not simply be a matter of wish fulfillment on his or her part? Skeptics might assert that anyone who believes in God is looking for a caring father figure in the midst of a hostile world and so resorts to belief in a supernatural being who is more powerful than all the threatening forces of the world. Other skeptics might assert that religious belief is a tool employed by the ruling classes to keep the lower classes conveniently humble, meek, and subservient.[50] More common today is the assertion that people come to believe in God in response to epistemic pressure applied by certain fundamentalist religious groups.

Enlightenment-inspired skeptics further suppose that belief in God could be warranted only by appeal to a large body of supporting evidence (i.e., culturally acceptable evidence). In the absence of such evidence, they contend that a rational person ought to suspend belief. By such reckoning, there is no such thing as a natural source of belief with respect to God.

If the analogy with perceptual beliefs is correct, this Enlightenment-inspired account is simply mistaken. It may be necessary in some instances to provide supporting evidence for one's belief in God (or disbelief in God), but if belief in God arises directly in some instances from a natural belief-producing mechanism within us, the call for evidence to support this belief may be out of order. If belief in God, like perceptual beliefs, is acquired in the proper circumstances as a result of the very makeup of our constitution, there would be no need for lengthy arguments of natural theology. It would be no more necessary to provide the sort of evidence the skeptic desires than it would be to provide evidence for our beliefs about the external world.

---

50. Arguments of this type were common among nineteenth-century intellectuals (e.g., Freud, Feuerbach, and Marx). Rudolf Otto offered an interesting suggestion that it is more natural and probable to suppose that finite and fallible individuals would *resist* belief in a holy God if left to their own devices than "dream God into existence," as the skeptic presumes; see *The Idea of the Holy* (New York: Oxford University Press, 1923).

However, there might be some cases in which it might be incumbent upon Christians to provide some evidence for their belief. It would be a fundamentally different kind of evidence than what the skeptic desires, however. We are created with certain natural sources of belief, among which we might list memory, perception, and instinct. Our only hope for knowledge is that these natural sources of belief are coherent and consistent with each other. And it seems likely that if the natural sources of our beliefs are consistent, then one source might provide evidence for the validity of another source. Suppose I was driving down the road and saw what appeared to be a large yellow balloon in the sky. Suppose I then stopped and asked some bystanders if they too saw a yellow balloon. If they assured me they did, and I was disposed to believe their testimony, I would take their statement as confirming my belief in the yellow balloon.[51] The mere questioning of the belief would not constitute an invalid inquiry.

Must I question my belief? Obviously it depends on circumstances. Sometimes there are reasons to doubt, but not always. Some perceptual beliefs may give us no reason to doubt their veracity (e.g., if I think I see a cloud floating in the sky as I drive down the road). Other perceptual beliefs may be so unusual that it would be quite reasonable to doubt them (e.g., if I think I see a giant toaster floating in the sky as I drive down the road). In the same way, there may be circumstances in which I feel no need for further verification of my belief in God, but it is not hard to imagine circumstances in which I might feel that a request for further evidence is entirely in order.

Suppose that both of Jack's parents are university professors who have consistently criticized the church for its witness to a supernatural being. Throughout Jack's formative years, they have made an effort to instill in him a critical stance toward beliefs about such a being. Would it not be quite "natural" for Jack, upon reaching the age of reflection, to consider belief in God implausible? Would it not take arguments that appeal to other beliefs he holds (or ought to hold) to convince him of the rationality of belief in God? One might be able to explain to him the repression of his initial impulse to believe in God, but to do so, one

---

51. Nicholas Wolterstorff refers to this as the "credulity disposition" — a concept he borrowed from Thomas Reid. See Wolterstorff, "Thomas Reid on Rationality," in *Rationality in the Calvinian Tradition*, ed. Hendrik Hart, Johan Van der Hoeven, and Nicholas Wolterstorff (Washington: University Press of America, 1983), pp. 43-69.

would have to appeal to evidence that he would find convincing — which would most likely be evidence that his culture has sanctioned. We would have to locate some beliefs of his that are inconsistent with his disbelief in God. Even so, these arguments would not finally be persuasive if he refused to give up a culturally sanctioned irrationality. However, if the grace of God were to break in upon his heart, Jack might be enabled to see these sanctions for what they are — mechanisms he had been using to avoid the proper claims of God upon his life.

Granting that the Spirit plays a substantial and decisive role in persuading us of the validity of belief in God, we might still ask what responsibility remains for us as Christians to those who do not yet believe. We must approach such individuals with an awareness of what it is that they are disposed to view as plausible. For example, we might find that in addition to believing that there is no God, Jack also believes that it is important to respect his fellow human beings, that it is not right to lie to others or to deprive them of basic human dignity. Not all cultures hold these beliefs explicitly, but Jack's culture does, and he accepts them as well. We might then suggest to Jack that a transcendent and redemptive God is the only means by which these assumptions make sense. Our argument might be long and drawn out, but it would follow parameters laid down by Jack's culture, affirming some culturally acceptable convictions while denying the validity of others.

This is to say that in the defense of a theological framework, certain Christian truth claims may require evidence while others do not. If Ruth finds belief in God to be irresistible, it is plausible to suggest that she is warranted in believing in God. If she sometimes encounters doubt, it should be evaluated in reference to other beliefs in her noetic structure. When belief in God is immediate and irresistible, this does not exclude a subsequent analysis of the evidence. In fact, such immediate belief in God may, at times, be eminently more plausible if it is combined with an assessment of the evidence (i.e., of truth claims made by other noetic faculties).

I must acknowledge that this line of reasoning allows for the possibility that people could claim a warrant for the belief that God does not exist if they experienced that belief as immediate and irresistible. However, using a distinction of Alvin Plantinga's, the Christian apologist ought to claim that despite the fact that there may be "prima facie warrant" for this belief, there is no "ultima facie warrant" for it.[52] There

---

52. See Plantinga, "Reason and Belief in God," in *Faith and Rationality,* pp. 16-93.

may be an initial warrant (cultural circumstances and expectations, etc.) for the belief that God does not exist, but it will ultimately be overridden. For if it is true that God does exist and that he is an omnipotent and benevolent Creator who desires that all his creatures know him, then it is right to assume that he will provide grounds for doubt that will ultimately override an individual's initial belief that he does not exist.[53] The mere fact that the belief that God does not exist is culturally acceptable does not mean that it is "ultimately warranted." The Christian apologist ought to be engaged in the task of showing why the belief that God does not exist ought not to be considered *properly* warranted. In this sense, my line of reasoning responds to the skeptic by leaving room for a limited assessment of the evidence.

The task of Christian apologetics may operate at several levels. It may be positive in nature and provide grounds of assurance for a person's belief in God. It may be primarily negative in nature and provide grounds of doubt for a person who believes that God does not exist. It may also provide an epistemic theory that warrants a person's belief in God without reference to any evidence whatsoever. In some ways these are three different tasks that have led to different apologetic methodologies and epistemic theories. If my line of reasoning is valid, these tasks can be accounted for under one apologetic umbrella.[54]

Internal and External Reason

The ramifications for the construction of a theological framework follow this pattern as well. There are several different levels at which reason may operate in the theological framework. The apologetic enterprise may rightly be construed as dealing with the assumptions from which

---

53. I would like to make two tentative suggestions as to the nature of this ultimate justification: it may lie in eternity, or it may lie so deep within the conscience of the unbeliever that it can be recovered only within a conversion experience. I surely do not want to claim that the grounds for doubt that may be provided to the unbeliever short of the ultimate warrant stimulated by the Spirit will necessarily be convincing in and of themselves. There are, after all, things more important to the the game of believing than mere epistemic reasons. The ultimate justification will take place only when one takes the full ramifications of sin into account and affirms the role of the Holy Spirit.

54. This is to suggest that the strategies of Calvinist epistemology (Plantinga and Wolterstorff), classic natural theology (Butler, Paley, Warfield, etc.), and even the presuppositionalist strategy of Cornelius Van Til need not be construed as mutually exclusive.

the theological framework is properly constructed. The movement from these assumptions into dogmatic conclusions has at least two aspects. The first of these concerns the proper construal of the biblical revelation, and the second concerns the manner in which that material is to be translated into the conceptuality of the modern world. The construal of the biblical revelation must be undertaken with a view of reason that is internal to the biblical text. This is to suggest that the proper rational framework for understanding the biblical material is contained in the text itself. Rationality is subservient to the text in some important sense. The Bible has its own plausibility structures, and the interpreter of the Scriptures must begin by locating these structures and identifying the impact they have on the theology of the entire canon.

The matter of translating the plausibility structures of the Scriptures into the structures of a particular culture involves what we might refer to as an external view of reason. We can expect to find that some scriptural plausibility structures will be similar to the cultural plausibility structures and others will stand in stark contrast. The evangelical belief in the final authority of the Scriptures establishes the principle that the internal use of reason must be normative in relation to the external use of reason. When the plausibility structures conflict, the internal use of reason must take precedence. This does not mean that evangelicals ignore the external use; they simply consider it to be subservient to the internal use.

A theological framework ought to strive to contextualize the gospel in the resultant theological vision. This assumes that one's native rationality allows for the possibility of understanding the gospel and accepting it as reasonable and plausible. If the plausibility structures of the gospel run counter to the structures of one's culture, the irresistible warrants of one's native rationality assume a priority. Ultimately, it is the evangelical's hope that native rationality undergirds the rational plausibility of the Scriptures, which in turn have a plausibility structure of their own. This latter structure will then provide the resources to resolve the conflict with the divergent plausibility structures of modern culture. The evangelical theological framework is constructed from the vantage point of the Scriptures, then, in an awareness of the conflicting views of reason but also in an awareness of the power of the Scriptures to interpret and resolve this conflict. It is a central task of the theological project to elucidate this gospel and its conflict with the rationality of modern culture in a language that is intelligible to the modern person.

The "problem" surrounding the two natures of Christ may serve as a helpful illustration. It has been argued frequently in modern times that it is not rational to believe that Jesus could be both fully human and fully divine. The divine characteristics of omniscience, omnipresence, and an incorporeal nature are incompatible with the limitations that are characteristic of human nature. It is argued that the traditional doctrine of the incarnation assumes both parts of this incompatibility and is therefore irrational. John Hick has gone so far as to suggest that this traditional affirmation of the church is akin to saying that a set of lines on a piece of paper could be both a circle and a square at the same time.[55] The biblical doctrine of the incarnation is intrinsically contradictory, he argues, and hence ought to be rejected.

How might an evangelical theological framework be constructed with this apparent problem in view? Briefly, one might begin by stressing the fundamental relationship between creature and Creator. If the knowledge of this relationship instinctively arises in the proper circumstances, then that knowledge must serve as the initial framework for the discussion of this "problem." Second, one might stress the foundational nature of the biblical material. It is the text itself that provides the parameters for rational discussion. If the Scriptures declare that Jesus was God incarnate, then it may be incumbent upon the believer to wrestle with the question of *how* this is possible rather than *if* it is possible. Some parameters may be laid out in Scripture, such as Jesus' actual birth in time, his physical development, his sinlessness, his relationship to the Father, and so on. These "facts" of Scripture will then inevitably push the "theory" of the incarnation in certain directions and away from others (e.g., toward a Chalcedonian definition and away from a kenotic theory). One might then proceed to look at Jesus Christ from the vantage point of the entire canon. What do the Scriptures themselves consider important about the person of Jesus Christ? How do they conceptualize his divinity and his humanity? A final step in the process might be to enlist modern conceptual tools as carefully and humbly as possible to clarify the incarnation for the modern person.[56]

---

55. Hick, "Jesus and the World's Religions," in *The Myth of God Incarnate*, ed. John Hick (London: SCM Press, 1977), p. 178.

56. The recent work of Thomas V. Morris is one very important effort in this direction. See especially *The Logic of God Incarnate* (Ithaca, N.Y.: Cornell University Press, 1986); see also his essay "Rationality and the Christian Revelation," in *Christian Faith and Practice in the Modern World: Theology from an Evangelical Point of View*, ed. Mark A. Noll and David F. Wells (Grand Rapids: William B. Eerdmans, 1988), pp. 119-38.

In summary, we must recognize that rational argumentation in the movement from the Scriptures to a contemporary expression of theology will be influenced by the dual nature of rationality as both native and cultural. I have argued that native rationality serves a foundational role for grasping the Scriptures. What is reasonable and plausible by the criteria of the Scriptures must then be expressed through the conceptual vehicles of one's culture. Certain parts of the theological framework will irresistibly arise from the Scriptures themselves, while others will arise in a less straightforward fashion. Both parts must be clothed in the concepts and language of a particular culture, though this will be a good deal more difficult at some points than at others.

We must seek to ensure that cultural expressions in the theological framework always remain open to correction by the Scriptures themselves. The framework of the Scriptures must take precedence over the cultural expressions of that framework. Therefore, the modern theological framework must remain ever sensitive and accountable to the original divine revelation. Theology must continually submit itself to the task of reformation — in accord not with cultural assumptions but with the touchstone of divine revelation.

PART II

THEOLOGY:
PAST AND PRESENT

CHAPTER 5

The Theological Past

Most of all, perhaps, we need intimate knowledge of the past. Not that the past has any magic about it, but because we cannot study the future, and yet need something to set against the present, to remind us that the basic assumptions have been quite different in different periods and that much which seems certain to the unedu-cated is merely temporary fashion. A man who has lived in many places is not likely to be deceived by the local errors of his native village: the scholar has lived in many times and is therefore in some degree immune from the great cataract of nonsense that pours from the press and the microphone of his own age.

C. S. Lewis[1]

INTRODUCTION

PART of the task of constructing a theological vision entails the ex-ploration of times when a vital theological vision guided the heart and mind of the church. In saying this, I am not advocating a search for a golden past. I simply think we will do well to try to learn from those who have gone before us. To be successful, the attempt will have to be grounded in humility — humility to recognize and to learn from our

1. Lewis, "Learning in War-Time," in *The Weight of Glory and Other Addresses,* ed. Walter Hooper (New York: Macmillan, 1980), pp. 28-29.

own historical limitations and from the wisdom of the church in ages past.

The cleansing value of the past ought not to be underestimated. It can challenge the cherished idols of the modern world and force our own community of faith to think seriously about its foundations. It may also help us to see the limitations of our respective theological traditions.

Our focus in this chapter will be on the movement from biblical text to doctrine in the thought of four significant theologians or theological movements. In order to understand how these representative theologians have moved from the biblical text to a contemporary expression of doctrine, we will have to begin with some groundwork in understanding the nature of the biblical text and the framework in which doctrine emerges from that text. Since these concerns are never embodied outside a concrete historical context, we will also have to explore the relationship between culture and theology as well as questions of doctrinal development. How have other cultures influenced the construction of a theological vision, and how has theology "developed" within a theological tradition? This will provide a context in which to raise the same issues in a pointed fashion with respect to the modern evangelical theological vision: How ought modern culture to influence the evangelical theological vision, and how might that vision develop from its own heritage?

Specifically, then, we will consider four case studies: (1) the magisterial reformers Luther and Calvin, (2) the Reformed scholastics of the sixteenth and early seventeenth centuries, (3) Jonathan Edwards, and (4) Geerhardus Vos. These thinkers and traditions provide a rich background against which to raise the issues at hand. They are different enough to teach modern theologians different lessons but similar enough to form a unified argument.[2]

I will be especially interested in framing these four case studies in terms of the revelatory trajectory sketched out in Chapters 3 and 4. Focusing on the movement from text to doctrine through the filters of tradition, culture, and reason will facilitate our understanding of the

---

2. The shape of this chapter has been influenced by my reading of David Kelsey's book *The Uses of Scripture in Recent Theology* (Philadelphia: Fortress Press, 1975), in which he presents case studies of seven representative contemporary Protestant theologians and then draws conclusions regarding the functional use of Scripture in theology. While I disagree with Kelsey's conclusions, I did find the framework of his inquiry to be worthwhile.

theological minds we consider. And I believe that these four case studies will also offer important insights into the modern construction of a theological framework insofar as they illuminate the revelatory trajectory.

It will be evident from the outset that the case studies are brief. It is not my intent here to try to unravel the depths of the theological vision of these thinkers. At issue is not historical detail but the broad outlines of the ways in which their theology developed. Nor is my selection of subjects meant to suggest that Protestant theology is somehow inherently superior. I simply felt that these case studies best anticipate many of the methodological conclusions I reach in the book's final two chapters.

A key to those methodological conclusions is the redemptive-historical use of Scripture in the construction of a theological framework and the application of a theological vision. The manner in which these thinkers conceive of the normative use of Scripture as historically redemptive is fundamental to their respective theological frameworks (and fundamental as well to the theological method I outline in the final two chapters). These are not the only four case studies that might have served to flesh out this particular insight, but they do offer instances of the self-conscious employment of the Scriptures and are therefore highly instructive for our purposes here.

These case studies are not meant to serve primarily as a lesson in the proper use of tradition in theology. I am not principally interested in getting at the historical lesson at this point, in understanding how accurately to describe and recover the past, although we will encounter some pointers regarding these issues along the way. Rather, it is my primary concern to enlist these thinkers as "conversation partners" for modern evangelicals. The need for such conversation is all the more important given the relative lack of serious reflective theological inquiry among modern evangelicals, especially on methodological matters. The modern community of interpreters would do well to increase the ranks of those it is willing to listen to and learn from.

These case studies are meant to highlight a part of the project of constructing a theological framework. The individuals I have selected bring unique insights to the theological task and for this reason are especially helpful to the contemporary evangelical community. I specifically looked for some representatives who played significant roles in shaping the evangelical heritage (Luther, Calvin, Jonathan Edwards) and some who remained outside the mainstream and are able to offer unique insights by virtue of that fact (the Reformed scholastics and Geerhardus Vos). We can be enriched by looking to both the center and the periphery, especially if we discover a degree of consensus between them regarding the normative use of Scripture.

I would ask you to be open to a consideration of these "heroes" even if they are not your own heroes. They are all connected in one fashion or another with the Reformed wing of Protestantism. Part of my reason for choosing them lies in the fact that the Reformed branch of the church (along with the Lutheran) has valued serious theological reflection more dearly than the other branches of Protestantism.[3] This branch of the church has been self-conscious in its concern for matters of method, of the framework in which one moves from the biblical text to doctrine. The principles of the construction of a theological framework have been uppermost in their minds, and as a result we can glean insights from their work in a straightforward manner. I am by no means suggesting that they constitute the only formative influence on evangelicalism, but, given the relative lack of methodological reflection (or consensus) within the movement as a whole, it would seem that there is much to be learned from this branch of Protestantism.

I do not mean to suggest either that there are no differences among these representative thinkers; in fact, they have much in common. But their differences are instructive. Although all four case studies give evidence of a central commitment to the redemptive-historical use of Scripture in theology, for example, each works out the commitment in a different way. This underscores some of the "diversity within unity" in Protestant thinking. Though the case studies are all fairly representative of thinking in the Reformed wing of the Protestant church, their theological vision is not blandly uniform or a simple repristination of earlier visions. Differences arise out of different philosophical assumptions and the diversity of their practical intent. As these thinkers wrestled with their own cultural and historical contexts, we must wrestle with the modern context. A simple reiteration or translation of a past theological vision will no more suffice today than it did in ages past.

The diversity of some matters of methodological detail evident in

---

3. See George Marsden, "Reformed and American," in *Reformed Theology in America: A History of Its Modern Development*, ed. David F. Wells (Grand Rapids: William B. Eerdmans, 1985), pp. 1-14.

these four case studies also indicates that in their search for a theological method, orthodox Protestants have more often been guided by a theological vision than by a consensus theological method. In other words, they typically start with the framework rather than the method. There are several general methodological principles that receive something approaching a consensus among these Protestant thinkers, but many methodological details remain beyond the reach of a consensus. This does not make the details any less important, however; in fact, it can endow them with a special importance. Luther and Calvin disagreed over interpretive principles with respect to certain gospel passages, and the distinctions between the doctrines that emerged from their different strategies were significant and have played a fundamental role in inter-Protestant dialogue.

Once again, then, I would stress that our objective in exploring theological visions from the past is not to devise ways by which we might simply recast them in modern language. Rather, we must look to them for insights into how we might better understand our own peculiar theological task in order to press on toward the goal of reestablishing a relevant biblical orthodoxy.[4] To this end, our attempts to recover and reappropriate these theologians will not follow strictly formal lines pertaining to matters of "theological method." They do not all make clear distinctions between matters of method and substance. While their particular views on the normative use of Scripture do exert a regulative influence on matters of substance for them, this influence amounts to more than just a methodological constraint. The authority of the biblical text more nearly approaches a part of the fabric in which the entire theological framework is woven. This authority is at once part of the theological framework and part of what holds the theological vision together.

The chief point I am trying to reach in this chapter is that theological frameworks are constructed not merely with the aid of formal constraints

---

4. In this regard, I must apologize for having failed to include either a patristic or a medieval theologian among the case studies. My principal excuse for the omission is that I simply am not as familiar with these earlier sources as I am with those I selected. Nevertheless, I would like to express my sincere conviction that evangelicals have paid far too little attention to the patristic and medieval periods. For a helpful entry into these areas from an evangelical perspective, see Gerald Bray, *Creeds, Councils and Christ* (Downers Grove, Ill.: InterVarsity Press, 1984). For further study, see J. N. D. Kelly's companion volumes *Early Christian Creeds*, 3d ed. (New York: D. McKay, 1972) and *Early Christian Doctrines* (New York: Harper & Row, 1978).

but also through a living experience of the Protestant doctrines. Methodological principles (e.g., principles of hermeneutics, contextualization, rationality) are present in every theological construction, but they are not normally chosen in a vacuum. As I have already suggested, the best theology is intensely personal. It is forged in a living encounter with the Scriptures, and therefore the use of the Scriptures in theology ought not to be merely an abstract principle. Certain abstract methodological principles undergird and shape this encounter, and in this role they are significant and absolutely necessary, but the theologians we will encounter in our four case studies remind us that theology in its ideal form is never abstracted from life. Theology is supposed to transform life — a point that is dramatically evident in the lives of these thinkers.

THE MAGISTERIAL REFORMATION

It is becoming increasingly difficult to define the Reformation as a movement.[5] The popular assumption that it began with Luther's famous nailing of the Ninety-five Theses to the door of the Castle Church in Wittenberg in 1517 is simply inadequate.[6] As with all cultural movements, the Reformation arose out of a complex of historical, cultural, economic, and political factors.

A variety of other significant reform movements within the Roman Catholic Church undoubtedly influenced the shape of the Protestant Reformation. The invention of the modern printing press in Germany facilitated the dissemination of Protestant ideas and as a result effected change across Northern Europe that would have been impossible a hundred years earlier.[7] The political environment influenced the degree

5. Many helpful introductions to the Reformation are available. One particularly accessible volume (which also shows familiarity with the most recent secondary literature on the subject) is Alister E. McGrath's *Reformation Thought: An Introduction* (Oxford: Basil Blackwell, 1988).

6. Though the nailing of the Ninety-five Theses to the door at the Castle Church is often popularly viewed as the event that pushed the Roman Catholic Church to the edge, it is important to remember that it was originally meant to provoke not revolt but discussion of the sale of indulgences. Erik Erikson rightly remarks that the posting was "not a defiant gesture in itself but rather scholastic routine" (*Young Man Luther: A Study in Psychoanalysis and History* [New York: W. W. Norton, 1958], p. 258).

7. This factor may partially explain the failure of the reform movements associated with John Wycliffe and John Hus in the century prior to Luther and Calvin.

of popular support for Luther and the other Reformers. The city states in southern Europe afforded fewer republican sentiments than those in the north. The political centers in the north had for some time been gradually detaching themselves from the authority of the Vatican. Given the ties between the political and ecclesiastical power of Rome, this helps to explain why the Reformation succeeded in Germany, failed in France, and never took root in Spain at all.

Recent studies have also suggested that popular religion was on the rise in the period immediately prior to the Reformation.[8] These new populist movements were almost always characterized by anticlerical and antipapal sentiments, and so we can assume that their adherents would have been that much more receptive to Luther's tirades against the centralized authority of the Roman Catholic Church.

Papal authority was further undermined by the Great Schism of 1378-1417 between the sees of France and Italy. For a while two, and then three, individuals claimed simultaneously to be the supreme head of the church. The resolution of this dilemma by the Council of Constance (1414-1418) left a nagging question for the Roman Catholic Church: Who had final ecclesiastical authority, popes or councils?

The intellectual movement known as the Renaissance was also a critical factor in shaping the Reformation.[9] The recovery of the classics of the Greco-Roman world during the Renaissance prompted a yearning for a return to primitive sources such as the Bible on the part of many of the Reformers. Renaissance-influenced thinkers such as Desiderius Erasmus sought to press reform of the church along lines spelled out by the early Church Fathers as well as the Bible.[10]

The first of our case studies will focus on two of the principal Reformation figures, Martin Luther and John Calvin. They are called *magisterial* Reformers because their reform movements were endorsed

---

8. See especially Bernd Moeller, "Piety in Germany around 1500," in *The Reformation in Medieval Perspective,* ed. Steven E. Ozment (Chicago: University of Chicago Press, 1971), pp. 50-75.

9. The link between the Renaissance and the Reformation is helpfully laid out by W. J. Bouwsma in "Renaissance and Reformation: An Essay in Their Affinities and Connections," in *Luther and the Dawn of the Modern Era: Papers for the Fourth International Congress for Luther Research,* ed. Heiko A. Oberman (Leiden: E. J. Brill, 1974), pp. 127-49.

10. It is no accident that Erasmus prepared the first critical edition of the Greek New Testament, for example. He sought to direct reform through the recovery of ancient sources.

and in part realized by magistrates, the ruling civil authorities. Again, the influence of social factors — in this case political — was critical to the success of the Reformation and to its enduring legacy in the Protestant lands.

In recovering the Reformation heritage, it is imperative that we understand the social forces that influenced and were influenced by these Reformers. Their theological visions did not form in a cultural vacuum. Social forces helped to shape what these men thought and how they lived, and hence they help to explain why the Reformation developed differently in Germany than it did in Geneva. We must not overlook the significance of these forces as we try to recover and learn from these seminal Protestant theologians.

On the other hand, it would be a grave mistake to discount the significance of the theological reasons that lay behind the Reformation. There were important differences between the Reformers and the papacy, which in part explains the intensity of sentiments aroused in Protestant lands.[11] This is simply to say that we cannot adequately account for the Reformation solely in terms of social factors, exclusive of any spiritual considerations. In an era such as ours, when scholars are keen to explain events and movements solely in terms of natural cultural forces, it seems almost anti-intellectual to suggest that there might be transcendent forces at work as well. And yet the Christian must not capitulate to this sort of pressure. God is at work in the world, and our thinking and acting occurs on the stage not only of the earthly drama but also of the eternal drama. So it was with the Reformers also.

Martin Luther

The briefest of outlines of Luther's life will suffice for our purposes.[12] He was born in Eisleben, Germany, of peasant stock. He trained for a time in law at the behest of his father but soon turned his mind to the

11. This is one of the differences between that age and our own: in the present climate, the level of theological interest and acuity among laypeople would prohibit a reformation *of the same kind* from taking place.

12. For further information, see Roland H. Bainton, *Here I Stand: A Life of Martin Luther* (Nashville: Abingdon Press, 1950) — still the best introductory volume. It is eminently readable and captures well the dynamism of its subject. A more contemporary and theological account of the life of Luther can be found in Walther von Loewenich's *Martin Luther: The Man and His Work* (Minneapolis: Augsburg, 1986).

study of theology and was trained to be a priest in the Augustinian monastery in Wittenberg. His primary training and early teaching responsibilities were in the field of Old Testament studies. He was captivated by the Psalms early on, but then, under the influence of his mentor Johann von Staupitz, young Martin turned his attention to the Pauline corpus of the New Testament. As a result of his early lectures on Paul's letters to the Galatians and the Romans, Luther wrestled with his own sense of unrighteousness and precariously arrived at the conviction that guided him during the remainder of his life — that he was justified before God by faith alone.

His own involvement with the reform movements within the Roman Catholic Church publicly began with the nailing of the Ninety-five Theses on Indulgences to the door of the Castle Church at the University of Wittenberg. Initially, he was upset with the Vatican's practice of selling indulgences as a means of building St. Peter's Church in Rome, but this concern developed into a much greater controversy over the very nature of church authority. Finally, after several now-famous public debates with representatives of the Vatican, Luther was excommunicated from the Roman Catholic Church.[13] He spent the remainder of his life providing public support and leadership for the burgeoning movement of religious dissent.

Possibly the single most influential act of Luther's later years was his translation of the Bible into the German vernacular. Literally and symbolically, he placed the Bible into the hands of the ordinary German peasant. The final infallible authority of the pope was undermined in German lands once and for all by this apparently innocent act of translation.

Consistent with his concern to place religion into the hands of the ordinary layperson once again, Luther composed hymns and catechisms in the language of the ordinary German. In this manner, the Lutheran Reformation was solidified in German lands, and Roman Catholic attempts to counter Luther's teaching with papal dictates or other hierarchical instruments of authority were thwarted. The simple and austere piety that Luther sought to exemplify proved effective in undercutting these external claims to religious authority.

Martin Luther was no sophisticated scholar, no "gymnast of the intellect"; he was "a man persevering rather than subtle and delicate in

---

13. Luther was actually excommunicated three times by Pope Leo X, as if to signal the importance and finality of the separation.

discrimination.... [He] had humor and loud laughter but not wit."[14] He was driven by an awareness of his own limitations and the reality of the grace of God. The particular form of both his written and spoken expression was undoubtedly shaped by his peasant upbringing, by his legal training, and by his lengthy tutelage in the Augustinian monastery under Johann von Staupitz. But it is his own spiritual struggle before God that stamped itself most indelibly on his theological framework.

Luther was consumed by an anxiety in the face of a holy and righteous God.[15] This was evident in his early monastic experience and is also manifest in his early lectures on the Psalms. It progressed even further as he lectured on the Pauline epistles of the New Testament and reached a climax, according to Luther himself, in his experience in the tower of the Augustinian cloister at Wittenberg. One day during the autumn of 1514, Luther struggled to understand the precise meaning of Romans 1:17.[16] In an emotional encounter with the text and, through the text, with God himself, Luther finally concluded that a sinner is justified through faith and that the righteousness of God no longer stands as a condemnation but rather as a means of grace. As he wrote in recalling this incident,

> At last by the mercy of God, meditating day and night, I gave heed to the context of the words, namely, 'In it the righteousness of God is revealed, as it is written, He who through faith is righteous shall live'. There I began to understand that the righteousness of God is that by which the righteous lives by a gift of God, namely by faith. And this is the meaning: the righteousness of God is revealed by the gospel, namely, the passive righteousness with which merciful God justifies us by faith as it is written, 'He who through faith is righteous shall live.' Here I felt that I was altogether born again and had entered paradise itself through open gates.[17]

14. Owen Chadwick, *The Reformation* (London: Pelican Books, 1972), p. 43.

15. I say "anxiety" here, but the German term that Luther typically uses — *anfectung* — is usually left untranslated in his works because it means more than simple anxiety. It connotes an all-encompassing dread in which one's very existence is at stake.

16. There is some controversy as to the exact date of the "tower experience." See A. Skevington Wood, *Captive to the Word: Martin Luther, Doctor of Sacred Scripture* (Grand Rapids: William B. Eerdmans, 1969), pp. 51-56.

17. *Luther's Works,* vol. 34: *Career of the Reformer IV,* ed. Lewis W. Spitz and Helmut T. Lehmann (Philadelphia: Fortress Press, 1960), p. 336.

Luther's understanding of this text was probably not novel even in his time, but it led to a personal transformation that in turn sparked a revolution in his theological vision. What is so significant in this incident is the manner in which the biblical text served as the medium through which he encountered God. The text neither opposed nor prevented the personal encounter (as it did in some later forms of Pietism), nor was his personal encounter mediated by any institutional forms of authority (as in Roman Catholicism of the Reformation period). The written word was a *living word*. It entered Luther by the power of the Holy Spirit.

Luther's personal appropriation of the doctrine of justification by faith changed the course of his life. The encounter with this doctrine in the Protestant church at large led to a fundamental shift in emphasis from the external act of religion (in cult, ritual, and ceremony) to the internal act of religion, to the domain of the mind and the heart, to *personal* faith.

It is no accident that Luther began to appeal to the Scriptures as the final authority in his debates with the Roman Catholic Church. His background in biblical exegesis convinced him of the priority of Scripture over all church authorities and ultimately led him to a rejection of the system of theology inherited from the medieval Roman Catholic tradition. As he grew in his resolve to believe only what the Scriptures taught, he grew more certain of the importance of placing the Scriptures in the hands of the layperson.

Luther is misrepresented if he is portrayed simply as a hot-tempered monk consumed by his own personal experience. It is true that he was in many ways incorrigible, and yet whatever the defects of his personality, they should not be allowed to diminish the validity of his devotion to the new understanding of the gospel. He did not indiscriminately revolt against all forms of authority; he opposed only those forms of authority that he believed impeded the revelation of God from having its proper impact on the heart and mind.

Luther grew in his own dependence on the Greek New Testament and the Hebrew Old Testament thanks in large measure to the work of the Renaissance humanists who had painstakingly sought to recover the manuscripts of Scripture in their original languages. In fact, given his appreciation for the humanist interest in the classical languages, Luther himself might be called a humanist. He was not a technical scholar by temperament, but he seems to have recognized the value of the linguistic and philological tools offered to him by the Renaissance humanist tradition. Thus he demonstrated a concern for the two poles of the theological project—the first horizon of Scripture in its original form and context and the second horizon of the Scriptures as captured in the vernacular of the German peasant. He was unwilling to compromise the importance of either of them.

Later in his life, Luther reveled in public denunciations of formal and rigid medieval scholastic theologians.[18] Even so, he never lost sight of the early classical scholastic training he had received. He may have railed publicly against the excessive dependence of medieval Roman Catholicism on Aristotelian philosophy in theological matters, but it is also true that his own writings were characterized by a technical scholastic precision. Owing in part to early training in law, Luther was proficient in making the sorts of fine distinctions (especially in regard to the doctrine of justification) that were typical of late medieval scholastic Augustinianism. He was not a scholastic in the medieval sense of that term, but this is not to say that he failed to make good use of some aspects of the tradition.

The rigors of his early monastic training exercised a significant influence on Luther. He was well suited to spending an extended period of isolation in the castle at Wartburg during the early 1520s. Though he undertook this seclusion principally because of the threats that had been made on his life, he made use of the time after the fashion of a monastic scribe, though with the obvious difference that his intention in working with the ancient texts was to translate the Bible into modern German.

Sola Scriptura is often hailed as *the* formal principle of the Reformation. Luther viewed it in terms of a rejection of the Vatican's claim to possess infallible authority in pronouncing on matters of doctrine—though, significantly, he did not view it as a rejection of authority per se. He had been trained to appeal to church tradition in arguments over points of doctrine, and he never fully abandoned that strategy, as his robust statements of approval regarding Augustine demonstrate.[19] The

18. For examples, see *Luther's Works*, vol. 54: *Table Talk*, ed. Theodore G. Tappert and Helmut T. Lehmann (Philadelphia: Fortress Press, 1967).

19. In 1517 Luther wrote to a friend, "my theology—which is St. Augustine's—is getting on, and is dominant in the university. God has done it. Aristotle is going downhill and perhaps he will go all the way down to hell. . . . Nobody will go to hear a lecture unless the lecturer is teaching my theology—which is the theology of the Bible, of St. Augustine, and of all true theologians of the Church" (quoted by Chadwick in *The Reformation*, p. 46).

important difference in Luther's strategy involved a subtle change in the criteria for the acceptance of doctrine. In much of the medieval tradition, a doctrine was accepted if it was commended by church tradition and was not contrary to the Scriptures. It was not enough for Luther that a doctrine merely avoid being inconsistent with Scripture; he sought a positive warrant for it in Scripture. He admitted the testimony of the Church Fathers only as a guide in establishing this positive warrant from Scripture.

Luther did not produce a systematic treatment of the major theological topics.[20] He preferred to write for particular situations with specific ends in mind. The Luther corpus is composed of a multitude of genres — commentaries, catechisms, polemical treatises, disputations, hymns, sermons, personal letters, and anecdotes. He was as competent to write a technical and learned commentary on the book of Galatians as he was to write a strong-tempered pamphlet condemning the political and worldly power of the pope. He did not draw the lines of distinction between academic theology and populist rhetoric. He believed that the very reform of Christendom was at stake, and he submitted himself in both mind and heart to this purpose.

Part of the legacy of Luther (and the other magisterial Reformers as well) was the return of preaching to a central place in the worshiping life of the church.[21] Luther's theology was nurtured in the long years of his exegetical training and teaching, but it found its classic expression in his preaching and popular writings. He did not become the sort of traveling itinerant that someone with his stature and intentions in our day might well become. In addition to serving as a university lecturer, Luther was an assistant at the parish church in Wittenberg from his ordination in 1510 to his death in 1546, and he did not stray often from the responsibilities of the parish.[22] It is remarkable how little evidence Luther ever gave of experiencing a tension between his university and parish obligations. As he saw it, they both drew on the same two funda-

---

20. Some might argue that his two catechisms constitute exceptions to this rule, but it should be remembered that these are summaries rather than extended expositions of doctrine.

21. For an able treatment of Luther's views on preaching, see Wood, *Captive to the Word*, pp. 85-95.

22. Gerhard Ebeling has counted well over two thousand complete sermons by Luther from this period that have survived (*Luther: An Introduction to His Thought*, trans. R. A. Wilson [Philadelphia: Fortress Press, 1970]), p. 53.

mental assumptions — first, that exposition of the message of the gospel always begins with the biblical text, and second, that one ought never to examine the text in isolation from the demands it makes on one's life.

Several overarching themes bind all of Luther's varied writings together.[23] It would be wrong to suggest that Luther thought through these themes systematically, however. Rather, he was consumed with a theological vision that inevitably focused on several dominant themes. He was convinced that these were the themes of Scripture. Evidence of this resides in the fact that his treatment of these themes could not always be reconciled with his theological framework when it came to the fine points: he was content to go as far as Scripture permitted him and no further. He was quick to acknowledge that there are mysteries in the gospel that a fallible and fallen mind cannot comprehend. He distrusted autonomous reason, although he did value the role of regenerate reason in efforts to defend and proclaim the gospel.[24] He sought to reconcile difficulties in Scripture through appeal to other Scriptures and only very infrequently speculated about the proper philosophical (i.e., nonscriptural) framework for understanding the doctrines of Scripture.

Luther's theological vision was intensely personal. It developed out of his own personal pilgrimage, and he most typically committed it to paper in the heat of controversy. He was concerned for theology not as a detached observer but as one thoroughly involved with his subject matter. Theology mattered in life, he felt, and no part of life was left untouched by the implications of theology. Luther might have offered a systematic defense of the gospel had he lived in another time, but the pressing needs of his day demanded a piecemeal defense for the divergent questions being asked.

The central issue of justification by faith was never very far from Luther's purposes. He viewed all of theology through this lens, and it clearly helped him to see things in Scripture that had previously been obscured. But it may also have exerted some negative influences on Luther's interpretive work.[25] For example, it seems unlikely that the

23. For a delineation of these themes and an assessment of Luther in terms of them, see chap. 2 of Timothy George's *Theology of the Reformers* (Nashville: Broadman Press, 1988).

24. The clearest study of Luther's view of reason is Brian A. Gerrish's *Grace and Reason: A Study in the Theology of Luther* (Oxford: Oxford University Press, 1962).

25. Daniel Fuller has argued that in focusing so resolutely on the doctrine of justification by faith as a theological lens for the interpretation of all Scripture, Luther

opponents of whom Paul speaks in his letter to the Romans were legalists in the sense envisioned by Luther. The apostle's argument was not directed at the claim (made by some Roman Catholics in Luther's day) that salvation could be achieved through good works but rather at the claim that salvation could not be achieved through one's ethnic identity as a Jew.[26] Additionally, Luther's overwhelming concern with the centrality of justification by faith led him to doubt the canonicity of the book of James for a time.

Luther conceived of the relationship between the Old and New Testaments largely in terms of the relationship between law and gospel. He saw the fundamental issue of justification underlying both Testaments and believed that the central difference between them lay in their understanding of the issue. He maintained that the Old Testament holds out the hope (unwarranted in his mind) that one might be justified before God on the basis of good works (i.e., obedience of the law). In the New Testament, he said, justification accrues to an individual solely on the basis of the merit of Christ received through faith. Luther imposed this framework on the Scriptures because he saw in it clear parallels to the theological claims being made in his own day. As a result, he sharply divided faith and works and left an enduring legacy of interpreting the New Testament's rejection of legalism as a rejection of the Old Testament's command to be obedient to the Mosaic Law.

While Luther undoubtedly understood the New Testament conception of justification, he misconstrued the Old Testament conception. The covenant enacted at Sinai rested as much on the sovereign initiative of God for its hope as did the concept of salvation in the New Testament. The central difference lies in the fact that the Sinai covenant looks forward expectantly to the fulfillment of its hope in the Messiah. The New Testament looks back on the actual fulfillment in the person of Jesus of the promise originally made to Abraham and renewed with Moses.

---

essentially established a canon within the canon, thereby violating a cardinal rule of Reformation theology — namely that Scripture be allowed to interpret Scripture. See Fuller, "Biblical Theology and the Analogy of Faith," in *Unity and Diversity in New Testament Theology: Essays in Honor of George E. Ladd,* ed. Robert Guelich (Grand Rapids: Eerdmans, 1978), pp. 195-213.

26. A vast new literature on Paul and the law has appeared in recent years. The groundbreaking work in this regard is E. P. Sanders's *Paul and Palestinian Judaism* (London: SCM Press, 1977). See also his *Paul, the Law and the Jewish People* (Philadelphia: Fortress Press, 1982).

The key point in this consideration of Luther is that his interpretive key (justification by faith) clarified many things in Scripture, but his own distinctive reading of the doctrine also prohibited him from seeing other important concerns in Scripture. His overriding commitment to the Scriptures was unfailing, and on this point even Luther himself desired to be judged. Contemporary evangelicals have much to learn from Luther — not because he was the perfect theologian but because he was a theologian willing to be judged by the Word.

John Calvin

Calvin was born in Noyon, France, a small town in Picardy just north of Paris. His father was an ecclesiastical lawyer who raised his son devoutly in the Roman Catholic Church. The elder Calvin initially guided his son toward a vocation in the church, but after he had been excommunicated from the church because of a financial quarrel, he decided that his son should not be ordained after all, but should rather pursue a career in law. The younger Calvin dutifully followed his father's wishes, though as a result of his studies in Paris and Bourges, he yearned for the quiet life of a humanist scholar rather than the active life of a lawyer. His father's death provided the opportunity to suspend his legal studies and undertake studies in the classics. His first book, published when he was only 23 years old, was an edition of Seneca's treatise *On Clemency,* complete with a textual apparatus and lengthy commentary. Though not a commercial success, the book did receive some positive critical notice. Had it not been for a conversion he experienced at some point during this period, Calvin would almost certainly have been content with the leisured life of a professor and scholar of the classics.[27]

Neither the times nor his personal circumstances permitted this, however. At some point during his stay in Paris, Calvin came into contact

27. The precise date and duration of Calvin's conversion remains a point of controversy among contemporary historians. The range of dates for the conversion given by scholars is between 1527 and 1534. There is no life of Calvin comparable to Bainton's life of Luther, *Here I Stand.* The single best work on Calvin and his historical context is François Wendel's *Calvin: The Origins and Development of His Religious Thought,* trans. Philip Mairet (Durham, N.C.: Labyrinth Press, 1987). The recent work of William J. Bouwsma, *John Calvin: A Sixteenth-Century Portrait* (New York: Oxford University Press, 1988), is a sympathetic attempt to render Calvin intelligible in the light of his sixteenth-century context.

with individuals advocating reform, and when persecutions of reforming individuals within France reached his own extended family, his sympathy for the reform movement grew. Increasing persecution eventually forced Calvin himself to flee France, a fact that lingered in his memory for the rest of his life.

He stayed for a time in Geneva at the insistence of the fervent Reformer William Farel. Exiled from the city for a period of three years for having pressed too great a moral reform on its citizens, Calvin went to Strasbourg and there spent a brief period that he described as the happiest time of his life. It was there that he met his wife, Idellete, and there that a strongly supportive French Reformed community nurtured his theological convictions. His stay in Strasbourg ended when the Genevans earnestly requested that he return to complete the reforms that had been derailed three years earlier. After some strong pleading by Farel, and then only reluctantly, Calvin returned to Geneva and there spent the remaining twenty-three years of his life.

The stamp that Calvin placed on Geneva during this time was profound. He was the senior pastor in the city as well as the senior teacher at the academy he founded to promote the teachings of the reform movement. He altered the entire social fabric of the city. Upon his return, he drafted a document entitled *The Ecclesiastical Ordinances* that was soon adopted by the city council as the effective constitution of the Genevan church and later the city. It structured the church under four orders — pastors, doctors, elders, and deacons — corresponding to the duties of doctrine, education, discipline, and social welfare. The principles laid out in this document were probably never put into force by the town fathers in quite the way Calvin had hoped, but even so it provided the definitive structure of the Reformation church as it spread far and wide under Calvin's influence. The influence of the *Ordinances* extended far beyond Geneva through the personal contact Calvin maintained with the large number of third-generation Reformers who came to Geneva to seek Calvin's counsel and who left deeply impressed with his program of theological and structural reform.

His most famous work, *The Institutes of the Christian Religion,* went through several editorial stages between 1536 and 1559 and proved almost from the start to be the most significant training manual of the Reformation. Calvin's writings were less intense and fiery than Luther's, but Calvin proved more able than Luther to consolidate the Reformed movement with a systematic work that laid out the framework of an overarching biblical theology. It is not an exaggeration to suggest that aside from the personal presence of Luther, Calvin's *Institutes* constituted the single most decisive influence on the Protestant churches at the time of the Reformation. And it remained fundamentally influential for over two hundred years, well into the seventeenth century. It was one of those rare documents that literally shaped a culture. Whether one agrees with its vision or not, its importance cannot be overestimated.

The Reformation may have owed its passion to Luther, but its order arose from the influence of Calvin. The Protestant movement would not have been the same without the distinctive contributions and personalities of these two men. And it is no accident that their influence extended far beyond their own lifetimes both within the Protestant churches and outside.

Calvin's theological vision, like Luther's, was driven by a sense of the greatness of God and the utter dependence of humanity upon God. On these essential points there is little difference between the two.[28] What differences there are is largely a matter of presentation: Luther aimed his convictions at the pressing problems of the day, while Calvin attempted to fit them systematically into a theological framework. Because of this approach, we find Calvin's methodological commitments nearer the surface in his writings.

It is apparent that Calvin's theology, no less than Luther's, was a response to the work of the Spirit mediated through the Word. Calvin's experience of this may not have been as intense as Luther's, but there is little doubt as to its profundity in his life. The fundamental unity between Spirit and Word was a hallmark of the Protestant church in both the Lutheran and the Reformed branches. The Spirit always acted in accord with the written Word (as opposed to the mediation of the papacy or of private experience). The fundamental question of the opening sections of the *Institutes* is "How can a person know God?" The answer lies in the systematic revelation of God in Scripture breaking in

---

28. Brian Gerrish insightfully remarks that Calvin "identified himself wholly with the common Protestant cause and never faced the Wittenbergers (Lutherans) as the sponsors of a rival movement" ("John Calvin on Luther," in *Interpreters of Luther: Essays in Honor of Wilhelm Pauck*, ed. Jaroslav Pelikan [Philadelphia: Fortress Press, 1968], p. 69). And Benjamin Warfield rightly noted that "it is misleading to find the formative principle of either type of Protestantism (Lutheranism and Calvinism) in its difference from the other; they have infinitely more in common than in distinction" (*Calvin and Calvinism* [New York: Oxford University Press, 1931], p. 357).

on the heart and mind of the individual through the power of the Spirit. This is the fundamental philosophical commitment of Calvin, that knowledge of God is found primarily in the written word and that it is from this starting point that all of theology begins. This is the methodological guideline that informs his entire work.

Both Luther and Calvin rejected what was to become the official Roman Catholic position on "tradition" at the Council of Trent (1540-1544). This two-source theory affirmed both a tradition of revelation in Scripture and an extrabiblical, oral tradition rooted in Jesus' postresurrection instructions to the apostles as passed down through the ages by the magisterium of the church. Luther and Calvin were equally insistent that no such revelatory tradition existed outside of Scripture. However, unlike sections of the radical Reformation, they also refused to *deny* the importance of tradition. Neither Calvin nor Luther simply threw out the preceding 1,500 years of church history. In representative fashion, Luther defended tradition in his treatise against the Anabaptists (1528): "We do not act as fanatically as the *Schwärmer*. We do not reject everything that is under the dominion of the Pope. For in that event we should also reject the Christian church. Much Christian good is to be found in the papacy and from there it descended to us."[29]

The indebtedness of Luther and Calvin to tradition can be seen clearly in their reliance on Augustine at central points.[30] Calvin was also profoundly indebted to the secular authors of antiquity. His form of argument in the *Institutes* shows striking parallels with those normally employed by classical authors such as Cicero and Seneca.[31] He drank deeply from the well of history, and the strength of his convictions was often a function of the clarity of the conviction he found in Scripture mediated through the patristic tradition. However, it is also clear that Calvin went to some lengths to distance himself from the classical humanist tradition in matters in which the humanists differed with Scripture. The most notable example is found in the first five chapters of Calvin's 1559 edition of the *Institutes,* where he demonstrates the weakness

29. *Luther's Works,* vol. 40: *Church and Ministry II*, ed. Conrad Bergendoff and Helmut T. Lehmann (Philadelphia: Fortress Press, 1958), p. 231.

30. Warfield remarked that "the Reformation, inwardly considered, was just the ultimate triumph of Augustine's doctrine of grace over Augustine's doctrine of the church" (*Calvin and Augustine* [Philadelphia: Presbyterian & Reformed, 1956], p. 322).

31. See Quirinus Breen, "John Calvin and the Rhetorical Tradition," *Church History* 26 (1957): 3-21.

of Cicero's position on the knowledge of God that can be acquired through nature alone. Without questioning the reality of such knowledge, Calvin goes to some lengths to show that it is merely preparatory to the "saving knowledge" of God that comes through the Scriptures.[32] In a manner reminiscent of Paul's argument with the Athenian philosophers in Acts 17, Calvin understood the background and philosophical assumptions of the humanist scholars of his day and effectively used that knowledge in his presentation of the gospel. He used their form of argument to substantiate biblical positions and was not ashamed of doing so.

While he had no compunction about borrowing certain methodological prescriptions (e.g., the form of proper argumentation) from extrabiblical traditions, however, Calvin was firm in his conviction that the *substance* of theology must extend no further than the limits of Scripture. A particularly acute example can be found in his understanding of appropriate worship. Unlike Luther, Calvin was convinced that the liturgy of the Protestant churches ought to include only what is expressly affirmed in Scripture. Luther, on the other hand, held that the church could include additional elements so long as they were not contrary to or expressly prohibited by Scripture. Thus, for instance, Luther was not averse to including sections of the medieval mass, whereas Calvin believed it was necessary to revamp the entire service based on explicit biblical injunctions. Calvin's "regulative" principle sought to distinguish more clearly the practices of the Protestant churches from those of the medieval church. His reverence for tradition was no less than that of Luther, but he believed it had to be filtered through Scripture more fully in matters of practice.[33]

On the troubling medieval issue of the relation between the canon of Scripture and the church, Calvin set forth the classic Protestant position in its clearest form. Specifically, he rejected the Roman Catholic

---

32. On this point, see E. Grislis, "Calvin's Use of Cicero in the Institutes I:1-5: A Case Study in Theological Method," *Archiv für Reformationsgeschichte* 62 (1971): 5-37. See also the brief treatment given to this topic by Alister McGrath in *The History of Christian Theology*, vol. 1: *The Science of Theology*, ed. Paul Avis (Grand Rapids: William B. Eerdmans, 1986), pp. 125-31. For an extended treatment of Calvin's doctrine of the knowledge of God, see T. H. L. Parker, *Calvin's Doctrine of the Knowledge of God*, rev. ed. (Edinburgh: Oliver and Boyd, 1969).

33. Calvin suggested at times that Luther's position on the eucharist was a result of his unwillingness to break fully with the medieval church. This is made especially clear in a short treatise he directed at Luther's disciple Joachim Westphal, *Second Defence of the Godly and Orthodox Faith concerning the Sacraments against the False Accusations of Joachim Westphal.*

position that the authority both to determine the extent of the canon and to interpret its message ultimately lay in the hands of the church.

Luther had raised this fundamental canonical issue by questioning the place of the epistle of James in the Bible. How were the Reformers going to resolve disputes like this without an authoritative ecclesiastical magisterium? Luther held that James contradicted the substance of the gospel as given in Paul's letters to the Galatians and the Romans. His implicit criterion for inclusion in the canon seemed to be a simple consistency with the gospel and more specifically with the doctrine of justification by faith. But this simply pushed the issue one step back: who is to determine whether a book is consistent with the gospel? The church? That would be to make the church authoritative, in some sense, over the Scriptures. Or should it be left to the individual? That would be to make the individual authoritative over the text — a recipe for anarchy. Luther may never have fully recognized the seriousness of the problem. In any event, it was not until Calvin came along that a fully Protestant response was developed.

Calvin argued that it was neither the church nor the individual that determined the canon but rather the Holy Spirit. It was the "internal testimony" of the Holy Spirit in the life of the believer in the church by which the extent of the canon could be discerned. This did not remove the issue from theological discussion in the church; it simply provided a framework in which the discussion might take place. And, importantly, it manifested Calvin's continuing concern to unite the Word and the Spirit.

Both Luther and Calvin denied that the interpretation of Scripture belongs exclusively to the magisterium of the church. They regularly championed the intrinsic perspicuity of the text: there is no need, they insisted, to interpose a papal representative between the laity and the biblical text. But again, this did not constitute a rejection of tradition. Both Luther and Calvin affirmed that tradition plays a vital role in the interpretive movement from Scripture to doctrine — and they included the contribution of the current community of believers in that tradition. They parted ways with medieval Roman Catholic views in asserting that the interpretive function belongs in the hands of the entire church (past and present) and not merely some elite part of it.[34]

---

34. Contrary to the views of many contemporary scholars, both the Roman Catholics and the Reformers denied that the meaning of the text is a creation of the church. Both affirmed that the meaning of the text resides not *in front of* the text but rather *in* the text. I develop this point further in Chapter 6.

On the other end of the spectrum, Calvin was also disinclined to make the Word captive to the individual. It is significant that in the second generation of the reform movement, Calvin set up structures in Geneva to guard against the abuses of the "right of private interpretation" — a right that Luther had championed in the first generation. Calvin seems to have been well aware of the dangers of the radical Reformation and its emphasis on the individual's right to interpret Scripture however he or she feels led by the Spirit. This "interpretive anarchy" was as much anathema to the Swiss Reformer as the "interpretive monarchy" of the pope. Calvin organized "congregations" in Geneva consisting of Reformed pastors from the surrounding territory and handfuls of devout laypeople. These congregations would gather on a weekly basis to discuss some prearranged passage of Scripture. The intent was that the congregation would wrestle in communal discourse over the proper interpretation of the text in preparation for the preaching of the passage on the following Sabbath. It was Calvin's firm belief that this was the only way to ensure responsible interpretation of Scripture. "For as long as there is no mutual exchange," he said, "each can teach . . . what he likes. Solitude provides too much liberty." This strategy of communal interpretation, doubtless a remnant of Calvin's days in Strasbourg, was eventually institutionalized in Geneva. Its significance for an evangelical theological method today cannot be overstated.

Calvin, like Luther, held that the Scriptures as interpreted by the community are brought to life in the preaching of the gospel. Calvin's theological vision in particular required the centrality of preaching. It is no quirk of history that the pulpit replaced the altar as the center of focus in the churches of Geneva and throughout Protestant Europe.[35] It is the gospel that brings life, and the gospel is indissolubly linked to the written Word, which in turn is brought to life in faithful preaching. In this practice, the Bible stands as the source and the standard for assessing all preaching. Like theology in general, said Calvin, the preaching of the church ought not to extend any further than Scripture permits. Preaching ought to focus on no less and no more than the entire counsel of the written Word. It must not speculate beyond the Scriptures, nor may it exclude parts of Scripture as unessential or unimportant.

Not all are called to preach, said Calvin. Those who are called to

---

35. An exemplary study of Calvin's doctrine of preaching can be found in T. H. L. Parker's *The Oracles of God.* I draw on Parker's insights in much of the following discussion.

preach are assured of this by the inner testimony of the Holy Spirit and by the external call of the fellowship of other pastors. There is in this sense a subjective and an objective aspect to the call required for preaching. Preachers bear a heavy burden and a tremendous privilege.

The centrality of preaching at Geneva also reflected Calvin's fundamental conviction that God can be "savingly known" only through his Word. God's initiative in salvation is mirrored in his initiative in revelation. It is God who comes to us, not the other way around. The three fundamental "layers" of this initiating revelation are the living Word, the written Word, and the preached word. Christ reveals most clearly who God is and how he can be known, the Bible serves as the effective channel for the transmission of the gospel of Christ, and the faithful preaching of the Bible is the instrument God has chosen to proclaim the gospel and make himself known. These functions are inseparable not because the church has authoritatively spoken but because God has ordained it. As Calvin put it, "We see how God works by the Word which is preached to us, that it is not a voice which only sounds in the air and then vanishes; but God adds to it the power of His Holy Spirit."[36] This obviously assumes that the preacher knows the living Word and the written Word. "None will ever be a good minister of the Word of God, except he first be a scholar [of the Word]."[37] With a contemporary ring, Calvin says,

> How many ministers of the Word one sees who are so poorly trained in Holy Scripture! . . . For they have never made a habit of moulding themselves entirely to the language of the Holy Spirit, as good scholars. If a scholar is a man of parts, and his master is a good teacher too, he will certainly not only remember what he has been taught, but will also retain some characteristic of his master so that it will be said: 'He was at such and such a school.'[38]

Calvin frequently uses the imagery of the "school" in his writings, for it captures well his conviction that serious study of the Word is absolutely essential to right and holy living. Unfortunately, many in our day seem to believe that serious study impairs one's ability and motivation to live a holy life. Serious and sustained reflection on the Scriptures

---

36. *Corpus Reformatum: Ioannis Calvini Opera quae supersunt omnia*, 59 vols., ed. Guilielmus Baum et al. (Braunschweig: C. A. Schwetschke, 1863-1900), 54:11.

37. *Calvini Opera*, 26:406.

38. *Calvini Opera*, 54:68.

forms the very heart of Jonathan Edwards's theological vision, but it is important to see the precedents of it in Calvin. To follow Christ is to immerse oneself in his Word. It is to think in biblical terms and in biblical ways. That is the starting point for holy living and the proper foundation for a theological vision.

THE REFORMED SCHOLASTICS

The Protestant scholastic period is generally thought to have begun with the death of the second generation of Reformers in general and Calvin in particular.[39] It lasted for nearly two centuries. The sons of the Reformers wrestled with a different age than their forefathers had, and it is likely that their impact on the larger culture did not match that of Luther or Calvin.

Many modern intellectual historians have suggested that this era of the Reformed church (and of the Lutheran church as well) was irrelevant and often downright obscurantist. A. C. McGiffert has suggested that the Protestant scholastic movement was characterized by a "rigid sterile rationalism lacking either religious warmth or intellectual originality."[40] If this analysis is correct, it is surprising that scholasticism should have remained the dominant form of Protestantism to the end of the eighteenth century.

The end of the Protestant scholastic era coincided with the consolidation of the Copernican revolution at the end of the seventeenth century with the work of Kepler, Galileo, and Newton. The influence of this scientific revolution extended into other areas of thought; increasingly, law, philosophy, science, and politics were drawn from nontheological first principles. The modern era baptized this monumental change without ever really noticing it. Thinkers in this new tradition such as Hobbes and Spinoza offered views of reality and society drastically different from those of traditional theology. Universities began to break free from the shackles of the church thanks in some measure to the

39. In the following discussion, I use the terms "Protestant scholasticism" and "Protestant orthodoxy" interchangeably to denote the dominant form of Protestantism on the European continent in the post-Reformation era. The terms "Reformed scholasticism" and "Reformed orthodoxy" are used interchangeably as well.

40. McGiffert, *Protestant Thought before Kant* (New York: Harper Torchbooks, 1961), p. 145.

reduction in its hegemonic power in the wake of the Reformation. When religious peace came in the seventeenth century, it proceeded on the assumption that the world was free to go ahead without religious leadership. As John W. Beardslee has suggested, "Luther's contemporary, Machiavelli, was the real victor in the war of the theologians."[41]

Theologians in the seventeenth century, Protestant and Catholic alike, still thought in premodern terms. Their confessions — most prominently the Canons of Dort and the Westminster Confession — echoed dogmatic formulations of ages past. For example, they reaffirmed the belief that the world owed its beginning and its ongoing sustenance to the hand of a personal and providential God and that this God had revealed himself faithfully in the Scriptures. They also affirmed that the fundamental task of the theologian is to spell out the *biblical* message as precisely as possible. They derived their axioms not from common human experience or the perceptions of the natural world but from a careful and cautious reading of Scripture. Their "dialogue partner" as they wrote their theology was not the new science but rather the Scriptures and the older philosophers. And by affirming these beliefs and adopting these strategies, say the historians of our day, they lost the battle for the modern mind.

The Protestant church of the seventeenth century consisted of three central parties — the Lutheran, the Reformed, and the Church of England. The Anabaptist wing was not influential in Continental Protestantism during this time except in isolated pockets, and in England it exercised influence only in modified form through the Puritans.[42] In terms of visible influence, it is not an exaggeration to say that Protestantism outside of England in the seventeenth century was dominated by the Reformed and Lutheran branches of the church. In the discussion that follows, we will focus on the Reformed branch, although given the remarkable similarities in theological method and ethos between the two branches, much of the analysis could easily be extended to include post-Reformation Lutheranism.[43]

41. Beardslee, Introduction to *Reformed Dogmatics: Wollebius, Voetius, and Turretin*, ed. and trans. John W. Beardslee (New York: Oxford University Press, 1965), p. 4.

42. Actually, the English Puritanism of the seventeenth century might more accurately be described as a curious blend of the Church of England, Reformed, and Anabaptist influences. Our discussion of Jonathan Edwards, the most formidable of the American Puritans, will bear this out.

43. For the finest and surely the most exhaustive study of post-Reformation Lutheranism to date, see Robert D. Preus, *The Theology of Post-Reformation Lutheranism*, 2

The post-Reformation era divides into three separate but overlapping stages.[44] Early orthodoxy runs from the time of the publication of the Heidelberg Catechism (1563) to the time when the theologians who sat at the Synod of Dort (1618/19) ceased to dominate Reformed theology (somewhere between 1630 and 1640). This was the period of confessional consolidation, when the movement was led by such men as Zacharias Ursinus, Caspar Olevianus, Jerome Zanchi, Theodore Beza, Francis Junius, and William Ames.

The second period runs from roughly 1640 to the end of the seventeenth century. Thinkers in this period did not create theological systems but modified, expanded, and elaborated extant systems. Prominent representatives of this period include Francis Turretin, Peter van Mastricht, Hermann Witsius, John Owen, and Benedict Pictet.

After 1700, Reformed scholasticism lost some of its vitality and ceased to be a dominant intellectual form in the churches and the Protestant universities of Europe. Systems of Reformed theology were still being produced by such individuals as Fredrich Stapfer and Bernhard de Moor, but increasingly these became peripheral to the mainstream theological discussions of the period.

Some modern analysts of the post-Reformation Reformed heritage have simplistically argued that the sons of the Reformation engaged in outright distortion of the vision of the Reformation propounded by their spiritual fathers — Calvin in particular. But the post-Reformation Reformed tradition is far more complex than most of these critics have suggested.[45] It may even be a misnomer to refer to the post-Reformation Reformed church as "Calvinistic," since Calvin was but one of the influences on this movement. Although he clearly exerted a more substantial influence over succeeding generations than any other single

vols. (St. Louis: Concordia, 1970). See especially the first volume of this work regarding the remarkable similarities between Reformed and Lutheran writers on the matters of prolegomena that I am treating in this study. All of this is not to deny the very real doctrinal differences between Lutheran and Reformed communions over such issues as the eucharist, justification, and predestination.

44. This division of the post-Reformation era follows the framework of Otto Weber, *Foundations of Dogmatics*, 2 vols. (Grand Rapids: William B. Eerdmans, 1981-1982), 1:120-27.

45. The following account of post-Reformation Reformed orthodoxy is deeply indebted to Richard Muller's marvelous *Post-Reformation Reformed Dogmatics*, vol. 1: *Theological Prolegomena* (Grand Rapids: Baker Book House, 1987).

individual, his contributions were significantly complemented by a host of first-generation Reformation pastors and scholars, including Peter Martyr Vermigli, Heinrich Bullinger, Martin Bucer, Jerome Zanchi, Theodore Beza, Andreas Gerardus Hyperius, and Wolfgang Musculus. Beyond any question, the account is far more complex than many quite common characterizations suggest in making straightforward declensions from Luther (a first-generation thinker) or Calvin (a second-generation thinker) to some particular later thinker (such as Theodore Beza) or group of thinkers. The fact that Calvin and Beza differed on some points does not in itself suggest that Beza was unfaithful to the Reformation vision. The Reformation proceeded from several fountainheads. In the century and a half after Calvin's death, the Reformed church was sustained through an extensive and variegated network of pastors and scholars. It would be a mistake to assume that all Reformed scholastics were the same, and it would be an egregious mistake to tar all the scholastics with the brush of a particular thinker's flaws.[46]

A fundamental concern of the scholastic period was the consolidation of a theological and religious movement, a movement that owed some of its original energy to the dominance of strong personalities and the perceived unjustness of certain Roman Catholic practices. As the new and burgeoning Reformed church temporally moved away from these cultural forces, it became important to develop mechanisms to propagate the Protestant theological framework within the changed environment. Theologians were focused no longer on reforming a church but rather on establishing and protecting a church. They gradually moved beyond primarily homiletical instruction to undertake the construction of a more thorough theological vision.[47] The two pressing

---

46. Unfortunately, so many scholars have followed this strategy that it has gained a certain credibility. Far too little attention has been paid to the very complex nature of the historical continuity and discontinuity of traditions. For examples of this flawed approach, see some of the older studies such as I. A. Dorner's *History of Protestant Theology*, trans. George Robson and Sophia Taylor (1871; reprint, New York: AMS Press, 1970), and A. C. McGiffert's *Protestant Thought before Kant*, as well as more recent studies such as Basil Hall's "Calvin against the Calvinists," in *John Calvin*, ed. Gervase Duffield (Grand Rapids: William B. Eerdmans, 1966), pp. 19-37, and Holmes Rolston III, *John Calvin versus the Westminster Confession* (Richmond: John Knox Press, 1972).

47. It is noteworthy that in the Protestant scholastic period, almost all of the academic scholars held dual posts — as university instructors and as pastors. These two vocations were separated only under the pressure of the secularizing tendencies of the Enlightenment in the eighteenth century.

concerns were polemical and pedagogical: there were new enemies against which to defend the gospel, and there were new institutions devoted to learning in the Reformed world.

The Reformed scholastics faced challenges from increasingly clear and well-articulated versions of Roman Catholicism and Lutheranism. In response, they felt the need to produce treatments of doctrine that were more refined and systematic than the introductory treatments that had been produced by the first and second generations of Reformers. Furthermore, unlike the earlier Reformers, the Reformed scholastics faced opposition from a group of free-thinkers who challenged settled christological and trinitarian doctrine.

Near the end of the sixteenth century, a group of Italian exiles known as the *erectici* opened up many questions of dogma that had been considered closed by the majority of theologians in the Lutheran, Reformed, and Roman Catholic traditions.[48] They seemed to challenge the very foundations of orthodoxy (both Protestant and Roman Catholic), and, for a number of cultural reasons, they progressively became a force with which the Protestant church had to reckon. The fundamental assumptions relating to the nature and character of God, the incarnation, and biblical infallibility that the Protestants had held in common with the Roman Catholics at the time of the Reformation came under severe attack in succeeding generations, calling for a response of a different sort than could be found in the work of either Luther or Calvin. Since the *eretici* challenge was couched in a rationalist framework, the scholastics responded with rationalist modes of argument.

The polemical cast of much of the scholastic writing of the period can also be attributed to pedagogical circumstances in Europe at the time. In the orthodox period, there was a movement toward institutionalization and the disciplined academic teaching of theology. The institutionalization of orthodoxy was founded on the principle that it had to have a form that could be passed on. It is in this sense that the theology of this period can appropriately be characterized as scholastic.[49]

---

48. For a helpful discussion of this group and their interaction with the Reformed scholastics, see John Patrick Donnelly, "Italian Influences in the Development of Calvinist Scholasticism," *Sixteenth Century Journal* 7 (1976): 81-101.

49. Richard Muller defends at some length his contention that this period cannot be identified simply with medieval or Aristotelian scholasticism. The Reformed scholastics were not fundamentally interested in theological speculation, nor was their dogmatics unduly reliant on human reason. See Muller, *Post-Reformation Reformed Dogmatics,* pp. 13-52,

This movement helped to define theology as a discipline with its own presuppositions and principles.[50] And in this setting, the theological framework developed on a highly technical level and in an extremely precise fashion. The early Protestant Reformers did not give systematic treatments of prolegomena matters because "they did not engage in the task of adapting the theological propositions of Protestantism to the needs of university-level training as system."[51] But the institutionalization of Protestant theology in the university context made rapprochement with philosophy necessary. Intellectual disciplines were still couched in a logical framework indebted to Aristotle. It was not uncommon for scholastic theologians to move in typical Aristotelian fashion from first cause to final goal, structuring their theological system in relation to first causal principles.[52] Nor was it unusual for scholastic theologians to note the fundamental difference between the orderly expression of the system based on an Aristotelian framework and the substance of the system based fundamentally on biblical principles. So, for example, Francis Turretin pointedly raised the question of the role of philosophy in theology and castigated those thinkers who were "more philosophical than theological, [who] rested more upon the reasoning of Aristotle and other philosophers than upon the testimonies of the Prophets and the Apostles."[53]

231-50. See also Muller, "Vera Philosophia cum sacra Theologia nusquam pugnat: Keckermann on Philosophy, Theology and the Problem of Double Truth," *Sixteenth Century Journal* 15 (1984): 343-65; and Lynne Courter Boughton, "Supralapsarianism and the Role of Metaphysics in Sixteenth-Century Reformed Theology," *Westminster Theological Journal* 58 (Spring 1986): 63-96. For a particularly cogent defense of this claim applied to the work of Francis Turretin, see Richard Muller, "Scholasticism Protestant and Catholic: Francis Turretin on the Object and Principles of Theology," *Church History* 55 (June 1986): 193-205.

50. For one of the relatively few English translations of extended passages from the work of European post-Reformation scholastics, see *Reformed Dogmatics: Wollebius, Voetius, and Turretin,* ed. and trans. John Beardslee. Francis Turretin's work on the doctrine of Scripture is available in English under the title *Francis Turretin on Scripture* (Grand Rapids: Baker Book House, 1985). The work of the English scholastics Ames, Perkins, Charnock, and Owen are all readily available in English.

51. Muller, "Scholasticism Protestant and Catholic," p. 173.

52. Indebtedness to Aristotelian logic is not without its detractors among the Protestant scholastics, however. This is especially so in the early period of orthodoxy and is voiced strongly by Perkins, Ames, and Polanus, who favored a discursive logic based on the work of Peter Ramus.

53. Turretin, quoted by Muller in "Scholasticism Protestant and Catholic," p. 200.

To varying degrees, the scholastics also argued against the Socinians that reason can never be the foundation or the norm of theology. Reason may be used to illustrate or collate theological arguments or scriptural passages, to draw out inferences, or to produce arguments concerning the orthodoxy or heterodoxy of a doctrinal position, but its uses are critically limited because, after the fall, it is fundamentally corrupt. Most scholastics gave every indication of believing that some questions simply cannot be answered by theology. Mystery played a crucial role in the systems of theology of this period, as is evidenced in the scholastics' well-known distinction between the "incomprehensible" (mysteries such as the Trinity and the resurrection) and the "incompossible" (contradictories such as transubstantiation and the ubiquity of Christ's body).

It is important to note that this period also brought the first extended discussion of theological method among Protestants (and, arguably, the last such discussion among conservative Protestants). This self-conscious concern for method marks a clear break from the early Reformers. It was not until the final 1559 edition of Calvin's *Institutes* that he gave evidence of anything approaching an overarching unity in his presentation of the Christian faith, and even here the structure derives not from the inherent nature of the doctrines discussed but rather from his desire to be faithful to the form of the Apostles' Creed. Calvin successively edited the *Institutes* to meet changing needs; the final form centered on the issue of our knowledge of God through natural and special revelation. All the later scholastics agreed with Calvin's fundamental premise on this point — namely, that the infinite God can be known in a salvific sense only through his revelation in Scripture. They went beyond Calvin, however, in giving greater prominence to the inner relationship of the doctrines. In doing so, they made the structure of the dogmatic system into a significant issue in its own right, in contrast with Calvin, who had simply borrowed his structure from an earlier tradition.

The first attempt to construct a systematic theology based on fundamental first principles was undertaken during the Protestant scholastic period. The scholastics moved from a discussion of first principles to doctrines that could be derived from these principles on a biblical basis. Typically, they structured their theological systems in one of two ways — according to the historical progress of redemption (God, creation, fall, redemption, glorification) or in an analytic manner (e.g., moving from the problem of sin to its resolution in redemption and faith and then to an exposition of the articles of faith). Both of these structures manifested

Calvin's initial concern with the doctrine of the knowledge of God as fundamental. One approach stressed the divine side of the issue, and the other stressed the human side. Regardless of whether one agrees with these approaches, it seems important to take the scholastic challenge seriously. What are the fundamental premises of Christian doctrine, and how do the doctrines of the Christian faith relate to one another?

With this methodological challenge came a host of other questions that had received virtually no attention early in the Reformation: What is theology? What are its divisions or parts? Is it a science? What are its causes and ends? Is it theoretical or practical? What are its *principia?*[54]

These questions were of fundamental importance because of the need to disclose the role of the Christian faith in the larger arena of human knowledge. Functionally, these questions operated the other way around for the scholastics: they asked not how divine revelation was related to human knowledge but how human knowledge was related to divine revelation. The orthodox tradition strongly affirmed the foundational role of Scripture — all true theology must begin there. And they maintained that the theology (i.e., the knowledge of God) revealed in Scripture is itself derived from the divine self-knowledge that only God possesses. Hence, human reason cannot serve as the cognitive foundation of theology because it has no access to knowledge of God in and of himself. Human reason is not an agent of divine revelation but only an instrument for understanding revelation. By thus sharply limiting the role of reason, the scholastics differed markedly with the dominant secular philosophers of the period. In this, the period marks a true though developed continuity with the Reformation slogan *sola Scriptura*. The scholastics affirmed that Scripture is the sole formative influence on the *substance* of the theological system.

We should take note of one final point concerning the relationship of these methodological matters to the substance (doctrines) of the Christian faith. Both Otto Weber and Richard Muller raise the interesting question of why discussions of prolegomena came fairly late in the life of the Reformation movement.[55] Why did several generations pass before

---

54. Richard Muller suggests these questions were first stamped on the orthodox tradition by Amandus Polanus in *Syntagma theologiae christianae* (1609). See Muller, *Post-Reformation Reformed Dogmatics*, p. 77.

55. See Weber, *Foundations of Dogmatics*, 1:4; and Muller, *Post-Reformation Reformed Dogmatics*, p. 53.

thinkers raised methodological concerns? Why was it only relatively late in the Reformation period that the movement from text to doctrine was discussed? Muller claims that the explicit formulation of prolegomena always comes relatively late in the life of a theological movement. Though all theology necessarily rests on presuppositions and principles, the clarification and codification of these principles come relatively late. If matters of prolegomena broadly concern the conceptuality needed to frame a theological system, then attention to the details of that conceptuality will normally not occur until after the substance of the theological framework itself has been stated and expounded.

There is another factor to be considered in this regard — the apparent paradox involved in using finite forms to discuss an infinite truth. The employment of human concepts in a discourse about an incomprehensible Being creates conundrums that are most difficult to fathom. In the nature of things, it is difficult to engage in an explicit discussion of the utter mystery of God's relation to his creation without having covered a good deal of preliminary material, and it is for this reason that such discussion will tend to come relatively late in the life of a theological movement. In any event, this clearly seems to have been the case in the Reformation context.

If this is in fact a general rule, then it is natural to suppose that matters of prolegomena are rarely ever "pre-dogmatic" in the sense that discussion of such matters precedes the doing of theology. It seems to have been the conviction of the post-Reformation scholastics that principles of method do not rest on prior nontheological ontological or anthropological presuppositions. The principles of method emerge from a properly constructed dogmatic system. The prolegomena of the Reformed scholastics were only an introduction to the theological framework, an introduction that shared in the presuppositions of the system of dogmatics as a whole. The prolegomena of the scholastics were not meant to be neutral philosophical statements that might somehow be theologically separated from the main body of the system. These foundational principles were meant to be dogmatic statements themselves (contra the Enlightenment) and therefore were not developed until after the rudiments of the system were already in place. If theology is essentially and necessarily connected with the biblical witness, then the very character and structure of that theology will be present only after the biblical witness is expounded. Speaking of the Reformed scholastics in this context, Muller says,

Theological prolegomena are never *vordogmitisch* (pre-dogmatic): they are an integral part of the dogmatic system that develops in dialogue with basic dogmatic conclusions after the system as a whole has been set forth. Thus, the Protestant scholastic prolegomena look back to medieval models — in the absence of clear statements of presuppositions and definitions by the Reformers — but do so in the context of an already established Protestant theological tradition as embodied in confessional norms.[56]

The Reformed scholastic tradition represents for modern evangelicals an attempt to spell out the methodological assumptions of a prior theological vision rooted in a momentous revival in the Christian church.[57] The very durability of the scholastic tradition ought to counsel us against dismissing it out of hand as a "rigid sterile rationalism lacking either religious warmth or intellectual originality." It adapted to a changing environment and spoke to pressing needs. It is remembered for its precise logical presentations of theological dogma. We must not forget that this precision was a virtue in an age when fundamental questions of the Christian worldview were at stake.

The Reformed scholastics did not abandon the faith of the first generation of the Reformers. If anything, they maintained the faith with vitality under circumstances that demanded institutionalization and a willingness to draw substantively from parts of the church tradition that had been cast aside only a century earlier. The proclamation and the protection of orthodoxy demanded nothing less.

JONATHAN EDWARDS

Jonathan Edwards is an imposing figure by any standard. The great American Puritan pastor and theologian stands as one of the most ominous theologians the church has ever produced. He towers over the American theological heritage, a figure whom Americans have both

---

56. Muller, *Post-Reformation Reformed Dogmatics*, p. 81.

57. J. I. Packer was simply wrong when he affirmed that one of the lasting legacies of the orthodox scholastics is their intellectualist defense of the truths of revelation apart from their pastoral and doxological motivations. Nothing could be further from the truth. See Packer, "Infallible Scripture and the Role of Hermeneutics," in *Scripture and Truth*, ed. D. A. Carson and John Woodbridge (Grand Rapids: Zondervan, 1983), p. 326.

greatly revered and greatly reviled. The late Harvard historian Perry Miller, the man most responsible for the revival of scholarly interest in Edwards, wrote in his now famous biography of Edwards, "The life of Edwards is a tragedy. . . . Because of his faith Edwards wrought incalculable harm."[58] A more recent and more temperate commentator, Henry May, said, "I have often found Edwards deeply interesting, sometimes repellent, often attractive and moving."[59]

The project of elucidating Edwards's theological vision is, to say the least, daunting, for his corpus is profound both in its depth and its breadth. He is arguably the most creative and the most orthodox theologian that America has yet produced. He was fascinated by the new learning of his day, and, although it may seem incompatible to most moderns, he was also bound by an unparalleled commitment of fidelity to the Scriptures.[60] Even those who do not agree with his conclusions would be hard pressed to find an individual more driven spiritually and intellectually by a commitment and devotion to God. He stands with Augustine and Luther in the depth of his analysis of religious experience. He stands with Aquinas and Calvin in the breadth of his intellectual grasp of the gospel. He may stand unmatched in his ability to have woven these two strands together effectively.

Given the vast scope and complexity of the Edwards corpus, I have elected to focus on just one aspect of one of his works — *A History of the Work of Redemption.*[61] My intent here is not to attempt anything approaching an exhaustive study of this work but simply to look at the way in which Edwards moves from text to doctrine in this great work — and specifically

---

58. Miller, *Jonathan Edwards* (New York: W. Sloane, 1949), p. 148.

59. May, "Jonathan Edwards and America," in *Jonathan Edwards and the American Experience,* ed. Nathan O. Hatch and Harry S. Stout (New York: Oxford University Press, 1988), p. 19.

60. Mark Noll has suggested that it was this tension that separated Edwards from his intellectual ancestors. Some who followed Edwards, such as the New England theologians Samuel Hopkins, Nathaniel Emmons, and N. W. Taylor, were bold and original thinkers but were less than faithful to their biblical heritage. Others, such as the Old Princetonians Charles Hodge and B. B. Warfield, wrote with a great sensitivity to biblical fidelity as interpreted in their tradition but were far from independent and original thinkers. See Noll, "Jonathan Edwards and Nineteenth-Century Theology," in *Jonathan Edwards and the American Experience,* pp. 260-87.

61. I will be working from the version of the text recently edited by John F. Wilson as volume 9 of the Yale edition of the *Works of Jonathan Edwards* (New Haven: Yale University Press, 1989); hereafter it will be referred to as *Work of Redemption.*

those aspects of his strategy that may be most helpful for modern evangelicalism. If in the process I whet your appetite for a further and more reflective reading of Edwards, I will have accomplished my purpose.

Jonathan Edwards was born in 1703 in East Windsor, Connecticut, the only son among eleven children.[62] His father was a respected clergyman and his maternal grandfather was the dominant religious personality of the Connecticut Valley and the pastor of the Congregational church in Northampton, Massachusetts.[63] After training at Yale, Edwards assumed the position of assistant pastor in the Northampton parish. He was there only a short time before his grandfather died, at which point Edwards, at the ripe age of 26, assumed the pulpit of the most prestigious church in the Connecticut Valley. Under his ministry, revival broke out in Northampton in 1734 and quickly spread throughout the Valley. Edwards was encouraged by the revival but wary of some of its excesses. Religion was not meant to destroy the social order, he insisted, but to revitalize it. He maintained that a learned religious establishment was entirely compatible with a heartfelt faith.[64]

Edwards labored for nearly twenty-five years at Northampton and gained a large measure of respect during his tenure. His sermons were well crafted, and though he may not have visited his parishioners as often as his grandfather had, he nonetheless assumed an admired position of leadership in the life of the Congregational churches in the Connecticut Valley.

A crisis came in his ministry at Northampton in the late 1740s, precipitated by Edwards's refusal to allow persons to receive the sacrament of the Lord's Supper without proper and manifest evidence of their conversion. This new policy ran contrary to the practice of his grand-

62. For those interested in further biographical information, I can recommend two recent works: Patricia Tracy's *Jonathan Edwards, Pastor* (New York: Hill & Wang, 1980), and Iain Murray's *Jonathan Edwards* (Edinburgh: Banner of Truth Trust, 1987). Tracy's book is more focused and critical, while Murray's is more popular and hagiographic.

63. This was Solomon Stoddard, who was referred to, with some accuracy, as the "Congregational Pope" from the Connecticut Valley.

64. This is a very important part of Edwards's theological vision from which contemporary evangelicals may fruitfully learn. I cannot expand on this point here, so I would urge you to consult the works in which Edwards treats these topics: *Religious Affections*, vol. 2 of *The Works of Jonathan Edwards*, ed. John E. Smith (New Haven: Yale University Press, 1959), and *The Great Awakening*, vol. 4 of *The Works of Jonathan Edwards*, ed. C. C. Goen (New Haven: Yale University Press, 1972).

father, and in 1751 he was asked to leave Northampton when he refused to relent on the matter.

With some despair and a great sense of humiliation, he accepted a call to minister to a pioneer group on the edge of the wilderness at Stockbridge, Massachusetts, and also to serve as a missionary to the nearby Housatonic Indians. But whether because or in spite of having been spurned by the religious establishment, these years in the wilderness proved to be the most productive period in Edwards's writing career. It was this period more than any other that may rightfully be said to account for the enduring influence he has exerted over American intellectual life. It was here that he produced his great works on the freedom of the will, on the nature of true virtue, and on original sin. And the influence of these writings began to spread far and wide almost immediately. By the fall of 1757, Edwards had accepted the offer of the presidency of the fledgling college at Princeton, New Jersey. He moved to Princeton in the spring of the following year and unfortunately died shortly thereafter from a smallpox inoculation.

The treatise that I have chosen to focus on here — *A History of the Work of Redemption* — was not actually assembled by Edwards himself. In the spring of 1739, he preached a series of thirty sermons that he hoped could later be edited and published under this title, but his untimely death prevented him from doing the work himself. There is ample evidence that this project had been a consuming passion for him shortly before his death, however. In fact, it is not too much to suggest, as recent commentators have, that he viewed this collection as the culmination of his life's work.[65] An analysis of his extant sermon manuscripts suggests that near the end of his life, he was gathering all the relevant materials from them in preparation for "a great work which I call a history of the Work of Redemption, a body of divinity in an entire new method, being thrown into the form of a history."[66]

The possibility that undertaking his duties at Princeton might delay his work on the preparation of this volume was the primary drawback

---

65. Much of the evidence for this conclusion can be gathered from Wilson Kimnack, "The Literary Techniques of Jonathan Edwards," Ph.D. diss., Univ. of Pennsylvania, 1971. On textual and editorial matters pertaining to the *Work of Redemption* project, I am indebted to John F. Wilson's introduction to *Work of Redemption* in the Yale edition, pp. 1-109.

66. Edwards, quoted by Sereno E. Dwight in *The Life of President Edwards* (New York, 1830), p. 569.

Edwards saw to accepting the call. In a letter to the trustees of the college, he expressed his reservation and then went on to give the clearest and most comprehensive extant formulation of his "new method":

> This history will be carried on with regard to all three worlds, heaven, earth and hell; considering the connected, successive events and alterations in each, so far as the scriptures give any light; introducing all parts of divinity in that order which is most scriptural and most natural; a method which appears to me the most beautiful and entertaining, wherein every divine doctrine will appear to the greatest advantage, in the brightest light in the most striking manner, showing the admirable contexture and harmony of the whole.[67]

Edwards was taken with the overwhelming sense of beauty in the presence of God, and it became one of the central organizing principles in his theology.[68] "God is God," he wrote, "and distinguished from all other beings, and exalted above 'em, chiefly by his divine beauty."[69] Beauty is the primary form of order in terms of which Edwards sought to understand all forms of order in the entire system of being under God. Note Edwards's language as he discusses the world of nature after his conversion experience: "The appearance of every thing was altered; there seemed to be, as it were, a calm, sweet cast, or appearance of divine glory, in almost every thing. God's excellency, his wisdom, his purity and love, seemed to appear in every thing; in the sun, moon and stars; in the clouds and blue sky; in the grass, flowers, trees; in the water, and all nature."[70]

It seemed natural to Edwards that this aesthetic sense also held the clue to the systematization of doctrine. Theology was not supposed to be merely a rational framework placed over the scriptural revelation in order to make the Scriptures intelligible to modern man, he believed. Rather, he saw the aesthetic harmony of the Scriptures as the underlying

---

67. Edwards, quoted by Dwight in *The Life of President Edwards*, p. 570.

68. The best short study of the place of beauty in the thought of Edwards is Roland Andre Delattre's "Beauty and Theology: A Reappraisal of Jonathan Edwards," *Soundings* 51 (Spring 1968): 60-79. For a most helpful analysis of the believer's perception of this beauty through an added "spiritual sense," see William Wainwright, "Jonathan Edwards and the Sense of the Heart," *Faith and Philosophy* 7 (January 1990): 43-62.

69. Edwards, *Religious Affections*, p. 298.

70. Edwards, "Personal Narrative," in *Jonathan Edwards: Representative Selections, with Introduction, Bibliography, and Notes*, rev. ed., ed. Clarence F. Faust and Thomas H. Johnson (New York: Hill & Wang, 1962), pp. 60-61.

fabric for the theological framework. Beauty was a structural concept for Edwards, held primarily not in the eye of the beholder but in the very mind of God. As the mind of God was discovered in the Scriptures, the beauty of his revelation became apparent, and an aesthetic or structured theology was possible.[71]

As Edwards conceived of the "body of divinity in an entire new method" that was to constitute his climactic project, his chief concern was how to convey the "beauty" of the model of revelation given in Scripture. He had to manifest some of the inherent structure of the revelation itself, and so in this sense his work would have to be primarily historical. However, it was not to be mere history as contemporary historians understand that term. It was to be a blending of sacred and secular history (the separation of which would have been utterly inconceivable to Edwards). His final and consummating theological project would be a manifestation of the structure and harmony of God's activity in relation to the world. It would be a theology fundamentally devoted to portraying the purposes and providence of God.

The Puritans generally and Edwards in particular held that God's redemption of his people is the fundamental thread tying all of history together. Redemption is the central concern of Edwards's first published work — *God Glorified in the Work of Redemption, by the Greatness of Man's Dependence upon Him in the Whole of It* (1731). He wrote of redemption as finally and fully directed at the goal of glorifying God. As John F. Wilson has suggested, "In effect, Edwards's argument was, so to speak, that if creation is a stage, the purpose of which is to permit the drama of redemption to be played out, the outcome of the drama (and thus the reason for creation) is God's self-glorification."[72] In Edwards's own words, "For God to glorify himself is to discover himself in his works, or to communicate himself in his works, which is all one."[73]

71. Edwards has sometimes been accused of mysticism in this regard, and there is an element of truth to the charge. But in his case, mysticism amounted to a belief in the importance of the vision of God that allows one to understand the world — as opposed to the type of vision that leads to retreat from the world.

72. Wilson, in his introduction to *Work of Redemption*, pp. 31-32. For a substantiation of this point, see Edwards, "Sermon One," in *Work of Redemption*, p. 125.

73. Edwards, quoted by Robert W. Jensen in *America's Theologian: A Recommendation of Jonathan Edwards* (New York: Oxford University Press, 1988), p. 39. For an interesting attempt at capturing this insight in a more popular vein, see John Piper, *Desiring God* (Portland: Multnomah Press, 1987). Piper is pointedly dependent on Edwards in this work.

Redemption also provided the clue to the clearest understanding of God's glory for Edwards. Therefore, the redemption of the world furnished the most suitable and the most "beautiful" framework for a "body of divinity." On this point, Edwards's theological assumptions assumed a very great role in determining the structure of his theological system.

The Puritans had shown a great concern for redemption, and in this Edwards was a typical Puritan. He treated this concern quite explicitly in his earlier works relating to the Great Awakening. In his later writings, Edwards departed from the typical Puritan emphasis on the subjective impact of redemption on the life of the individual and emphasized instead its objective nature. The Puritan approach often translated into a narrow concern for a "morphology of conversion." Part of Edwards's genius lay in applying this concern to history as a whole. As he saw it, history manifested in large the experiences of the individual soul undergoing the regenerative process. Therefore, the category of redemption helps make sense of the world and its history, even serving to explain the role of the individual's experience in that history. Edwards's theological vision in this final proposed treatise was shaped by the merging of the motions of nature, history, and the saint's private self into one theological drama, "showing the admirable contexture and harmony of the whole."[74] This was the "new method" of which Edwards had written to the trustees of the Princeton college.

The sermons that provide the basis for *A History of the Work of Redemption* followed the typical Puritan form.[75] The preacher would begin with a reading of the text and some explanation of its literary and historical setting, its meaning and context. Next would come the implications of the text for an understanding of doctrine, a consideration of how the text ought to affect the believer's understanding. Finally, there would be a lengthy discussion of the ramifications of the text for the behavior of the congregation.[76] Although Edwards tended to concentrate

74. On this point, see William J. Scheick "The Grand Design: Jonathan Edwards' *History of the Work of Redemption,*" in *Critical Essays on Jonathan Edwards,* ed. William J. Scheick (Boston: G. K. Hall, 1980), p. 178.

75. For an excellent overview of the shape of these early sermons, see Wilson's introduction to *Work of Redemption,* pp. 34-40.

76. For an analysis of the Puritan sermon and its role in the cultural life of colonial New England, I heartily recommend Harry S. Stout's *The New England Soul: Preaching and Religious Culture in Colonial New England* (New York: Oxford University Press, 1986).

on the second aspect — doctrine — in his initial sermon series on the history of redemption, he did not omit lengthy sections of application or "improvement," and there is little reason to suspect that he would have omitted such material from his proposed treatise had he completed the work of editing it himself. The Puritans believed that doctrine properly moves life, and Edwards was clearly a Puritan in this respect. The interesting thing about the proposed treatise was that Edwards envisioned it as an entire "body of divinity" that would "improve" the soul.

Edwards set out to identify stages in God's redemptive plan in history. In standard Protestant fashion, he identified three fundamental stages: (1) the period from the fall of man to the incarnation of Jesus, (2) the period from Christ's incarnation to his resurrection, and (3) the period from the resurrection to the end of the world. The terms he used to characterize these stages are, respectively, "preparation," "imputation," and "application."[77]

Edwards's treatment of the first two stages appears very consistent with his own Reformed and Puritan tradition. He envisioned the Old Testament as consisting of identifiable periods, each of which prepared for the coming of Christ. More than Luther or Calvin, Edwards tied the Testaments together through the use of typologies. He viewed persons and events in the Old Testament as "types" or shadows that pointed to and found their fulfillment in some aspect of the person and work of Christ. For example, Edwards proposed that the skins Adam and Eve used to to hide their nakedness in the Garden of Eden were types of the righteousness of Christ in which Christians hide themselves.[78]

Edwards also offers a consistently high and conventional christology in the overview of the second period. He upholds the ancient creeds in affirmation of the full humanity and full divinity of Christ. He makes full use of the language of "covenant" — both in respect of Christ's original covenant with the Father and Christ's covenant with his people — a framework inherited from the Reformed scholastics. There is little that appears innovative in this section.

We might note briefly that Edwards was leery of applying Christ's subjective life to the contemporary experience of the believer. Christ manifested certain virtues as a part of his obedience, but Edwards did not believe that faithful believers ought to try to imitate them as such

---

77. See Edwards, "Sermon One," in *Work of Redemption*, p. 117.
78. See Edwards, "Sermon Two," in *Work of Redemption*, p. 136.

in their own lives. The point of Christ's life was not to provide a pattern but rather to secure redemption. It was in the purchase of redemption, said Edwards, that Christ established his fundamental link with the contemporary believer.

It is in his examination of the final period of history that Edwards manifests his greatest theological and philosophical innovation. He believed that the future of the world could be known through the prophetic literature of the Bible. His use of typology in analyzing the third period extends not only to figures and events in the apocalyptic literature of the Scriptures but also to figures and events in the extrabiblical world. For example, he places a good deal of emphasis on Constantine's conversion in the fourth century as a manifestation of God's intention for the spread of the kingdom here on earth.

Edwards categorized the present age under six headings, which he derived from his own application of principles to modern history rather than from any explicit categorization within Scripture itself.[79] The significance of the stages he outlined lies not in each successively but in the whole as understood through the parts. It was as if Edwards was conducting a symphony in which each note was magnified in importance because of its role in the score of music.[80] He had rehearsed each individual part of the score before, in front of his New England congregation, but he must have felt that something was still missing from their purview — something they needed for a fuller understanding of their own redemption. The omission lay in the view of the parts as an orchestral whole. The events he pointed to were basic themes already established for his hearers, but in their perfection, the whole was enriched by skillful anticipation of later themes and extensive elaboration of earlier themes as the consummation of all things approaches.

It was a different sense of architectonic structure than had been present in some of his theological ancestors, but Edwards would have

79. In developing this sixfold scheme, Edwards may have had in mind some sort of link to the six days of creation or the six stages of the Old Testament covenant, though he never makes the link explicit. I would simply note that his concern for harmony might well have urged him to make such connections.

80. Robert Jensen has made much of the fact that Edwards saw "beauty" exemplified preeminently in music, that he found in the organic relationship of the notes a type of excellence that was unparalleled elsewhere and that served as a forceful illustration (though only in shadow form) of the beauty of God. See chap. 4 of *America's Theologian*.

seen no discrepancy between the early and later structures. If anything, he believed, his proposed treatise would complement and supplement the earlier doctrinal efforts. The key for Edwards lay in the beauty of the work of redemption. Unfortunately, he provided only a cursory treatment of this subject in the sermons he preached in the spring of 1739.

Pointing to the fundamental principle of purpose of the series, Edwards said in the first sermon,

> The Work of Redemption with respect to the grand design . . . is carried on from the fall [of man to the end of the world] in a different manner, not merely by the repeating and renewing the same effect on the different subjects of it, but by many successive works and dispensations of God, all tending to one great end and effect, all united as the several parts of a scheme, and altogether making up one great work. Like an house or temple that is building, first the workmen are sent forth, then the materials are gathered, then the ground fitted, then the foundation is laid, then the superstructure erected one part after another, till at length the topstone is laid. And all is finished.[81]

The final point we should note about the proposed treatise is that Edwards hoped to impress the beauty of the work of redemption on the hearts and the minds of his readers by manifesting it in the treatise itself. His chief goal was to engage the lives of his readers. The *History of the Work of Redemption* was an exhortation to members of the community that they might experience a work of redemption in their own lives. Edwards wished to isolate the sort of knowledge that transformed understanding and apprehension into new behavior — "the taste of honey attracting the palate."[82] The changed heart would then value the glory, the beauty, and the love of God. And though this altered sense could come only as a supernatural gift, Edwards nonetheless believed that it was his duty to write about it as clearly and as passionately as he could using his natural abilities and the "divine and supernatural light" that had been granted to him in his own conversion. Was he successful in this project? Henry May writes that "perhaps Edwards' greatest achievement as a writer is that he comes close through his poetic powers to achieving the im-

81. Edwards, *Work of Redemption*, p. 121.
82. Bruce Kuklick, *Churchmen and Philosophers: From Jonathan Edwards to John Dewey* (New Haven: Yale University Press, 1985), p. 31.

possible. He almost manages to prove to the unilluminated the logical necessity of this supernatural illumination, and even to tell us what it is like."[83]

GEERHARDUS VOS

Geerhardus Vos was a professor of biblical theology at Princeton Seminary for nearly forty years.[84] Though an important voice at the staunchly orthodox seminary, Vos has received scant attention in comparison to his colleagues B. B. Warfield and the stalwart of Old Princeton, Charles Hodge.[85] This is all the more glaring in light of Vos's huge literary output and his complete support of the Princeton cause in its battle with modernity.[86] Vos was not as deeply indebted to the reigning Common Sense philosophy as were the other professors at Princeton and therefore may not have fit the neat categories usually associated with the philosophical positions at the seminary during this period. His approach to theology also looks different in form from that of Hodge and Warfield, and this too may account for his being excluded from summary accounts of this very influential conservative nineteenth-century seminary.[87]

Geerhardus Vos was born in Heerenveen, the Netherlands, in 1862.

83. May, "Jonathan Edwards and America," p. 31.

84. Specifically, Vos served from 1893 to 1932. The period from the founding of Princeton Seminary in 1812 to the creation of Westminster Theological Seminary in 1929 as a result of a conservative/liberal split in the Princeton faculty is often referred to as the era of "Old Princeton." During this period, the institution's theology was uniformly conservative and Reformed, its ecclesiology was Presbyterian, and it represented a significant part of the evangelical coalition during the nineteenth century.

85. It is interesting that in two recent volumes devoted to Old Princeton that are largely sympathetic to its theological vision, scarcely a word is said of Vos. See *Reformed Theology in America: A History of Its Modern Development*, ed. David F. Wells (Grand Rapids: William B. Eerdmans, 1985), and *The Princeton Theology, 1812-1921: Scripture, Science, and Theological Method from Archibald Alexander to Benjamin Warfield*, ed. Mark A. Noll (Grand Rapids: Baker Book House, 1983).

86. For a complete bibliography of Vos's works, see James T. Dennison, "A Bibliography of the Writings of Geerhardus Vos, 1862-1949," *Westminster Theological Journal* 38 (Spring 1976): 350-67.

87. For a comparison of Vos and Warfield on the nature of theology, see my essay "Two Theologies or One? Warfield and Vos on the Nature of Theology," *Westminster Theological Journal* 54 (Fall 1992): 235-53. Some of what follows originally appeared in this article.

He came to the United States in 1881, when his father was called to be the pastor of a Christian Reformed Church in Grand Rapids, Michigan. He studied at the Christian Reformed college and then the Theological School of the Christian Reformed Church (now called Calvin College and Seminary). In 1884 he matriculated at Princeton Seminary. His early studies were confined to the Old Testament. At the urging of his mentor at Princeton, W. H. Green, Vos published his senior thesis, entitled the *The Mosaic Origin of the Pentateuchal Codes* (1886). He undertook doctoral studies in Europe at Berlin and Strasbourg.

Abraham Kuyper offered Vos the first chair in biblical theology at the fledgling Free University of Amsterdam. Reluctantly, Vos declined the offer and accepted a post at what is now Calvin Theological Seminary as Professor of Didactic and Exegetical Theology. His tenure there was curtailed in 1893 when he acceded to pleas from the faculty at Princeton that he join them as Professor of Biblical Theology, a post he held until he retired in 1932.[88]

Vos is the first evangelical proponent of what has come to be called "biblical theology."[89] Although there is no indication that Vos understood his task to be in conflict with traditional systematic theology, his methodology nonetheless looks very different. His theological method provided a significant antidote to the critical histories of the Bible that arose during the era of heightened historical consciousness at the turn of the century. Unfortunately, his work was little noticed at the time and is only now gaining some partial recognition.[90] Its impact on the disci-

88. Vos's role in the split that occurred at Princeton Seminary in 1929 as a result of J. Gresham Machen's activities has received very little attention. Vos clearly sided with the conservatives in the debate but, probably owing to the nearness of his retirement, decided to stay at Princeton instead of joining Machen and the others at Westminster Theological Seminary.

89. Vos preferred to use the phrase "history of special revelation" in connection with his theological method, but because of its ungainliness, he eventually settled for the designation "biblical theology." He seemed particularly concerned to distinguish his practice of this method from that of others who did not accept his view of biblical inspiration. We should also take care to distinguish Vos's method from that of such individuals as Floyd V. Filson and Balmer H. Kelly associated with the establishment of the journal *Interpretation* in 1947. For a careful description of this latter movement, see Krister Stendahl, "Biblical Theology, Contemporary," in the *Interpreter's Dictionary of the Bible* (Nashville: Abingdon, 1962); for a decisive critique of the movement, see James Barr, *Semantics of Biblical Language* (London: Oxford University Press, 1961).

90. Vos has begun to receive attention through the writings of several representatives of the evangelical movement, including Herman Ridderbos, Meredith Kline, and

pline of theology was little understood by conservative evangelicals at the time; even Warfield, his colleague for over twenty-five years in the department of theology, did not imagine theology to have been much affected by Vos's insights.[91]

In the tradition of nineteenth-century evangelicalism, systematic theology was construed as a science that operates on principles common to other sciences. As science brings order and harmony to a part of observable nature, it was assumed, theology seeks to bring order and harmony to the whole of the biblical revelation. In an oft-quoted passage from the opening pages of his *Systematic Theology*, Charles Hodge says,

> The Bible is to the theologian what nature is to the man of science. It is his store-house of facts; and his method of ascertaining what the Bible teaches is the same as that which the natural philosopher adopts to ascertain what nature teaches. . . . Theology is a jumble of human speculations, not worth a straw when men refuse to apply the same principle [of induction] to the study of the Word of God.[92]

Hodge viewed theology as an inductive science with a methodology much like that of the natural sciences. Theologians gather a body of data through exegesis of Scripture and use it as a basis for building a proper system.[93] Systematic theology then became "that department or section of theological science which is concerned with setting forth systemati-

George Eldon Ladd. Also of interest is some recent work by David F. Wells, Henri Blocher, E. P. Clowney, Richard B. Gaffin, Vern Poythress, and others who write on theological topics with a decidedly Vosian methodology. Unfortunately, he has received virtually no attention among nonevangelicals.

91. See my "Two Theologies or One?"

92. Hodge, *Systematic Theology*, vol. 1 (1872; reprint, Grand Rapids: William B. Eerdmans, 1946), pp. 10, 15.

93. In the hands of the later fundamentalists, this inductive approach begins to look much like proof-texting. And indeed, there are sections in Hodge's *Systematic Theology* that come perilously close to proof-texting as well. One very interesting indication of this from within the Old Princeton tradition itself can be found in Warfield's comments on Hodge as a practitioner of exegesis. In a little article entitled "Dr. Hodge as a Teacher of Exegesis" (originally published in A. A. Hodge's *Life of Charles Hodge* [New York, Scribners, 1880], pp. 588-91), Warfield suggests that Hodge had a wooden approach to the text in the teaching of theology. He further charges that Hodge frequently lost sight of the meaning of the whole text and as a result got lost in the morass of details. These are remarkable comments, especially in light of the fact that Warfield continued to use Hodge's *Systematic Theology* as a text in his classes.

cally, that is to say, as a concatenated whole, what is known concerning God."[94] The data for systematic theology were not individual texts or individual results of exegesis of individual texts but rather the complete conception of revealed truth offered by Scripture.

In the address he offered when he accepted the chair in biblical theology at Princeton Seminary in 1893, Vos began to mark out the relationship between biblical and systematic theology.[95] Contrary to the reigning biblical criticism of his day, Vos argued that there is nothing in the nature or aims of biblical theology that justifies the claim that systematic theology is somehow unbiblical. When rightly cultivated, he insisted, systematic theology is as truly biblical and as truly scientific as biblical theology. The fundamental difference between the two disciplines is simply the mode in which the material is organized. Biblical theology organizes the material in a historical framework, whereas systematic theology organizes its material in a thematic or topical fashion.[96] However, Vos went on to argue that systematic theology ought to be structurally dependent on biblical theology.

Vos understood biblical theology as the study of the actual self-disclosures of God in time and space — those made prior to the first committal to writing of the biblical documents and those made during the extended process of inscripturation. In this sense, biblical theology is centered in the attempt to understand the redemptive and revelatory activity of God in its *historical unfolding*. It is not concerned with the text

94. Benjamin B. Warfield, "The Task and Method of Systematic Theology," in *Studies in Theology* (New York: Oxford University Press, 1932), p. 91.

95. The majority of the address was concerned with spelling out the differences between biblical theology as it was practiced in the critical schools and the way it ought to be understood by conservative scholars. The text of the address has been reprinted as "The Idea of Biblical Theology as a Science and as a Theological Discipline," in *Redemptive History and Biblical Interpretation: The Shorter Writings of Geerhardus Vos*, ed. Richard B. Gaffin, Jr. (Phillipsburg, N.J.: Presbyterian & Reformed, 1980), pp. 3-24. It is somewhat remarkable that the chair of biblical theology Vos accepted when he agreed to come to Princeton Seminary in 1893 had just been created: there was no such element in the curriculum prior to Vos's arrival. And it is safe to say that Princeton was relatively ahead of its time in the creation of this chair, at least among conservative theological seminaries.

96. Vos does not specifically discuss the mode of organization practiced by systematic theology in his inaugural address, but elsewhere he describes it as "logical" or "topical" organization (see his *Biblical Theology* [Grand Rapids: William B. Eerdmans, 1948], pp. 4-5).

per se but rather with what the text reveals to us about the redemptive activity of God in history.[97]

In like manner, systematic theology is not concerned with the text per se but rather with what the text reveals to us about God. It extrapolates from the historical context (and literary context) to a synchronic understanding of God and his activities. Both disciplines transform the biblical material, but, says Vos, "Biblical Theology draws a *line* of development. Systematic Theology draws a *circle*."[98] Biblical theology discloses the inherent and organic structure in the history of redemption revealed in the Scriptures; systematic theology presents the redemptive and revelatory activity of God as a completed project.

Vos held that the discipline of biblical theology should be regulated both in its content and in its structure by the biblical text. The text comes to us as a historical document marked by epochs of both redemptive activity and redemptive revelation. Biblical theology ought to be structured to mirror this in some important sense.

Systematic theology, on the other hand, while recognizing the inherent structure of the text as a whole, presents its material in a form further abstracted from this structure. Though there are points in the text "in which the beginnings of the systematizing process can be discerned,"[99] these are not central to its overall structure. The text may give the original impetus to systematic theology, but the logical structure by which systematic theology organizes the biblical material is not identical with the structure of the text. As Vos says, "The Bible is not a

97. Although Vos makes no mention of Edwards, and the historical record gives no indication that he was familiar with Edwards's work, there are some remarkable similarities between the two on this point of emphasizing the centrality of redemption. On the other hand, Vos differs from Edwards in that he deals more explicitly with his methodology and emphasizes the relationship of systematic theology to biblical theology more than Edwards does. Moreover, there is little indication that Vos operated within the philosophical framework that motivated Edwards to write *A History of the Work of Redemption*. Vos's appreciation for the historical character of revelation and redemption can be traced in part to Herman Bavinck and Abraham Kuyper (see Richard B. Gaffin, Jr., "Geerhardus Vos and the Interpretation of Paul," in *Jerusalem and Athens: Critical Discussions on the Theology and Apologetics of Cornelius Van Til*, ed. E. R. Geehan [Nutley, N.J.: Presbyterian & Reformed, 1971], pp. 228-37).

98. Vos, *Biblical Theology*, p. 16.

99. Vos, *Biblical Theology*, p. 16. Vos may have downplayed the importance of the Pauline epistles, for example, with their dogmatic concerns. These are not largely historical narratives but rather theological letters. I will take this up at greater length in Chap. 7.

dogmatic handbook but a historical book full of dramatic interest."[100] In this sense, biblical theology more nearly embodies the historical framework in which the various biblical texts are produced. Systematics provides a framework for understanding the totality of the redemptive revelation found in the Scriptures, but this framework is abstracted from the historical development of the revelation found in the text. If we were to compare the theological disciplines in a Vosian manner, we might say that exegetical theology unearths the literary and historical structure (i.e., the context) of the text, biblical theology portrays the redemptive activity of God in its historical context, and systematic theology analyzes the activity of God through the dominant themes that arise in that activity.[101]

It was one of Vos's central concerns, then, to understand the relationship between the methodologies of biblical theology and systematic theology. If biblical theology organizes its material in a historical framework and systematic theology organizes its material in a topical framework, how is systematic theology actually to enlist the organization of biblical theology in its construction? In what sense is systematic theology dependent on biblical theology? This is clearly an important issue with respect to our concerns in this book as well: if systematic theology is the presentation of the theological vision in modern terms, and if systematic theology is dependent on biblical theology, then a determination of the nature of this dependence might well be crucial to defining how we should proceed in our efforts to construct a contemporary evangelical theological vision.

---

100. Vos, *Biblical Theology*, p. 17. Even so, there remain criteria for assessing the relative faithfulness of systematic theology to the substantive message of the text.

101. A consideration of the resurrection of Christ provides an interesting case study at this point. Vos presents the resurrection as the culminating event in the history of redemption. He sees it primarily in its eschatological perspective — i.e., how it fits into God's unfolding plan of bringing history to its proper consummation. He develops this at some length in the last half of his book *The Pauline Eschatology* (Princeton: Princeton University Press, 1930). As B. B. Warfield develops the "doctrine" of the resurrection (in "The Resurrection of Christ: A Fundamental Doctrine," *Homiletic Review* 32 [1896]: 291-98), he points to this culminating event not in eschatological terms but rather in soteriological terms. He focuses on the significance of the resurrection for a theory of the atonement. I am thankful to Richard Gaffin for his suggestion that this same point is made very clear when one compares Vos's treatment of the use of "resurrection" in Romans 1:3-4 with that of Warfield. For a discussion of this intriguing comparison, see Gaffin, *The Centrality of the Resurrection* (Grand Rapids: Baker Book House, 1978), p. 98-106.

Vos emphasized the notion of the historical "epoch," which he employed as the central category for dividing biblical history. He contended that these epochs or stages of redemptive history are clearly marked out in the biblical text. He suggested that the author of Genesis used the phrase "these are the generations" to mark out distinct epochs, for example. Each stage is characterized by certain important events that are peculiar to that epoch but not completely discontinuous with other epochs: there is an important sense of continuity linking all epochs in the larger biblical story of redemption.

The imagery of the mature tree growing from a seed was a favorite illustration of the Old Princeton theologians, and Vos was no exception. He used the illustration to describe the history of redemption and underscore the reality of historical development in Scripture, a fundamental fact for which theology must account. Vos believed that theology must deal with revelation in the active sense, as an act of God, and try to understand and trace and describe this act.

Vos argued that the historical progression of the revelation process manifests itself most clearly in the different epochs found in the pages of Scripture. These epochs are not creative impositions on the text, he insisted, but are located "in strict agreement with the lines of cleavage drawn by revelation itself."[102] Within each epoch there is a grouping of central themes. These themes then tie different epochs together so that the story is coherent from beginning to end. It is in understanding the stories themselves that these themes become visible. Again, Vos warns that these doctrinal themes must "not be imported into the minds of the original recipients of revelation."[103] His concern with respect to biblical theology is to permit Scripture to set its own agenda. Theology, in its content and its form, ought to be what Scripture irresistibly demands.

Vos contends that the Bible's ability to reveal is necessarily conditioned by the actual redeeming activity of God that takes place in and through history.[104] He goes so far as to suggest that the biblical revelation shows historical progress and development because God well understood the limits of our ability to understand his activities and purposes all at once.

---

102. Vos, *Biblical Theology*, p. 16.
103. Vos, *Biblical Theology*, p. 16.
104. In this regard, see especially the opening pages of "The Idea of Biblical Theology as a Science and as a Theological Discipline."

Vos was concerned to emphasize the organic character of this historical development in the structure and content of the Scriptures. "The Bible is, as it were, conscious of its own organism; it feels, what we cannot always say of ourselves, its own anatomy."[105] The facts of Scripture ought not to be construed in isolation from one another or as inventions of the mind but rather as truths found clearly within the great eschatological framework of Scripture.

Vos considered an awareness of the epochal character of the Scriptures to be absolutely essential to exegesis of the biblical text. The meaning of the text is wrapped up with both its actual historical context and its place in the epochal unfolding of redemptive history. The part has meaning within the whole, and the whole gains its meaning from the parts. If this sounds circular, in a certain fashion it is. Borrowing a phrase from contemporary scholarship, Vos affirmed the reality of the "hermeneutical circle," though not in the sense that later thinkers use that term. The "horizons" in Vos's project are the individual text and the entirety of the text. The exegete must allow the two to dialogue with one another continually, each helping to explain and clarify the meaning of the other.

The impact of these principles on Vos's actual practice of exegesis is enormous. Texts do not stand in isolation, only later to find their correlation and concatenation in the theological vision of the church. Rather, the texts stand in a teleological relation to one another because they have one divine author who has brought the facts of history into teleological relation to one another. Vos manifests this "purposeful" reading of the biblical text when he exegetes some of the historical writings of the Old Testament:

> The true principle of history writing, that which makes history more than a chronicling of events, because it discovers a plan and posits a goal, was thus grasped, not first by the Greek historians, but by the prophets of Israel. Hence, we find also that the activity among these circles includes sacred historiography, the production of books like the Books of Samuel and Kings in which the course of events is placed

---

105. Vos, *Biblical Theology*, p. 16. It is this concern to emphasize the biblical revelation in its organic unity that distinguishes biblical theology from technical exegesis. Though exegesis properly construed must take the historical context of any particular passage seriously, the purview of the exegete is not at once the entirety of the revelation. On the other hand, the totality of the revelation *is* the proper purview of the biblical theologian.

in the light of an unfolding divine plan. Good meaning can thus be found in the ancient canonical custom of calling these historical writings 'the earlier prophets'.[106]

Another example can be found in the manner in which he understood the bridge between the Testaments (a major theological theme in Vos). Here he pointed to the centrality of John the Baptist, who brought together the two Old Testament redemptive elements of law and prophecy in his constant repetition of the phrase "repent, for the kingdom of God is at hand." The Baptist brought this redemption to the brink of its consummation (in Jesus) by uniquely and finally conjoining these two elements with the simple conjunction *for:* "repent, *for* the kingdom of God is at hand." Law and prophecy were not finally in tension but rather stood in a teleological relationship to each other. The law prepared the way for the gospel, and the gospel subsumed the law within itself. John pointed to this bridge, which was finally realized in the person and work of Jesus.

This means that we cannot fully grasp the nature of the person and work of Jesus until we see this historical development and preparation.[107] Of fundamental importance for the exegesis of the New Testament is the manner in which the Old Testament formed the context for the purpose of the mission of Jesus. Jesus, wrote Vos, "was the confirmation and consummation of the Old Testament in His own Person, and this yielded the one substratum of His interpretation of Himself in the world of religion."[108]

Vos raised several questions of a straightforward theological nature from the vantage point of systematic theology (concerning the Trinity, predestination, the self-knowledge of Jesus, etc.), but he did not do so in the context of exegesis of individual texts; rather, he grounded such questions in the correlation of many texts across several different biblical epochs. It must also be admitted that Vos did not produce a detailed agenda of topics in systematic theology. Still, one cannot read Vos without getting the impression that any systematic theology would be poorer that failed to harvest the fields he had sown. A theological vision must be shaped by a careful and purposeful reading of the revelation of

106. Vos, *Biblical Theology*, p. 190; italics mine.
107. See Vos, *Biblical Theology*, pp. 311-29.
108. Vos, *Biblical Theology*, p. 358.

God's redemptive activity. We will understand ourselves only if we first understand Scripture. Once we understand the framework of Scripture, we may then interpret our own place in the historical unfolding of the redemptive activity of God. The Scriptures ought to interpret the modern era rather than vice versa. This is a lesson from which modern evangelicals might greatly benefit.

CHAPTER 6

The Theological Present

We live in an age that cannot name itself. For some, we are still in the age of modernity and the triumph of the bourgeois subject. For others, we are in a time of the levelling of all traditions and await the return of the repressed traditional and communal subject. For yet others, we are in a post-modern moment where the death of the subject is now upon us as the last receding wave of the death of God.

David Tracy[1]

INTRODUCTION

WE ARE living in a time of unprecedented cultural crisis.[2] The breakdown of Western cultural hegemony in the past three decades has been remarkable with respect to both the depth it has reached and the speed with which it has proceeded. The world has grown increasingly smaller in direct proportion to the increase in the awareness of the diverse cultures of the globe. Eurocentrism is on the way out and ethnocentrism is on the way in. The marrow of modern culture no longer resides in

---

1. Tracy, "On Naming the Present," in *On the Threshold of the Third Millennium*, ed. Philip Hillyer, Concilium series (London: SCM Press, 1990), pp. 66-85.
2. For a clear development of this thesis, see James Davison Hunter, *Cultural Wars* (New York: Basic Books, 1992).

191

the white middle class of America but in all the emergent groups of the First and Third Worlds. The superpowers of the twentieth century no longer demand the respect they once did. In the decade of the 1980s the walls of the Soviet bloc, the greatest system of political tyranny of the twentieth century, came crashing down. In that same period, the moral shallowness of the American character was manifest as never before. Following fast on the heels of Watergate, the Reagan presidency came to symbolize the selfishness and shallowness of modern democratic capitalism even while it provided corrosive forces that led to the collapse of the failed utopia of Soviet communism.

In an era such as ours, what has happened to theology? By some indicators it has made a surprising comeback. Theologians occupy places of increasing prestige in the modern secular university. A recent study suggests that the writing of theology is actually undergoing a period of great revival if judged solely by the number of systematic theologies written and published in the past decade.[3] Philosophers of religion, sociologists of religion, and historians of religion also seem to be gaining a better hearing in the modern university. Churches with interest in such historic doctrines as the incarnation and the resurrection have flourished in recent decades.

By other indicators the picture is not nearly so rosy, however. The clergy (both conservative and liberal) of modern America are more nearly dominated by the model of the therapist and the manager than by the model of the pastor/theologian.[4] Pastors no longer serve as purveyors of God's truth but rather as maestros orchestrating the self-fulfillment of the church community. Higher education in general and theological education in particular are both in a state of serious upheaval as a result of having been gradually marginalized in modern culture to the point that they no longer serve as shapers of that culture in any real sense.[5] Increasingly, moral and religious questions are being divorced

3. Gabriel Fackre made this assertion in his presidential address to the American Theological Society, "The State of Systematics: Research and Commentary," 12 April 1991, reprinted in *Dialog* 31 (Winter 1992): 54-61.

4. A compelling case for this indictment is presented by David F. Wells in *No Place For Truth; or, Whatever Happened to Evangelical Theology* (Grand Rapids: William B. Eerdmans, 1993).

5. Regarding university education, see the important work *The Secularization of the Academy*, ed. George Marsden and Bradley Longfield (New York: Oxford University Press, 1992). Regarding theological education, see David Kelsey, *To Understand God Truly: What's Theological about a Theological School* (Louisville: Westminster/John Knox, 1992).

from the discourse of the public arena as the culture becomes progressively more hostile to truth in all its varieties — especially biblical truth.[6] Even conservative Christians no longer think in categories defined by the imagery of the Bible; instead, they draw on the images provided by the great god of modern civilization — television.

If evangelicals are going to recover a theological vision, they will have to reflect on the impact of this current state of affairs with some care and caution. In states of cultural crisis, theological identity is often transformed as well, and the transformation is often blind and irrational. But it need not be this way. In a world growing ever more discontent with modernity, a growing chorus of disaffected modern theologians now call themselves "postmodern." In such a context, we would do well to look into how the evangelical theological vision is being influenced by and is responding to this brave new world.

WHAT IS POSTMODERN THEOLOGY?

The sheer diversity of the present state of theology as practiced in the academy makes the task of defining postmodern theology seem well nigh impossible. If it is safe to say anything by way of defining the contemporary state of the theological discipline, it is that it is intractably fragmented. There seem to be no rules governing the discipline any longer, nor even any dominant paradigms — beyond the central paradigmatic characteristic of postmodernity itself, of course — namely, diversity.

Modern consciousness has presumed a movement from fate to choice. The vast array of new possibilities afforded by modern technology has encouraged the assumption by modern individuals that they can pretty much do anything imaginable, that they are no longer bound by the fates of history.[7] Modernity pluralizes both institutions and plausibility struc-

---

6. See John Richard Neuhaus, *The Naked Public Square: Religion and Democracy in America* (Grand Rapids: William B. Eerdmans, 1984).

7. One example of the new sociological reality that has been produced by modern technology can be found in the rhetoric of the whole debate surrounding human reproduction. Modern birth control techniques have led naturally — perhaps even necessarily — to a characterization of one side of the debate as "pro-choice." The language of "choice" is broadly indicative of the subjective turn in morality, the assumption that morality arises from the human subject alone.

tures.[8] Those seeking to move beyond modernity have not only accepted this pluralization as a brute fact but have proceeded to baptize it as a good in itself. Cultural diversity is not something to be feared, they maintain, but is rather a virtue of enlightened (i.e., postmodern) societies.

In the modern American academy, competing visions of the theological task vie for attention in religion departments all across the country. Process theologians contend with liberation theologians, who in turn contend with narrative theologians, who in turn contend with hermeneutical theologians, all of whom contend with their colleagues in biblical studies. No one theological vision commands anything like universal respect, let alone universal consent. Part of the reason we have come to this pass is that we have gradually abandoned the goal of attempting to establish an "objective" reading of the Bible and have as a result stranded theology in the quagmire of a thousand different frameworks. Some illustrations are in order.

Liberation theology is sometimes characterized as the dominant mode of theologizing today, although this would be hard to substantiate on empirical grounds. While many departments of religion offer some sort of lip service in support of liberation theology, very few have anything approaching a consensus coalition of liberation theologians. Nor are there many departments in which a "minority" grouping has become a majority bloc. An astute observer of the modern theological landscape, Martin Marty, has written, "Most theological schools of my acquaintance have only 'a' liberation-minded feminist, or black, or Third-Worlder, or would-be any of the three. And that is it. The professional societies of theologians will schedule an occasional paper on the topic (liberation). But most of the concern now is technical: for texts, interpretation, hermeneutics, publicness, universalism-relativism-pluralism, and issues of that sort."[9] Moreover, the body of liberation theologians is itself fragmented. The Latin American Roman Catholic theologians are now coming under critical scrutiny by their North American and Asian counterparts for sustaining patriarchal traditions that have largely been discredited elsewhere. Liberation theology appears to be fragmenting further as the difficult task of defining oppression in a religiously significant manner becomes ever more complicated.

8. See Peter Berger, *The Heretical Imperative* (Garden City, N.Y.: Doubleday, 1979).
9. Marty, "Introduction: How Their Minds Have Changed," in *Theologians in Transition*, ed. James Wall (New York: Crossroad, 1981), p. 17.

And just as there is no single dominant theological movement at this time, so there is no single figure or even group of figures that towers over the theological field in the manner that a Barth or a Bultmann or a Tillich did a generation ago. The plethora of "conversation partners" in the theological journals testifies to the death of the "three theological giants" of the first half of this century.

Perhaps ironically, an increasing number of contemporary theologians are suggesting that the current theological chaos signifies that one era has come to an end and another is beginning, that for the past three decades theology has been undergoing a transformation of radical proportions.[10] They typically associate the birth of the new era with the sudden emergence and the equally sudden demise of the "death of God" theologies in the 1960s. Stanley T. Sutphin has written that "when honest and sensitive men assert that God has been crowded out of the world of human experience, that the biblical vision of the love of God is contradicted by the vast evil apparent in the world, and that the Biblical notion of God threatens human dignity and freedom, theologians must take notice."[11] The radical secularization of theology introduced by the death-of-God movement sounded the death knell to theology done in the manner of the nineteenth and early twentieth centuries.

The death-of-God theologians suggested that Christians should abandon belief in God in favor of the Enlightenment belief in reason, science, politics, and human achievement — all in the name of Christianity. They "foresaw a world of rather sunny agnostics who might somehow be moved by a few retrieved liberating themes from the Christian story and symbolic pool."[12] The consequent abandonment of transcendent meaning and purpose precipitated a deep sense of questioning. This questioning extended to both the Enlightenment ideals underlying the movement and the legacy of its theology in the previous century

---

10. Not all theologians are certain that fundamental changes are afoot. While he grants the possibility that we are in the midst of a theological sea change, Langdon Gilkey has urged a wait-and-see attitude: "Those who like brisker language might wish to define this new scene not as one merely of re-evaluation but as the beginning of the 'disintegration of secular culture' — but that judgment is probably quite premature" ("Theology for a Time of Troubles," in *Theologians in Transition*, p. 31). Only history will be able to determine how revolutionary this period has in fact been.

11. Sutphin, *Options in Contemporary Theology* (Lanham, Md.: University Press of America, 1987), p. 5.

12. Marty, "Introduction: How Their Minds Have Changed," p. 8.

and a half. The disenchantment with modernity signaled a new era that has come to be called "postmodernism."[13]

Commentators are suggesting that this transition into the postmodern era is roughly akin to the revolutions in theology that took place in the sixteenth and nineteenth centuries.[14] In the sixteenth century the medieval vision of theology was overturned by the Reformation, and the Reformation vision of theology was likewise overturned as a result of Enlightenment influences in the eighteenth and nineteenth centuries.[15] During each of these periods, a new paradigm emerged, characterized by a new set of ideals, a new set of methods, and new criteria of success in theology. An analogous change of paradigm, ideals, methods, and criteria of success lies behind the current "revolution" in theology.

The modern era has not so much been rejected by postmodernism as it has turned in on itself.[16] The assumptions that shaped it have also shared in its demise. Modern theology has been relativized by its own commitment to relativism. It is viewed as historically conditioned by its own sense of historical consciousness.

But the fact that postmodern theologians have rejected the modern Enlightenment-inspired mode of doing theology does not mean that they have any desire to return to the orthodox model of theology of pre-

13. There is a very real debate as to whether we are beyond modernity or still in the throes of it. If modernity is defined by its social institutions — industrialization, urbanization, and democratic capitalism — then clearly we are still in high modernity. If modernity consists in an identifiable complex of ideologies — Cartesian epistemology, Marxist social theory, Freudian pyschology, and classic liberal theology (à la Schleiermacher) — then clearly we are entering the postmodern era.

14. It is highly illuminating when a contemporary theologian refers to the period before the Enlightenment as the "Constantinian" era, from which the Enlightenment provided a "great deliverance." See, e.g., D. M. Mackinnon, "Theology as a Discipline of the University," in *The Rules of the Game: Cross-Disciplinary Essays on Models in Scholarly Thought*, ed. Teodor Shanin (London: Tavistock Publications, 1972), p. 172.

15. Among those who have employed this fourfold categorization (medieval, Reformation, modern, and postmodern) are Gillian R. Evans, Alister E. McGrath, and Allan D. Galloway in *The Science of Theology*, vol. 1 of *The History of Christian Theology*, ed. Paul Avis (Grand Rapids: William B. Eerdmans, 1986), though these authors concern themselves with only the first three categories in this book. The same categorization is implicitly present in John S. Kent's *The End of The Line: The Development of Christian Theology in the Last Two Centuries* (Philadelphia: Fortress Press, 1982).

16. To clarify, when I speak of the "modern era," I am referring to the period from the end of American revolutionary period until the end of the Vietnam war (roughly, 1800-1970). When I speak of the "postmodern era," in theology, I am referring to the period after the tumult of the 1960s.

Enlightenment times.[17] Despite what appears to be some evidence to the contrary (e.g., in the trenchant postmodern attack on modernity), the tide of current theology flows ever forward, not backward. The primitivist impulse current in some evangelical circles is not characteristic of postmodern theology. Contemporary theologians are postmodern, not premodern. External authority has not replaced the authority of human experience. Objective truth has not replaced subjective assumptions.

The fundamental methodological shift in the present era has been a movement away from a detached, disinterested, scientific, and critical theology toward a subjective, reader-response, literary, and critical theology. It presents a set of challenges to an evangelical vision of theology quite distinct from those offered by the older liberal theologians. In a manner analogous but not equivalent to the way in which orthodox theologians of the nineteenth century faced the onslaught of theological liberalism, the contemporary evangelical must understand and face squarely the challenge of postmodern theology.

But, unlike the situation in the nineteenth century, today there is no single theological vision "out there" offering the challenge. Nor is it clear that evangelicalism ought simply to reject out of hand the myriad insights of the pantheon of theological visions in postmodern theology. If my assertions about the nature and character of evangelicalism are at least partially correct, evangelicalism has had an uneasy relationship with modernity itself, and the critique of modernity originating in postmodern theology may just be instructive for evangelicals. As Martin Marty has suggested, "Fundamentalists who might scorn [postmodern theologians] for playing into the 'spirit of the times' are the ones who have the *Zeitgeist* in their pocket. Any market tester can prove that instantly."[18]

In what follows I want to offer some general characterizations of themes that have motivated the transition from modern to postmodern theology. These themes do not characterize every postmodern theology, but to the extent that there are family resemblances among the divergent theological visions of the postmodern movement, there will also be certain patterns or themes that receive greater or lesser emphasis in these

17. Even the relatively conservative Old Testament scholar Brevard Childs says, "To suggest a new approach is needed [in biblical scholarship] is not to propose a return to a traditional pre-Enlightenment understanding of the Bible. Such an endeavor is not only wrong in concept, but impossible in practice" (*The New Testament as Canon* [Philadelphia: Fortress Press, 1985], p. 35).

18. Marty, "Introduction: How Their Minds Have Changed," p. 14.

visions.[19] There are family resemblances largely because the one constant among the plethora of postmodern theologies is that they have
rejected modernity in some form or fashion.[20] Emerging from the matrix
of modernity, these theologies all gained their force in the midst of the
cultural crisis of the revolutionary decade of the 1960s. Black theology
arose in conjunction with the civil rights and black power movements.[21]
Feminist theology emerged from the sixties' sexual revolution.[22] Roman
Catholic liberation theology arose in the aftermath of the Second Vatican

19. There is a lively controversy as to the essential character of postmodern
ideology: does it lie with the radical pragmatism of Richard Rorty, the radical literary
theory of Stanley Fish, and the deconstructionism of Michel Foucault, or does it lie with
the more tempered hermeneutical theories of Paul Ricoeur, the revisionist theology of
David Tracy, and the liberation ideology of such feminists as Elisabeth Schüssler
Fiorenza. Revealing his own intuitions, David Ray Griffin characterizes the radical
postmoderns as proponents of "eliminative postmodernism" or "ultramodernism," and
he refers to the other kind of postmodernists as proponents of "constructive postmodernism." The essential difference between these two outlooks resides in a disagreement over
whether the death of modernism entails the elimination of a worldview. See *God and
Religion in the Postmodern World: Essays in Postmodern Theology,* ed. David Ray Griffin (Albany:
State University of New York Press, 1989). Without minimizing the debate over these
substantial issues, I will interpret postmodernity in its fundamentally constructive form
— i.e., I take postmodernity to refer to the general discontent with the epistemological
and theological framework of the eighteenth-century Enlightenment while in a significant way appreciating some advances of this framework.

20. Three of the clearest and most important defenses of postmodernism in
theology are David Tracy's *The Analogical Imagination: Christian Theology and the Culture of
Pluralism* (New York: Crossroad, 1981), Edward Farley's *Ecclesial Reflection: An Anatomy of
Theological Method* (Philadelphia: Fortress Press, 1982), and George Lindbeck's *The Nature
of Doctrine: Religion and Theology in a Postliberal Age* (Philadelphia: Westminster Press, 1984).
The conceptual framework of this chapter reflects in large measure the influence of
these three works. In saying this, I am not overlooking the very real and substantial
differences among the works. See William C. Placher's *Unapologetic Theology: A Christian
Voice in a Pluralistic Conversation* (Philadelphia: Westminster Press, 1989) for a sensitive
discussion of the differences between Tracy (whom Placher refers to as a revisionist)
and Lindbeck (whom he refers to as a postliberal). Tracy himself calls Lindbeck an
"antimodern" ("On Naming the Present," pp. 73-77).

21. For treatments of the history of black theology, see James Cone, *For My People:
Black Theology and the Black Church* (Maryknoll, N.Y.: Orbis Books, 1984), pp. 5-31; and
Gayraud Wilmore and James Cone, *Black Theology: A Documentary History* (Maryknoll,
N.Y.: Orbis Books, 1979).

22. On the origins of feminist theology, see Elisabeth Schüssler Fiorenza, *In
Memory of Her: A Feminist Theological Reconstruction of Christian Origins* (New York:
Crossroad, 1983), and Rosemary Radford Ruether, *Sexism and God-Talk: Toward a Feminist
Theology* (Boston: Beacon Press, 1983).

Council (1961-1964).[23] One might go so far as to suggest that the conservative religious response to the decade of the 1960s was the charismatic movement — which only now is in the initial stages of theological construction.[24] The rise of narrative theology is less clearly related to any specific crisis of the 1960s, but it is undoubtedly linked to the despair felt by those confronted with the loss of community in the face of modern technology and individualism.[25]

What are some of the family resemblances of these divergent theological visions? One obvious candidate is pluralism. Intrinsic to the postmodern critique of modernity is the rejection of the goal of a unified science and correspondingly of a unified theology. The anthropological foundation of Enlightenment theology was betrayed in the search for a "common human experience" that might serve as the basis of theological reflection. Postmodern theology has not jettisoned the anthropological foundation; it has simply recognized and welcomed the pluralism that comes with it.

Another family resemblance is the prophetic role accorded theology in culture. There is sharp disagreement over the shape of this prophetic role, but there is some consensus that theology must not simply follow culture but must rather serve as a corrective to it. The contemporary Roman Catholic theologian David Tracy has forcefully argued for the "public" role of theology as opposed to the largely privatized role it played in modern theology. But if it is to be public, it must contribute to the public discussion, and it cannot do this if it simply echoes the convictions of mainstream culture. There is a consensus that theology has a distinctive role to play in questioning the foundations of modern Western culture, even if the nature of the questions to be asked is a matter of some dispute.[26]

---

23. The classic text of liberation theology is Gustavo Gutiérrez's *Theology of Liberation* (Maryknoll, N.Y.: Orbis Books, 1973).

24. For a recent attempt to develop a charismatic theology, see J. Rodman Williams, *Renewal Theology*, 3 vols. (Grand Rapids: Zondervan, 1988-1992).

25. No one has yet traced the history of the narrative movement. Gabriel Fackre has perhaps come closest to doing so in his essay "Narrative Theology: An Overview," *Interpretation* 37 (Fall 1983): 340-52. For clear expressions of the movement's concerns, see Hans Frei, *The Eclipse of Biblical Narrative: A Study in Eighteenth and Nineteenth Century Hermeneutics* (New Haven: Yale University Press, 1974); and George Lindbeck, *The Nature of Doctrine: Religion and Theology in a Postliberal Age* (Philadelphia: Westminster Press, 1984). For a good summary, see Placher, *Unapologetic Theology*.

26. In saying this, I do not mean to pass over the dispute between postmoderns such as Tracy and postliberals such as George Lindbeck regarding the nature of theology. Lindbeck argues that theology itself is not public in Tracy's sense, although he neverthe-

A final theme that ought to be highlighted is the emergence of epistemic pragmatism among postmodern theologians. It is much in vogue in current theological discussion to attack foundationalism as a theory of knowledge. It is no longer considered acceptable to think of knowledge as a pyramid built on some unshakable foundation. The search for this foundation (whether in the Bible, following medieval and Reformation thinkers, or in science, following modern thinkers) has been abandoned. It is held that every belief is potentially (and ought practically to be) revisable. The epistemological enterprise is less like building a house than like engaging in a conversation or telling a story.

We need to consider each of these themes in greater detail. After we have done so, we can turn to a consideration of what sort of postmodern theological method might arise from this critique of modernity. Finally, we will view the postmodern impulse through the filters of the evangelical convictions enunciated in previous chapters.

THE CULTURAL SETTING
OF POSTMODERN THEOLOGY

As with modern evangelicalism, definitional analyses of postmodern theology must echo the ambiguity present in the movement at large. But unlike evangelicalism, a case could be made that the diversity present in postmodern theology is intrinsic to the vision of theology being pursued by postmoderns. Part of the very character of a postmodernism is its pluralism, its radical diversity. There are no longer any overarching goals to which theology must faithfully aim. Neither are there any overarching authorities that might determine the proper shape of the theological vision.

The radical pluralism extends not simply to theological conclusions but also to methodological constraints. Theologians self-consciously begin with divergent sets of assumptions about the nature of the theological task. One theologian may view the problem of patriarchalism as the fundamental issue to which a relevant theology must respond.[27] Such

---

less asserts that it must speak to public issues and thus it must retain a prophetic stance toward culture.

27. See, e.g., Rosemary Radford Ruether, *New Woman — New Earth: Sexist Ideologies and Human Liberation* (New York: Crossroad, 1975); and Mary Daly, *Beyond God the Father: Toward a Philosophy of Women's Liberation* (Boston: Beacon Press 1973).

an individual will likely view the experience of sexism and gender oppression as the touchstone of a genuine theology. Another theologian may view the radical movement underlying reality itself as the fundamental issue to which a theology must respond. Such an individual will likely view the critique of a static metaphysics as the touchstone of a genuine theology.[28] Still another theologian may begin with the complexity of deriving meaning from one's own historically conditioned experience.[29] Such an individual may well consider community-defined purpose (commensurate with the realization that the community constantly changes) as the touchstone for theology and hence view theology as a means to relate the community's history to the individual's identity through the telling of the story.

To understand the nature of diversity in postmodern theology, we have to sort out two concerns. The first involves the philosophical and theological factors that engender a fascination with diversity; the second involves the social and cultural factors that give rise to this theological diversity. Theology evolves in response both to factors internal to the discipline itself and to social factors external to the conceptual project. A theological vision might develop, for example, (1) from the assumption that the self is the touchstone of meaning and (2) in the context of a surrounding democratic culture that tends to elevate the individual over the community. One set of factors need not exclude the other.

Isolating the cultural factors first, it is ironic to note that one of the central unifying factors of postmodern theology is also one of its strongest influences toward diversity. For all its diversity, postmodern theology is unified in the extent to which it remains largely an activity pursued in the outpost of the modern university. It remains an academic discipline pursued by professionals in their field. There may be more cross-pollination among the disciplines today, but it is no less true today than it was fifty years ago or even one hundred years ago that the current vision of theology is largely molded in an academic context. In 1898 Abraham Kuyper wrote that "until the middle of the last century Theology received its impulse from the Church. . . . Since that time, however, Theology has not allowed itself to be governed by the life of the Church,

28. See, e.g., John B. Cobb and David Ray Griffin, *Process Theology: An Introductory Treatment* (Philadelphia: Westminster Press, 1976); and Schubert Ogden, *The Reality of God, and Other Essays* (New York: Harper & Row, 1966).

29. See, e.g., *Why Narrative? Readings in Narrative Theology*, ed. Stanley Hauerwas and L. Gregory Jones (Grand Rapids: William B. Eerdmans, 1989).

but by the mighty development of philosophy" — which is to say, by the university.[30] And that is as true today as it was then. With its commitment to the university setting, postmodern theology remains a technical discipline with a language peculiar to itself. It also carries itself on as a "school" theology — built around the reigning paradigms of a select group of academic centers here and abroad. The "new Yale" theology is distinct from the theology associated with the "Chicago school," and this in turn is distinct from the "Claremont vision."

In many respects, the "scholastic" (or school-based) character of theology provides an institutional sanction for theological diversity. The strong and separate identities of the prestigious universities effectively authorize a radical pluralism of theological visions.[31]

Some would argue that theology is currently being fashioned from the ground up and from the fringes inward. They could point to the fact that the cultural outposts of Latin America and Asia are now thriving centers of postmodern theology.[32] However, it should not be forgotten that the dominant theologians in these lands originally studied either in North America or Western Europe and remain connected with select universities there.[33] Moreover, the technical jargon of theological treatises coming out of the Third World still bears a strong resemblance to the technical language of the major Western academic centers. In this sense, the major universities have served as a unifying conduit for postmodern theological discussion while at the same time functioning as the means to further the pluralistic goals of the postmodern theological vision.

A second cultural factor that has shaped the diverse parameters of

30. Kuyper, *Principles of Sacred Theology*, trans. J. Hendrik DeVries (Grand Rapids: William B. Eerdmans, 1954), p. 51. This is an abridged translation of the three-volume Dutch work originally published in 1898.

31. Tenure decisions in large universities are often based to a significant degree on the quantity of a candidate's creative and pioneering literary production — another way in which institutions sanction and encourage diversity.

32. Harvey Cox has asserted that the theology of the twenty-first century will arise from the Two-Thirds World and as a result will look much different than it presently does. He points to the importance of the small lay-led base communities (intensive discussion groups) for present-day Latin American liberation theology as one significant sign of this trend. See *Religion in the Secular City: Toward a Post-Modern Theology* (New York: Simon & Schuster, 1984).

33. Andrew Kirk offers a forceful reminder of this in *Liberation Theology: An Evangelical View from the Third World* (Atlanta: John Knox Press, 1979).

the postmodern theological vision has been the relative failure of ecumenical discussions in this century. Gone are the heady days when the ecumenical movement employed a lowest-common-denominator approach in its efforts to develop a universal theology and a universal church. The failure to reach the elusive goal of ecclesiastical unity has slowly brought the recognition that the deeply entrenched differences in the separate sectors of Christendom and the rest of the world's religions cannot merely be talked away.

Ecumenical dialogue now consists not merely in recognizing the differences among the divergent church communions and the different world religions but in embracing this pluralism. The movement now seeks to maintain theological distinctives without absolutism and to initiate honest dialogue without relativism. The postmodern theologian seeks to avoid both the extreme of ignoring pluralism (e.g., by asserting the exclusive truth of one religion over another) and the extreme of wallowing in pluralism (e.g., by denying the validity of all religious traditions). The failure of past ecumenical discussions to bring genuine unity has undoubtedly influenced this change.

Surely the emergence of modern mass communication has applied tremendous (though indirect) pressure toward the pluralization of theology. The social consciousness of ethnic and religious diversity around the globe has increased by quantum leaps in the era of the jet airplane and satellite telecommunications. These technological innovations have helped to place an enormous burden on theologians to think in globally sensitive terms, which itself has undergirded the move toward diversity and pluralism. Though few theologians have taken to the airwaves, most of them have taken to the air and found themselves wrestling very immediately with the reality of a religiously pluralistic world.

These cultural factors inevitably move a definition of the postmodern theological movement in the direction of a studied ambiguity. It is difficult to define the parameters of the postmodern theological vision because of the social context that has given rise to postmodernism in the first place. A world with an ever-increasing appreciation of its social diversity will not applaud a theology that lacks an ever-increasing sense of creedal diversity. This ambiguity may be partially clarified (though not thereby removed) by a consideration of the theological and philosophical reasons that influence this infatuation with diversity. Such a consideration must begin with the fundamental critique of the Enlightenment ideal reflected in much of postmodern theology.

THE ROOTS OF POSTMODERN THEOLOGY

In many ways this critique is actually an extension of the Enlightenment critique of the premodern vision of theology. "What remains constant in the shift from modernity to post-modernity," writes David Tracy, "is the fact that such contemporary critiques of modernity deepen the fundamental commitment to those purely secular standards for knowledge and action initiated by the Enlightenment."[34] If we look at the roots of the postmodern vision of theology in the Enlightenment ideal and its critique, it becomes apparent that postmodern theology is continuous with modern theology in some important respects and discontinuous in other respects.[35] In order to extend our understanding of postmodern theology, I believe it will be beneficial to take a closer look at the Enlightenment ideal and its critique of an earlier theological vision.[36] In the following section we will concentrate on two aspects of this critique — the Enlightenment rejection of a divinely inspired revelatory authority and a divinely providential teleology. An assessment of the ways in which postmodern theology has echoed and transformed the Enlightenment influence in these areas will give us some important insights into the general shape of the postmodern theological method.

The Enlightenment Legacy: The Critique of Authority

In a number of ways, the Enlightenment of the seventeenth and eighteenth centuries amounted to a critique of external authority.[37] During

34. Tracy, *Blessed Rage for Order: The New Pluralism in Theology* (New York: Seabury Press, 1978), p. 8.

35. Any accounts that do not reflect historical continuity and discontinuity are probably not sufficiently nuanced to capture the true spirit of any historically conditioned change.

36. The shape of the study of theology after the Enlightenment is helpfully laid out by Steven W. Sykes in "Theological Study: The Nineteenth Century and After," in *The Philosophical Frontiers of Christian Theology*, ed. Brian Hebblethwaite and Stewart Sutherland (Cambridge: Cambridge University Press, 1982), pp. 95-118.

37. David Ray Griffin suggests that the heart of the Enlightenment lay in its claim that the Supernatural God — i.e. the God of traditional Western (Augustinian) Christian theology — had died. The rejection of the fundamental authority of God entailed the rejection of other, institutional forms of authority, such as the church and the king. See his "Introduction: Varieties of Postmodern Theology" and "Postmodern Theology and A/Theology: A Response to Mark C. Taylor," in *Varieties of Postmodern Theology*, ed. David

this period, a suspicion of all cultural authorities except the individual's own reason was launched in the academic centers of Europe. External authority was replaced by subjective authority — critical human reason. This has often been referred to as the "subjective turn," and from it arose the historical consciousness that was so characteristic of the age.[38]

The rise of modern science in this period challenged the reigning philosophical conceptions of that endeavor. The political revolutions of the period helped shed the reliance on monarchical forms of authority in favor of democratic ideals. The philosophers of this period likewise questioned the dominant metaphysical and epistemological schemes of the medieval era. The individual subject (or at least those individual subjects who happened to be teaching in prestigious universities of Europe) became the preeminent authority in matters pertaining to the constituents of the real world and how that world was known. The working assumption was that an objective scholar was in a far superior position to know the world as it really is than was any religious cleric of the premodern period. Ecclesiastical commitments simply prejudiced one's view of reality. It was predicted by the early ideologues of the Enlightenment that the removal of this functioning authority over science would lead to a new era of scientific progress.[39]

Ray Griffin, William A. Beardslee, and Joe Holland (Albany: State University of New York Press, 1989), pp. 1-7, 29-61.

38. For a generally critical account of this "subjective turn," see Jeffrey Stout, *The Flight from Authority: Religion, Morality and the Quest for Autonomy* (Notre Dame, Ind.: University of Notre Dame Press, 1981). For an interpretive essay with a concern for the larger social implications, see Henry F. May, *The Enlightenment in America* (New York: Oxford University Press, 1976). Standard histories of philosophy normally see this "subjective turn" as the explanatory key for understanding modern philosophy starting with René Descartes in the seventeenth century. See, e.g., Frederick J. Copleston, *A History of Philosophy*, vols. 4-6 (Garden City, N.Y.: Doubleday, 1985). See also the highly influential set of essays gathered together in the collection entitled *The Linguistic Turn: Recent Essays in Philosophic Method*, ed. Richard Rorty (Chicago: University of Chicago Press, 1967), which charts the extension of the "subjective turn" in twentieth-century Anglo-American philosophical circles in the form of a "linguistic turn." Given the assumption that language shapes our world (and culture), some forms of postmodern theology point to the relative arbitrariness of language as an argument for the arbitrariness of divergent theologies.

39. It must be remembered that the inspiration for the Enlightenment was largely intellectual and that for a long time the movement remained isolated among a relatively few university-related people. The implications of the Enlightenment were not felt (or accented) on a popular level for well over a century. As James Turner has noted, "Despite the perils supposed to beset belief [in God], unbelief in fact remained unthinkable to

It is no accident that biblical criticism arose in this environment and flourished in the century after the European academy had rounded the "subjective turn."[40] Biblical criticism was founded on the assumption that all human thought (including and most especially that reflected in the Scriptures) is historically conditioned. This intuition received ready acceptance among "enlightened" Western biblical scholars. They set themselves to the task of separating the real history behind the Bible from its mythological and dogmatic accretions by uncovering the many discrepancies in the text and critically reconstructing the many sources from which each part of the discrepancies arose. The diversity of the sources they identified and revealed constituted a potent argument for the utter humanity of the text, void of a unifying transcendent author.

Nineteenth-century biblical critics focused much of their energy on locating the authentic oral and written sources that lay behind the biblical documents. They believed that the historical "life" of these texts pointed to the true nature of the biblical message and would lead to a fundamental reassessment of the meaning and importance of these texts in the life of the church. Whatever their intent, however, the fundamental symbols that the critical scholars discovered behind and before the canonical text actually said far more about the ethical and religious ideals of nineteenth-century academics than they did about the "real" Jesus.[41]

In modified form, this quest for the real Jesus continued into the twentieth century. Each successive critical attempt tried to locate the authentic Jesus or at least a Jesus that might revolutionize the church and society (as, it was assumed, Jesus had originally intended to do). Eventually, the Jesus of faith was separated from the Jesus of history, and scholarship moved correspondingly in two directions. Behind both paths was the fundamental conviction that there is in fact only one Jesus worth finding. There might be divergence on how that objective can be

---

all but a tiny handful" in the eighteenth century (*Without God, without Creed: The Origins of Unbelief in America* [Baltimore: The Johns Hopkins University Press, 1985], p. 35). Turner's work and May's *Enlightenment in America* are both helpful treatments of the diffusion of the Enlightenment into popular American culture over the past two centuries.

40. The best brief account of biblical criticism in the past two centuries can be found in John Rogerson, Christopher Rowland, and Barnabas Lindars's *The Study and Use of the Bible*, vol. 2 of *The History of Christian Theology*, ed. Paul Avis (Grand Rapids: William B. Eerdmans, 1988); see especially pp. 318-80.

41. Albert Schweitzer reminded the theological world of this in his important work *The Quest of the Historical Jesus* (London: A. & C. Black, 1910).

found, but after all is said and done, there is only one Jesus who might rightly be reclaimed — the historical Jesus who is of no benefit for modern faith or the Jesus of modern faith who has no real roots in history.

The Enlightenment Legacy: The Critique of Purpose

The Enlightenment also brought with it an attack on biblical teleology — the conviction that history moves in keeping with the purposeful plan of God. The "history of salvation" approach was rejected in favor of a "scientific" reading of biblical history. There was one and only one history behind the Bible, and it was clear to Enlightenment-inspired theologians that this history was not and could not be providentially guided. Events such as the creation and the fall could no longer be accepted as historical *because of* the teleological role they played in the Bible — a role that exposed their fundamentally mythic character.

The model of the world as an organism was replaced by the model of the world as a mechanism. Some of the early "mechanical philosophers" such as Gassendi, Boyle, and Newton were self-conscious in their Christian profession and saw this mechanization of nature as a means to protect the independence and the sovereignty of God.[42] But a growing number of philosophers argued to the contrary that the mechanization of nature provided a means to explain the events in the world without recourse to God.

The old dualism of earth and heavens was slowly dismantled as the earth became simply one of the planets included under the same scientific rubric with the rest of the heavens, all of which became subject to universal laws of mechanics. All of nature was reduced to one large machine, void of any transcendent purpose. Appeals to a "plan of God" were rejected in favor of appeals to natural forces at work in the world. The discussion of final causes was replaced by a discussion of efficient causes.

This "new nature" replaced the traditional Greek-Christian conception of nature as possessing spiritual or personal characteristics. The

---

42. There is a vast literature addressing the controversy surrounding the influence of Christianity on the development of modern science. For a good overview of the issues involved, see R. Hooykaas, *Religion and the Rise of Modern Science* (Grand Rapids: William B. Eerdmans, 1972). These issues are largely beside the point in the context of our discussion, however; for our purposes, the only really germane point is that the mindset of modern science helped Enlightenment-inspired thinkers to conceive of the world as operating apart from the direct agency of God.

world under Copernicus, Galileo, and Bacon became a mechanism. Thus originated the famous "clockwork" image that dominated Europe in the seventeenth and eighteenth centuries. The world moved with mathematical precision because it operated under the quantifiable laws of mathematics. Galileo put the matter this way:

> Philosophy is written in the grand book, the universe, which stands continually open to our gaze. But the book cannot be understood unless one first learns to comprehend the language and read the letters in which it is composed. It is written in the language of mathematics, and its characters are triangles, circles, and other geometric figures without which it is humanly impossible to understand a single word of it; without these one wanders about in a dark labyrinth.[43]

This conception of nature led in turn to a doctrine of primary qualities (characteristics that can be quantified — figure, magnitude, position, and motion) and secondary qualities (characteristics that cannot be quantified — smell, taste, color, etc.). It was held that primary qualities truly exist in the object, whereas secondary qualities exist only in the subjective perception of the objects.

With this picture of the universe, it no longer seemed reasonable to suppose that God was constantly tinkering with his machine or that he was moving the world in any direct sense. God may have been in charge in some sense, but for those committed to a mechanistic science he became at best a sort of absentee landlord. In the eighteenth century, natural law was seen as the divine mechanism by which the world is maintained on its proper course. In the nineteenth century, natural law was seen as the glue that holds the world together, and it became increasingly more difficult to suppose that God is the gluemaster.

But if God were dropped out of the picture entirely, as some of the more radical Enlightenment thinkers had hoped he might be, there remained the puzzling question of the purpose and origin of the world. As it stood, this riddle served as a powerful apologetic tool in the hands of Christians during the age of the Enlightenment. They hailed the intricate design of the machine as evidence of its divine origin (and, some maintained, the continued divine maintenance of the world). Chris-

---

43. Galileo, *The Assayer* (1623), as quoted by Franklin Baumer in *The History of Modern European Thought* (New York: Macmillan, 1977), p. 50.

tian apologists of this era believed that science provided strong evidence for the existence of God, often using the analogy of the relationship of a watch and the watchmaker as the philosophical underpinning of the argument.[44]

However, as the nineteenth century wore on, the argument from design proved increasingly less compelling. The emergence of the theory of evolution in the last third of the nineteenth century leveled an especially serious blow.[45] The inherent forces of random mutation and natural selection supplanted the notion of a divine designer as an explanation for the complexity and regularity of the biological world around us. And soon enough the theory of evolution was broadened by analogy to account for other processes in the physical and social worlds, further diminishing popular reliance on the notion of divine teleology. In this regard, the role that the theory of evolution played philosophically was as large if not larger than the role it played scientifically. In large part, this development accounts for the popular perception that science is at war with religion.[46] It remains astonishing how quickly the theory was embraced by both the academy and American culture at large.

Darwin provided the missing link in the Enlightenment critique of a divine teleology and thus played an absolutely central role in the development of modernity. His theory of evolution suggested that appeals could be made simply and solely to internally functioning forces as ways to explain the apparent teleology of the world. Modernity was finally able to abandon the framework of divine providence in favor of a powerful and sophisticated alternative — biological evolution.

As the argument from design fell into increasing disfavor, God was increasingly marginalized. Among those who affirmed the Enlightenment agenda, he became a God of the gaps, a means to account for the remaining gaps in the catalogue of scientific knowledge about the world. But as science continued to push out the lingering mysteries, it continued to push out God as well. And in the writings of Feuerbach, Marx, and Freud, he was pushed inward, too — rendered a projection of human needs and desires.

44. The classic rehearsal of the argument from design and the watchmaker analogy can be found in William Paley's *Lectures on Natural Theology* (1802).

45. Darwin published *The Origin of Species* in 1859 and *The Descent of Man* in 1871.

46. Andrew D. White's immensely influential (if thinly argued) volume *A History of the Warfare of Science and Religion in Christendom* (1896) provides an apt illustration of these perceptions.

In connection with all these developments, eighteenth- and nineteenth-century theologians launched an offensive against the prophetic literature of the Bible. They argued that it was no longer acceptable to interpret the prophecies of the Old Testament as predating the events in which they were fulfilled. For example, Isaiah 45:1 contains a reference to the Persian King Cyrus. Premodern theologians had uniformly interpreted this reference as a prophecy. They maintained that the author of this verse had lived as much as a century before the reign of the King Cyrus to whom he refers. The new critics began with the assumption that this could not have been prophecy, however, and hence concluded that this part of the book of Isaiah must have been composed much later than had traditionally been assumed — that it must in fact have been composed after the reign of Cyrus. They demystified the text by dint of their critical assumptions.

Why was predictive prophecy of the sort traditionally associated with Isaiah 45 rejected out of hand? Because it assumed a God who was providentially involved in the world — an assumption no longer shared by many Enlightenment-inspired biblical critics. In the absence of such a God, there could have been no way to determine with any certainty what the future would hold, and therefore no way that the literature of that or any time could have been predictive in its specific intent. In keeping with their principles, the new biblical critics proceeded with a radical reconstruction of the dating of much of the Old Testament.

THE CHARACTER OF POSTMODERN THEOLOGY

It is undeniably the case that the "critical consciousness" of the Enlightenment continues in postmodern theology. There has been no return to external authority as a viable source for the construction of a theological framework.[47] It is assumed that theology is and must be constructed from

47. The radical postmodern theologian Mark C. Taylor goes so far as to suggest that even subjective authority must be jettisoned in the postmodern vision. If the being of God — and, as a result, divine authority — were rejected in the Enlightenment, then the ideas of the self allied with God must likewise be rejected. And if there is no self, then there can be no authority arising from the self. This is not yet the majority opinion among postmoderns, but for a compelling defense of this position based on Enlightenment-inspired assumptions, see Taylor, *Erring: A Postmodern A/Theology* (Chicago: University of Chicago Press, 1984).

the ground of human experience up. The fundamentally anthropological cast of modern theology has been strongly reaffirmed in postmodern theology. The "critical consciousness" is now critical of the conclusions — but not the assumptions — of earlier Enlightenment-inspired criticism.

In the postmodern framework, criticism extends not only to the religious authority of the premodern era but also to the revered realm of modern science. The core of the modern era's hope and meaning lay in the advancing claims of science in general and technology in particular.[48] Technological advances were the key for the eschatological hope of the modern West. With the steady advance of modern science came an increasing reliance on inanimate sources of power — sources of power considered by the modern person to be good in and of themselves. The postmoderns pride themselves on their awareness of the previously unrecognized presence of human bias in the use of these inanimate sources of power. Given their awareness, postmoderns view technology, like science generally, with great suspicion because of the ways in which it is used to serve the interests of dominant cultural prejudices. Technology holds great potential for good, but it has manifestly realized its potential for evil.[49] As the Enlightenment had sought to free the West from ecclesiastically vested biblical authority, so the postmodern revolution seeks to free the West from culturally vested scientific authority.

The appropriation of biblical symbols has undergone a transformation of rather radical proportions in the postmodern vision. The modern theologian had sought to locate a kerygmatic core of the canonical witness in hopes of finding and translating symbols that might revitalize modern culture. With the aid of significant filters, the Bible could still serve academically approved purposes. This concern has been transformed in the hands of postmodern theologians, who now go to great lengths to point to the "dark underside of Scripture" — the ways in which Scripture has been used to engender obscurantism, racism, sexism, authoritarianism, and "book religion" — a veneration of the book as a

48. For a clear analysis of the impact of modern technology on culture in general and religion in particular, see Jacques Ellul, *The Technological Society* (New York: Alfred A. Knopf, 1964).

49. Skepticism about technology among postmodern theologians is typically linked to expressions of concern about nuclear weapons and environmental pollution. See, e.g., J. B. Cobb, Jr., *Is It Too Late? A Theology of Ecology* (Milwaukee: Bruce Publications, 1971).

holy object.[50] The cultural blinders of modernity successfully prevented Western culture from seeing this darker side of the canonical witness, say the postmodern theologians. But they also concede that no age can successfully throw off the entire yoke of its immediate predecessors — and for evidence they point to a latent reverence for the "biblical morality" espoused by liberal theologians in the modern era that has persisted into the postmodern era despite the fact that the framework that produced it has been shed in much of postmodern theology.

Postmodern thinkers have attempted to throw off the cultural blinders of modernity and face the full reality of the prejudice inherent in the biblical tradition and all religious traditions arising from the biblical record. Such characteristic attitudes as patriarchalism, monarchicalism, racism, and sexism of the classical salvation-history scheme are now widely viewed as discredited. In this context, the biblical criticism of the modern era has been supplanted by ideological criticism — critique not of the historical sections of the Bible but of many of its moral and religious assumptions. Sandra Schneiders has offered a representative criticism:

> The Bible was written in a patriarchal society by the people, mostly men, whom that system kept on top. It embodies the androcentric, that is, male-centered presuppositions of that social world, and it legitimates the patriarchal, that is, male-dominant, social structures that held that world together. Its language is overwhelmingly male-oriented, both in reference to God and in reference to people. In short, the Bible is a book written by men in order to tell their story for their advantage. As such, it confronts both women and justice-inspired men with an enormous problem. It is not at all certain that the Bible can survive this challenge, that it can retain the allegiance of people called to justice and freedom in a postmodern world.[51]

It is not simply the Bible that the postmodern subjects to this type of criticism but modern culture as well. The biblical tradition exerted a

---

50. No one has spelled this concern out more clearly than Edward Farley in *Ecclesial Reflection*, especially chap. 6.

51. Schneiders, "Does the Bible Have a Postmodern Message?" in *Postmodern Theology: Christian Faith in a Pluralist World*, ed. Frederick Burnham (New York: Harper & Row, 1989), p. 65. For a longer and more trenchant critique along similar lines, see Mary Ann Tolbert, "Defining the Problem: The Bible and Feminist Hermeneutics," *Semeia* 28 (1983): 113-26.

substantial influence on the rise of the West, and so the West inevitably continues to give evidence of the prejudices of that tradition. Representative of the biblical tradition in the medieval context was Augustine, who, in the fourth century, supposed that the Bible contained an important critique of culture. Representative of the modern response to that perspective was Adolf Harnack, who, in the nineteenth century, supposed that culture contained an important critique of the Bible. The revolutionary aspect of the postmodern theologian is the supposition that both the Bible and the culture stand in need of critique.

To this end, David Tracy has argued that postmodern theology must engage in the kind of interpretation now known as a "hermeneutics of critique and suspicion" as well as a "hermeneutics of retrieval."[52] Theology must seek to retrieve those traditions that have not flourished or survived in the cultural crucible of the West. Theology must also interpret with suspicion those aspects of the biblical tradition that have survived and that serve a destructive purpose in the modern world. The postmodern theologian cannot forfeit the Enlightenment heritage of criticism, even if it extends to the very culture that nourished it.

Postmodern theologians maintain that there is no innocent interpretation, no unambiguous tradition, no historyless, subjectless interpreter. Theology occurs in a cultural context, the critique of which lies at the heart of the Bible. But that Bible's own critique must itself be criticized. The postmodern must engage in the critique of modernity — even if it is painful to do so.

Ecclesial Authority

From where does this critique arise? The answer most often is ecclesial reflection, from the community of believers attempting to be faithful to the purposes of their faith. Edward Farley has given the clearest clues as to the nature of this ecclesial existence.[53] It is not a community committed to a divinely inspired revelation by which it endures and gains its purpose; rather, it is a community shaped by the redemptive presence of the transcendent, which transforms any and all provincial attitudes whether based on ethnic, geographical, cultic, racial, sexual,

---

52. See Tracy, *The Analogical Imagination: Christian Theology and the Culture of Pluralism* (New York: Crossroad, 1981), especially chaps. 3 and 4.

53. See Farley, *Ecclesial Reflection*, especially part 2.

political, social, or doctrinal considerations. The redemptive presence transforms the community in the direction of a universal community, yet without losing the particularity intrinsic to the human being.[54] Redemption is openness to human pluralism in all its richness, a pluralism that cannot be denied through absolutism or denigrated into relativism. People are to be accepted for what they are, however different they may be from us. In the affirmation of these differences comes the possibility of dialogue and an increasing understanding of the differences.

The events by which this redemptive presence is communicated are often "sedimented" in the literature in which they survive. Both biblical and ideological criticism are required to unearth these events and to turn them into religiously significant symbols. Religious texts may witness to these transformative events, but they ought never to be seen as substitutes for them or as infallible interpretations of them. Sallie McFague puts it this way:

> The essential core [of Christianity] is not any book or doctrine or interpretation, but the transformative *event* of new life, a new way of being in the world. . . . Scripture is testimony to this event; doctrines are consensus attempts to formulate its significance; theologies are interpretation of it; but *as event* it stands behind, beneath, and before all our constructions of it.[55]

The event is unique in that its religious and redemptive significance cannot be stated in solely doctrinal or conceptual terms. As Edward Farley and Peter C. Hodgson put it, "Biblical language portrays new ways of being in a world transformed by grace; its meaning is a function of symbolic and metaphorical uses of language that cannot be directly translated into conceptual terms."[56] As a result, the move from biblical text to theology does not occur along traditional lines from exegesis to doctrinal conceptualization to systematization and finally to confession-

---

54. For an Enlightenment-era expression of a similar conviction, see book 3 of Kant's *Religion within the Limits of Reason Alone.*

55. McFague, "An Epilogue: The Christian Paradigm," in *Christian Theology: An Introduction to Its Traditions and Tasks,* 2d ed., ed. Peter C. Hodgson and Robert H. King (Philadelphia: Fortress Press, 1985), p. 378.

56. Farley and Hodgson, "Scripture and Tradition," in *Christian Theology: An Introduction to Its Traditions and Tasks,* p. 74.

ally oriented theology.[57] Rather, the theological framework is constructed in the empowering experience of ecclesial community as members of the community use the event-symbols of the various religious traditions to open themselves up to others.

The religious and redemptive authority of the religious literature (primarily though not exclusively the Bible) therefore resides in the way it is used by the ecclesial community, the ways in which a new kind of corporate existence is brought about. Religious texts are authoritative not because of any intrinsic quality but only to the extent to which they function in the church to shape new human identities and transform individuals and communal life. The Bible assumes authority because it can facilitate communities to function in redemptive ways, and it is this religious authority by which human beings are redemptively transformed.

Ecclesial process as such (the redemptive use of religious literature and tradition) is the salvific work of God in history. God saves *through* the historical manifestation of human possibility, not *from* history or in spite of it. "The ecclesial community, moreover, is nonethnic, universal, and culturally pluralistic, so that purely ethnic, provincial, and culturally relative elements of scripture cannot be authoritative."[58]

The authority of Scripture derives not from its content but from its power to occasion new occurrences of revelation (i.e., new understandings of openness to others) and new experiences of redemptive transformation when used in situations of proclamation, theological reflection, and personal self-understanding. These "revelations" and "redemptive experiences" cannot be directly translated into theological concepts. Rather, the theologian "redescribes" what has been expressed biblically, employing a contemporary idiom that allows the modern person to gain an "imaginative construal" of the essence of Christian faith.

The goal that drives the postmodern project, then, is the desire to be open to the diversity of religious experience, not the "modern" desire to find a common human religious experience on which a universal theological framework might be constructed. But it is still an anthropological vision in contradistinction to the premodern and clas-

---

57. For the clearest available statement of this traditional approach, see David F. Wells, "The Nature and Function of Theology," in *The Use of the Bible in Theology: Evangelical Options,* ed. Robert K. Johnston (Atlanta: John Knox Press, 1985), pp. 175-99.

58. Farley and Hodgson, "Scripture and Tradition," p. 75.

sical theological vision. Its fundamental assumptions begin in critical human reflection.

Theological Realism

Another significant theme in the postmodern vision is the demise of modernity's triumphalism. Echoing many of the transforming themes of the neo-orthodox movement of the 1940s and 1950s, postmodern theologians are often skeptical about the optimism that characterized much of liberal theology. The liberal tradition trumpeted the superiority of Western enlightened religion and promised prosperity (normally of the intellectual variety) for all other parts of the globe that would follow in its wake. It proclaimed the virtues of a European education and the need for the undeveloped world to mirror the strategies of the West. Colonialism often served as a handmaiden to this vision.

However, the commitment to Enlightenment-inspired science and technology did not result in the world peace called for by the liberal theologians of modernity. The "modern wars" in Vietnam, the Middle East, and South Africa gradually changed the way many conceived of the West (and its liberal vision). In particular these wars were painful reminders of the dark side of the Enlightenment hope of making an absolute out of any one culture or set of cultural norms. Indeed, humanity's dark side has become a recurring theme in the developing postmodern literature — not in the form of a doctrine of sin but rather as a corrective to the imperialism of liberal culture and liberal theology.

Once again in this context, as postmodern theology jettisoned dominant themes in modern theology, it did not replace them with premodern perspectives. Though the optimism of modern theology has largely been rejected, it has not been supplanted with the premodern (and neo-orthodox) hope in the providence of God. Postmoderns repudiate the triumphalism expressed both in the assertion that history is headed toward a humanly inspired utopia and the assertion that it is headed toward a divinely inspired heavenly kingdom.

Postmodern theologians share a conviction that there is no thread of extrinsic or even intrinsic purpose holding history together. Good does not necessarily triumph over evil. The men in the white hats do not always arrive in time to save the town from the men in the black hats. It is not even clear any longer which of those two groups represents good and which represents evil. The reality and irrepressible nature of evil is an overwhelming theological theme in the postmodern vision.[59] The optimism of the modern era and the "hope in God" of the premodern era have been forsaken in the postmodern vision.

According to postmodern theologians, triumphalism of either variety founders on the rock of theodicy. In light of the horrific suffering experienced during the past century, it is very difficult to sustain a belief that God somehow maintains control over this world. Theology has shifted from a model of divine causality to a model of divine influence and in the postmodern vision to a model of benign influence at best. Events cannot be interpreted as coming from the divine hand any longer, nor can the realities of modern culture be viewed as products of a basically virtuous humanity. Finite human freedom cannot be violated, and finite human evil cannot be concealed. Failure to see this perpetuates a myth that ironically "mundanizes the divine and sacralizes the nondivine."[60] Robert King speaks for most postmodern theologians when he asks, "How can we suppose God is divinely sovereign over history when history issues in the mass extermination of innocent men and women? Can we assume that all things are ordered to human good when the relentless pursuit of human good leads to the destruction of the environment and the disruption of the ecological balance in nature?"[61]

The task of affirming meaning and purpose for the human community without a transcendent source, first undertaken by the death-of-God theologians, is part of the very fabric of postmodern theology. But the postmodern theologians have set themselves the more difficult task of creating *transcendent* meaning and purpose for the human community without a transcendent source.

The fabric of postmodern theology is by no means uniform or even regularly patterned; it is a patchwork quilt in which are stitched together bits and pieces of the variety and richness of human experience. The remnants of which the quilt is constructed can be traced not to divine revelation but to a diverse range of other religious experiences. Undergirding this theological project is the philosophical conviction that religious knowledge begins not with a set of "givens" or "foundations" but

59. For a representative postmodern treatment of the problem of evil, see Wendy Farley, *Tragic Vision and Divine Compassion: A Contemporary Theodicy* (Louisville: John Knox/Westminster Press, 1990).

60. Farley and Hodgson, "Scripture and Tradition," p. 76.

61. King, "The Task of Theology," in *Christian Theology: An Introduction to Its Traditions and Tasks,* p. 27.

rather with conversation and dialogue. In more technical terms, this may be referred to as a theory of *epistemic pragmatism.*

Epistemic Pragmatism

The Enlightenment initiated a critique of the foundations of knowledge by calling into question the fundamental principles of orthodox theology. No longer were the dictates of revelation allowed to settle questions by their very presence. In the Enlightenment project, every theological conclusion had to be justified on nontheological grounds.[62] And many modern thinkers argued that there simply was not sufficient evidence to support the claims of traditional orthodoxy.

But liberal theology failed to take account of its own unsupported belief in human reason. According to the Enlightenment ideal, every belief needed a reason, except one — the belief in reason. But what about this belief? Why does it not need a warrant? Why should one believe in reason without any supporting reasons? With these questions came the recognition of the dogmatic (and therefore irrational) character of the Enlightenment's belief in reason — a belief much closer to a fundamental act of faith than to a scientific and critical act of reason. When it was acknowledged that the foundations were unsupported, they collapsed.[63] Specifically, it precipitated the demise of logical positivism, the philosophical movement that had most nearly tied the hopes of human culture to the progress of modern science. The logical positivists maintained that natural science provides the surest foundation for human knowledge.

62. Nicholas Wolterstorff makes the interesting claim that orthodox Christianity was also radically affected by this challenge. During this period, orthodox theologians also sought to ground their faith in secular evidence — a strategy he refers to as "evidentialism." See "The Migration of Theistic Arguments: From Natural Theology to Evidentialist Apologetics," in *Rationality, Religious Belief, and Moral Commitment: New Essays in the Philosophy of Religion,* ed. Robert Audi and William J. Wainwright (Ithaca, N.Y.: Cornell University Press, 1986), pp. 38-81.

63. The most influential recent attack on the Enlightenment commitment to Reason and the resultant foundationalist epistemology can be found in Richard Rorty's *Philosophy and the Mirror of Nature* (Princeton: Princeton University Press, 1979). The seeds of this demise are most clearly evident in the literature surrounding the death of logical positivism. See in particular Willard van Orman Quine, "Two Dogmas of Empiricism," in *From a Logical Point of View: Nine Logico-Philosophical Essays* (Cambridge: Harvard University Press, 1953), pp. 20-46; Wilfred Sellars, *Science, Perception and Reality* (London: Routledge & Kegan Paul, 1963); and Ludwig Wittgenstein, *Philosophical Investigations* (New York: Macmillan, 1953).

It was not long after the cracks began to turn up in this foundational assumption that the whole edifice came tumbling down. Science itself is not nearly as objective as the logical positivists had supposed.[64] Nor were the foundations of human knowledge in general free of fundamental biases. History is full of examples in which "knowledge" of this sort has given rise to various traditions of oppression.

Postmodern theology has also been influenced by sociological critiques of this Enlightenment picture of knowledge. The argument is that people do not ordinarily think with rational foundations in mind and that in fact no human being is or can be purely objective or form hypotheses based solely on rational considerations. The process of forming theories involves far more than simply locating the proper foundations and building upward from there. Unspoken political and ideological assumptions exert a greater influence than reason itself on the construction of reigning paradigms of knowledge.[65]

It is not clear what kind of epistemology will eventually replace Enlightenment foundationalism, but the postmodern movement is at least united in the conviction that foundationalism is inadequate as a theory of knowledge.[66] No longer is it permissible to think of human knowledge (of whatever variety) as consisting of sets of beliefs that rest indubitably upon other sets of beliefs and that the whole structure of beliefs ultimately rests on a set of privileged and irrevisible foundational beliefs. Postmoderns reject the assertion that knowledge is like a house built on sure and steady foundations and that the only philosophically interesting task is the search for the most reliable foundation.

The most prominent proponent of a "postmodern epistemology," Richard Rorty, has suggested that philosophy began a rapid descent when it turned its fundamental attention to epistemological questions. The descent began with René Descartes, continued with John Locke, and culminated in Kant and the later Kantian (i.e., Enlightenment) tradition.

---

64. On this, see Thomas Kuhn's landmark work *The Structure of Scientific Revolutions* (Chicago: University of Chicago Press, 1962) and Paul Feyerabend's *Against Method: Outline of an Anarchist Theory of Knowledge* (New York: Schocken Books, 1978).

65. See Michel Foucault, *The Order of Things: An Archaeology of the Human Sciences* (New York: Vintage, 1973); and Jürgen Habermas, *Knowledge and Human Interests* (Boston: Beacon Press, 1968).

66. Antifoundationalist sympathies are evident in the work of a whole range of postmoderns, from the relatively conservative Jeffrey Stout (*The Flight from Authority*) to the very radical Mark Taylor (*Deconstructing Theology* [New York: Crossroad, 1982]).

Descartes mistakenly invented the modern notion of the mind, says Rorty, Locke got wrapped up in getting from the mind to the real world, and Kant reduced epistemology to the problem of understanding the relation between sense impressions and the interpretation that the knowing mind puts on them.

Rorty has described his own program as an attempt "to undermine . . . confidence in the 'the mind' as something about which one should have a 'philosophical' view, in 'knowledge' as something about which there ought to be a 'theory' and which has 'foundations,' and in 'philosophy' as it has been conceived since Kant."[67] He contends that knowledge should not be construed as a mental process that mirrors or represents reality. Knowledge is not a set of privileged representations of the external world, he argues, and the mind is not like a ball of wax getting imprinted in an objective and unbiased fashion by that world, as Locke had presumed. It is not clear what role Rorty assigns to the mind in connection with knowledge or whether he conceives of the mind getting imprinted by anything external to it. He maintains that the metaphor of the "web of belief" is a much more helpful explanation of mental processes than that of a "house built upon foundations" for explaining mental processes.[68]

Beliefs are connected only to other beliefs, not to a world "out there." Knowledge is a matter not of explicating a word-world relationship but rather of understanding how epistemic subjects (i.e., human beings) function in their respective believing communities. One is justified in believing a particular theory not by locating rationally supporting evidence for the belief but rather by receiving permission from a relevant social community to hold the theory. To be justified in such belief is a "matter of victory in argument rather than of a relation to an object known." Furthermore, says Rorty, "our certainty will be a matter of conversation between persons rather than a matter of interaction with non-human reality."[69]

As human beings, we are never able to get outside our own web of belief, and hence nothing can count as a reason in support of our beliefs except another one of our beliefs. We cannot appeal to privileged

67. Rorty, *Philosophy and the Mirror of Nature*, p. 7.
68. Rorty borrows this phrase and its conceptualization from Willard van Orman Quine and Joseph S. Ullian, *The Web of Belief* (New York: Random House, 1970).
69. Rorty, *Philosophy and the Mirror of Nature*, p. 157.

access to a word-world relationship. The authority for any belief is always internal, to our own beliefs or to a relevant community of knowers. The question of the proper foundations of knowledge (e.g., the Bible, tradition, science, etc.) is thus jettisoned in favor of the question of the social approbation of any and all knowledge claims.

This is a fairly radical pragmatism, and it characterizes much of postmodernism.[70] Unlike pure skepticism, it does not hold that there is no world out there (or no real historical Jesus) to which the knowing (or believing) mind must somehow get related. The postmodern pragmatists have simply made the claim that this is a rather fruitless and uninteresting concern.

> Pragmatism . . . does not erect Science as an idol to fill the place once held by God. It views science as one genre of literature — or, put the other way around, literature and the arts as inquiries, on the same footing as scientific inquiries. . . . The question of what propositions to assert, which pictures to look at, what narratives to listen to and comment on and retell, are all questions about what will help us get what we want (or about what we *should* want).[71]

An important product of this new pragmatism for postmodern theology is its suggestion that the present global encounter with other religions is both a necessity and a virtue. It is necessary because it precludes from the outset the possibility of returning to a monolithic, homogeneous vision of theology. It is a virtue because it forces us to see the richness of the variety of religious traditions missing from earlier theological traditions that supposed there to be but one truth "out there."

If these are the dominant themes, can there be any methodological norms for the construction of a postmodern theological framework? Can

70. William Placher offers a tempered critique of Rorty from the vantage point of the "New Yale" school and helpfully reminds the reader that Rorty's pragmatism is not shared by the mainstream theological establishment (*Unapologetic Theology: A Christian Voice in a Pluralistic Conversation* [Philadelphia: Westminster Press, 1989]). Placher is undoubtedly right in this contention. Yet it is also the case that some form of moderate pragmatism reigns in most theological circles today. Rorty may draw more radical conclusions from the death of foundationalism than most, but all postmodern theologians join him in having abandoned the older foundationalist epistemology. The consensus is that some form of pragmatism must be embraced.

71. Rorty, *The Consequences of Pragmatism (Essays: 1972-1980)* (Minneapolis: University of Minnesota Press, 1982), p. xliii.

there be guidelines to which all theologies must adhere? How is it possible to steer clear of an absolute view of truth and avoid a crippling relativism at the same time? If theology begins from below (i.e., with a consideration of human experience), is it reasonable to hope that there might be any means for resolving religious disputes? The perplexing nature of these questions in the light of the entrenched pluralism of postmodern theology helps explain why methodological questions have been the consuming passion of many contemporary theologians during the past two decades. At times it seems as though postmodern theologians talk about nothing other than methodology. To this concern we now turn more directly.

Theology as Hermeneutic

There is a renewed interest in the "Christian tradition" within the movement I have been calling postmodern theology. The interest has been fueled by desires to retrieve lost traditions while also debunking much of the dominant Western tradition. The interest in retrieving the past has also been motivated in part by a desire to move beyond the all-consuming "now" of modernity. There has also been a concern to debunk the past of its legacy of oppressive traditions, but this is typically just the flip side of the same coin. Retrieval themes are most often rooted in a desire to recover traditions that have not survived the cultural crucible of the West. Debunking themes are rooted in a desire to uncover the prejudices in the traditions that have survived the cultural crucible and therefore continue to taint the modern world. Patriarchy and racism are the prejudices that have received the most significant critiques.

Much of the postmodern theological scene fosters a troubling alienation from the central written classic of the Christian tradition, the Bible. The critique of racist, sexist, and classist elements in Scripture by liberation, feminist, and ethnic theologians today contributes to the perceived chasm between the modern world and the Scriptures. The breakdown of Western Christianity's parochialism in the face of a global culture widens this gap between the horizons of the modern world and the Scriptures. The upshot is that the postmodern theologians create more distance from the past than they manage to eliminate, because they emphasize the chasm between modernity and postmodernity and compound it by retaining the Enlightenment chasm between the Scriptures and the modern world.

Despite the realities of these cultural chasms, there is a growing recognition of the influence exerted on modern Christians by the Scriptures and the traditions that emerged from them in the West. There is a growing consensus that individuals come to the theological task with a set of assumptions by which they make sense of the world. Normally, these are not assumptions of which we are formally conscious, but they nonetheless play a formative role in the development of our theological outlook. The retrieval and examination of the traditions out of which many of these assumptions arise has become a critical element for the postmodern thinker in forging a new theological vision. Put another way, this concern for the retrieval of "tradition" arises from the sentiment that the theological framework is shaped by two "horizons" — tradition and experience. As David Tracy puts it, "Whenever we interpret contemporary experience theologically, the history of effects of the Christian tradition is also present in the interpretation itself. Whenever we interpret the Christian message theologically, we inevitably also apply it to our contemporary experience in order to understand it at all."[72]

In contrast to modern theologians, who wanted to talk only of the interpretation of the tradition by the criteria of modern rationality, and in contrast to premodern theologians, who wanted to talk only of the interpretation of experience by the tradition (the biblical text preeminently), postmodern theologians encourage the discussion of the interaction of these two horizons. The retrieval of the culturally distant Scriptures of the Christian tradition helps in understanding the theological visions that have emerged from those Scriptures in the West and that are present in varying forms in the modern world. It also aids in beginning the task of reforming those traditions.[73]

72. Tracy, "Theological Method," in *Christian Theology: An Introduction to Its Traditions and Tasks*, p. 56. I take Tracy's comments on theological method to be both representative of postmodern theology and influential in setting its agenda. In what follows I employ Tracy's framework to help clarify the methodological convictions of postmodern theology. This is not to accord Tracy the status that Barth or Bultmann or Tillich had a generation ago; it is merely to say that Tracy has provided some helpful clarification of postmodern theological method(s).

73. Postmodern theology has demonstrated a renewed interest in the church. The sentiment seems to be that the church ought not to be abandoned (or equated with the larger culture) but ought rather to be reformed from within. It is striking that the group of postmodern Roman Catholic theologians who were very supportive of Vatican II and its reforms and who initiated the journal *Concilium* — individual such as Hans Küng, Edward Schillebeeckx, David Tracy, Gustavo Guttiérrez, Leonardo Boff, and Elisabeth Schüssler Fiorenza — have stayed within the Church even as it has become more conservative under Pope John Paul II.

And yet there is reason to be suspicious of the apparent deference that postmoderns pay to "tradition," for they view it not as divine revelation or as authoritative but merely as revelatory of the modern predicament. Tradition is valuable, they say, to the extent to which it helps us to understand ourselves and our assumptions about the world. In this, the postmodern vision remains modern (as opposed to premodern) in its fundamental fidelity to the anthropological character of theology. Gordon Kaufman is representative in his persistent argument that theology is not descriptive or expository with regard to some being called *God* but rather that it is a "construct of the imagination which helps to tie together, unify and interpret the totality of experience."[74]

In this manner, postmodern theology extends the modern vision rather than moving against it or undermining it. In the postmodern vision, theology remains secondary to all concrete interpretations of the concrete symbols of the tradition — that is to say, theology remains secondary to the interpretative guidelines of modern experience. The present community of faith is the final touchstone of truth as it interacts and interprets the tradition in order that the community's own future might move beyond the "destructive tendencies" of the present.[75]

Though dedicated to an anthropological starting point, postmoderns nevertheless insist that theology consists in some measure of the movement from text (i.e., tradition) to doctrine (i.e., theological reflection).[76] However, unlike most evangelicals, postmodern theologians insist that the path between text and doctrine is fundamentally bi-directional, that theology is a movement from text to doctrine *and* from doctrine to text, from the past to the present *and* from the present to the past. Contemporary experience helps reform the tradition, and the tradition may help reform contemporary experience or at least uncover fundamental assumptions of modern culture.

74. Kaufman, *An Essay on Theological Method* (Missoula, Mont.: Scholars Press, 1979), p. 43.

75. The entrenched pluralism in postmodern theology leads to widely divergent interpretations of the nature of "destructive" tendencies. Note, e.g., the extremely disparate interpretations of "oppression" even among various theologies of liberation — feminist, black, Latin American, *minyung*, etc.

76. The postmodern is normally fearful of "doctrine" in the orthodox sense of that term, meaning a group of beliefs to which assent is given or required. However, it remains the case that there are some "constants" in the postmodern theological vision (some of which we will consider shortly), and they play a role similar to that which doctrine plays in the orthodox vision.

Many postmodern theologians have suggested that theology should be more like a conversation than a lecture. The text (the tradition, the past, the classic) does not simply tell the theologian what to believe. Rather, the text may aid the theologian in reflecting critically on the life-situation of the present-day religious community. The theologian in turn helps determine what aspects of the tradition are in need of reformation. According to David Tracy, "Theology is the attempt to establish *mutually critical* correlations between an interpretation of the Christian tradition and an interpretation of the contemporary situation."[77]

The dictates of contemporary experience and/or the hidden traditions of the past will often challenge earlier dominant theological interpretations of the meaning and truth of the Christian message. For example, in the nineteenth century, evolutionary theory challenged the assumptions of evangelical readings of the opening chapters of Genesis and the traditional Christian apologetic argument from design.[78] More recently, methodologies from the social sciences and philosophy have been used to challenge traditional christological formulations.[79]

At other times, the analysis of the Christian message will confront reigning understandings of contemporary experience. For example, liberation theologians have hailed the Exodus event as a challenge to modern forms of oppression such as sexism and racism,[80] and they have cited Old Testament conceptions of justice in critiques of materialistic consumerism.

The interaction of these two horizons — the Christian tradition and contemporary experience — gives shape to several fundamental methodological tasks in the project of theology. One of these is the

77. Tracy, "Theological Method," p. 36; italics mine.

78. Two works illustrate this well: the theologically liberal but tempered work of Frederick Temple, *The Relations between Religion and Science* (London: Macmillan, 1884), and the more radical work by Andrew D. White, *A History of the Warfare of Science and Theology in Christendom* (New York: D. Appleton, 1896).

79. The controversy created by *The Myth of God Incarnate*, ed. John Hick (London: SCM Press, 1977), can be understood as a reaction to the way in which the framework of modern experience was used to challenge the traditional notion of the Incarnation. The flood of literature that followed the publication of this book can helpfully be interpreted as defenses of two ways of viewing the Incarnation — one traditional and the other modern.

80. For a good case study in this type of biblical interpretation, see Gustavo Gutiérrez's now-classic theological text *A Theology of Liberation*, especially chap. 9.

location and contemporary interpretation of the central symbols of the Christian tradition for an appropriate construal of the present situation. The interpretations are not limited by past interpretations but apparently must risk abandoning the insights of past generations in the hopes of challenging the biases of the present generation. These interpretations are inevitably concerned with envisioning a Christian future along eschatological lines enunciated by such contemporary cultural theologies as feminist and black theologies. They give voice to the conviction that elitism of any sort has no part to play in the community of the future. Radical egalitarianism is the operative goal, and an affirmation of theological pluralism is the means of achieving that goal — and both the goal and the means are seen to be grounded in the identity and presence of Jesus Christ.

Postmodern theologians focus on the contemporary situation when it comes to the application of biblical norms. This is the sense in which they contend that interpretation of biblical symbols must occur from the ground up — that is to say, beginning from the needs and dilemmas of the modern world. The present community of faith defines its problems, and the biblical text may then speak to them as defined.

An awkward question arises for this type of interpretation, however: Whose norms govern the process of locating and defining the problems? Those of the feminist? The black? The Asian? The process theologian? The radical pluralism in the modern community leaves postmodern theologians without any sufficiently encompassing criterion of adequacy for these interpretations.[81] There is no simple touchstone test as there was in the context of premodern theology — where theological interpretation strove to be faithful to the data of Scripture, and the problems of the modern world were dealt with as analogues to those described in the Bible. The postmodern theologian's need to challenge diverse sectors of modern society gives rise to a plurality of touchstones, all competing

---

81. For a clear exposition of this dilemma, see Schubert M. Ogden, *On Theology* (San Francisco: Harper & Row, 1986). Ogden believes that there is a genuine dilemma but is nonetheless convinced that it is possible to state in very broad terms some criteria of credibility for a full theological method and to do so on more than simply Christian grounds. On the other hand, many theologians influenced by the New Yale school are not so nearly convinced as Ogden that there is (or ought to be) any hope of finding criteria of credibility outside of Christian theology itself that do not beg important questions. See Charles M. Wood, *The Formation of Christian Understanding: An Essay in Theological Hermeneutics* (Philadelphia: Westminster Press, 1981).

with one another. How can theological interpretation and discourse be controlled in this environment?

The historical-critical methods of the older biblical critics will not suffice in setting the proper limits on possible interpretations of the tradition. They may help in understanding the biblical text's own historicity, but a mere reconstruction of the history of the biblical text along historical-critical lines will not make it relevant to the modern world. The historical-critical reading of Scripture does not produce an adequate theological understanding of either the questions of the modern world or Scripture's creative responses to these problems. Historical-critical interpretations leave the Bible in the past. The challenge for the postmodern is to bring the Bible into the present by asking questions of it that very few in previous generations have asked. The modern use of the Bible did not challenge the present; in many cases it did not even challenge the past.[82]

More than "mere" history must lie behind the impact of the Christian Scriptures. The fact that they have given a religious identity to the church through the ages indicates that they constitute more than a merely historical document. The power (and relevance) of the Scriptures transcend all merely historical treatments that attempt to separate out the "fact" from the "fiction" in the canon.

What is needed is the realization that the task of interpretation is not religiously neutral. The Bible cannot be read simply like any other book. Its evocative power is lost without some recognition of the inter-

---

82. Severe criticism of the historical-critical method of exegesis began in the early 1970s and has continued with increasing strength. Representative of this concern was the issue of *Interpretation* (vol. 25, 1971) devoted entirely to the question of the relation of Scripture to theology. The most influential criticism of the historical-critical method was that of Gerhard Maier in *The End of the Historical-Critical Method* (St. Louis: Concordia, 1974). It should be noted that Maier's criticisms of the historical-critical method are largely premodern, not postmodern. He argued for a return to a notion of divine revelation and thus to an intrinsically authoritative Scripture. For a postmodern critique of the method see Frank Kermode, *The Genesis of Secrecy* (Cambridge: Harvard University Press, 1979), and David Kelsey, *The Uses of Scripture in Recent Theology* (Philadelphia: Fortress Press, 1975). Kelsey argues for a strongly "functional" view of Scripture, positing its authority in the "uses" to which it is put in the religious community. Kelsey's colleague at Yale Hans Frei provided a keen historical analysis of the rise (and demise) of historical-critical exegesis in the eighteenth and nineteenth centuries in *The Eclipse of Biblical Narrative: A Study of Eighteenth and Nineteenth Century Hermeneutics* (New Haven: Yale University Press, 1974). Frei's historical argument clearly foreshadowed Kelsey's functionalist argument.

play of the religious horizon of the text with the religious horizon of the modern interpreter. The historical-critical method is concerned only with the preunderstanding (intention) of the original author or editor. But this is only half the story. Both the interpreter and the text possess a preunderstanding, and the power of the classic religious text lies in the challenge that each brings to the other. Properly understood, the task of interpretation entails keeping both horizons in view.

A classic religious text such as the Bible has a certain permanence and may have a certain range of possible interpretations marked out by the historical context. But as postmodern theologians periodically say, the classic text has an "excess" of meaning.[83] Its meaning is not fixed and determined by its original context. It is religiously "pregnant" in that its challenges are not fully formed by the historical context in which it was conceived. This is to say that the text may occasion challenges for the reader that were never imagined in the original setting, challenges framed by the life experiences of the modern reader, not by a recon-struction of the life experiences of the original authors and editors. The text grows beyond its original historical context and reaches out in different ways to new situations. Specifically, the text challenges the present community to move toward redemption.[84] It elicits a response on the part of the community of interpreters to the community's unique problems. This is what makes it religiously significant.

The postmodern vision also seeks a means to remove any distor-tions and illusions that are native to the classic text. The original context of the Scriptures undoubtedly influenced the writing of the texts, say the postmoderns, and the biases of the original authors are undoubtedly echoed in the writings that bear their imprint. It is the responsibility of the modern interpreter to recognize these flaws in the text and to prevent them from influencing the modern community of faith. This is possible when the problems themselves have been defined by the modern situa-tion and when this framework serves as the filter through which the ancient text is examined. For example, postmodern theologians maintain that patriarchalism is evident throughout the pages of Scriptures, and

83. In this regard see especially Edgar V. McKnight, *The Postmodern Use of the Bible: The Emergence of Reader-Oriented Criticism* (Nashville: Abingdon Press, 1988).
84. I would underscore the ambiguity of the term *redemption* in postmodern usage. It is not typically used to denote an objective activity of God in bringing people out of a state of bondage to sin; rather, it tends to be suggestive of a "new way of living in the world"—and it seldom receives any more clarification than that.

no interpretation (or application) of the Christian Scriptures will be complete until this has been recognized and removed.

The task of the interpreter is thus to strike up a "conversation" with the text, to demonstrate a willingness to learn from the text and be challenged by it as well as remain critical of it. We cannot engage in honest conversation if we leave the text in its own historical context or if we strip it of its central historical challenges. We must embrace both the text's historical limitations and its historical possibilities, and we cannot do so unless we enter into a critical — that is to say, postmodern — conversation with the text.

There is a lively debate under way among postmodern theologians concerning the precise nature of this conversation with the text. The controversy centers on the modern interpreter's ability (or lack thereof) to know what is true about the biblical text. Some have argued that the interpretive conversation cannot be critical in the sense that it judges what is finally true about the text, that the modern interpreter cannot stand in judgment over the text.[85] Others have argued that criticism of the text is absolutely central to the conversation. According to these postmoderns, the modern interpreter must make a decision as to what is finally true about the text and what should be rejected. At stake is the appropriation (or rejection) of the truth claims of the original text.[86]

To the first camp of postmodern theologians, it remains an open question whether a *critical* conversation with the biblical text is possible in principle. They argue that any attempt to undo the illusions and the systematic distortions of the original contexts of the Scriptures presupposes a privileged position from which these criticisms may be launched. But it is precisely this notion of a privileged position that many postmodern theologians want to reject in principle because it assumes that

85. See, e.g., George Lindbeck's *The Nature of Doctrine*. Lindbeck is representative of what has sometimes been called the "New Yale School." On this rendering, the text is understood in a regulative manner — i.e., as not making first-order truth claims but rather as providing a sociolinguistic framework that defines and gives identity to the Christian community.

86. In this regard see especially the proposals put forward by David Tracy. He takes specific issue with Gadamer on this point, arguing that the postmodern must not lose sight of the crisis of cognitive claims occasioned by the Enlightenment. The theologian must still engage in argument to establish what is finally true about the text; the theologian cannot stop being "critical." See Tracy, *The Analogical Imagination*, chap. 1, sect. iii.

knowledge can be gained from a distortion-free platform.[87] The post-modern who rejects this notion of a distortion-free platform concludes that modern interpreters are bound by their own distortions and thus can stand in judgment over the text only in a limited sense. Finally and ultimately, questions of criticism become unimportant to this camp of postmoderns. It is not of great consequence to them whether the Bible is true or not; what is fundamentally important is the use to which the Bible is put in the modern community.

The second camp of postmoderns contend that the interpreter must engage in a kind of ideological critique of the text in order to isolate the distortions of the text and of the traditions that have emerged from the text. The nature and character of this "critique" will vary depending on the life situation of the interpreter. But to shun this "critical" task, they say, is to lose the genuine insight of the Enlightenment — namely, that questions of truth must be a matter of utmost importance. As David Tracy puts it, "What remains constant in the shift from modernity to post-modernity is the fact that such contemporary critiques of modernity deepen the fundamental commitment to those purely secular standards for knowledge and action initiated by the Enlightenment."[88]

This second strategy manifests a concern to show the adequacy (or inadequacy) of the truth claims (usually cognitive) of a given religious tradition and its unique interpretation of the Scriptures. In order to accomplish this, some paradigm for what constitutes objective argumentation is requisite. This will normally take the form of argumentation in some acknowledged discipline in the wider academic community. Typically that discipline will be philosophy or the philosophical dimension of one of the social sciences or humanities.

On either reading, the postmodern use of the text is meant to bring challenges to the contemporary community in a "prophetic manner" — prophetic in the sense that it dares to raise doubts about the secularizing influence of the religious institutions of culture. As Jesus chastened the moneylenders in the temple, so the postmodern theologian chastens those who have fashioned the gospel in keeping with the ideals of modern culture. The reigning paradigms of cultural values ought not to serve as

---

87. See especially the second part of Hans-Georg Gadamer's *Truth and Method* (New York: Crossroad, 1975). See also Lindbeck's *The Nature of Doctrine.*
88. Tracy, *Blessed Rage for Order*, p. 8.

sanctions of religious institutions, and when the association between the two becomes too close, as it has in modern America, the community of the faithful must rise to challenge the equation of cultural values with religious values.

This challenge has little to do with the belief systems of the original author or editor of the Scriptures but much to do with the way the contemporary community has appropriated those Scriptures and lives accordingly in the modern world — how it treats people, how it treats the environment, and so on. The interpretation that most effectively occasions this challenge may be judged most adequate, at least in part. Interpretation then may be said to be guided by a concern to change the lifestyle of the present-day community.

Furthermore, a classic religious text such as the Bible ought intrinsically to challenge the ways in which it is traditionally read. Even more broadly, religion ought to be inherently self-reforming: a tradition should be suspicious of itself on its own religious grounds. Postmodern theologians suggest that Bultmann may have been correct after all in his insistence that the prophetic-eschatological strand of Christianity (and not merely modernity itself) demands the demythologizing of Christianity by Christianity. This is to say that the Scriptures cannot finally be "captured" by any set of theologians but must continually debunk dogmatic status quo interpretations. This may take the form of challenging a supernatural reading of the text, for example, or challenging the historical-critical method.[89] The appropriation of the text in the modern situation ought to continue to challenge the way the text has been appropriated in earlier times.

Stepping aside from these methodological concerns for a moment, it is important to ask a couple of questions about the nature of the theological project as a whole in postmodernism. Does the Bible play any unique role as a classic religious text? How does the interpreter determine which texts are religiously significant? Do not different texts

---

89. Thus the postmodern historian Brian A. Gerrish makes the interesting argument that Protestant liberal theology in the nineteenth century was carrying on the task of "reformation" begun by Luther by challenging the status quo and forging new ways of looking at the text (*Tradition and the Modern World: Reformed Theology in the Nineteenth Century* [Chicago: University of Chicago Press, 1978]). Far from being unfaithful to the Protestant tradition, these liberal theologians were actually more consistent with the tradition than were their orthodox counterparts, says Gerrish. I doubt that Luther would have seen the situation in this way, however.

have different effects on different people? The answers to these questions provide important insights into the nature of postmodern theological method.

The religious classic is a religious classic because it provokes some fundamental existential question for the human spirit — questions of finitude or fault, of fundamental trust or meaning, estrangement, alienation, oppression, loyalty, anxiety, mortality, or the like.[90] What is the meaning of death? What gives life purpose? What is oppression? Postmodern theology has sought to discern and interpret these kinds of fundamental questions as they disclose a genuinely religious dimension in our contemporary experience and language. That a given text provokes these kinds of questions is the first indication that it is a classic. A second indication would be evidence that it possesses a sense of "otherness" or "strangeness," a sense that heightens the reader's consciousness and challenges the reader's preunderstanding of life in the modern world. Does the text force the reader to ask hard questions about his or her own life?

The Bible is unique in that it poses these types of questions on almost every page. It raises fundamental questions and challenges the status quo continually. It is unique in the depth of its insight. It has not defined the fundamental questions; it merely raises them in a variety of settings, and in this it provides a much-needed corrective in a culture that has demonstrated an inclination to avoid dealing with these issues at all costs. The Bible (and Jesus as the main figure in the Bible) is still religiously and culturally significant to the extent to which it brings unique and essential challenges to the modern world. Its profundity and vitality in this regard help to account for why most postmodern theologians refuse to give up the label of "Christian" even if they have rejected much of the traditional doctrinal understanding of Christianity.

As a classic text, the Bible produces its world of meaning in front of the text as a possible way-of-being-in-the-world. This way-of-being-in-the-world challenges accepted cultural mores (especially those in the West, it would seem). The text thus challenges the interpreter to think in new ways and to imagine new possibilities. This would seem to indicate that the important interpretive task is not to know as much as possible about the original historical context and meaning of the Bible

90. See chaps. 4–5 of Tracy's *Analogical Imagination*.

but rather to know how it might "creatively and imaginatively" challenge destructive mores in our culture. Its being a classic is determined by its impact, not by its historical roots in principle.

The interpretation of the "Christian tradition" (or the "second constant," as it sometimes called in postmodern theology) has likewise manifested a variety of interpretive keys, ranging from "the historical Jesus" to the "original apostolic kerygma" to the "praxis of the Exodus event." These divergent keys, which are meant to unlock the door of Scripture, all compete at one level. Yet at another, deeper level, they manifest the pluralism present in the Scriptures themselves, a pluralism that postmodern theology heartily affirms.

This pluralism is circumscribed by the demand that theologians also make their interpretation available to the entire community of theological inquiry for assessment.[91] What might be the grounds of the community's assessment? The present hope is that some grounds will emerge from the conversation, inspired by a community-wide discussion of theological interpretation. Whether this is a reasonable hope still remains to be seen.[92] In the following pages, we will take a look at whether the yearning for a criterion of adequacy (i.e., a means to determine whether a theology is adequate, true, appropriate, etc.) is consistent with the fundamental commitment to methodological and theological pluralism in the postmodern vision. But I would note here simply that many postmodern theologians do seem to want some matrix that would both permit a common assessment of theological interpretations and prevent any single model of theology from attaining cultural hegemony. It is their hope that a responsible theological community will provide plausible theological warrants for its proposals while also recognizing the culture-dependency of those warrants.

---

91. Interesting in this regard is Clodovis Boff's recent study *Theology and Praxis: Epistemological Foundations* (Maryknoll, N.Y.: Orbis Books, 1987), in which a younger Latin American liberation theologian has sought to provide an objective warrant (arising from the social sciences) for liberation theology and thereby a matrix for the assessment of theology in general. This is in contrast to earlier expressions of Latin American liberation theologians that sought to *proclaim* the truth rather than to *defend* it.

92. There are some who doubt whether any such criteria of adequacy will ever (or should ever) be found in the present climate. See George Lindbeck, "Scripture, Consensus, and Community," in *Biblical Interpretation in Crisis: The Ratzinger Conference on Bible and Church,* ed. Richard John Neuhaus (Grand Rapids: William B. Eerdmans, 1989), pp. 74–101.

EVANGELICAL AND POSTMODERN THEOLOGY

Clark Pinnock and Thomas Oden have recently and independently of one another issued a call for the construction of a "postmodern orthodoxy."[93] Given the constraints we have considered thus far, we might ask whether such a thing is possible. Are the fundamental methodological commitments of postmodern theology consistent with the vision of theology in classical Protestantism? Surely the answer is Yes — and No.

No adequate assessment of postmodern theology can deny the challenge it presents for evangelicalism. One obvious area of insight in this regard is the postmodern critique of modernity. Evangelicals have lacked the critical tools and often the desire to critique the modern world effectively. On the whole, the evangelical subculture tends to be more profoundly influenced by the spirit of the age than resistant to it. The postmodern vision(s) may at least provide enough distance from the modern Enlightenment-inspired era to permit asking the difficult questions that evangelicals have not yet dared to ask.

On the other hand, it must be remembered that the postmodern vision has largely been shaped as an extension (a radical extension at points) of the older liberal theological vision. For that reason, uncritical acceptance of dominant trends in this vision may sound prophetic today but look like little more than theological faddishness in the future.

I have tried to describe the postmodern theological vision by isolating those themes common to theologians who characterize themselves as postmodern. Central among these themes is the critique of culture. The individual critiques brought by the various theologians differ markedly in their details, but there is some commonality in the extent to which the postmodern vision has been energized by its prophetic role within Enlightenment-inspired Western modernity. This has manifested itself in two directions — in an affirmation of the global demands placed on theology in the present era and in a denial of the older foundationalist modes of knowledge.

Theological method inspired by these postmodern themes is hermeneutical at its core. Interpretation in this theological sense is successful when it effectively merges the horizons of the text of the Bible (or of

93. See Pinnock, *Tracking the Maze: Finding Our Way through Modern Theology from an Evangelical Perspective* (New York: Harper & Row, 1990), p. 118; and Oden, *After Modernity, What? Agenda for Theology* (Grand Rapids: Zondervan, 1990).

some other classic religious text) and of the modern situation. Postmodern theologians are uniformly insistent that no dogmatic constraints be placed on the outcome of this interpretative process and that there can be no fully objective answer to the predicaments of the modern situation.

In what follows, I want to enter into a "conversation" with five fundamental methodological commitments of the postmodern vision on the one hand and the parameters of the evangelical vision enunciated in previous chapters on the other. The postmodern "conversation partners" I will be introducing are the postmodern conception of the discipline of theology, the critique of modernity, the commitment to pluralism and liberation, and the use of the Bible.

Theology and Publicness

As I noted at the outset of this chapter, postmodern theology, like modern theology, is primarily an academic pursuit. Its identity has been forged largely in the classroom rather than in the pews. As a result, it is constrained by a technical language as well as by the ideological tools current in the academy. Postmodern theology has clearly sought to be responsive to the contemporary marketplace of ideas. But in order to take its place as an academic discipline in the classic arena of the university, theology has had to strive for a certain precision and differentiation from other disciplines that it has not always been able to attain.[94]

Whatever else may be said of the postmodern theological vision, it clearly is an enterprise committed to inclusion in the university curriculum. It yearns for respect in the academy — a respect largely denied it in the West over the past fifty years.[95] In some measure as a response to the lack of respect it receives across the curriculum, postmodern theology has become a cross-disciplinary study, borrowing its

94. Edward Farley suggests that the paradigm of knowledge in the university is largely technocratic and that this demands quantification and objectivity, two values that theology in particular does not possess. See *The Fragility of Knowledge: Theological Education in the Church and the University* (Philadelphia: Fortress Press, 1988), especially chap. 4.

95. Evidence for this can be found in part in the fact that graduate studies in religion are often relegated to a university divinity school, which, like business, law, and medical schools, is a professional school outside the traditional university undergraduate curriculum. In other words, the identity of theology is now parasitic on the university and no longer central to it.

methods from other disciplines. Seeking inclusion in this manner, postmodern theology has actually landed itself in a state of limbo without any clearly demarcated place in the curriculum it might rightfully call its own.

This dislocation is evident in the cultural critique that lies at the heart of the postmodern vision. The critique arises as much from the social sciences as it does from any commitment to specifically theological principles. Much of the postmodern critique of culture begins with an understanding of secularism that is largely defined in terms established by the social sciences. Postmodern theologians locate the causes of secularism by appeal to purely natural and social forces. This may actually be of some benefit in clarifying the elements of the natural and social orders that have contributed to secularism, but it seems strange that theologians are unwilling to avail themselves of any other tools. Is it really inappropriate to suppose that such biblical categories as sin, unbelief, and idolatry might helpfully enter into the analysis?

Part of the identity problem that theology faces in the postmodern vision is precisely this — that it has no unique role to play in the universe of disciplines. It seems largely parasitic on the other disciplines, increasingly the social sciences. Its methods, if valid, are borrowed from the social sciences and the natural sciences. It stands not as a unique discipline but as a derivative discipline. In Enlightenment-sounding prose, David Tracy puts it this way:

> In any and every case, the fundamental ethical commitment of the theologian *qua* theologian remains to that community of scientific inquiry whose province logically includes whatever issue is under investigation. . . . In principle, the fundamental loyalty of the theologian *qua* theologian is to that morality of scientific knowledge which he shares with his colleagues, the philosophers, historians, and social scientists. No more than they, can he allow his own — or his tradition's — beliefs to serve as warrants for his arguments. In fact, in all properly theological inquiry, the analysis should be characterized by those same ethical stances of autonomous judgment, critical reflection, and properly skeptical hard-mindedness that characterize analysis in other fields. . . . [The postmodern] theologian finds that his basic faith, his fundamental attitude towards reality, is the same faith shared implicitly or explicitly by his secular contemporaries. No more than they, can he allow belief in a "supernatural realm of ultimate significance"

or in a supernatural God who seems, in the end, indifferent to the ultimate significance of our actions.[96]

In one sense this is very peculiar. Tracy suggests that the identity of theology is bound up with self-consciously critical and autonomous disciplines. But why should self-consciously autonomous methods be proper for theology? Should not the fundamental reality for the theologian be a dependence on the God who creates and redeems? And if that is the case, would it not be more proper for the theologian to seek to reflect on this situation with an attitude of dependence rather than autonomy?[97] Should not the fundamental loyalty of the theologian be to God rather than to colleagues? The "new scientific morality" seems to me to be an inauspicious starting point for systematic reflection on the revelation of God because it assumes methodologically that God is not a proper "conversation partner" in theological discourse. God neither speaks nor reveals himself in many expressions of the postmodern theological vision and as a result is effectively removed from the theological project altogether. This seems strange indeed.[98] Even if there were such a thing as a commonly agreed upon set of procedures among most philosophers, historians, and social scientists, why should a Christian theologian give ultimate allegiance to those procedures rather than to God or to the fundamental truths of Christianity?

Ironically, it may be the case that an appreciation of the *critical* stance of the postmodern theologian will facilitate the reemergence of an evangelical theological vision in culture and in the academy. God and his revelation may actually be the fundamental point of departure for evangelical theological reflection, but we must also reckon with the reality of sin and its effect on the mind. Any sense of easy confidence in the dictates of theology is out of place in a world in which sin is pervasive in both the individual and the culture. And for this reason, evangelical theologians must remain ever *critical* of theological visions.

96. Tracy, *Blessed Rage for Order*, pp. 7-8.

97. For further argument to this effect, see Alvin Plantinga, "Advice to Christian Philosophers," *Faith and Philosophy* 1 (July 1984): 253-71. For a sharp though not particularly enlightening dialogue on these issues between Plantinga and J. Wesley Robbins, see "On Christian Philosophy," *Journal of the American Academy of Religion* 57 (Fall 1989): 617-24.

98. This characteristic seems entirely consistent with the older theological modernism.

However, they must engage in a form of criticism founded not on the autonomy of human reason (as in theological liberalism) nor on the historical conditionedness of human reason (as in postmodern theology) but on the normative stance of revelation in the face of sin and unbelief of all varieties, even evangelical forms.

In the face of sin, critical reflection may serve a positive function. Is this not the fundamental lesson of Protestantism — that the reality of sin presupposes the right and responsibility of Christians to ask continually whether they are being faithful to the gospel? Critical reflection (i.e., the sort of reflection that refuses to stop asking difficult questions of accepted norms) must be an important element of the theological task, but it must be a fundamentally dependent critical reflection rather than an autonomous critical reflection. It must be critical of the human overlays on the gospel rather than of the gospel itself. Its criteria of truthfulness must lie not in the consent of the community nor in fidelity to the methodological procedures of the university but rather in faithful reflection of divine revelation.

An important part of this task is the realization that Christian theology is a public discipline and therefore ought to abide by the rules of public discourse. By "public discipline" I mean a discipline that makes claims of truthfulness applicable to all. If Christian theology is public in this sense, then it ought not to be privatized away into isolation from outside scrutiny. The biblical revelation that forms its basis is a public revelation recording events that took place on the field of observable history. It is a historical narrative in large measure. This entails that the claims of theology are not mystical argument based on private intuition. The public nature of the discipline guards against abuse from private opinion that may construe the gospel however it pleases. If a theology is immune to criticism, its warrant has probably been shaped more from private opinion than the public revelation of God.

It is important to the evangelical to be involved in public discourse. In part this means that it is important to take part in conversation with nonevangelicals about the nature of theology. The warrant for the evangelical vision does not arise from the consent of this larger and largely academic community, but the public aspect of this discourse, which evangelical theologians have shunned over the course of the past century, will bring a critical edge to their theological vision — a critical edge that is vital in the face of sin.

With this in mind, let me suggest that after meeting its primary obligation to engage in conversation with God, the evangelical theological vision ought properly to engage in conversation with three different worlds: the church, the academy, and the world.[99] Evangelical theologians can meet their primary obligation to remain in conversation with God by keeping their feet firmly planted in the Scriptures. The questions and the projects that they pursue ought to arise in the first instance because of a radical confrontation of the Word; theological work should not be circumscribed by the larger theological world, nor should it be motivated in its inception by a desire for inclusion in that larger world. Having met its primary obligation to God, theologians can take up their secondary loyalty to the church as the community of the faithful, in which context their communal identity is established. Beyond this, they should be only derivatively loyal to the world and to the academy. They must not shun these public realms, but neither should they grant them fundamental loyalty. Engaging in this fourfold conversation (with God, church, world, and academy) will provide evangelical theologians with opportunities for critical reflection on the foundations of their theological vision, which in turn will facilitate the difficult task of assessing the degree to which that theological vision maintains its fidelity to the Scriptures and its awareness of the human overlays that are placed on the Scriptures.

We should note that the evangelical theologian has significantly different motives for carrying out this "conversation" in the public realm than does the postmodern theologian. Postmodern theologians are typically motivated by an affirmation of theological universalism (the assertion that all religions are salvific/redemptive/liberating to some extent) to enter into the world and specifically into public discussion with it. They maintain that it is wrong to pretend that their only audience is the elect of God, that Christian theologians have an obligation to bring their redemptive wisdom to the table along with representatives of all the other religions of the world. The evangelical might agree that it is a good thing to come to the table, but not for that reason. The evangelical theological framework is not driven by the conviction of universalism. In fact it is driven by just the opposite — exclusivism with respect to

99. For an endorsement of conversation with these three publics in the postmodern context, see Tracy, *Analogical Imagination,* chaps. 1-2. David F. Wells has presented a summary endorsement in the evangelical context in an unpublished paper entitled "Theology in Culture: The Fragmenting Vision." I discuss these three publics in greater detail in Chap. 8 herein.

redemptive truth. As a result, it is driven by a desire to uncover the deceptive influences of sin, whatever their source may be — personal, cultural, traditional, or the like. And such influences are most easily detected in encounters with people who are different. This provides their motivation to be involved in the public discourse of the academy and the world.

An addendum is important here. The impulse to be engaged in the public discourse of the academy and society should be theologically and not apologetically motivated. That is to say, the warrant for doing theology in a specifically evangelical fashion is not grounded in the success that that kind of theological vision enjoys in the nonevangelical community. Contrary to the Enlightenment ideal, it is not the case that theological arguments are "adequate" only when "reasonable persons" recognize them as reasonable.[100] Theological arguments are adequate when they are faithful to the revelation of God. But that is not to say that we might not enter into discussion with those who differ with us in order to facilitate an assessment of our faithfulness.

Theology and the Critique of Modernity

One of the most helpful things that has arisen in the public conversation concerning theology is the growing awareness of the profound influence of modernity on theological visions, including the evangelical vision over the past two centuries. With respect to the peculiar shape of the modern evangelical theological framework, this perception did not arise among evangelical theologians themselves, who have been in relative hibernation during the past fifty years.[101] Rather, it emerged among evangelical historians and social scientists who have recently appropriated the modern critical tools of their disciplines.[102] Modern historiographical insights have helped evangelicals understand their own cul-

100. The inverse of this principle is more obviously fallacious — A theological argument is inadequate if it is the case that not all "reasonable persons" (normally defined as good and upstanding university professors) will recognize them as reasonable. In the jargon of the academy, I am arguing for a logical notion of epistemic justification and against a purely social notion of epistemic justification.

101. It may be added that evangelical apologists tended to be even more deeply in hibernation — with some notable exceptions, such as C. S. Lewis and Francis Schaeffer.

102. I have in mind here the penetrating criticisms of the movement offered by evangelical historians George Marsden, Nathan Hatch, and Mark Noll and by evangelical social scientists Robert Wuthnow and James Hunter.

tural roots, and the social sciences have offered categories that help establish the place of the theological subculture of evangelicalism within the larger matrix of Western culture. These are not substitutes for theological categories but complements to them. In somewhat startling and at times disturbing ways, evangelicals have begun to see themselves in the mirror and learned that parts of their identity are profoundly rooted in their culture.

One might add that the encounter with non-Western cultures has also helped American evangelicals to understand their peculiar cultural matrix. Missionary anthropology has proved a useful tool in the evaluation of cultural influences when American evangelicals have sought to present the gospel in other societies. It is not an exaggeration to suggest that earlier efforts to contextualize the evangelical message were often haphazard and seldom consciously evaluated. Proclaiming the gospel on foreign soil, evangelicals often assumed that the values of the Bible were identical with those of the white North American middle class — including a fascination with the self, a reliance on technology, and an eschatological hope of prosperity.

In the encounter with the critique of modernity by postmodern theology, evangelicals may actually begin to set about the project of contextualization in a more controlled and deliberate fashion. The values of any cultural context should never be identified strictly with the values of the gospel, even though the gospel by necessity must go into all cultures with a cultural garb. For this reason it is desperately necessary to recognize those elements of evangelical theology and practice rooted in modern American culture as opposed to those rooted in Scripture. A closer analysis of the biblical text may be part of that story, but another important part of the story lies in the nuanced evaluation of modernity, a task that may be facilitated by the postmodern critique of modernity.

As we have seen, this critique begins with an evaluation of the Enlightenment ideal of the scholar as an objective, detached, and disinterested observer. Enlightenment-inspired scholars found truth in the impersonal and scientific approach to life. Freed from the oppressive weight of established authorities, they introduced new authorities of their own — the methods of rational and scientific inquiry originating in the Enlightenment paradigm. The "enlightened" scholar was a "modern pagan" who sought to retrieve classical paganism's restrained and rational attitude toward the possibilities of self-fulfillment. And it was assumed that the surest way to achieve this goal was through the wholesale application of scientific method to natural and social reality.[103]

Theology was reduced in large measure to a study of the history of religions. The eschatological hope of the Enlightenment ideal lay in its optimistic view of humanity's capacity both to find and solve its own problems. Postmodern thinkers have persuasively argued that we as a civilization are no richer as a result of this strategy than we were previous to it. There are no fewer wars, no fewer torn families, no fewer suicides. Culture's hope in its own raw native abilities has foundered on the rock of reality.

For a time evangelicals imbibed some of this Enlightenment ideal as well. They sought to give theology the appearance of a science and were optimistic about the emergence of those great Enlightenment-inspired creations democracy and the market economy. This evangelical cultural optimism ebbed markedly during the modernist-fundamentalist wars of the 1920s, but it was strangely resurrected during the cold war period. Evangelicals in the 1870s and the 1970s both foresaw a nation that would return to its Christian roots and thereby more nearly achieve its manifest destiny. In both these periods the evangelical movement lost its prophetic edge. It is no accident that this happened when it ceased to challenge accepted cultural mores of democracy and the market economy. This is not to suggest that democracy and the free market ought to be abandoned or criticized from the vantage point of another competing political and/or economic system; it is simply to suggest that evangelicals have to come to grips with the fact that democracy and the free-market economy, like all social, political, and economic systems, are flawed as a result of the fall. An illustration may help explain.

Modern evangelicalism is in part characterized by a deeply populist impulse rooted in the democratic ideals of the West. Theology is presumed to be for the people, by the people, and of the people. In determining what it is that the Bible is saying, popular consent has become the final acceptable authority, and those who most clearly have popular consent (the revivalists of the 1870s and the TV preachers of the 1970s)

103. Harvey Cox's influential work *The Secular City: Secularization and Urbanization in Theological Perspective* (New York: Macmillan, 1965) may be best understood as a theological affirmation of this vision of secularism (which is why it created such a stir originally). Cox argued that the historical basis for the secular world can actually be found in the Bible and that the secularity of the present age is a good and healthy situation.

are therefore the most authoritative. The result is that biblical authority is now filtered through the pronouncements of a populist set of popes. As George Lindbeck notes, "Playing fast and loose with the Bible needed a liberal audience in the days of Norman Vincent Peale, but now, as the case of Robert Schuller indicates, professed conservatives eat it up."[104]

We should also take note of the way in which the nature of evangelical theological discourse has changed in the modern era. It has been well chronicled that evangelicalism was at the forefront of the transition during the past century from a print-based society to an image-based society.[105] Less noticed has been the abandonment of sustained rational inquiry, a virtue in the earlier print-based society. Evangelicals now seem content with thinking in fragments and pictures. They engage far less in argumentation on the basis of closely reasoned biblical demonstration and engage far more in attempts to persuade with appeals to word-pictures and stories from current cultural circumstances. The theological thinking of evangelicalism is too often simplistic and superficial. Complexity is shunned and sometimes actually denounced as a vice. Those who would construct an evangelical theological framework must be fully aware of this situation and associated problems created by the evangelicals' attachment to a modern, technologically inspired, image-based culture.

Liberal theology always struggled with the transition to an image-based culture. It never seemed to come to grips with television, and in recent times it has quite successfully led the criticism of the evangelical televangelists. But the postmodern critique has moved this challenge a step further. Questioning the unflinching confidence in modern science that has long characterized Enlightenment-inspired cultures, it has refused to hang its own hopes on modern technology. It has raised doubts about how value-free science and technology really are and similarly critiqued the attendant political and economic systems of modernity. Evangelicals would do well to pay heed.

But while the postmodern critique of modernity may be helpful to the evangelical theologian at significant points, it should also be resisted at several points. Having critiqued secularism, many postmoderns have proposed replacing it with a religious secularism that in many ways is little

---

104. Lindbeck, "The Church's Mission to a Postmodern Culture," in *Postmodern Theology*, p. 45.

105. For a perceptive analysis of this transition, see Neil Postman, *Amusing Ourselves to Death: Public Discourse in the Age of Show Business* (New York: Viking Press, 1985).

different from the secularism that they condemn. While the postmoderns inveigh against the radical this-worldliness of Enlightenment secularism, they have not shown any interest in returning to the sort of supernaturalism that lies at the very heart of the evangelical framework. They have criticized modernity's stress on the temporal, the here-and-now, the immediate, the sensate of this world of space and time, but they still maintain that all things are relative, mortal, conditioned, and finite. The distinctive hope of the postmodern is that even though these fundamental tenets of secularism are true, life is still meaningful. As David Tracy characteristically says of postmodern theologians, "They believe that neither secularism nor supernaturalism can adequately reflect or appropriately ensure our commitment to final [human] worthwhileness."[106]

The postmoderns object to the way in which the secular model carried out its critique of traditional Christianity: it presumed that it could conduct its business within a framework of value-free inquiry. The postmoderns insist that no such critique can be value-free. This is not to say that the postmoderns have abandoned the critique, however. Indeed, they pursue it vigorously; they simply assume a value-laden posture in doing so — a posture laden with the values of the morally enlightened academic.

The death-of-God theologians argued that theology does not need the concept of "God," especially a God who creates, sustains, governs, and redeems the world. Postmodern theologians often retain the symbol of "God" to which the ancient creeds attest, although they radically reinterpret it on the basis of their own moral norms. The postmodern "God" stands on the side of the oppressed against the oppressor, on the side of the Two-Thirds World against the West, on the side of females against males, and so on. This moral critique (or "ideological critique," as it is sometimes called) of the traditional concept of God occurs not from the neutral platform of scientific rationality but from the admittedly predisposed platform of modern moral sensibilities. The evangelical vision of theology must not succumb to this type of critique.

The disenchantment with Western culture that is so characteristic of postmodern theology carries an implicit affirmation of non-Western culture. The postmoderns presume that they are abandoning the elitist values of the Enlightenment-inspired West in favor of an egalitarian approach to truth. They insist that no one person or group of persons is

106. Tracy, *Blessed Rage for Order*, p. 9.

fundamentally in a better situation than anyone else to pursue the truth (except for postmodern theologians?). In making this argument, they are not denying differences in native intellectual faculties from one individual to another, nor are they denying that one person might be better trained than another in the pursuit of truth. Rather, their assertion is grounded in their understanding of the nature of truth. Unlike moderns and premoderns, postmodern thinkers reject the notion that truth is "out there" to be found. They forsake the correspondence theory of truth — the assertion that a sentence is true if it adequately corresponds to a real state of affairs — in favor of "dynamic" theories of truth. The precise nature of a "dynamic" theory of truth is not immediately obvious, but we can get a better sense of it by looking at its fundamental implication, theological pluralism.

Theology and Pluralism

Each evening the entire globe is brought into our living rooms on television. Afghanistan and Iran are no longer very far away. American neighborhoods also manifest this global character. No longer is the blend simply that of Scotch Presbyterians residing beside Irish Catholics. Nowadays the mix has been extended to include Vietnamese Buddhists and Egyptian Muslims and Indian Hindus among many others. Economies are likewise becoming global in structure. Interest rate rises in America are tied (if indirectly) to fluctuations in Pacific Rim stock markets and flare-ups in Middle East ethnic conflicts.

The postmoderns welcome and embrace the new globalism, and in particular the reality of religious pluralism. They maintain that this pluralism has enlarged the moral vision of modernity and challenged the exclusivistic claims of traditional Christianity. We will defer a consideration of the first claim for a bit, but at this point let us take a closer look at the second claim — that an exclusivistic view of truth ought to be abandoned in the face of modern religious pluralism.

Why should we regard the reality of many different faiths as a warrant for rejecting the particular truth claims of any single faith? No one doubts the empirical facts at this point. There are many different religious communities in the world, all distinct from one another. And it cannot be denied that these various religious communities make competing truth claims. Traditional Christianity claims that God actually became a man in the person of Jesus Christ. The Jewish and Islamic communities believe this proposition to be false. But why should one suppose that these fundamental disagreements ought to lead to an acceptance of pluralism with regard to truth? Why should one agree with the assertion of John Hick that

> at its best, each of the great world faiths constitutes a perception of and a response to the ultimate divine reality which they all in their different ways affirm; and also that within each there are to be found true saints through whom the Transcendent shines within the fabric of our human life. . . . Considering them as totalities we can only acknowledge that within each the process of salvation/liberation/ human-perfecting can and does take place.[107]

The great (and not so great) world religions do affirm the reality of the Transcendent, but why should we suppose with Hick that all these affirmations are equally true? There are sophisticated arguments in the literature providing philosophical warrants for such a view of pluralism,[108] but I believe there is an underlying assumption driving all these justificatory projects — namely, that all religions are fundamentally rooted in culture, that the shape of a given religion's unique claims derives in large measure from the cultural context out of which those claims are made.[109] There is no position of privileged access from which one religion can justifiably claim to be nearer the truth than any other religion. All religions begin from that great equalizer, human culture, and that common thread prohibits any one of them from having an advantage in the pursuit of truth, especially if truth is viewed as timeless and transcultural.

The golden rule of postmodernism is "Grant to all other religions the same presumption of truth as you grant to your own religion." All religions are created equal. It is their varied cultural contexts that cause them to develop apparently competing claims to truth. But it remains an article of faith among postmodern theologians that all religions are

---

107. Hick, "Pluralism and the Reality of the Transcendent," in *Theologians in Transition*, p. 61.

108. For a representative selection (both positive and negative), see the October 1988 issue of *Faith and Philosophy*.

109. In *The Heretical Imperative*, Peter Berger has marked out the cultural influences that have brought the modern world to this view of religious pluralism. In his words, "Modernity pluralizes institutions and plausibility structures" (p. 8).

equally situated in the pursuit of truth and therefore are to be treated equally.[110]

This point may not actually be original with the postmodern theological vision. The concept of the golden rule of truth is found in Hinduism and several other syncretistic East Asian religions. This could be viewed as evidence of inequality among world religions, since it would seem to suggest that some are nearer the truth than others (at least with respect to a doctrine of "truth").[111] And yet this would cut across the truth of the claim itself, for if it is possible to say that some religions are closer than others to the truth about truth, then there must be a truth "out there" somewhere to which they are closer. But this is simply to recall a well-worn criticism of relativistic theories of truth: it is logically meaningless to claim that all truth is relative if by this you mean that no truth is absolute, for this claim is itself an assertion of absolute truth. If all truth is relative, then you cannot deny the validity of an exclusivistic conception of truth. If no truth is absolute, then you cannot affirm that all truth is relative. In this sense, a relativistic view of truth is self-referentially incoherent.

More important for our concerns, however, is the postmodern assumption of the cultural rootedness of all religions. This assumption demands a fundamental reassessment of the notion of revelation, as is readily apparent in postmodern literature today. It also calls into question the transcultural character of divine revelation. Edward Farley has offered some revealing insights into theological method in this regard, arguing that Christianity's commitment to a divine and authoritative Scripture may best be understood as a culturally conditioned response to the identity crisis of exilic Judaism in the fourth century B.C.[112] Farley covers very standard ground concerning the "history of religions" and argues that the notion of a divine revelation arose during the Babylonian

110. In point of fact, while the postmoderns grant that all religions are created equal, are equally situated to pursue the truth, and should be treated equally, they may nonetheless decline to grant them all an equal value, since they vary in the extent to which they satisfy postmodern moral sensibilities.

111. I mention this not to take issue with the merits of a relativistic view of truth but simply to establish the point that postmodern theology does not constitute quite so major a revolution as some of its proponents contend. The syncretist (Hinduism being the most prominent syncretistic world religion) has always sounded like a postmodern theologian in this regard, which is to say that the notion is very old indeed.

112. See Farley, *Ecclesial Reflection.* Clark Pinnock says of this book, "I have never encountered a more devastating refutation of historic Christian belief in the authority of the Bible and its related assumptions" (*Tracking the Maze,* p. 31n.13).

exile of the Jews in response to their need for an instrument of community identity. Lacking a state, the Jewish people had to look to some other source for communal identity. Following certain Jewish leaders, they turned to the Torah. Before long they accorded it the character of a timeless, transcultural revelation in order to guarantee Jewish identity regardless of the political situation of the Jewish community. Farley argues that the same sort of strategy was adopted early in the Christian era in response to the precariousness of the fledgling Christian community. The twin concerns of maintaining unity and identity persisted in the early church, encouraging the construction of the doctrine of a divinely authoritative set of writings. According to Farley, the essential diversity of the apostolic writings was subsidiary to the sense of unity imposed by belief that they had all been divinely inspired. Whatever the apparent disparities of the apostolic writings, the greater truth was that a single divine Author stood behind the text. It was subsequently asserted that this divine authorship ensured a hidden unity to the Scriptures that could be unlocked only by those authorized by the original apostles — namely, the magisterium of the church.

There is nothing particularly new or original about this argument, but Farley does make the striking claim that he can make the "Scripture principle" come crashing down simply by telling the real historical and cultural story behind it. Elsewhere, he quotes D. F. Strauss affirmingly: "The true criticism of dogma is its history."[113]

The mere fact that there are cultural influences suggests to Farley that the doctrine of divine revelation could not possibly be true, because he immediately jumps to the conclusion that the *only possible* influences on the rise of a religion are cultural. As a result, he assumes that the telling of the cultural story of a religion provides a refutation of its transcultural claims. But if there *are* transcultural as well as cultural forces at work in the history of religion, Farley's description is only half of the story.[114] One

113. Straus, quoted by Farley and Hodgson in "Scripture and Tradition," p. 72.

114. George Marsden reminds us of this helpfully in the afterword to his masterly history of the evangelical movement, *Fundamentalism and American Culture: The Shaping of Twentieth-Century Evangelicalism, 1870-1925* (New York: Oxford University Press, 1980). "Since God works among imperfect human beings in historical settings," he says, "'pure' or 'perfect' Christianity can seldom if ever exist in this world. God in his grace works through our limitations; for that very reason we should ask for the grace to recognize what those limitations are. So we may — and ought to — carefully identify the cultural forces which affect the current versions of Christianity" (p. 230).

should expect there to be cultural forces at work in the development of the Christian religion, but this is far from establishing that the *only* forces at work in the history of Christianity (or any other religion for that matter) are cultural. Traditional theism has always argued that God himself is actively involved in the affairs of the world. The presence of cultural influences does not by itself prove anything to the contrary.

I am stressing this point because there has been a recent surge in interest in global religious pluralism. The beginnings of this interest can be traced to the nineteenth-century interest in naturalistic explanations of religious phenomena. Marx's explanatory hypothesis of religion as "the opium of the people" is not fundamentally different from Farley's. Freud went to some length to offer a speculative history of religion, and, though the details are different, his purpose was not far removed from Farley's. Hume's attack on miracles incorporates a cultural attack on the primitive Christians as naive and anti-intellectual. Farley's historical reconstruction is far more nuanced than Hume's, but his point is the same: belief in traditional religion can be attributed wholly to cultural circumstances and limitations. In different cultural circumstances, religion will correspondingly look very different.

Evangelicals have too frequently denied the presence of cultural influences on their religion, and the postmodern theological vision may be of some benefit in helping to correct this weakness. However, the gain seems to me small in comparison to what would be lost by a wholesale adoption of the postmodern vision — namely, the reality of the transcultural character of divine activity and divine revelation. On this point evangelicals properly reject the modern (and postmodern) insistence that religion derives in the first and only instance from cultural factors.

I have a second level of concern with regard to this issue of religious pluralism, involving the ways in which evangelicals from different confessional backgrounds interact. There is a growing sentiment among evangelicals who disagree with one another on one issue or another that all such divisive issues should be relegated to the background and that their interest should be focused instead only on the things they have in common. We have already taken a look at some of the cultural forces that account for the development of this strategy (in Chap. 2). Now I would like to take a closer look at the ways in which it has affected the evangelical theological vision.

Apart from essential defining issues, theology has become something of a smorgasbord for evangelicals. Having entered the evangelical theological restaurant, an individual is permitted to make choices from the menu according to personal tastes. Even recent systematic theologies of an evangelical stripe have displayed this strategy.[115] Four basic views are presented on, say, the issue of baptism, and readers are left to decide for themselves which one they would like. Too often the implication seems to be that the theological issue itself is unimportant. More serious yet, evangelical theologians are attributing the origins of theological issues to sets of culturally conditioned circumstances and abandoning them there. For example, an author may trace a given baptismal tradition to its origins in sixteenth-century Protestantism and then end the discussion there, without making any effort to introduce issues of the biblical witness to the sacrament. The result is that the practice of the evangelical faith is impoverished with respect to a whole host of issues, including church polity, eschatology, election, liturgy, the doctrine of the Holy Spirit, and the like.

The fabric of theology is thus torn, reduced to a simple recitation of the smallest set of common doctrines to which a socially defined group adheres. To prevent this, evangelicals must resist the postmodern fascination with pluralism which downplays the importance of truth. The pluralist inclination to abandon the centrality of truth is simply not worthy of serious intellectual commitment, and it has demonstrated its corrosive effects on the evangelical fidelity to the gospel of Jesus Christ.

Theology and Liberation

Liberation is a common theme in the writings of postmodern theologians. Though disagreeing in some of the particulars, they do share several tendencies in the employment of this concept. Normally, they substitute the concept of liberation for the theological notion of salvation in one way or another, translating that ancient theological concept onto the modern conceptual map. The translation of "salvation" into "liberation" has significant doctrinal consequences, however. Liberation is more often than not defined as "humanization" — the process by which people discover and realize forms of common life that can reverse the dehuman-

---

115. For all its other strengths, the recent three-volume systematic theology produced by Millard Erickson, *Christian Theology* (Grand Rapids: Baker Book House, 1983-85), suffers from this serious defect.

izing tendencies of the present age.[116] Liberation strives to treat people as subjects rather than as objects of manipulation. It seeks to shape a supportive community that encourages the process of humanization. All of this is to say that liberation theology focuses on an overwhelmingly this-worldly understanding of the work of God in people's lives.

The deeply social or corporate character of liberation theology is the feature that makes it attractive to the postmoderns. Frustrated with the ever-present corrupting individualism in modern society, postmodern theologians have begun to question the foundations of the social and political order of the modern world and the modern West in particular. Their ideological critique is rooted in the conviction that Western individualism is dehumanizing because it isolates people from their native social structures. It permits and even encourages oppression by condoning the assertion that the individual reigns supreme over all else, even over other individuals. The executive who is climbing the corporate ladder must of necessity trample others on the way up. In a world where everyone is out to claim his or her own piece of the pie, it is inevitable that some will have to settle for scraps, that some will be oppressed in their attempts to reach the goal. This oppression typically falls along either social (i.e., racial, sexual, and ethnic) or economic (i.e., class) lines.

The fundamental methodological preference associated with this conception of liberation (salvation) draws on an essentially inductive and social scientific conception of theology. Theology begins with the concrete expressions of those aspects of a society that impede freedom and humanization. These concrete expressions are then analyzed with the aid of tools from the social sciences. The resulting information serves as the basis for a new interpretation of the religious tradition and the Scriptures. The interpretation of these sources contains elements of both "suspicion" and "retrieval" — a sifting of those parts of the tradition and the Scriptures pertinent to the modern understanding of the oppressive

---

116. This is most readily evident in the material that authors specifically refer to as liberation theologies (e.g., Gustavo Gutiérrez's *A Theology of Liberation* and José Míguez Bonino's *Doing Theology in a Revolutionary Context* [Philadelphia: Westminster Press, 1975]), but it is also evident in works of process theology (e.g., John B. Cobb Jr.'s *Christ in a Pluralistic Age* [Philadelphia: Westminster Press, 1975]), works of feminist theology (e.g., Rosemary Radford Ruether's *Sexism and God-Talk*), and the work of ordinary Western academic theological liberals (e.g., Don Cupitt, *Taking Leave of God* [London: SCM Press, 1980], and Gordon Kaufman, *The Theological Imagination: Constructing the Concept of God* [Philadelphia: Westminster Press, 1981]).

social structures of the particular situation in which the theological reflection arose.

The general parameters of this method include the conviction that the biblical message demands the liberation of all people in the present age. We ought no longer to draw lines of distinction between Christians and non-Christians but only between oppressed and oppressors. The way we draw these lines will depend on the unique shape of oppression that has arisen in the specific situation we are considering. Having accomplished this analysis, liberation theologians are typically quick to adapt and apply a range of social and political ideologies to promote the proper forms of liberation. They have demonstrated a special fondness for Marxist political theory, deconstructionist literary theory, and other ideologies that provide a means to criticize the entrenched social and political order of the West, but these are not the only ideological stances from which the postmodern critique can arise. Nevertheless, inasmuch as postmoderns tend to view Western capitalist consumerism as the fundamental source of contemporary dehumanization, they will naturally tend to root their critique in non-Western ideologies. The challenge for evangelicals is to root their critique in biblical ideology — an ideology that is no less trenchant than Marxism in its critique of consumerist individualism.

Human experience serves as the fundamental touchstone for postmodern theology because salvation is defined in terms of humanization. Harvey Cox has suggested that theologians must "rethink the Gospel from the viewpoint of those who have been excluded from or trampled by the modern world."[117] Theology then becomes the means for explaining how to do so. Postmodern theology has to be "from below" because the gospel is "from below." The postmoderns will brook no compromise on this point — which is why there will always remain a theological chasm between the evangelical and the postmodern theological visions. The fundamental methodological movement of the evangelical theological framework is not from the ground of human experience to the superstructure of ideology but rather from the interpretive superstructure of biblical ideology to an understanding of human experience.

On the other hand, evangelicals would do well to take note of postmodern concerns about the impact of the actual social and economic structures on life. Evangelicals must finally come to terms with the

117. Cox, *Religion in the Secular City*, p. 154.

manner in which the structures of society influence the way we view the world and live our lives. Modern technology is not theologically neutral. It influences the ways in which churches are run and the values of the people in those churches. This must not be ignored. Evangelicals capitulate to the spirit of the age in supposing that their range of choices is limited to various enculturations of the gospel instead of believing that the gospel offers a critique of every culture. The object is not to substitute a Marxist or a feminist or a Latin American enculturation of the gospel for a North American capitalist enculturation of the gospel but rather to see the gospel in its critique of North American capitalism *and* Marxism *and* feminism *and* Latin American liberation theology.

Theology, Language, and the Bible

Postmodern theologians have been deeply influenced by the "linguistic turn" in modern philosophy that occurred sometime around the beginning of the twentieth century, when the philosophical disciplines began to reflect more carefully on the use of language in the shaping of knowledge.[118] Since the time of Descartes, modern philosophy had traditionally conceived of a person's mental life as consisting in bare concepts or mental pictures. Only after reflection would people clothe these concepts and ideas in language. Philosophers in this century have become increasingly convinced that human thought cannot occur without language. As a result, words have come to be viewed as the fundamental building blocks of knowledge. Recently, that has been expanded to include not simply words but the entire languages in which those words are embedded. All people think and live in a language, and each language imposes its own unique structures on their thinking and living.

The implications of this linguistic turn for religion and theology are vast, especially in connection with our understanding of the ways in which language changes. It is not a matter of reality shaping language but of language shaping reality. To the extent that language is influenced by external factors, these factors are most likely to be cultural. Language does not change when it bumps up against a thing called the "world"; rather, it changes when it bumps up against itself in the form of a thing called "culture." The process is complicated by the fact that culture itself

118. For helpful discussions of this philosophical transition, see the essays in *The Linguistic Turn*.

is in part a function of language.[119] Postmodern theologians refer to this as the dialogical relationship of language and culture. Different theologies may be viewed simply as functions of different languages and different grammars.[120]

Postmodern theologians pursue their reappropriation of the Bible in the context of these sociolinguistic concerns. Edward Farley and Peter Hodgson have stressed the importance of drawing on the whole range of established and new language theories in order to uncover the vast array of meanings and motives that are otherwise hidden in the biblical text. These methods allow the modern community of interpreters to see the text in a completely different light than the traditional grammatical-historical modes of exegesis permitted. Questions of historicity (e.g., was Jonah actually swallowed by a large fish) are still important to some postmodern theologians but only in a tangential sense. Contemporary literary-critical methods of reading the Scriptures free postmodern theologians from the straightforward historical reading of the text that was so common in the church during its first eighteen centuries of existence. Having removed "history" from the Scriptures, the postmoderns "are now able to enter into the intentionality of the writings with a kind of second-order or postcritical naiveté, in that way sharing in their evocation of the power of being and the new ways of being in the world associated with it."[121] The biblical text becomes the window of opportunity through which all sorts of new worlds can be entered. The worlds are shaped by the ideological critique of the postmodern theologian, but it is the text that provides the powerful symbols and images by which these brave new worlds can be enacted.

Unfortunately, this process allows the Bible to end up saying anything the critic wants it to say. Too often the new methods simply provide ways to circumvent the obvious and plain meaning of the text. It seems patently true that these new methods of exegesis are shaped more by

119. These twin assumptions — that language is a function of culture and that culture is a function of language — can be traced in part to the later work of Ludwig Wittgenstein. His clearest work in this area can be found in *Culture and Value* (Oxford: Basil Blackwell, 1980); his most influential work is *Philosophical Investigations* (New York: Macmillan, 1957).

120. For a clear example of this approach, see Lindbeck's *The Nature of Doctrine.* He refers to his theory as a cultural-linguistic view of religion and a regulative theory of doctrine.

121. Farley and Hodgson, "Scripture and Tradition," p. 83.

the assumptions of the interpreter than by the assumptions of the text. It is scarcely surprising that the text inevitably turns out to support whatever ideological conclusions happen to be dear to the critic.

David Kelsey is so bold as to suggest that while the results of biblical scholarship are clearly relevant to doing theology, they are not ultimately decisive, since every theological proposal and every sermon is shaped by a prior imaginative construal of what Christian faith is all about, a construal that determines how biblical texts and other sources will be selected and interpreted.[122] I wonder how these postmodern theologians would respond to interpreters approaching their own works in the manner they advocate, uncovering in them much that they neither intended nor desired.

CONCLUSION

The neoevangelical resurgence of the 1940s and 1950s led by Billy Graham, Carl F. H. Henry, and Harold John Ockenga was built on the conviction that cultural isolation is neither a viable nor a biblical strategy. In the ensuing decades, evangelicalism began to mirror the broader culture in disturbing ways, though this is not to say that it did not foster significant points of resistance during this time as well.

It has become increasingly clear to evangelicals during the past decade, however, that they have to develop a clear cultural strategy, which entails grappling with the impact that culture has exerted on the movement. I have tried to suggest that in this endeavor there is much to be learned from postmodern theology in all of its diverse forms. In particular, evangelicals have to struggle more seriously with the public character of theology and a strong prophetic confrontation with mo-

---

122. See part 3 of Kelsey's *Uses of Scripture in Recent Theology.* Brevard Childs, Kelsey's Old Testament colleague at Yale, disputes this point (somewhat ironically in my estimation, owing to the similarity of their two approaches): "For a variety of theological reasons I find it basically unsatisfactory to assign the Bible a subordinate role within the creative imagination of the church where it functions merely as a souce of imagery without a determinate meaning. If there is anything still left of the legacy of the Reformation for the church, it lies in the insistence that the enterprise of Christian theology must be carried on in an intensive wrestling with the scriptures, without which it can be neither true nor faithful" (*The New Testament as Canon* [Philadelphia: Fortress Press, 1985], p. 546).

dernity. Evangelicals are taking a great risk by remaining silent in the face of challenges from pluralism and liberation theologies. Furthermore, the postmodern use of the Bible might actually encourage evangelicals to think about both the final authority of Scripture and its functioning authority in theology and the life of the church.

Doubtless many evangelicals will be tempted to take the easier route of simply dismissing postmodern theology as a new form of the old theological liberalism. It is true that in many ways postmodern theology is an extension of that older theological vision, especially in its anthropological assumptions. But evangelicals have a lot to lose by abandoning conversation with the postmoderns altogether.

Modernity continues to rage around us. There are no signs on the horizon suggesting the end of the high-tech, information, communication age. There are signs that the human response to these forces may be changing, however. An earlier generation believed that science was the key to the hope of the future. Today that hope is far more guarded. We still see boundless possibilities in the computer, but we are also aware of its dehumanizing impact on culture. New phone technology, beepers, and fax machines have greatly facilitated communication, but they have also introduced whole new levels of stress into our lives by keeping us plugged into the system wherever we go. The world has been gathered together into the global village through mass communication, but in coming closer we are able to see at closer range not only our similarities but also our differences, in ways that are not always pleasant or edifying.

These challenges all find focus in the burgeoning movement called postmodern theology. Evangelicals who neglect either the cultural crisis or this significant cultural response to the crisis are thereby failing to be faithful to the mandate to take the gospel into all the world and failing to meet the challenges that the crisis and the response demand of those who steadfastly preach redemption in an age of despair. Conversation with postmodern theologians will stretch evangelicalism as it has never been stretched before. There is no guarantee that evangelicalism will not break — except for God's promise to be faithful. For a people whose collective memory includes the cross as well as the resurrection of Christ, this may well be a discomfiting comfort.

PART III

THEOLOGY: FRAMEWORKS AND VISIONS

CHAPTER 7

The Theological Nature of the Bible

The medieval theory of levels of meaning in the biblical text, with all its undoubted defects, flourished because it is true, while the modern theory of a single meaning, with all its demonstrable virtues, is false. Until the historical-critical method becomes critical of its own theoretical foundations and develops a hermeneutical theory adequate to the nature of the text which it is interpreting, it will remain restricted — as it deserves to be — to the guild and the academy, where the question of truth can endlessly be deferred.

David C. Steinmetz[1]

INTRODUCTION

IN THE remaining three chapters of the book, I want to offer a concrete proposal for constructing a theological framework and appropriating a theological vision. The evangelical tradition has not been nurtured to think methodologically, and that is why I felt it was necessary to lay the groundwork in the previous chapters requisite for such a methodological discussion. The nature of the evangelical tradition, with its own theological and cultural diversity, underscores the need for such a preliminary discussion to preliminary matters.

1. Steinmetz, "The Superiority of Pre-Critical Exegesis," *Theology Today* 37 (April 1980): 27.

To this end I have suggested that it is vitally important to begin to look outside the contemporary evangelical setting in order to understand the task at hand. I presented the case studies in Chapter 5 and the extended survey of postmodernism in Chapter 6 with the intent of establishing a vantage point from which we might take a new look at the evangelical theological task and in particular to assess the current disarray and fragmentation of the evangelical movement.

It is my conviction that the nature of the theological task has changed significantly in our day. This change has led some evangelicals to think about the theological task in categories quite different from those of traditional Protestant orthodoxy.[2] Others have gone so far as to abandon the theological task altogether in favor of a retreat to an anti-intellectual praxis and absorption into the modern self movement.[3] A quick browse through most Christian bookstores will swiftly confirm the dominance of the second strategy.

The preceding chapters should have established my belief that it is neither wise nor biblical to abandon the theological task. It is not wise because the refusal to think theologically will inevitably lead to the loss of the modern mind, which in turn will lead to the loss of the modern soul. And such a loss would be especially tragic at this time, when the world is seriously engaged in a battle of competing visions.[4] Our world is reminiscent of that of the first-century Christians, when the church was simply one theological competitor among many. The early church was continually engaged in major apologetic battles, as evidenced in the fact that almost every book in the New Testament grapples with some major controversy. The New Testament authors give ample testimony to clear-headed thinking about cultural alternatives to the gospel. This biblical witness should be a vivid reminder to

2. Recent attempts by evangelicals to construe the task of systematic theology look very different from the traditional evangelical systematic theologies of Hodge, Berkhof, and Erickson, for example. For examples of such recent attempts, see Bruce Demarest and Gordon Lewis, *Integrative Theology* (Grand Rapids: Zondervan, 1987); Gabriel Fackre, *The Christian Story: A Pastoral Systematics,* 2 vols. (Grand Rapids: William B. Eerdmans, 1984, 1987); and Thomas Finger, *Christian Theology: An Eschatological Approach* (Nashville: Thomas Nelson, 1985).

3. See Philip Rieff, *The Triumph of the Therapeutic: Uses of Faith after Freud* (New York: Harper & Row, 1966).

4. This phenomenon is as readily recognizable in the politics of our time as in its theology. See Thomas Sowell, *A Conflict of Visions: Ideological Origins of Political Struggles* (New York: William Morrow, 1987).

us that a coherent theological framework is vital to the health of the church.

If we can agree that the theological project ought not to be abandoned, we might nonetheless do well to ask if it might not benefit from being reshaped in the present climate. I make this suggestion not out of a careless disregard for history but, to the contrary, because I am sensitive to the lessons history has for us on this score. Models and structures of theological frameworks from the past should remind contemporary evangelicals that there are other ways to "package" theology than what they may be used to.

If there are stress points in the movement at large, these might be addressed in part by rethinking the "shape" of the theological framework as well as its content. The fragmentation of the evangelical community can be attributed at least in part to this generation's fragmented theological vision. And part of the fragmentation of this vision can be attributed to the fragmenting "structure" of theological thinking in the evangelical community. It is important to ask seriously whether the conception of doing theology by stringing together Christian doctrines like pearls in a necklace might not be undermining the essential unity of the biblical message. As it stands, evangelical theology tends to deal with each component part individually, at best stitching things together after the fashion of a patchwork quilt. There may be interesting patterns evident in each of the individual pieces, but there is no pattern that holds the quilt together overall, other than its diversity. Evangelical theology tends to be as haphazard in assembling individual doctrines as television is in assembling individual images: there is no encompassing framework or intrinsic consistency.

In the final three chapters, I want to discuss the theological nature of Scripture, the movement from Scripture to a theological framework, and, finally, the principles that turn a theological framework into a theological vision. It is important to see the theological project as embedded in the Scriptures themselves rather than as merely an overlay on them, for this will make it easier to see how the theological project can be restructured to more nearly mirror the structure of Scripture — a point I made initially in the earlier discussion of Edwards and Vos.[5]

---

5. This strategy has also been defended in our century in a different way by the neo-orthodox school of biblical theology aligned with the figure of Oscar Cullmann. See *Salvation in History*, trans. Sidney G. Sowers (New York: Harper & Row, 1967).

Such a strategy will also help us to maintain fidelity, in the structure and substance of theology, to the material norm of the Protestant Reformation — namely, Scripture itself.

In Chapter 8, I elaborate principles for the actual construction of a theological framework built on redemptive-historical lines. The principles themselves concern the three interpretive horizons of the theological project — the exegetical, the epochal, and the canonical. In the final chapter, I discuss the process of turning a theological framework into a theological vision by understanding the cultural context that the framework is entering. I pay particular attention here to the biblical critique of contemporary culture and its fundamental values. A theological framework ought effectively to situate us in redemptive history and by doing so provide the grounds for us to remain prophetic within our unique cultural setting. These are the programmatic principles that address the need for theology to speak to its three modern audiences — the church, popular culture, and the academy.

[A theological framework remains constant over time, while a theological vision properly changes as culture changes] The challenge for the contemporary evangelical community is not simply to repeat the theological vision of our forebears but to appropriate their theological framework by means of a new theological vision that is equal to the daunting tasks facing us today in our own culture.[Our theological vision will be different from that of our forebears not because the foundation of that vision (the theological framework of redemptive history) has changed but because culture has changed.]

REDEMPTIVE HISTORY

A fundamental fact about the Scriptures is that they constitute a text with a developing story. It is a story that clearly progresses toward the accomplishment of specific goals. Redemption is an activity of God that unfolds over time. This unfolding movement in the biblical text is profoundly important to the accomplishment of its purposes. We must remember that Scripture not only witnesses to God's redemption but is an effective agent of that redemption. Biblical revelation progresses because it mirrors the progressive nature of redemption. The "story" of God's involvement with and redemption of his people is acted out on the stage of history with many distinct but related parts. And it is vital to our understanding of this history that we take note of the fact that God acts in and through history. He is not simply the grand professor at the head of the class who stands and lectures. He is integrally involved in human history, serving not only as the author of the "story" of redemptive history but also as a genuine character in the story.

The covenantal relation between God and his people has a history to it, and in order to understand the relationship between God and his people, one must understand their history together. Redemption does not happen all at once, nor does it evolve uniformly. Rather it develops with strange twists and turns in separate but related epochs. These epochs are demarcated largely by God's acts and redemptive covenants. The epoch of creation ends with the judgment on Adam and Eve and God driving them from the Garden. The epoch of the patriarchs begins with the divine call to Abraham to enter into a covenant with God and ends with the climactic story of Joseph being placed in a position of prominence by the providential hand of God. Later epochs can likewise be demarcated by the covenantal purposes and activity of God.[6] The central redemptive epoch in the New Testament begins with the incarnation by which God personally enters into history in human form, and it reaches a culmination in Jesus' death, resurrection, and ascension.

The identity of the early Christian communities was rooted in a purposeful reading of Old Testament history. God was preeminently the Lord of history. He was the God of Abraham, Isaac, and Jacob. He was the God who brought the Israelites up out of the land of Egypt. He was the God who gave the Law at Sinai. He was the God who acted on the plane of history. And he was constantly reminding Israel that, as he had acted in the past, so he would continue to act in the future. God had always been the primary actor on the stage of history, shaping that history according to his will, and he would continue to be.

With the incarnation, ministry, death, resurrection, and ascension of Christ, it became evident to the New Testament apostles that history had moved to a climax before their very eyes and that it would reach

6. For a helpful overview of the usefulness of thinking in terms of "redemptive epochs" for the hermeneutical task, see chap. 14 of Richard Pratt's *He Gave Us Stories* (Brentwood, Tenn.: Wolgemuth & Hyatt, 1990).

its proper consummation at the end of time. God had given them eyes to see his plan at work in their midst. They were transformed by this revelation; their view of the world was transformed. An evangelical theological vision must likewise be embedded in the framework of God's lordship over all of history.[7]

The framework of redemptive history includes not only God's actions in history and the revelatory power of those actions but also the divine interpretations that have been placed on those actions in the pages of the Scriptures. God discloses himself and his purposes through his words and actions. It is imperative that these not be separated in the formation of a theological framework.[8] We must also remember that while God accommodates us by using our language, his words can serve different purposes in different contexts. Some words describe, others evoke emotions, still others command action. The purposes of human language are multifarious, and so we should expect the divine purposes in using human language to be multifarious. Not all of the Scriptures are meant to describe historical facts, and therefore not all Scriptures play a truth-telling function. And while we ought not to make too much of this fact, neither should we forget it. I will return to this point at greater length later in this chapter.

We should note one further point in regard to the framework of redemptive history. The Bible neither relegates human beings to insignificance nor elevates us to godhood. God thinks enough of us to interact with us, but he does so by meeting us on our level, not raising us up to his. We remain rooted in history, and yet this neither impedes God's redemptive activity nor supplants his lordship over all of history. He speaks and acts in cultural settings in such a manner that his words and acts have significance for all of history.

7. For this point I am indebted to O. Palmer Robertson, "The Outlook for Biblical Theology," in *Toward a Theology for the Future*, ed. David F. Wells and Clark Pinnock (Carol Stream, Ill.: Creation House, 1971), pp. 65-91.

8. Evangelicals have traditionally emphasized the *speech* of God by encapsulating it in doctrinal formulations. In doing so, they have neglected the *acts* of God. They have ably defended the historicity of these acts, but they have virtually ignored the centrality of their theological character. It is one of the fundamental principles of biblical interpretation in any standard evangelical text that "didactic material interprets historical material." This is simply another way of saying that the speech of God is more important than the acts of God. For a helpful clarification of this point as applied to the writings of Luke, see chap. 1 of Roger Stronstad's *The Charismatic Theology of St. Luke* (Peabody, Mass.: Hendrickson, 1984).

REDEMPTIVE REVELATION

The fundamental framework of the Scriptures is the revelation of the creative and redemptive activity of God. This is not revelation in an abstract sense — a simple communication of certain propositions — but rather a revelation deeply embedded in God's speaking and acting and our hearing and seeing. God does sometimes speak through propositions, but these are not typically straightforward statements of timeless truths. Rather they are propositions that demand the obedience and transformation of all who understand them. They are propositions loaded with implications for a person's entire being, because God himself is being revealed in and through them.

God acts in redemptive ways in history and reveals himself in and through those acts. The biblical record testifies that God's activity in the history recorded in Scripture is itself revelatory of the very character of God. Geerhardus Vos goes so far as to suggest that "the process of revelation is not only concomitant with history, but it becomes incarnate in history. The facts of history themselves acquire a revealing significance."[9] God is not known in abstraction but rather in and through redemptive history as it comes interpreted in the Scriptures. Biblical history reveals, by the appointment of God, God himself.

But God reveals himself not merely as our Creator and the one to whom we are ultimately accountable for all of our words and actions. God is also our Redeemer, bringing redemption in the face of human rebellion. As God's character provides the moral fabric to the universe, it also brings grace when we his creatures reject that moral fabric. This is to say that God brings both judgment and mercy. Judgment comes in response to rebellion; mercy is made manifest in the face of rebellion because of God's good pleasure. Together they form the very heart of the picture of God. He is both righteous and gracious. He acts to bring both condemnation and redemption. His word is a two-edged blade; sword and scalpel, it both cuts and heals.

"God reveals himself in the Old Testament as a God who acted according to principles (promises may be a better word) that would not change as long as the sun and moon endured," said Francis Foulkes in a classic essay. "The people of the Old Testament could assume therefore, that as He had acted in the past He could and would act in the

---

9. Vos, *Biblical Theology* (Grand Rapids: William B. Eerdmans, 1948), p. 6.

future. By such an assumption the whole of the Old Testament is bound together and given unity."[10] This assumption gives unity to the Old Testament and is central in the New Testament in the person and promise of Jesus. He is the fulfillment of God's promises of the Old Testament, but, with the Holy Spirit, he is also the guarantor of God's consummating actions at the end of time, when every part of his creation will finally and completely bring him glory and thereby make his perfect character manifest.

The present generation must understand that God will most certainly be glorified at the end of time. This is the hope of creation that continues to provide purpose to life. We must also remember, however, that we will glorify God at the end of time as recipients of either his redemption or his judgment. At the end of time, "every knee shall bow and every tongue shall confess that Jesus is Lord to the glory of God the Father" (Phil. 2:10-11). The condemned will pay a grudging homage, while the redeemed will praise him with rejoicing, but God will be glorified by both. And in his judgment on those who bow the knee contrary to their natural inclinations, God will bring sin to its proper and righteous end. In this, his redemption will be a perfect redemption, and his judgment will be a perfect judgment. And as those perfect acts are performed, God will be made manifest as God. He will be glorified.

Part of God's glory consists in his redemption of a people for himself. God's redemptive activity is what gives identity to the people of God from beginning to end. It is also what reveals the identity of God to his people. His people know who they are to be because they know who their God is.

Christ constitutes the apex of God's redemption and redemptive revelation. In the New Testament, Christ is the source of hope for those who are his disciples. In its attachment to Christ, the early church experienced the forgiveness of sins before its God and rested in the promise of eternal life with him. Importantly, Christ also served as the source of the church's hope in the face of its enemies. Christ provided his church with an identity distinct from that of the surrounding hostile world.

The theological identity of the church was rooted in the continuing unfolding of the divinely appointed history of redemption through the

---

10. Foulkes, *The Acts of God: A Study of the Basis of Typology in the Old Testament* (London: Tyndale Press, 1940), pp. 1-2.

death and resurrection of Christ. This was the defining principle for the Christian challenge to the pagan world of the first century. God's redemptive history had begun in the Old Testament and reached a climax in the mission of Jesus. It was this consistent thread of God's redemptive activity in history, both in its past development and its present state, that provided the early church with the resources for an effective response to the pagan communities surrounding it.

For whatever reasons, God has chosen to bring redemption to his people in a progressive and epochal manner. This being the case, it should come as no surprise that the revelation of God's redemptive activity also has an epochal structure, manifested and marked in the canonical Scriptures. It would be hard to miss the distinct episodes in the Scriptures. The epochal structure is perhaps most clearly evident in the accounts of three of the central characters in the Old Testament — Abraham, Moses, and David. The vital importance of these characters is reflected in the length of time they occupy center stage in the Bible and by the considerable numbers of references that are made to them and their time periods in the later pages of Scripture. Biblical history is obviously not intended to be an exhaustive account of human history from creation to the end of time. Much is left out, and many seemingly minor events are so emphasized that the modern interpreter cannot but help to affirm the "theological" purposes implicit in the telling of the story. God communicates by emphasizing certain themes, and the modern reader must be sensitive to them.

The epochs of redemptive revelation are knit together because there is one God who holds redemptive history together. The linkage between epochs is evident in the complex manner in which Jesus relied on the central figures of the Old Testament to communicate an understanding of his own person and mission. The Old Testament "story" was key to Jesus' communication of his real identity to his disciples. The earlier epochs helped to "interpret" the ministry and mission of Jesus. It is the connection with the past that makes the present and future explicable.

The Mosaic period contained laws and prescriptions peculiar to its own historical setting, but it also contained important links with Christ. The most obvious link is the manner in which the Mosaic law provided the seed from which grew the later Davidic kingdom, which in turn provided the seed from which the messianic kingdom of Jesus would come. A less obvious (though no less important) link was Moses' plea in Exodus 32 that he might serve as the mediator between God and his people. In this role, Moses asked that he might receive the full wrath of God in place of the people of Israel, who rightly deserved it because of the unbelief they demonstrated in their worship of the golden calf. God refused Moses' request. Such mediation did not take place until much later, in Christ's atoning death on the cross.[11] God revealed the identity of the Messiah in the person and work of Christ, but the process of revelation began much earlier, with Moses and Abraham and even back to Adam. Our own understanding of Christ will be greatly impoverished if we fail to relate it to the stories of Moses and Abraham and Adam.[12]

REDEMPTIVE THEOLOGY

The essence of theology is the interpretation of the history of redemption. Correspondingly, our theological framework must see the totality of the movement of scriptural revelation as progressing toward a goal. No point in the history of redemption can be understood aright until

11. For an elaboration of this theme, see Edmund Clowney, *The Unfolding Mystery: Discovering Christ in the Old Testament* (Colorado Springs: Navpress, 1988).

12. On this point and with regard to the christology of the Old Testament, it is illustrative to compare Benjamin Warfield (a systematic theologian) with Geerhardus Vos (a biblical theologian). In an essay entitled "The Divine Messiah in the Old Testament," Warfield investigates what sort of witness the Old Testament makes to the deity of the Messiah. He gives some sense of the developing nature to the doctrine of the divine Messiah but little appreciation of the manner in which this development within the canon shapes the doctrine itself. He tries to argue that the author of the letter to the Hebrews shows dependence on three Psalms and in this dependence affirms the presence in foreshadowed form of the doctrine of the deity of the Messiah in the Old Testament. He cites Isaiah 9:6 and Daniel 7:13 and argues on the basis of these passages that there is a clear sense in the Old Testament of the character of the Messiah as divine and as redeemer. What is striking here is the unconnected character of Warfield's argument. He gleans the Old Testament doctrine of the Messiah in a straightforward manner from three individual texts. The developing nature of the Old Testament conception of the Messiah plays little role in his theologizing here. The relationship of the New Testament epoch to these Old Testament epochs does not play a significant role in his conclusions at all. By contrast, Vos characterizes the Old Testament witness to the messiahship of Christ as an essential element in its eschatological system and an inseparable part of the hope of the coming of God to his kingdom that formed the heart of the Israelite religion from its origin. See part 2 of Vos's *Biblical Theology*. For a contemporary and more accessible treatment of these same themes, see Clowney, *The Unfolding Mystery*.

its relationship to the origin and the consummation of this movement has been understood. The epochal framework of the Scriptures helps us interpret the present in terms not only of the past but also of the future.

Old Testament history is written theologically. Behind this history writing lay the practice of the rehearsal of the former acts of God. In the hands of the Old Testament prophets, history was instruction in the ways of God. Prophets were interpreters of history and of its relevance for the present and future. History was recorded because history could be repeated — not in detail, of course, but according to the principle that the past acts of God provided the hope that he would continue to be faithful to his people and his promises.

The theological framework of modern evangelicals has to engage this purposeful reading of history. It has to make an effort not merely to exhibit the historicity of the events of Scripture but to provide its own account of the present and future by drawing on the interpretive grid that Scripture uses to interpret events of the past, present, and future. A theological framework dedicated to this sort of interpretation would be able to rise above being a mere set of "dogmatic flags" that warn us about errant theological views. It would provide us with a teleological framework that would point out the meaning in events that might otherwise appear to be "secular." It would attempt to explain why human history is important by virtue of where it has come from and where it is going. It would make sense of the present because it would make sense of the past, preeminently in and through the Scriptures. The Scriptures provide the interpretive matrix that explains human history in global terms and enables us to understand our own role in that history — which, for those with eyes to see and ears to hear, is ultimately purposeful.

Our interpretive matrix should be the interpretive matrix of the Scriptures. It should make sense of the past and the present and the future in the same manner that the Scriptures do. In order to do this, a theological framework cannot simply mine the Scriptures looking for answers to a set of specific questions that arise uniquely in the modern era. It should seek out the questions that the Scriptures are asking, for these remain the questions that are important for understanding the past and present and future.

Many evangelical theologians have supposed that the task of systematic theology (what I have been referring to as the task of constructing a theological framework) consists in the search for doctrinal models and keys that fit the Bible's complex locks and open them up to the reader. This is often compared to the role that scientific theories play in organizing data.[13] Since data can be organized in any number of ways, the important part of the scientific project is to find a theory that renders them intelligible to the modern scientific community. The theologian operating on this sort of model will try to develop doctrines that can render the data of biblical phenomena intelligible.[14]

But this model of the theological framework betrays in significant ways the central insight of the Protestant reformers — *sola Scriptura*. If we fail to link the structure of theology to the structure of Scripture carefully, we undermine the normative role of Scripture. This is not to say that a theological framework ought simply to repeat the scriptural text, but it is to urge that great care be taken to ensure that the conceptual categories of the theological framework adequately reflect the phenomena of Scripture. It is only by reflecting the Scriptures both in structure and content that a theological framework can be genuinely faithful to those Scriptures.

Structure and Content

Theology has typically been divided into exegetical, biblical, and systematic categories — exegetical theology dealing with the literary analysis of the text, biblical theology dealing with a historical analysis of the text, and systematic theology dealing with a topical arrangement of the data of the Scriptures. Often, little attention is paid to the structural overlap of the three categories. In concert with several recent commentators, I want to suggest that the structure of systematic theology ought to mirror in some important way the structure of biblical theology. The

13. This is most clearly evident in nineteenth-century evangelical defenses of theology as a "science," abiding by all the rules of induction and observation of normal science. See, e.g., vol. 1, part 1, chap. 1 of Charles Hodge's *Systematic Theology* (1872; reprint, Grand Rapids: William B. Eerdmans, 1946).

14. For a clear statement of this conception of the theological task see Clark Pinnock, "How I Use the Bible in Doing Theology," in *The Use of the Bible in Theology: Evangelical Options*, ed. Robert K. Johnston (Atlanta: John Knox Press, 1985), pp. 18-34. Pinnock's essay in many other ways is most commendable, but in advocating this sort of approach to the doing of theology, I fear it may actually impede the progress for which he so passionately calls. For reasons I have already spelled out in some detail, I find this approach wrongheaded.

dominant themes of redemptive revelation ought to be the dominant themes of systematic theology.[15]

The theological framework ought to be linked to the actual *structure* of the biblical text itself and not merely to the *content* of the Bible. The questions that the biblical text asks ought to be the primary questions of the theological framework. The dominant themes of the biblical text ought to be the dominant themes of the theological framework. The sense of movement so critical to the biblical text ought to be part and parcel of the theological framework. The organic relations between the different episodes (or epochs) of the Scriptures ought to be developed in such a manner as to envelop the modern epoch and thereby bring the entirety of history under the interpretive umbrella of the Scriptures.

As we have seen, shortly before his death, Jonathan Edwards indicated that he was at work on developing a theological framework along these lines that was to have been modeled on a "history of the work of redemption" and would have been a "body of divinity in an entire new method, being thrown into the form of a history."[16] Though Edwards never completed the work, he pointed to a methodological principle later developed by Geer-hardus Vos — that theology ought to be developed in a pattern that closely follows the structure of the biblical text. Edwards and Vos were both deeply committed to traditional Calvinistic theology, and it was not part of their intention to overthrow the substance of that theological framework. Rather, they sought to reconceptualize the theological framework using categories that arise more naturally from the biblical text. The historical movement in the biblical text is notably missing as a structural element in most systematic theologies, and both Edwards and Vos sought to recapture that movement in their respective theological frameworks.[17]

---

15. "Surely it does not become systematic theology to unravel what has been synthesized to a degree even in the Scriptures," Meredith Kline has representatively suggested. "Systematic theology ought rather to weave together the related strands yet more systematically" (*By Oath Consigned: A Reinterpretation of the Covenant Signs of Circumcision and Baptism* [Grand Rapids: William B. Eerdmans, 1968], p. 29). See also Richard B. Gaffin, "Systematic Theology and Biblical Theology," *Westminster Theological Journal* 38 (1975-1976): 284-88.

16. Sereno E. Dwight, *The Life of President Edwards* (New York, 1830), p. 569.

17. Since neither Edwards nor Vos ever wrote a complete systematic theology, we can only speculate about what shape they might have taken. I have worked on the premise (spelled out in particular by Vos) that systematic theology must be structurally dependent on biblical theology and hence would need to undergo a major change from its traditional categories of presentation.

Unfortunately, most evangelical theology remains caught up in a "topical" presentation of the biblical material that is largely oblivious to the biblical derivation of those "topics." For example, evangelical theologians may be inclined to make a logical consideration of the attributes of God central to their theological framework, despite the fact that a description of God's activity plays a more central role in the Scriptures than does a description of his attributes. It is my contention that they should construct their theological framework more with an eye to what is central in the Scriptures than with an eye to what may be attractive but extraneous categories for organizing the biblical materials.[18]

The topical treatment of the biblical data is proper when and only when the exegetical and redemptive-historical concerns are kept in view. The three theological categories ought not to be discreet and independent sciences, each dealing with the biblical data in its own way. Exegetical, redemptive-historical, and systematic theologies are all integrally related to each other. Each must grapple with what the others have to offer. Exegetes who do not properly take into account the conceptual categories of the systematic theologians may well prematurely foreclose on certain exegetical options in the analysis of a text. Likewise, biblical theologians may well "moralize" a text if they fail to appreciate its place in the redemptive history of the biblical text. The exegete and the biblical theologian and the systematic theologian ought not to operate in isolation from one another.[19]

If an exegete assembles two or three equally plausible interpretations of a given text, it may be the case that the results of systematic and/or biblical theology will exclude all but one option. Similarly, an exegete might correctly interpret elements of the story regarding Cornelius's conversion in Acts 10 but miss something of the richness of the

---

18. I am not suggesting here that nothing can be said about the attributes of God. I am simply suggesting that such discussions have often proceeded badly in evangelical systematic theologies, serving as a starting point or a primary organizing principle, as a ground for the development and justification of other doctrines in the system, rather than as a derivation from the scriptural starting point of divine actions.

19. The specialization of disciplines in the modern university structure has quite obviously influenced the specialization in the theological disciplines. Indeed, the professionalization of theology has extended to the point that professionals are inclined to feel that the work they do has to be independent of other disciplines and even subdisciplines within a larger discipline. On the professionalization of the theological disciplines, see Martin Marty, "The Clergy," in *The Professions in American History*, ed. Nathan O. Hatch (Notre Dame, Ind.: University of Notre Dame Press, 1988), pp. 73-91.

passage by overlooking the larger contextual issue of the gospel going to the Gentiles for the first time. The Scriptures as a whole must be the defining point for all exegesis, and proper exegesis must take seriously the entire canon as its interpretive horizon.[20]

The key point here is that biblical texts do not stand in isolation from one another, depending on an external theological framework to provide some sort of unity. Theology can be found in the biblical text itself; it contains its own principles of organization as it explains the past, present, and future.[21] All of the individual texts of the Scriptures stand in a teleological relation to one another because they have one divine author who has brought the facts of history into teleological relation to one another. And if redemption and revelation are to stand as closely related concepts in a theological framework, it is imperative that revelation be understood in its organic wholeness even as redemption is so understood. To find the interpretive keys that will unlock the theological framework, we must turn not to some set of isolated passages but rather to the entirety of the canon as understood on its own terms. The task of systematic theology is to locate the doctrinal models and keys that fit the Bible's complex locks and open them up to the modern reader — those being the keys that Scripture as a whole provides.

It is the totality of redemptive history and revelation that inform each portion of Scripture and bind the whole together. And since the accom-

---

20. Brevard Childs has forcefully argued against a "canon within a canon" on the grounds that the Scriptures fulfill a certain function of granting identity to the church. This identity arises not from isolated passages but from the canon as a whole. The church's exegesis must therefore arise from this standpoint as well. See *The New Testament as Canon: An Introduction* (Philadelphia: Fortress Press, 1985).

21. J. I. Packer says in characteristic fashion (and with justification) that evangelicalism claims "that the conceptual categories, arguments, and analyses in terms of which biblical authors present to us God, man, Christ, the Holy Spirit, Satan, sin, salvation, the church and all else on which they give teaching are in truth God-taught and so have abiding validity" ("Infallible Scriptures and the Role of Hermeneutics," in *Scripture and Truth*, ed. D. A. Carson and John Woodbridge [Grand Rapids: Zondervan, 1983], p. 327). What is illuminating about this assertion is the scant structural relationships among the topics that Packer lists. The organic relationships so characteristic of the biblical text itself are relatively absent from the evangelical set of topics — contrary to the claim Packer is making. He goes on rightly to suggest that "evangelicalism ought to allow the Bible to speak for itself in terms of its own interests, viewpoints, and emphases, in other words by a method that is thoroughly and consistently a posteriori" (p. 328). I am in wholehearted agreement with this concern, though not with the way it is realized in much of modern evangelical theology.

plishment of redemption was the fundamental reason why the books were written in the first place, it provides the fundamental key to interpreting the texts as a whole. It is the revelation of redemption that underscores every biblical text and therefore ought to underscore every exegetical and theological enterprise that seeks to be faithful to the biblical text.

This is to suggest, contra Luther, that there is no dogmatic criterion that finally determines the meaning of every biblical text. Luther applied his principle of *ob sie Christum treiben* ("what urges Christ") to the question of what books ought rightfully to be included in the canon. And yet the canon itself properly determines what it means to urge Christ.[22] No criterion ought to be admitted that excludes some canonical texts from the meaning of or membership in the scriptural revelation. The interpretive matrix of Scripture is all of Scripture.[23] All biblical texts are related to one another by the redemptive purposes that underlie the canon as a whole. The canon in its entirety gives the meaning of those redemptive purposes.

Theological Narrative

If the Scriptures are to serve in some fundamental sense as the norm of theology and the primary basis on which a contemporary theological framework is to be shaped, then the simple insight that the Scriptures have a "story-like" character will be important. God's revelation was not given at one time, nor in the form of a theological dictionary. The Bible, as Vos reminds us, is not a dogmatic treatise. It is a book full of dramatic interest and comes complete with major and minor plots. It not only reveals God's redemptive purposes but is an agent in those redemptive purposes as well.[24] It possesses great literary diversity and, in its own unique way, accomplishes many different tasks, the giving of information

22. Herman Ridderbos makes this point forcefully in *Redemptive History and the New Testament Scriptures*, trans. H. DeJongste and Richard B. Gaffin, Jr. (Phillipsburg, N.J.: Presbyterian & Reformed, 1988), pp. 36-40.

23. On this point, see Robertson, "The Outlook for Biblical Theology."

24. "Special revelation as deposited in Scripture is redemptive," noted John Murray. "It not only provides us with the history of God's redemptive accomplishments, not only does it interpret for us the meaning of these redemptive events; it is itself also an abiding and for us indispensable organ in the fulfilment of God's redemptive will. Without it we should have no encounter with redemptive revelation and therefore no experience of redemption" ("Systematic Theology, Second Article," in *The Collected Writings of John Murray*, vol. 4 [Edinburgh: Banner of Truth Trust, 1982], p. 4).

being only one among many. If a contemporary theological framework isolates its task as being simply one of faithfully repeating the information contained in the Scriptures, it may accomplish something important, but it will miss out on much else that the Scriptures are trying to accomplish. A form of gnosticism results when revelation is considered by itself, as providing a set of general truths that are to be believed independent of the other parts of the redemptive process.[25]

It ought to be remembered that the book that gives identity to the contemporary Christian is multi-faceted. The Bible was written over the course of many centuries, and its "story" develops progressively. In form it has the characteristic parts of a story — features such as tension and vision, pain and hope, movement and consummation. It is a story with real characters who develop and a God who actually discloses himself on the pages of history. It would be a mistake, however, simply to equate the form of the Scriptures with the form of a great novel. The Scriptures contain much more than simple historical narrative. But it would also be a mistake to ignore the great similarity. The Scriptures have a primary plot running through them, and the Bible weaves many different strands of literature together to form a coherent message. This message becomes increasingly clear through both the acts and the words of God, which are strangely, at times, the acts and words of men. The Scriptures have many authors, and yet they also have one author. Careful attention reveals Scripture to be a masterpiece, complex beyond imagination and yet, paradoxically, simple enough for children to read.

Traditional systematic theology has often employed abstract language to bring greater precision to the vast amount of data and information recorded in the Scriptures, and much has been gained by this precision. But we must be aware that the translation of biblical information into an abstract theological language may take away clarity as well as providing it, if in fact the Scriptures are written not only to communicate certain facts but also to accomplish certain tasks.[26] God's fundamental task is the accomplishing of redemption. The means of achieving this is in part fulfilled in and through the historical Scriptures.

---

25. I owe this point to Richard B. Gaffin, *The Centrality of the Resurrection: A Study in Paul's Soteriology* (Grand Rapids: Baker Book House, 1978), pp. 15-17.

26. This point is made helpfully by Gabriel Fackre in *The Christian Story*, vol. 1: *A Narrative Interpretation of Basic Christian Doctrine* (Grand Rapids: William B. Eerdmans, 1984); see especially pp. 4-10.

The attempt to capture the "vision" of the Scriptures is analogous to an attempt to capture the vision of a medieval tale in order to communicate it to children of the modern era. Three strategies present themselves with regard to this difficult task: (1) one might explain the imagery contained in the medieval tale with the help of abstract concepts; (2) one might try to capture the imagery in the conceptual framework of the modern child; or (3) one might try to help the child understand the imagery of the tale and thereby allow the child to be captured by it. The first two strategies have fairly obvious drawbacks. Most children would lose something if they were simply told, in lecture format, what the characters of the tale represent in modern psychological jargon. The second strategy would likely be more effective, and yet the value system of most modern children would limit their capacity to grasp the challenge that the tale was meant to bring. A far more effective way to facilitate their "understanding" of the tale would be to help them think within the conceptual categories of the tale itself. That is to say, it would likely prove more effective to bring the child into the medieval world than to attempt to bring the medieval tale into the child's world. Transported into the world of the tale, children would be able to enter into its sense of wonder, fascination, fear, horror, and sadness.

In an analogous way, a contemporary theological vision might be helpfully construed as an attempt to take the modern reader back into the plot of the Bible in all its richness and thereby challenge the way the reader thinks about the modern world. Instead of translating out the categories of the original story, theology ought to bring the modern person into the conceptual world of the Scriptures.

Organic Unity

A contemporary theological framework must focus centrally on our "redemptive-historical index," by which I mean the understanding of our place in the historical unfolding of the purposes of God. We stand in a unique epoch of God's redemptive dealings with humankind, and until we have understood the relationship between our epoch and those that have preceded it and will follow it, we will retain a hopelessly fragmented conception of ourselves and our culture. We must understand where we have come from and where we are headed if we are to understand who we are right now. We must understand the unity of the past, present, and future if our lives are to possess any unity and coherence. Our sense of place is dependent on the coherence of redemptive history, and this begins with the unity of redemptive history as recorded and interpreted in the Scriptures.

However, our theological framework must recognize that the unity of the Bible is not to be found in the first instance in the biblical documents themselves but in the continuity of the history of the Creator-creature covenantal relationship (including Israel and later the mass of Gentile believers drawn into the scope of that relationship through the Christian mission). In his covenant with his people, Yahweh bound himself to them with respect to the present and future and obligated them to live by faith in him and obedience toward him.

The unity of salvation history throughout various epochs is considered problematic by many twentieth-century theologians. They see more disunity than unity between the Old and New Testaments.[27] Evangelicals (and orthodox Christians more generally) tend to focus on the unity between the Testaments centered in God's continuing activity. I would suggest that the working assumption of an evangelical theological framework ought to be the unity-in-diversity of the Testaments — with unity being prior to the diversity since it is one God who manifests himself in the diversity of historical epochs. A theological framework that fails to acknowledge the coherence and the cohesion of the Testaments in God's creative and redemptive character and activity will not do full justice to the Scriptures themselves. Nor will a theological framework that fails to grant the historical progression in God's redemptive activity be adequate. The historical development and unfolding of the divine plan is a persistent theme in all of the Scriptures.

One of the fundamental questions with which the discipline of biblical theology wrestles is that of the relationship between the epochs. How is Moses related to Abraham? What light does Isaiah shed on the "day of the Lord" inaugurated at Pentecost? How are central themes in one epoch carried over into and/or transformed by another epoch? How is an epoch understood in its own terms and how is it understood by later epochs?

In order to understand any particular epoch, we have to understand its relationships to other epochs both in terms of redemptive and reve-

---

27. David L. Baker offers the best available survey of the twentieth-century frameworks through which the Old and New Testaments have been related in *Two Testaments: One Bible* (Downers Grove, Ill.: InterVarsity Press, 1977).

latory activity. There is a "flow" to redemptive history that is paralleled in the history of revelation. A theological framework that fails to capture the "organic unity" in this flow of redemptive and revelatory history will likely be guilty of unnecessary abstraction from the text of Scripture. Normally one of two errors is committed by modern evangelical interpreters who take this route. Some overstress the continuity between the epochs (à la theonomy); others overstress the discontinuity of the epochs (à la dispensationalism). I concur with Edmund Clowney's observation that "modern dispensationalism rightly recognizes that there are great divisions in the history of redemption; it errs in failing to grasp the organic relation of these successive eras, as developing manifestations of one gracious design."[28] The theonomic movement rightfully recognizes the underlying unity of the Old and New Testaments but fails to notice the organic progression present between the two Testaments.[29] While I cannot settle all of the exegetical questions that arise in this context, I do think it is important to remember that an interpretive framework built on the assumption of divine authorship in history will seek to make clear the *organic relations* among the divergent epochs of the Bible. This need not result in a bland uniformity or essential contradictions of principles across epochs; rather, it should help the reader to see overarching purpose progressively revealed through the different epochs of the Scriptures.

Which epoch is the modern church in? Clearly, we are in the period between the two comings of Christ, between the incarnation and the parousia — the same place in the history of redemption in which Paul composed his letters. In this sense, we are in the same context as Paul; we share the same redemptive-historical index. Given this fact, the Pauline epistles ought undoubtedly to play a central role in expounding and clarifying the history of redemption for us in the twentieth century. However, it is not proper to interpret the Pauline epistles without due regard for the larger narrative context in which they fit and to which they are self-consciously related — namely, the entire canon. Paul defends his own apostleship by drawing a link to Moses.[30] As the apostle

---

28. Clowney, *Preaching and Biblical Theology* (Grand Rapids: William B. Eerdmans, 1961), p. 15.

29. See Richard B. Gaffin, Jr., "Theonomy and Eschatology: Reflections on Postmillennialism," in *Theonomy: A Reformed Critique*, ed. William S. Barker and W. Robert Godfrey (Grand Rapids: Zondervan, 1990), pp. 197-224.

30. See Scott Hafemann, *Paul and Moses* (Tübingen: J. C. B. Mohr, forthcoming).

to the Gentiles, Paul saw the breaking of the Spirit into the present age as a fulfillment of the Abrahamic covenant (see Rom. 4; Gal. 3). All of which underscores the point that a theological system cannot be constructed properly without due attention to the full canon in all of its organic relationships.

As we seek to construct our own theological framework, whatever its scope and final shape, we can do no better than to follow in Paul's footsteps, explaining and interpreting the redemptive-historical tension that characterizes the contemporary believer's existence by expounding and elucidating "the mystery hidden for long ages past, but now revealed" (Rom. 16:25-26). Our theological framework ought to be conditioned by redemptive history — which is simply to say that with Paul, Luke, John, and Peter, we should look to the death, resurrection, and ascension of Christ for the interpretive key to the meaning of our past, present, and future. The divine and apostolic interpretation of these key events in history forms the theological context of our own times. These events, in this sense, have an "epochal reach" that enables them to determine the way we are to think and to live even in the twentieth century and beyond.

A Note on Method

It is normal to settle methodological issues before making any positive assertions about the actual theological commitments of the biblical text. It seems obvious to many that before one can ask "What does the Bible say?" it is necessary to ask "How do we find out what the Bible says?" Before one does theology, one must know how to do theology. Another way to put this apparent truism is that a volume on theological method ought to appear before volumes on theological topics.[31] Without wanting to supplant that intuition entirely, I think it is important to recall a point we established in the context of our consideration of the Reformed scholastics in Chapter 5 — namely, that methodological considerations are normally postdogmatic rather than predogmatic. It is more often the case that one first establishes the substance of a theological framework and only afterward reflects on the methods used to substantiate that vision. Otto Weber was right in suggesting that theology should have no

31. Working on that assumption, most systematic theology texts present a discussion of theological method before proceeding to the discussion of theology proper.

true prolegomena in the sense of having nontheological, anthropological, or ontological presuppositions that do not share in the assumptions of the system as a whole.[32] Methodological considerations should serve only as a heuristic introduction and should possess the same presuppositions as the system of dogmatics as a whole.

Contemporary philosopher Roderick Chisholm pointed to a dilemma of sorts when he suggested that there are two essential questions to be asked in making any assertions about the world (theological or otherwise):

1. What is the *extent* of knowledge? (What do we know?)
2. What are the *criteria* of knowledge? (How do we know that we know?)

More often than not, it is assumed that question 2 must be answered before question 1. But, in an intriguing essay, Chisholm argues that question 1 holds greater promise as a starting point.[33] Though it is normal to think that there must a *method* for picking out "good beliefs," in fact we cannot decide on a method unless we actually know that it picks out genuine instances of "good beliefs" in the first place. Any method will be relatively useless unless it is apparent that the beliefs it picks out are in fact "good beliefs" — and how can we know that unless we already know what a "good belief" is?

"And in favor of our approach," says Chisholm unabashedly, "there is the fact that we do know many things, after all."[34] He observes that human knowledge normally reasons *backward,* from the belief to the processes by which the belief is picked out. Human reflection is simply the process by which belief-formation is analyzed retroactively. However beliefs may be formed in the first place, it is only on the basis of those beliefs that one is able to reflect on the belief-formation process itself.

From a theological vantage point this is important. As one looks at the biblical text as a whole, it ought to be apparent that certain beliefs (about God, humanity, sin, etc.) inevitably form. On the basis of those

---

32. See Weber, *Foundations of Dogmatics,* 2 vols., trans. Darrell L. Guder (Grand Rapids: William B. Eerdmans, 1981-82), 1:4-5.

33. Chisholm, *The Problem of the Criteria* (Milwaukee: Marquette University Press, 1974).

34. Chisholm, *The Problem of the Criteria,* p. 48.

beliefs, the belief-formation process itself becomes susceptible to critical scrutiny. Only after the process has worked is one able to develop some methodological insights into how the process ought to work.

In this regard, theological prolegomena are not on a different epistemological level from what follows the prolegomena. The fundamental hope of the theologian (and we are all theologians) is that God will work through his Word making himself manifest through the biblical revelation by the power of his Spirit. The theological framework that arises from a careful reading of the Scriptures will in some sense arise because of the faithful witness of the Spirit through those Scriptures to shape the mind and the heart in accord with it. Ever cognizant of the distorting influence of sin, we hope that God will illuminate our minds by the Word through the power of the Spirit in spite of the distorting influences. It is God who breaks through to us, not we who through mental effort jump out of our own skins and become bias-free in our reading of the Scriptures.

All of this is not an attempt simply to baptize our distorted readings of the biblical text in the name of the Father, Son, and Holy Spirit. God does illuminate our minds with his truth — but this does not remove from interpreters the obligation to be perpetually willing to challenge the methodological assumptions that have led them to their beliefs. Granted that this challenge will come from within the circle of beliefs already formed on the basis of their interaction with the Scriptures, it is nonetheless important to remember that these beliefs themselves are revisable. Beliefs do not attain a status of indubitability or irrevisibility simply because they are formed in interaction with the Scriptures on the basis of certain methodological guidelines. In principle they are open to challenge — even to the point that the methodological parameters themselves might be changed.

THE REDEMPTIVE THEOLOGIAN

The evangelical response to the rampant and deeply ingrained paganism of the present day ought not to begin with a set of disparate doctrines that separate "us" from "them." Rather, it ought to begin with redemptive history, which both unites and separates Christians and pagans. Redemptive history begins with the God's act of creation, an event that shapes a collective human identity. When God creates, he shows himself to be

Lord over all of history, both sacred and secular. His lordship is rooted in the reality of his creative act, and we are all absolutely dependent on him as a result of that fact.[35] All human beings are linked by having been created in God's image, and, as the divine image bearers, we all share a responsibility to make God manifest in and through our lives. The "image" language of Genesis 1:26 also points to the reality that we are radically dependent on God. We are only images of the original. Our very existence is derivative from God's existence. Our character is derivative of his, and our purpose is wrapped up with his plan. Humanity remains categorically lower than its Creator and sustains a strong bond with the rest of the created order as creatures. The writer of Ecclesiastes reminds us that "God is in heaven and you are on earth" (4:2). No amount of philosophical sleight of hand can alter this reality.

However, this is only one side of the collective human identity that is rooted in God's creative act. The biblical text reminds us that in all of creation, humankind alone bears God's image. Neither animals nor even angels are anywhere said to be made in the divine image. The principal aim of the "image" language is to exalt the human person. The creation of Adam and Eve is clearly the apex of the Genesis 1 account. The story of this unique creative act is brought to its proper consummation in the Sabbath relationship between God and his human creatures. No other part of creation stands in such a high and exalted relationship with God.[36]

God's creation of humankind invokes upon the person, at one and the same time, absolute obligation and irrevocable dignity. These are two sides of the same coin. One is not possible without the other. The language of the "image" is suggestive of visibility, and therefore it is proper to understand human obligations and human dignity as the means by which God's perfect character is manifested in creation's history. We are special not by virtue of who we are but by virtue of whom we have been created by and whom we stand in relation to. Our uniqueness

---

35. This may in part explain the entrenched nature of the controversy over creation and evolution. Setting aside the merits of any of the individual arguments involved, it is amazing that this controversy has raged for well over a hundred years and shows no signs of abating. In part, the explanation for this must be found in the fact that human identity is rooted in God's creative act, and if this is denied, humans become mere cosmic accidents.

36. Henri Blocher marks out this characterization of the *imago Dei* with great clarity and force in *In the Beginning: The Opening Chapters of Genesis*, trans. David G. Preston (Downers Grove, Ill.: InterVarsity Press, 1984); see especially pp. 79-94.

consists in being the divine representatives on the plane of space and time. It is a uniqueness shared by all humans, and it is this "common first story" in history from which our theological framework for the present generation must be formed.

Contemporary evangelicals must understand this historical trajectory of God's actions as well as the accompanying interpretation of those actions in order to understand their own identity. Without a sense of where they have come from, they will have little sense of who they are in the present or of where they are going in the future. If redemption develops along a historical timeline, then the evangelical corporate identity will be found on that timeline as well. Would that evangelicals understood not only the theological concept of redemption but their place in redemptive history as well.

Interpretive Expectations

It is important to realize that our own peculiar context will influence what patterns we look for and which patterns we will actually find in the Scriptures. Gestalt psychologists often remind us that perception is greatly influenced by expectation. Two different people may perceive two very different patterns in the same picture depending on their respective expectations and backgrounds. The same is vitally true in theology as well. One must be sensitized to cultural and contextual expectations as one comes to the text of Scripture.

The overall design of redemptive history becomes apparent only when one is looking for it. Eyes not looking for a forest might see only trees. The patterns of a design are often complex and hidden to the eye that is not looking for them. It is also true that patterns will not be seen by the eye that has been trained to assume that the landscape is devoid of them.[37]

---

37. This latter flaw is apparent in the following remarks by James Barr: "My account of the formation of the biblical tradition is an account of a human work. It is man's statement of his beliefs, the events he has experienced, the stories he has been told, and so on. It has long been customary to align the Bible with concepts like 'Word of God', or 'revelation', and the effect of this has been to align the Bible with a movement from God to man. It is man who developed the Biblical tradition and man who decided when it might be suitably fixed and made canonical. If one wants to use the Word-of-God type of language, the proper term for the bible would be Word of Israel, Word of some leading early Christians" (*The Bible in the Modern World* [New York: Harper & Row, 1973], p. 120).

Like a great novel, the Scriptures can be read on a number of different levels. One can often gain insight into the text by comparing two seemingly different sections of the story and finding amazingly similar themes developed. Since God is the Lord of history, it is natural that we should find patterns and themes in his redemptive activity interspersed throughout that history. There is a consistency to God's contrary-to-human-expectations activity in redemption. Eternal life is granted through the death of one man. The youngest rather than the oldest son receives the covenant benefits in the patriarchal period. One gains her soul by giving it up. The first shall be last and the last shall be first. The foolishness of the world is the wisdom of God, and so on. Would it not be odd in this contrary-to-human-expectations pattern if God declared *explicitly*, as in lecture form, exactly how and in what direction his redemptive "tree" grew from its "seed"? It would seem far more natural to expect that redemptive patterns are largely implicit in the text, interwoven in and through the "natural" history of the text. Is this not the reason for the frequent scriptural call for those who have eyes to see and those who have ears to hear (Deut. 29:4; Isa. 6:10; 11:3; 32:3; Jer. 5:21; Ezek. 12:2; 40:4; 44:5; Matt. 13:16; Mark 8:18; Rom. 11:8)?

Vos and Edwards sought to call attention to the fact that theological patterns are intrinsic to the Bible itself rather than arbitrary creations of the interpreter. One is not free to find any pattern in the text that suits one's fancy.[38] The significance of the biblical text does not lie merely in the changes it occasions in the life of the reader nor in some chance element in the text that a given reader happens to see because of his or her bias.[39] The significance lies in the reality of the redemptive (and therefore purposeful) activity of God to which the Scriptures are providing witness. The patterns are intrinsic to redemptive revelation itself — although that is not to say that they are therefore obvious to all human eyes.

The implications for a theological framework are important. Doctrinal categories ought to be neither artificial, imposing an order on the biblical revelation that is not itself a part of the revelation, nor

38. In Chap. 8 I argue that this marks an essential difference between typology and allegory: typological patterns are intrinsic to the text, whereas allegorical patterns are arbitrary creations of the interpreter.

39. Radical postmodern reader-response criticism errs on precisely this point. For a presentation of this sort of error, see Edgar V. McKnight, *The Postmodern Use of the Bible: The Emergence of Reader-Oriented Criticism* (Nashville: Abingdon Press, 1988).

wooden, excluding testimony from Scripture that does not fall within some preconceived pattern. The doctrinal form must arise from and faithfully represent the revelatory content and structure that the theological framework is seeking to present.[40] This is to say that a theological framework must be committed to serious and sustained exegesis of individual passages — an exegesis that is itself guided by a sense of the whole of Scripture. Theology will desert its vocation when it divorces itself from either the small picture of individual texts or the large picture in which those smaller parts fit. Our theological framework cannot simply compile the small pieces of individual epochs in any way it deems suitable; it must seek to capture the pieces in something akin to the arrangement of the parts in the original painting. It should especially seek to bring to the surface patterns in the original work that might otherwise not be apparent to modern eyes.

It is important to see that both biblical parts and biblical patterns are necessary to the construction of a theological framework. Theologians should not be content with simply bringing to their readers' attention individual pieces of the text in isolation from the patterns into which those pieces fit. This means that it is important to convey something of the original context of passages but also something of both the "epochal fit" of the text and the "canonical fit" of the passage. A passage in this sense may be said to have three contexts: its immediate setting, its setting in a particular epoch, and its setting in the entirety of God's redemptive revelation. There is a general awareness that theologians cannot do justice to the meaning of a given passage if they try to explain (or use) it without reference to its immediate context, but we should realize that they may do equal exegetical damage if they seek to explain (or use) it without reference to the epochal and canonical contexts.

It is wise to construe the task of the exegete as uncovering the meaning of a passage in its immediate context. Biblical theologians concern themselves with the meanings of passages in their epochal and canonical contexts. Systematic theologians then construct theological frameworks by appropriating the work of the exegete and the biblical

40. I take this to be David F. Wells's main point in his essay "The Nature and Function of Theology," in *The Use of the Bible in Theology: Evangelical Options*, ed. Robert K. Johnston (Atlanta: John Knox Press, 1985), pp. 175-99. Though I spell out the implications of this insight with a greater emphasis on the structure of a theological vision rather while Wells focuses on the content of the vision, much of what he says undergirds the convictions I have expressed here.

theologian and explaining the conceptual categories of the Scriptures to the contemporary audience in ways that are intelligible to them.

In the present climate, a large challenge to theology is the temptation to allow the concern for "relevance" (i.e., a narrow concern for the applicability of the text to the pressing issues of our own time) to dominate the theological framework and thereby edge out considerations of the flow of redemptive history. An evangelical theological framework ought to speak anew in each generation, effectively reminding us of the patterns of redemptive history and our own place within it, which implies an associated critique of contemporary culture. The task is not to remake the gospel anew in every generation but to communicate anew the claims of the eternal gospel on every individual and every culture.

The Community

It is important that we keep in mind the fact that the construction of a theological framework and the appropriation of a theological vision are properly tasks of the Christian community and not of isolated individuals. Meaningful dialogue within the Christian community is essential to this work. We must join Luther and Calvin in affirming that the interpretive task is a communal project. The image of individual exegetes in solitary study with nothing but the Scriptures before them or the picture of modern evangelicals with Bible in hand sitting apart from others on the tops of grass-covered hills are flawed portrayals of the interpretive project. Personal biases are as likely to be revealed as are personal insights when interpretation is simply and solely private.

The communal character of interpretation serves to suppress the tendency of an ecclesiastical aristocracy or an academic elite to reign supreme in matters pertaining to the Bible. The proper province of interpretation and the construction of a theological framework is the church as a whole. Undoubtedly the church will contain some individuals who are more gifted in technical matters of grammar and literary analysis and others who are uniquely gifted in historical and theological analysis. However, the church must be on guard against so isolating these individuals that they operate outside the bounds of the church as a whole. And we must also be on guard against encouraging every layperson to see in the text whatever he or she wants to see. The task of interpretation, like the other tasks of the church, ought to manifest the organic functioning of the body, all the parts being interrelated and dependent on each other. The foot cannot say to the hand that it is not needed; each has its distinct and vital duties to perform. Similarly, those gifted in an understanding of biblical languages have special tasks to perform, but they ought never to do so without a proper purview of the church as a whole.

THE REDEMPTIVE MATRIX: A SUGGESTION

The following is a suggested structure for a theological framework. It still needs to be fleshed out much further and qualified in important ways, but it may nonetheless serve an illustrative function at this point in our discussion of constructing a theological framework.

An Interpretive Matrix of Scripture
Umbrella Theme — The God Who Creates and Re-creates for His Glory

  I. The God Who Creates
    A. The Revelation of Creation
    B. The Covenant of Creation
      1. God as Covenant-King
        a. The Principle of Election
        b. The Principle of Judgment
      2. *Imago Dei*
        a. The Creator/Creature Structure
        b. The Creature as Only an Image and the Only Image
    C. The Glory of God in Creation
  II. God Who Re-creates (Redeems)
    A. The Revelation of Redemption
      1. Redemptive History
      2. Redemptive History Interpreted — Old Testament/New Testament
        a. Authority and Inspiration
        b. Literary Diversity → Theological Structure
        c. Hermeneutics
          a. Narrative — Historicity
          (1) Didactic — Theological Exegesis
          (2) Typology — Eschatology
      3. The Living Word — The Incarnation (Christology)
    B. The Covenant of Redemption
      1. The Covenant Promised — Abraham

    2. The Interim Covenant—Moses

    3. The Fulfillment Inaugurated—Christ

       a. Union with Christ (Soteriology)

       b. The Application of the Work of Christ (Pneumatology)

       c. New Covenant Community (Ecclesiology)

    4. Redemption Consummated

       a. The Final Judgment

       b. The New Heavens and the New Earth

  C. The Glory of God in Redemption

This framework suggests that both a structure and a set of issues are prominent in the Scriptures as a whole and bring unity to otherwise diverse concerns of the biblical witness. It is fundamentally God's activity as Creator, Sustainer, and Redeemer that holds the book together and infuses meaning into its diverse episodes and literature.

The above matrix is meant to offer a theological framework that respects the way Scripture operates not simply as a collection of books but as a canon of redemptive revelation for the people of God. The unity-in-diversity of the framework mirrors the tension of God's activity in human history present in the text itself. It asks how the past is relevant with respect to the present and how the future gives meaning to the present in the biblical record.

The framework may have to be modified in important ways as new exegetical and biblical-theological work arises. Like any other confessional and/or theological framework, it is properly subject to reform and correction in the light of new scholarship. However, the fact that this framework is properly subject to reform should in no way be taken to imply that the Scriptures themselves contain data that may be organized in any number of conflicting fashions or indeed that there are a variety of competing frameworks in the Scriptures themselves.[41] It is tempting to offer different or competing frameworks because of the relative difficulty of subsuming a huge amount of literature in a single interpretive framework. Indeed, this side of paradise we should expect that this task will never be completed. Before that time, we will continue to lack a completely exhaustive framework—not because there is no

41. On this point, I strongly disagree with Richard Pratt (*He Gave Us Stories*, pp. 79-84) and John Frame (*The Doctrine of the Knowledge of God* [Phillipsburg, N.J.: Presbyterian & Reformed, 1987], pp. 206-14).

such framework but because our eyes do not see as they ought and our ears do not hear as they ought. Our hope is that the apostle Paul was right when he wrote that "now we see but a poor reflection; then we shall see face to face. Now I know in part; then I shall know fully, even as I am fully known" (1 Cor. 13:12).

We can assume that an exhaustive interpretive framework will be as complicated and as simple as is the biblical text. Interpretive frameworks must be carefully nuanced to guard against oversimplifications, but they must not lose sight of the fact that it is the function of the biblical revelation to shape the identity of the people of God as they are founded on his redemptive work. We must not lose sight of either the meaning or the purpose of the book.

Before we accept the outline I have presented as a "type" of an interpretive matrix, we might legitimately ask how it was formulated, how it functions in the formation of a modern theological framework, and how it might change the nature of the evangelical vision in our day. To these questions the final two chapters are devoted.

CHAPTER 8

From Biblical Text
to Theological Framework

*A biblical scholar's product may have to be sometimes as dry as dust.
But dust has its place, especially when it is gold dust.*

John Murray[1]

SOLA SCRIPTURA

IF WE want to respect the principle that a modern theological frame-work should seek to mirror more nearly the structure of the canonical Scriptures, we should establish some general parameters for the process of moving from text to theological framework. Our fundamental concern should be to find theologically relevant principles that will help locate those structures in the Scriptures themselves. We have to search those patterns that form the framework by which the Scriptures themselves understand the past, present, and future.

At the heart of the theological project lies a hermeneutical inter-action between the text and the interpreter. It is a kind of interaction in which their respective theological visions engage or intersect each other. It is a meeting between two different "ways to put the world together."

---

1. Murray, "Systematic Theology," in *The Collected Writings of John Murray*, vol. 4 (Edinburgh: Banner of Truth Trust, 1982), p. 16.

290

In this meeting, the interpreters must realize that as they ask questions of the text, the text is also asking questions of them and showing them an alternative way to put the world together. This should force the interpreters to rethink many of their fundamental assumptions and ways of thinking.[2] Therefore, the interpreters are obligated (1) to find ways to find the questions that the text is asking them to ask and (2) to find the framework in which those questions are being asked. How can those questions and that framework be found? How might one let the biblical text more nearly serve as the fundamental source of both the structure and the substance of a theological framework? In this chapter and the next, we will explore a set of preliminary answers to these questions.

Sola Scriptura was a rallying cry for our Protestant forebears. As we have already seen, neither Luther nor Calvin ever intended that this principle serve as the means by which individual interpreters might bypass the contributions of the larger interpretive community, either past or present. The Reformers maintained that interpretation of the biblical text is a responsibility not of the individual but of the community of believers gathered. It must be a corporate enterprise.

There are manifold indications that individualism, so characteristic of the modern West, wreaked havoc on biblical interpretation in the generations after the Reformers. Even so, Protestantism has managed to preserve a sense that Scripture is the final authority for the life of the believer; it has simply failed to affirm the hermeneutical parameters that are properly implicit in the principle of *sola Scriptura*. If Scripture is the final authority, then in some important sense Scripture must be allowed to interpret Scripture — which entails another fundamental principle of the Reformers, the *analogia fidei* (the analogy of faith). The faith defined in any given scriptural passage is to be interpreted by the faith defined in the whole of the Scriptures. The authority of the Scriptures is integrally connected with a proper understanding of those Scriptures, and the final court of appeals in interpretive matters must be the Scriptures themselves. Protestants have given less than unswerving fidelity to these principles, and as a result the Protestant movement has never achieved

---

2. J. I. Packer makes this point, though for different purposes and in a different context, in his essay "Infallible Scriptures and the Role of Hermeneutics," in *Scripture and Truth*, ed. D. A. Carson and John Woodbridge (Grand Rapids: Zondervan, 1983), p. 339. There is a parallel here in Gadamer's proposal that the distancing of horizons (understanding the differences between them) must precede the fusing of horizons; see *Truth and Method* (New York: Crossroad, 1975).

a unified expression. Luther's opponents at the Diet of Worms promised him that there would be a thousand different interpretations of the Bible and a thousand different churches if Christians were to embrace the principles of *sola Scriptura* (contrary to the Roman Catholic conviction that the ecclesiastical magisterium was an equal authority alongside the Scriptures) and *analogia fidei* (contrary the Roman Catholic conviction that the pope alone can define the faith of the church). The prediction proved only too accurate.

My purposes in raising this particular methodological consideration should be obvious. The formation of a theological framework requires both a final touchstone of authority on matters of substance and a final touchstone of interpretation on matters of structure. What we are to believe and how we are to live are inextricably bound up with the structures of belief and life — that is, with how those beliefs and lives are connected to one another. The Scriptures seem clear in their testimony to the actual physical death of Jesus on the cross, but unless we understand the significance of that event, we will miss something central about the message of Scripture. Further, unless we understand the structural relationships between the symbols and events that preceded the death of Christ and the event of his death itself, our faith will be greatly impoverished. It is not enough simply to understand that Christ died on a cross, for any number of people have died on crosses. And it is not enough simply to understand that Jesus died as both God and man on the cross, for then one might declare with Friedrich Nietzsche (and Paul Van Buren and Thomas Altizer) that God has died. In order to understand the death of Christ, we must understand the biblical significance of the event. We have to understand it in the light of the Old Testament covenants and the consummation of history at the end of time. The doctrine of Christ's death is hermeneutically connected with both the past and the future. It is not until we make this linkage that the doctrine will be significant for us in our time. Scripture must serve not only as the evangelical's final authority in doctrine and life but also as the final interpretive lens through which that authority is mediated to and for us.

To that end, let me suggest that there are three significant movements in the biblical text's interpretation of itself. It will be on the basis of these three movements that we can proceed to construct our theological framework and apply it to our present situation. The movement from Scripture to doctrine (theological framework) and from doctrine to the present situation (the theological vision) will occupy us in the remainder of the book and serve as an appropriate context in which to complete our discussion of the renewing of the modern evangelical theological vision.

THE THREE HORIZONS
OF REDEMPTIVE INTERPRETATION

Edmund Clowney has suggested that the biblical text has three interpretive horizons: the immediate context of the book (or passage), the context of the period of revelation in which the book (or passage) falls, and the context of the entirety of revelation.[3] I will be referring to these as the textual horizon, the epochal horizon, and the canonical horizon, respectively.

It is signally important that we take each horizon seriously if we want to understand the biblical material properly. While no horizon takes precedence over the others, each must nonetheless be regulative of the other two.[4] The meaning of any given passage will depend to a great extent on its place in its own particular epoch and its place in the entirety of redemptive revelation. The theological interpreter of Scripture must allow the three horizons to dialogue with one another continually, helping to explain and clarify the meaning of the others.

It is when we keep all three horizons in dialogue that Scripture begins to inform us about what questions it considers important and the framework necessary to find answers to those questions. The Scriptures in their entirety and in their particularity clarify which questions are important and which questions are not. A modern theological framework ought to be correspondingly careful in distinguishing between what is important and what is not. It ought to seek answers from the biblical text that the text itself is asking. And though it might seem to modern readers

3. Clowney, *Preaching and Biblical Theology* (Grand Rapids: William B. Eerdmans, 1961), p. 16.
4. This intuition lies behind Vos's conviction that biblical theology (as a discipline) must regulate exegesis. This is not to say that a given passage should not be analyzed in terms of its genre and literary setting but rather that part of the meaning of the text lies in its connection with the rest of the biblical material and hence that part of the interpretive horizon of any individual text is the entirety of the biblical text. See Vos, *Biblical Theology* (Grand Rapids: William B. Eerdmans, 1948), pp. 14-18; and Murray, "Systematic Theology," p. 17.

that a given passage is asking one set of questions, if they were to approach it from the vantage point of the epoch in which the text is set or from the vantage point of the redemptive revelation as a whole, they might find that a different set of questions is more important to the passage itself.

The meaning of a text like Exodus 32 (the episode of the golden calf in which Moses apparently pleads with God and changes God's mind) is intimately wrapped up with the epochal significance of Moses as a mediator of the covenant and the canonical significance of his action as a foreshadowing of Christ, the final mediator of the covenant with God's people. The epochal and canonical horizons help to determine which questions are important to the passage and which are not. Failure to pay attention to the epochal and canonical horizons might lead the modern reader into the mistake of reading the passage too narrowly — for instance, focusing on the question of whether prayer can change God's mind. This is *not* the fundamental question of the text.[5] The question that the epochal and the canonical horizon want to ask of the passage is who might be an acceptable mediator between God (who is faithful) and the Israelites (who are unfaithful). This is the thread that links this particular passage to the rest of the Scriptures, and we must not lose sight of that as we attempt to build a biblical theological framework.

The upshot is that we ought to be leery of attempts to isolate the meaning of texts from their epochal and canonical horizons. We have to do more than merely skim the surface of individual texts, and we have to look beyond our own immediate concerns as we approach the text. What the modern eye sees as central to a particular episode may actually be peripheral to the episode from the vantage point of the epochal or canonical horizons. The problem here is not that a superficial reading of the text wreaks havoc by infusing it with foreign meaning but that it misses the larger meaning that resides in the text. Since meaning is a holistic concept, and God is the author of the Scriptures, a faithful interpreter must take the whole of God's horizon (the canonical horizon) and the reality of the progressive nature of that horizon (its epochal

---

5. It would be strange if this were the fundamental question of the text given the Jews' hope that God would remain faithful to his promises despite the behavior of his people — specifically, that he would not change his mind about the covenant he had originally established with Abraham.

significance) into account. This task is further complicated by the factor of human authorship, which makes it necessary for us to include the horizon of the immediate passage as one of the interpretive horizons in the theological project.

If the meaning of a text is bound together with the meaning of other texts, then it is imperative that we reflect on the three horizons and the relationships among them.

The Textual Horizon

It is easy enough to affirm that any given passage in Scripture means simply what it says. But it can be a good deal more difficult to determine exactly what it is that the passage is saying, for one thing because of the often knotty issue of its literary features — notably questions about its genre, the intent of the author, the way it may have been used in the original receiving community — as well as issues associated with the two broader horizons (epochal and canonical) that we have already mentioned. The situation is further complicated by the fact that biblical passages have at least two authors (one divine and one human) and hence authorial intention may move in two directions.

Keeping all of these complicated factors in view may be difficult, but it is important nonetheless. I would like to propose a framework for the theological analysis of texts that seeks to take this complexity into account without losing a sense of the essential perspicuity of the biblical text.

The Scriptures of the Old and New Testaments are the redemptive revelation of God. They do not simply reveal truths about the world and God (though they surely do not do less than this). The biblical text is meant both to describe God and the world and to accomplish God's redemptive purposes. Biblical truth is a truth that transforms. We should expect that a great diversity of styles and genres would be required to accomplish the task of bringing redemption to the entire person from the entire Godhead.

Biblical texts contain statements that purport to describe actual states of affairs in the world (past, present, and future). They also offer commands, which are neither true nor false, though they are not insignificant as a result. Rich imagery is often used to capture the mind and to bring home important concepts to people who frame their own conceptual life in terms of those images. The New Testament church is compared to a bride and to the human body. The authors did not employ these images because they couldn't come up with any more precise language. Far from it. Evocative conceptual images such as the body and the bride convey much more than narrowly technical language could. Such language was used to shape the way people related to the church with their entire being. The imagery of the human body suggested that the people in the church were to be organically related to one another. The imagery of the bride suggested that there was a sense of intimacy between Christ and his church. The apostle Paul obviously thought these images better captured the dynamic of the church than more abstract and precise philosophical terminology. The New Testament church was not identical to a bride; Christ did not leave the symbol of sexual intercourse as a lasting sacrament of the church. But the image of the bride did serve to capture the imaginative constructs of the original readers and presumably moved them to think and to act in different ways than they had previously.

This suggests that a theological analysis of texts ought to be careful not simply to "translate out" the imagery and symbolism used in the texts. Far more important for the theological framework and vision is the mining of the imagery and symbolism for the wealth that they convey. It is important to understand the imagery as well as to understand the limitations of the imagery in the original context. A theological analysis of a particular text must be careful not simply to tell us what the text "means" but must also seek to capture the manner in which that meaning is conveyed and the impact it is to have on life. We must not drain away the life of the text by abstracting its meaning. Part of the meaning of the text is the transformation of life that it occasions.[6]

The grammatical-historical exegesis that has traditionally been favored by the Protestant communities has been helpful in focusing on the grammatical structure of the biblical text and its historical setting. The Reformers used this type of exegesis to undercut fanciful and often far-fetched allegorical interpretations that extracted purely accidental meanings from the symbols of a text. It seeks to bring the interpreter back down to earth by more carefully focusing on the descriptive content of a passage,

---

6. This is to say that the meaning of a sentence involves more than the connection that might be made to a declarative proposition. Meaning involves more than mere reference as in the logical positivist's scheme. For a classic statement of the theory that meaning is identical with reference, see Ludwig Wittgenstein, *Tractatus Logico-Philosophicus,* trans. D. F. Pears and B. F. McGuinness (London: Routledge & Kegan Paul, 1974).

"explaining out" the grammatical structure of the text, isolating any peculiarities of the historical setting that have assigned special meanings to words, and evaluating as thoroughly as possible the symbols of the text. It assumes that the meaning of a text can be determined by locating the factual state of affairs that can be described on the basis of the text.

This is part of the theological task, but contemporary Protestants must remember that it is only part of it. The diversity of genres in the Bible ought to draw attention to the diversity of tasks being accomplished through the Bible. The Bible describes states of affairs but it also commands actions, evokes emotions, offers worship, denounces unbelief. We should approach individual passages with the assumption that the text has been formulated to capture the richness of the tasks it has been designed to accomplish.

Kevin Van Hoozer has suggested that we might gain insights into the richness of biblical language by analyzing each sentence (or passage) for the presence of four fundamental factors: the propositional, the purpose, the presence, and the power.[7] Each sentence is *about* something (the proposition); it points to a fact and makes reference to a particular state of affairs. Each sentence also has a particular function to fulfill (the purpose); it seeks to accomplish a given task, such as describing a state of affairs, commanding an action, expressing an emotion, or the like. Each sentence seeks to express the purpose in a particular form (presence). The form of the sentence gives a clearer sense of its purpose; the "vehicle of delivery" indicates to some degree the direction in which the sentence is going and hence provides clues for discovering its purpose. Finally, each sentence possesses a power to accomplish its task — the power being a function of the combination of the proposition, the purpose, and the particular form in which the author has written.

The supposition behind this analysis is that a sentence is a complicated entity and that in order to understand it carefully and sensitively, one must come to grips with its multifaceted nature.[8] A theologian must be

---

7. Van Hoozer, "The Semantics of Biblical Literature," in *Hermeneutics, Authority and Canon,* ed. D. A. Carson and John Woodbridge (Grand Rapids: Zondervan, 1986), pp. 53-104.

8. Van Hoozer does make the mistake of inferring that the diversity of literary forms, and thus the force of a literary unit, should be attributed to the human side of the divine/human matrix of Scripture. It seems far more reasonable to me to suppose that God, as a primary author of the Bible, intends the diversity of literary forms for the accomplishment of his purposes.

especially careful not to look at Scripture in a one-dimensional fashion, as simply a source of information about history or a book of moral principles or even a doctrinal textbook describing the attributes of God. As with the interpretation of literary texts in general, the theological interpretation of biblical texts ought to seek to enrich our understanding of the central purpose of Scripture — namely, the revelation of redemption and the actual act of redeeming. The Bible *brings* redemption as well as *describes* it.

It is imperative, then, that the theological interpreter of the biblical text understand the multifaceted character of the sentences in Scripture as well as the multitude of different forms of sentences in the Scripture. The sheer diversity of biblical genres suggests that there are likely to be significant nuances of meaning peculiar to each of the different forms of literature in the Scriptures. The gospels are different in form and purpose from the epistles, which in turn are different from Old Testament historical narratives. All of these are different from the poetic and apocalyptic literature.[9] The same string of words in these different genres will have different purposes and likely have different meanings. The same string of words may actually be two different sentences. Therefore a theological case for a specific truth must differentiate the way a psalm and a proverb support the doctrinal truth. And the doctrinal truth ought to be cast not in abstraction but with as much "life" in it as in the original biblical texts. This seems only commonsensical, and yet evangelical textbooks tend to assemble doctrines from diverse texts in such a fashion as to make them all look quite the same. A finer analysis of biblical texts requires common sense and hard work — virtues unfortunately not seen often enough in evangelical theology. The literature of the Bible is exceedingly rich in its complexity; a theological framework and vision should take this into account.

One significant implication of this sort of analysis is that the symbols and images of the biblical text should be considered part of the very fabric of the meaning (and therefore purpose) of the biblical material. The Bible should not be stripped of its symbols, rendered into a kind of neutered theology-speak, and then reinvested with symbols from the contemporary culture. This sort of theological translation work subverts the actual meaning of the biblical material. A "literalistic" theology that

9. For a helpful primer delineating the interpretive task along these genre lines, see Gordon Fee and Douglas Stuart, *How to Read the Bible for All Its Worth* (Grand Rapids: Zondervan, 1982).

removes the images and symbols will inevitably be an impoverished one. A "contextual" theology that substitutes modern symbols for all of the biblical symbols will inevitably reshape the biblical message.

This is not to suggest that theological interpretation ought not to be literal or contextual. The biblical text ought to be understood as it was literally meant to be understood. And surely it is the case that the rich symbols of the Bible are used not because the writers (and God) were insufficiently sophisticated theologians but rather because they well understood the power of symbols to move people and to hold the conceptual framework of those people together. Biblical symbols provided the glue for the worldview of the people of God.

The symbols and images of the Bible (e.g., the burning bush, the parable of the sower, the imagery of the bride and bridegroom) are woven into the fabric of biblical literature, a literature that purports to describe the world in a manner *contrary* to normal human conceptualizations. The symbols are often reminders that the world may not be as it seems and that the thinking of the world may be in need of transformation.

The symbol is distinct from that which it represents, but it seeks to draw the reader (and hearer) to that which it represents. The exodus deliverance of the Old Testament is a symbol of the redemption wrought in the New Testament, but it is not to be identified with New Testament redemption.[10] The bread and the wine are not identical with the body and the blood of Christ.[11] The miracles of the New Testament not only exhibit Jesus' power over nature but also fundamentally illustrate and point to the redemption that he brings to his people. He gives sight to the blind, he heals the lame, he turns water into wine, and he raises people from the dead. All these symbols point to the nature and transformative power of the redemption that Christ purchased for his people through his death and resurrection.[12] The theological framework will lose something of its own transformative power if it reduces these symbols to mere historical events. They *are* historical events, but they have significance beyond this in that they seek not only to transform nature

---

10. Some Israelites who passed through the Red Sea subsequently perished in the Judean wilderness as a result of their unbelief.

11. The church's early apologists Aristides, Justin Martyr, and Athenagoras of Athens were quick to defend the church against the charges of cannibalism arising from "literalistic" understandings of passages such as Matthew 26:26-29.

12. See Colin Brown, *Miracles and the Critical Mind* (Grand Rapids: William B. Eerdmans, 1984), pp. 293-326.

but also to transform the human mind. When we genuinely understand the miracle, the way we conceptualize the world is changed.

The symbols of the biblical text are meaningful because they are grounded in relationships that the Creator has established in creation. The organic unity-in-diversity of the human body is a powerful symbol of the church because God has made both. It is important that we understand the symbols in creation that point to the Creator and his redemption, and in doing so it is also important that we take care not to confuse the symbol with what it is meant to symbolize. For example, the language of "image" in Genesis 1 is a reminder that there is a unique relationship between humankind and God, and yet we must take care to remember that the image is not identical with the original. To equate the creature with the Creator would be to commit the sin of idolatry.

The divine establishment of both the symbol and the link between the symbol and that which is symbolized is an important part of redemptive revelation. Symbols root particular passages in the entirety of revelation. God has so correlated the symbol and what is symbolized that the human mind naturally moves from the one to the other. And it is this natural and intuitive move from symbol to what is symbolized that a theological framework must capture and represent for the modern mind.

To the extent that modern readers have become oblivious to the theological significance of symbols, they have cut themselves off from a full understanding of individual texts. Their literalistic and abstracted approaches inhibit the natural inclination of the mind to be carried from symbol to that which is symbolized and thereby impoverish their understanding of Scripture. Importantly, such approaches have also debilitated theology, draining away its ability to motivate action in the present world. Theological exegesis cannot simply translate out the symbols of the biblical text; the symbol must be recaptured in its unique ability to point beyond itself to what is true and noble and right and pure and lovely and admirable. Theology must help the modern person to "think on these things."

The Epochal Horizon

The second interpretive horizon we have to consider is the epochal. The Scriptures possess a unified theological framework, but it is a framework that is progressively revealed in history. God's redemptive revelation progresses in stages, through different epochs. These epochs are distinguished by the different ways in which God has revealed himself and in which his people have understood him. Neither God himself nor his promises change from epoch to epoch, but his progressive revelation of himself and his redemptive plan do take on different appearances in different periods. The seed grows through stages until it becomes a tree. The movement of redemptive revelation is from perfect seed to perfect tree, not from imperfect to perfect nor from flawed to flawless.

The epochs of Scripture do not embody different plans of God, any of which may be chosen for application today. The point of the epochal character of redemptive revelation is that God's revelation of his redemption develops over time. There is a unity within this development because God holds the epochs together. But this fundamental unity should not lead us to minimize the differences among the epochs. In Galatians 3, Paul argues that the Mosaic covenant was a caretaker covenant that made the character of sin evident. In fulfilling this task, the Mosaic covenant was very successful, but it did not bring redemption: it foreshadowed redemption, but it did not secure it. The Mosaic covenant prepared the way for the mission and ministry of Jesus. But we ought not then to look back on the Mosaic epoch and conclude that it contained an essentially flawed covenant that was powerless to fulfill its promises. No, the power of the Mosaic epoch lay in its ability to prepare for the redemption that was to come in Christ. Each of the biblical epochs must be understood in its own right as well as in relationship to the others.[13]

Certainly an understanding of the epochal character of divine revelation should inform the construction of the contemporary theological framework. The first step toward ensuring that this happens should be to mark out the historical epochs of God's redemptive revelation. The most basic division is obviously between Old Testament and New Testament, but there are other divisions. Some of these are delineated in the Scriptures themselves. There are noticeable differences between the time preceding Christ's death, resurrection, and ascension and the time

---

13. I am defending a certain view of the relationship between the Testaments here. Admittedly, this is a matter of some controversy for evangelicals (for a helpful discussion of the controversy, see *Continuity and Discontinuity: Perspectives on the Relationship between the Old and New Testaments*, ed. John Feinberg (Westchester, Ill.: Crossway, 1988), and in making these comments I do not mean to suggest that it is settled. But regardless of the status of this fundamental issue, it seems clear that the relation of the biblical epochs remains a *central* theological issue for the construction of a theological framework. In fact, I suspect that almost all major controversies in evangelical theology could be reduced in the end to a difference concerning the relationship of the Testaments.

following, for instance. The preaching of Acts assumes such an epochal division, as Peter's sermon in Acts 2 and his dream in Acts 9 make clear.

The New Testament identifies several epochs in the Old Testament period. In Romans 5, Paul focuses on the division of time before and after the giving of the law at Sinai, for example. In 2 Peter 3, Peter divides redemptive history into three distinct epochs: the period before the flood, the period after the flood, and the period of the new world to come. Stephen's speech in Acts 7 likewise identifies three distinct periods: the age of the patriarchs, the Mosaic age (the time of the exodus and conquest of the Promised Land), and the age of the monarchy (David and Solomon).

The later prophets of the Old Testament also point to several of these same time periods. The importance attached to the events surrounding the promise made to Abraham, the giving of the law at Sinai, and the renewal of the promise to David are prominent in the pages of these later prophets.[14] Isaiah speaks of God's promises to his people in the time of Abraham and in the time of Moses and the apparent abandonment of those promises in the time of the exile (Isa. 63). Jeremiah points to the continuity of the covenants established with Abraham, Isaac, Jacob, Moses, and David and also points to the discontinuity of the time of the law of Moses and the time when God would put his law in his people's minds and write it on their hearts (Jer. 31–33). Malachi points back to the time of the giving of the law to Moses at Horeb and points ahead to the time of the promised day of the Lord (Mal. 4).

The Old Testament is vast and complex, and the epochal divisions that Paul, Peter, Stephen, and the Old Testament authors themselves marked out manifest different but complementary perspectives in looking at redemptive history in the Old Testament. Each had distinct theological purposes in view and drew divisions in redemptive history that were relevant to their particular concerns. All of the authors sought to draw out the implications of God's covenantal working throughout all of history by investigating the significant differences as well as significant continuities between previous epochs and their own.

14. For demarcations of the Old Testament epochs similar to those suggested by Jonathan Edwards (in *A History of the Work of Redemption*) and Geerhardus Vos (in *Biblical Theology*), see Meredith G. Kline, *The Structure of Biblical Authority*, rev. ed. (Grand Rapids: William B. Eerdmans, 1975); O. Palmer Robertson, *The Christ of the Covenants* (Grand Rapids: Baker Book House, 1981); Thomas McComiskey, *The Covenants of Promise* (Grand Rapids: Baker Book House, 1985); and E. Earle Ellis, *Prophecy and Hermeneutic in Early Christianity: New Testament Essays* (Grand Rapids: William B. Eerdmans, 1978).

In addition to marking the significant epochs, we should devote some care and attention to isolating the central themes and concerns of each epoch. What are the central covenantal terms of the period? What are the particular intentions of the author(s) in that epoch? Why are certain issues repeated time and again in particular periods? How do the central themes of one epoch relate to the central themes of another epoch? Rather than imposing conceptual categories on the various epochs, we would do better to adopt a more inductive method, letting the emphasis of the text be the emphasis of the theological framework and letting the central themes of that framework be the central themes of the biblical epochs.

The Canonical Horizon

Essential to the canonical horizon of biblical interpretation is the continuity between the promises of God and his fulfillment of those promises. This is the principal glue holding the diverse epochs together. The biblical authors frame their writings with the assertion that God has been faithful to his promises in times past, and so he shall be faithful in the future. The promise-fulfillment model is a thread that secures the unity of the diverse collection of these writings. It provides meaning in the midst of present circumstances and hope for future deliverance.

This underlying stratum of the biblical writings focuses our attention on the divine plan of history — a plan that holds past, present, and future together and therefore appropriately lies at the heart of a contemporary theological framework. Biblical history provides instruction in the ways of God. Prophets were interpreters of history and of its relevance for the present and future. History is recorded in the Scriptures to show us how it can be repeated — not in precise detail but according to the patterns of God's interaction with humankind.

Rudolf Bultmann was wrong when he suggested that biblical history is cyclical, a mere repetition of patterns established in the past. He was correct, however, in pointing to the pattern-like framework of the Bible.[15] The present is tied to the past in the Scriptures not as mere

15. Bultmann expresses these views most clearly in "Ursprung und Sinn der Typologie als hermeneutischer Methode," *Theologischer Literaturzeitung* 75 (1950): 206-11. Leonhard Goppelt offers the most extensive and cogent response to Bultmann along the lines I have suggested here in *Typos: The Typological Interpretation of the Old Testament in the New,* trans. D. H. Madvig (Grand Rapids: William B. Eerdmans, 1982).

repetition but as development. The sacramental system develops from symbolic animal sacrifice in the Old Testament to the atoning death of Christ in the New Testament. He is the sacrifice offered once for all (Heb. 9–10). The institution of the temple and the priesthood and the animal sacrifices are not carried over; these elements are "fulfilled" in Christ.

One significant biblical means of presenting the promise-fulfillment model is through the use of typology.[16] Typology is simply symbolism with a prospective reference to fulfillment in a later epoch of biblical history. It involves a fundamentally organic relation between events, persons, and institutions in one epoch and their counterparts in later epochs. The early event, person, or institution is called the "type," and the later one is called the "antitype." A "typical" relation, then, links some event, person, or institution in one epoch to another event, person, or institution in another epoch in some fundamental and essential way.[17]

The typological relation is a central means by which particular epochal and textual horizons are linked to later horizons in redemptive revelation. It links the present to the future, and it retroactively links the present with the past. It is founded on the organic connection of God's promises with his fulfillment of those promises.

In the Old Testament, the Babylonian captivity was interpreted through the lens of the Exodus event. God would bring release from captivity in Babylon just as he had in Egypt. However, the release from Babylon would be far greater than the release from Egypt because the situation was so much more severe: Israel was now in rebellion against God. The new deliverance would be not merely a political deliverance

---

16. The two most helpful sources relating to typology are Goppelt's *Typos* and Clowney's *Preaching and Biblical Theology.* Goppelt's study is more massive and technical; Clowney is primarily concerned with the impact of typology on the contemporary expression of the Christian faith. Both are significant in their own right. See also the relatively recent discussion of this issue by Richard M. Davidson, *Typology in Scripture: A Study of Hermeneutical 'Tupoß' Structures,* Andrews University Doctoral Dissertation Series, no. 2 (Berrien Springs, Mich.: Andrews University Press, 1981). While I do not entirely agree with Davidson's methodology, I do admire his defense of typological relations between Old and New Testaments. See also David Baker's discussion of typology in chap. 6 of *Two Testaments: One Bible* (Downers Grove, Ill.: InterVarsity Press, 1977).

17. The difference between typology and allegory is that typology involves a relationship between some "essential" aspect of the type and antitype, whereas allegory involves a relationship stemming from some accidental or peripheral aspect of the original event, person, or insitution.

but also a deliverance from rebellion and sin. This added deliverance enriched the concept of redemption and offered to Israel a greater sense of identity in that it afforded a greater sense of the providential activity of God.

This points to the twofold character to the pattern of typology.[18] First, there was a repetition of the promise-fulfillment pattern of redemptive history: God would be continually faithful to his people and to his promises. Second, there was a difference of degree between the former acts of God and the new ones: the fulfillment of God's promises would be even better than the recipients of the original promise had foreseen.

If this is true, then genuine theological analysis of the canonical horizon will necessarily involve a consideration of the links of progressive fulfillment between the epochs — of the continuity of the promise-fulfillment pattern but also of the progression in which the latter was even greater than the former. Theological construction must begin to wrestle with the fact that this progressive fulfillment lies at the heart of a theological framework. The meaning of past epochs is invested into later epochs in the Scriptures, and the meaning of those epochs is in turn invested into future epochs.[19] This might be referred to as the "epochal reach" of typology.

The promises of God often have two or more fulfillment horizons, one relatively immediate and the other at some distance in the future. The promise to Abraham regarding descendants and a great nation was given miraculous fulfillment in the birth of his son Isaac. It also reached fulfillment to some extent in the next epoch, the age of Moses, when Israel became a great nation. The promise also found fulfillment in the expanding group of descendants who came to faith following the death and resurrection of Jesus.[20] Finally, it is quite correct to say that this

18. On the twofold character of typology, see Francis Foulkes, *The Acts of God: A Study of the Basis of Typology in the Old Testament* (London: Tyndale Press, 1940).

19. I should restate at this point a caution that Jonathan Edwards raised in this regard. While it is permissible to view postbiblical history in the light of established typology, we should not seek to establish new relationships between biblical types and postbiblical antitypes. To do so would be to embrace the sort of "signs of the times" mentality that Jesus forbids in Matthew 24.

20. In John 8, Jesus tells the scribes and Pharisees that they are not the true children of Abraham, that those who hear and abide by the word of God are the true inheritors of the promises to Abraham.

promise given originally to Abraham will find its ultimate fulfillment in the new heavens and the new earth. The original promise given to Abraham can thus be said to have four fulfillment horizons, all of which are clearly identified in the Scriptures (Gen. 12; 17; Exod. 3; 33; John 8; Acts 7; Gal. 3; Rev. 21–22).

We should also note that there is significant progression between these fulfillment phases. The first (the birth of the son Isaac) was but a taste of the miraculous power of God to fulfill his promises. The second (the rebirth of the nation under the leadership of Moses) seemed even greater than the first inasmuch as the descendants of Abraham received a national identity and a land that they could call their own. The third (the birth of the church following Jesus' death and resurrection) was climactic. In the offering of the ultimate sacrifice of God's own Son, the New Testament saw the fulfillment of the Mosaic sacramental system as well as the fulfillment of the original command that Abraham sacrifice his son. Christ also broke down the national and ethnic boundaries of the Mosaic epoch in his disciples, who were the true descendants of Abraham. The fourth phase of fulfillment (the inauguration of the new heavens and the new earth) will consummate the promise finally and fully in such a manner that "at the name of Jesus every knee should bow, in heaven and on earth and under the earth, and every tongue confess that Jesus Christ is Lord, to the glory of God the Father" (Phil. 2:10-11). God will no longer be present to his people indirectly but, as John wrote in the book of Revelation of the new heavens and the new earth, "'now the dwelling of God is with men, and he will live with them. They will be his people, and God himself will be with them and be their God. He will wipe every tear from their eyes. There will be no more death or mourning or crying or pain, for the old order of things has passed away.' He who was seated on the throne said, 'I am making everything new!'" (Rev. 21:3-5).

Typology is founded on the notions of providence and prophecy. While the type does have significance for its own time, its greater significance is directed toward the future. It testifies to something greater than itself that is yet to come. The future antitype will surely come, because God will providentially bring it to pass. It is God's ability to hold history together that serves as the foundation of typology. The prophetic fulfillment of the original type is as certain as the God who providentially orders that fulfillment. As typology is the foundation of the theological interpretation of redemptive revelation, so divine providence is the foundation of the theological interpretation of typology.

Adam was a type of Christ in his federal representation of humankind.[21] As Paul is quick to remind his readers in Romans 5, the link is not simply one of similarity. There are significant and important differences, all the more important because of the similarities. Both Adam and Christ act on behalf of those whom they represent. Through Adam, condemnation and death spread to all people, whereas through Christ, justification and life spread to the many.

Moses was also a type of Christ in his federal representation of the people of God. Exodus 32 tells how Moses offered himself up on behalf of the people. The Israelites had sinned greatly in constructing the golden calf. Moses asked that his own name might be blotted out of the book of life in order that the Israelites might be forgiven their sin. The similarities with Christ are striking, and yet so are the differences. God did not accept Moses' offering, vowing instead to avenge the sin of the people in due course. Even the author of Deuteronomy seems to have been well aware that there would be another greater than Moses who would bring God's word to his people (18:15-19). The letter to the Hebrews reflects on the respective leadership of Moses and Christ, concluding that "Moses was faithful as a servant in all God's house, testifying to what would be said in the future. But Christ is faithful as a son over God's house. And we are his house, if we hold on to our courage and the hope of which we boast" (3:5-6).

It is the unmistakable conviction of the New Testament that Moses prepared the way for Christ. Moses pointed to Christ. This was no mere accident of history but was the outworking of the providential plan by which God brought redemption to his people. The concept of providence is what lies behind the New Testament connection of Moses and Christ, and providence ought therefore to be foundational in our theological framework as well.

Christ is also connected with the past through the figures of David and Solomon. David stands as the Lord's anointed to rule in power and justice. Solomon was the prince of peace and the representative of the highest wisdom in ancient Israel. It was clear that the promises to David would be fulfilled in the heir to the throne — though, as the New Testament reminds us, not in the line of the monarchy that immediately followed David (Matt. 22:41-41; Acts 2:22-36). The "anointed one" of

21. The Greek term τύπος, translated in the Revised Standard Version as "type," is used directly in this regard in Rom. 5:14.

the line of David was often described as one greater than David. Christ inherited those promises and brought them to their fulfillment. Jesus clearly understood his own mission and ministry in light of David and Solomon. He was the true king, and his kingdom will know no end. There was no more dominant motif in the ministry of Jesus than that of the "kingdom of God."[22] The original type of this kingdom was most surely the kingdom of David. Christ's kingdom shall be perfect, though David's kingdom was not. The inauguration of Christ's kingdom occurred at Pentecost in Acts as a result of the ascension of Jesus recorded in Acts 1 and as predicted in John 14–16. When Jesus ascended to heaven, he ascended to be crowned king. His kingdom was established now in the hearts of those whom he called and calls to himself and will later be established in the new heavens and the new earth. Unless we understand the earlier kingdom (David's and Solomon's), we will not understand the king of kings or the present and future shape of his kingdom.[23]

Canonical analysis seeks to bring to light this sort of historical matrix that holds biblical history together and provides the conceptual framework through which all of history is to be understood. The Old Testament believers hoped not only that God would continue to act as he had in the past but that he would do so on an unprecedented scale. The faith of Israel was forward-looking — specifically, looking forward to the fulfillment of the promises made to Abraham and the promises made to David. People looked forward to something more than a mere repetition of God's acts in history, for this would have brought only joy mixed with suffering. They awaited the "day of the Lord" when Israel would be exalted more gloriously than ever before and the other nations would be judged.

Old Testament passages are often "recast" in the New Testament. This is not to say that the New Testament authors dismissed the original event of redemptive significance as no longer useful; rather, in light of the new revelation, they moved aspects that had formerly gone unnoticed into the foreground, thereby creating a broader horizon of interpretation. In this sense, they completed or refined the meaning of the original

---

22. Matthew, writing to a Jewish audience that would not pronounce the name of God, used the phrase "kingdom of heaven" predominantly but equivalently.

23. Other possible types of Christ include the temple, the tabernacle, the passover, creation, Noah, and Jonah. The list could go on, and it would be greatly enriching to the theological project if these were to be explored in much greater depth.

events. Later interpretations do not invalidate earlier interpretations.[24] There is an organic relation between the type and the antitype and therefore a development in the very meaning of the original type when the antitype appears. After we have come to an understanding of the original symbol in the context of its original horizon, we can safely proceed to determine the significance of its eschatological realization; its original meaning will "naturally" expand.

Without a hermeneutical method that brings together providence and prophecy in this way, we can safely use typology only where the New Testament sanctions it explicitly. But typology is much richer than this, as are the relations of the epochs of redemptive history.[25] Redemptive revelation is woven into that fabric of history with significant threads holding the different epochs together. The affirmation of typological hermeneutics is an affirmation of the fabric-like character of redemptive revelation. It is an affirmation that the horizon of the entire canon must enter as one significant horizon in the theological analysis of the biblical material.

Biblical history is prophetic in the sense that all history, understood *sub specie aeternitatis,* teaches us the principles on which God rules and will rule as Lord of history. The Old Testament record of history is prophetic in the sense that it describes a revelation and divine action that are as yet incomplete. And the New Testament points to a consummation of history that now we understand only in part, as through a glass darkly.

Until we grasp the past and future, we will not be able to make sense of the present. We will not be able to improve the impoverished character of evangelical theology in general until we pay far greater regard to the past and future — and this means the past, present, and future framework of the redemptive revelation of God. Theology informs evangelicalism only tangentially today. Until evangelicals conceive of the present as existing on a continuum with the past and the future of redemptive history, theology will continue to play only a small role in the evangelical community. If we could but see the transformation of the present as a function of its relation to the past and the future, then

24. See G. K. Beale, "Did Jesus and His Followers Preach the Right Doctrine from the Wrong Text? An Examination of the Presuppositions of Jesus' and the Apostles' Exegetical Method," *Themelios* 14 (April 1989): 89-96. For a more general treatment of this topic, see Oscar Cullmann, *Salvation in History,* trans. Sidney G. Sowers (New York: Harper & Row, 1967).

25. For a defense of this thesis, see Goppelt, *Typos;* and Clowney, *Preaching and Biblical Theology.*

theology would more nearly live up to its calling. As Francis Foulkes
has eloquently suggested, "Revelation is wrought out in history and to
the eyes of faith, history is revelation."[26]

THE TASK OF MIRRORING

The modern evangelical theological framework ought to seek to mirror
the interpretive matrix that is found in the redemptive revelation of the
Scriptures. Having gained some insights into the nature of that interpretive matrix and some of the tasks associated with locating the matrix,
we must remember that this task is not an exact science. Some will see
intricate patterns in the matrix that are not immediately apparent to less
trained eyes. The more perspectives the church brings to bear on this
project, the more adequate its theological framework will be.

The church cannot simply mine the Scriptures looking for answers
to a set of specific questions that arise uniquely in the modern era. The
Scriptures have an integrity of their own that must be respected.
Granting this, however, the church must nonetheless understand that
the Scriptures transform all of history by interpreting it in the light of
God's redemptive purposes and intentions. The church may get a better
understanding of these purposes and intentions by asking a number of
important questions:

1. What are the important issues in Scriptures?
   a. What are the important issues in the work of a particular
      writer?
   b. What are the important issues in a particular epoch?
   c. What are the important issues in the entire canon?

2. What are the structural relationships between issues?
   a. What are the structural relationships between issues raised by
      a particular writer?
   b. What are the structural relationships between issues raised in
      a particular epoch?
   c. What are the structural relationships between issues raised in
      the entire canon?

26. Foulkes, *The Acts of God*, p. 35.

3. What is the significance of the relationships between issues in the Scriptures?
   a. What is the significance of the relationships between issues in each writer?
   b. What is the significance of the relationships between issues in a particular epoch?
   c. What is the significance of the relationships between issues in the entire canon?

The church has to grapple with these sorts of framework questions before it can confront the Scriptures with questions of relevance. Only on the basis of answers to these sorts of questions will we be able to construct an adequate theological framework. Only a biblically adequate theological framework will be able effectively to transform the conceptual categories of the present day and thereby transform those who think and live in the present day.

CHAPTER 9

From Theological Framework to Theological Vision

Not even the people of God in our epoch of redemptive history are called to create a holy culture, because Christians are called to go out into every culture with the gospel. We are a people, to be sure, but our peoplehood is spiritual. Culturally, we are Jew and Gentile, Greek and Roman, European and African.

Ken Myers[1]

INTRODUCTION

A THEOLOGICAL framework ought to be shaped through the careful and purposeful reading of the revelation of God's redemptive activity. It is only when that is understood that a theological vision will develop. It is by that vision that we can understand the proper identity of the modern individual and the modern community of interpreters and the proper place of the modern era in redemptive history. As we come to understand the theological framework of the Scriptures, we can use it to interpret our own place in the historical unfolding of the redemptive activity of God. In this sense, the Scriptures are to be the primary interpreters of the modern era.

---

1. Myers, *All God's Children and Blue Suede Shoes: Christians and Popular Culture* (Westchester, Ill.: Crossway Books, 1989), p. 51.

The biblical thought world is foreign to modern culture; it can seem oppressive and even barbaric to modern sensibilities. It may seem natural in an age such as ours to ask why we should attempt to let the Bible interpret us. Why is the Bible even important in an age such as ours? The inability to answer these all-important questions plagues modern biblical scholarship. Modern academic study of the Bible manifests the lack of an underlying framework affirming that redemptive history is not finished and hence that we live in the midst of it. The Bible does not end with the death and resurrection of Jesus in the third decade of the first century of the common era. Jesus is the Lord who reigns over biblical history and postbiblical history. Redemption is attached to the same Lord yesterday, today, and tomorrow. It is this same Lord who initiated salvation history and will consummate it at the end of time. The Bible is relevant because the present situation is but another episode in the story of the Bible — a story that has begun and climaxed and awaits a consummation foretold in the Scriptures. The Scriptures offer a framework for interpreting this past, present, and future, including our own past, present, and future.

The interpretation of the present era involves not only understanding and critiquing the tasks and responsibilities of the Christian community but also developing a framework by which we can understand modern communities of unbelief. Both kinds of communities lie within and are subject to interpretation by the redemptive historical matrix of the Scriptures. The matrix is universal in its scope in this regard.

The universality of this historical matrix is rooted in the soil of Genesis 1. Believer and unbeliever alike are created by God. There is a fundamental relationship of creature to Creator that marks believer and unbeliever as one. The *imago Dei* informs humanity's very existence because of God's attachment to humanity through the act of creation. Human beings are God's fleshly representatives in the created order — a representation that no other part of creation shares but that all of humankind holds in common.

The *imago Dei* provides a theological bridge between peoples of apparently different cultures and times, even of different places in redemptive history. It permits communication across cultures and across history. It is an essential bond uniting us at the very depth of our being. The *imago Dei* confers on all of humanity a common character of experience that is unique to it in all of creation. Our fundamental identity as human beings lies not in our cultural or historical particularity but in our common origin, the creative activity of God.

The past two centuries have witnessed a virtual ideological assault on this conviction. The onslaught has focused most clearly on historicism as a movement and as a theme in several other ideological movements. Historicism is an attempt to reject moral and theological absolutes by suggesting that all people are fundamentally rooted in the particularity of their own historical circumstances, that there are no transcultural principles applying to all people in all times and all places. The critics of transcultural and transhistorical linkage deny the linkage, typically by eroding the concept of the *imago Dei*. Responding to this kind of criticism, J. I. Packer says, "The truth seems to be . . . that, as most people have always thought, what is deepest in human experience is also most universal and that such experiences as loving a spouse, admiring a hero, feeling the pity and terror of tragedy, and knowing the unchanging God are among the deepest of all, so that in principle they are the most fully communicable across historical and cultural divides to those who are capable of tuning in to such things."[2]

In addition to being rooted in God's creative activity, the common identity of humankind is also rooted in the events of Genesis 3. Humankind shares not only in the creaturely aspects of the *imago Dei* but also in the common experience of the fall. Human rebellion and sin are perfectly universal in their scope. There are no individuals who escape the impact of the fall on the strength of their own character. After Genesis 3, there is no indication that even God's people are created without a fallen nature or that they are redeemed into a state of sinlessness. Believers and unbelievers alike are rebellious.

A third significant common characteristic of modern humanity lies in our relatively similar redemptive-historical index: we stand on common ground in relation to Scripture and the consummation of redemptive history. The identities of peoples of all the modern cultures are wrapped up with the epoch stretching from Pentecost to the second coming of Christ. We all live between these two significant events — events that Scripture designates as having defined a new epoch. This redemptive-historical index gives modern people some indication of how they are to relate to the earlier epochs of Scripture and also how those earlier epochs shed light upon the daunting tasks of the present epoch. It is only on this basis that Scripture can be effectively applied

---

2. Packer, "Infallible Scripture and the Role of Hermeneutics," in *Scripture and Truth,* ed. D. A. Carson and John Woodbridge (Grand Rapids: Zondervan, 1983), p. 332.

to the modern world. The past, present, and future of Scripture must inform our own past, present, and future and thereby shape our collective identity.

Unbelievers are located on the redemptive historical index just as believers are. There is a distinction between the two: the unbeliever faces a prospective judgment — a judgment that is still to come — whereas the believer's judgment has come already on the cross of Christ. Nevertheless, believers like unbelievers are infected by sin that reaches to the very core of their being. Therefore, the present cultural flowering of sin (which comes, after all, in many diverse cultural manifestations) stands in need of the sort of transformation that can be effected only by the power of the radical redemptive work of God in and through history.

Interpretation and critique of the modern era ought to be a part of the character of a modern theological vision. Such critique should proceed on the assumption that we have a common identity with people in biblical times, that what God said and did in the biblical text ought to inform what he says to us and what he is doing and will do for us in our circumstances. This is to say once more that the theological framework of the Scriptures should be the foundation of our theological vision. The question of the relevance of the biblical text presumes that the flow of redemptive history in the biblical theological framework can appropriately give birth to a modern theological vision.

While affirming the essential identity of humanity across cultures and history, it is still necessary to affirm that sin manifests itself in a variety of ways. The *imago Dei* itself consists of a multitude of diverse expressions. Consequently, the critique of culture and of every human person (including ourselves) will inevitably be complicated and diverse, a task that we must therefore undertake with the utmost seriousness, care, and caution.

THEOLOGY AND THE PIECES OF CULTURE

Let us turn now to a consideration of the principles by which the theological framework might relate to the modern world and thereby form a theological vision. The movement from theological framework to modern culture begins with questions such as the following: What is modern culture? Which impulses of modern culture(s) are to be criticized? How and why are they to be critiqued? Which parts of our culture ought to be affirmed? How and why are they to be affirmed? How does the redemptive matrix of Scripture transform the present and the future?

As we noted in Chapter 2, culture is nothing more (or less) than the constant and curious conversation that takes place between each of us and the environment in which we reside, we ourselves being part of that environment. On this model, the theological task can be broken down into aspects associated with different segments of this conversation. The conversation can be sliced into three pieces — the church, popular culture, and the academy — and we can view theology as having the task of maintaining conversation with and critiquing each piece individually. To a certain extent the divisions are arbitrary, but they do serve the purpose of slicing a very complex pie into conceptually manageable pieces. The divisions are points of entry into the discussion of the movement from theological framework to theological vision.

Within each of these pieces of culture, the theological task has a twofold responsibility: exposition and application. The task of exposition begins with the recognition that we have to express the theological vision of the biblical witness in a language that is intelligible to the modern mind. Theologians must be able to speak the language of the modern world. Part of their task is to help transport modern individuals back into the thought world of the Bible, to help them understand its sense of history, to help them appreciate biblical symbols, images, and metaphors. They have to explain how God actually manifested himself in biblical times and show what the reign of God meant in those contexts. And their task goes beyond mere translation; they must also present a challenge. By transporting the modern person back into the conceptual world of the Scriptures, theology brings a challenge to the very assumptions that undergird cultural life today.

It is this challenge that forms the basis of the application part of the theological task. The theological framework turns into a theological vision when it enables modern people to understand anew their own world. A theological vision allows them to see their culture in a way different than they had ever been able to see it before. The vision gives them new eyes on the world and forces them to take a prophetic stance in each of the pieces of culture that are addressed. Those who are empowered by the theological vision do not simply stand against the mainstream impulses of the culture but take the initiative both to understand and speak to that culture from the framework of the Scriptures. This will inevitably entail speaking against our culture (since sin is an integral part of humankind and all of the cultures that derive from fallen humanity). The modern theological vision must seek to bring the entire counsel of God into the world of its time in order that its time might be transformed.

Part of the intended goal of a theological vision, then, is the demythologization of modern cultures. The myths of modern cultures are to be unmasked and exposed for what they are. This can be done only through the agency of divine revelation. This debunking of the values of modern cultures includes uncovering the accretions to biblical faith within the community of believers as well as the perversions perpetuated as truth within the larger culture. The end result is that present communities are freed not from the demands of the gospel but from the distortions of modern culture. This includes the church, the academy, and the popular culture. These are the audiences for evangelical theology. They are spheres of culture to which a theological vision ought to speak.

The first of the three audiences for a theological vision is the church. It is in the community of believers that a vibrant theological vision ought to arise. The process begins with a transformation of the identity of the community and with a transformation of the identity of the believer within that community. The church is invested with the responsibility to protect and to proclaim the whole counsel of God. The second audience is popular culture, the largest and most complicated of the three. Popular culture has influenced the evangelical movement more profoundly than many dare to imagine. It is also the source of most of the values held in the world today and therefore stands in greatest need of a biblical critique. The academy is the third audience for a theological vision — an audience that was largely abandoned by evangelicals in the early part of the twentieth century. There are signs that they are beginning to recover and appreciate the importance of this audience, but with this renewal there comes a temptation to embrace the values of the academy rather than the values of the gospel.

It is worth paying careful attention not only whom theology is speaking to but also which audience theology is arising from when it speaks. Theology must be prophetic in the modern culture. Christianity is a countercultural movement at heart. Our theological vision must bring God's word to bear on modern culture and supply the church with eyes to see and ears to hear. In order to do this, theology must reflect on the audience to which it is speaking and the audience from which it speaks.

Theology and the Church

Until the end of the eighteenth and the beginning of the nineteenth centuries, the church was the prime recipient of theological endeavors and was the prime context in which theological visions were constructed. That is no longer the case for a number of reasons, as we have seen. The parachurch character of evangelicalism subverts the possibility of a churchly theology. The depth of revivalism in the evangelical movement has undermined the distinction between church and nonchurch and therefore blurred the lines within which theology might be nurtured. The growing professionalization of theological education has placed most seminaries in the hands not of churches but of private enterprise.[3] And finally the breakdown of ecclesiology as a significant category of the theological framework has contributed to shifting the prime context of theology from the church to popular culture.

Though the reasons for this shift are diverse and diffuse, the impact has been focused and intense. Evangelicals have broken the fundamental connections between theology and worship and mission. As the primary context of theological construction has moved outside the church, it has lost sight of the God who called out a people for his own, that they might worship him and proclaim his name in all the world. It is God who grants to his people a theological vision, and the church is the fundamental context he has chosen to carry forth that vision. The church was not a nebulous entity in the New Testament, nor were the people of God left without a vision in those days. The church had particular shape, structure, and spiritual location. Its privileges and responsibilities were spelled out in great detail. As the apostles addressed particular churches or groups of churches, they delivered a common theological framework that was meant to infuse the people with a new way-of-looking-at-the world — a theological vision.

In the epoch of the new covenant, the church is the primary organ of God's activity. The covenant promises to Abraham, fulfilled ultimately through the person and work of Christ, are applied in the context of the church in this new era. The true seed of Abraham are the disciples of Christ. As God was faithful to Abraham, so he will be faithful to Abraham's seed. It is this reality that should serve as the starting point

---

3. Many of the larger evangelical seminaries — e.g., Fuller, Gordon-Conwell, Dallas, Reformed, Westminster, Talbot, Asbury — remain unaffiliated with a church.

for our own theological vision in the twentieth century. The promise is climactically fulfilled in Christ, and it is for this reason that Christ is the cornerstone of our theological framework, even as the apostles and prophets are the foundation (Eph. 2:20).

The biblical canon serves as the effective witness to the work of God in history and as the constitution of the church. It is Scripture in which the identity of the church is grounded. The church is meant to be the effective witness to the work of God in the postcanonical period. After the book of Revelation was completed, the church became the primary window through which the work of God is seen in the world. This is not to say that the church has taken the place of the Scriptures but rather that the church is founded on the framework of the Scriptures. In her life and in her words, the church is meant to give faithful proclamation to the work of God today and in the future as she has in the past.

The promise of God's covenant is "I will be your God, and you will be my people" (Lev. 26:12; 2 Cor. 6:16). The church is the possession of God. It consists of those whom he has formed for himself that they might show forth his praise. Undoubtedly the focus of the church ought to be the God who has brought her forth and through whom and unto whom are all things. But the church must wrestle with how this praise of God is to go forth. She must constantly be on guard against allowing her proclamation to become self-praise instead of the praise of God. If the church is the context for the praise of God, it is also the proper context for the protection of that praise. Theology likewise reflects two purposes when it functions with a church identity: it sets forth a framework for the praise of God, and it declares the boundaries of that praise.

The church abandons theology only at great peril to herself, but likewise theology abandons the church only at great peril to itself. Evangelical theology was greatly impoverished when it lost sight of the foundational institution of God's activity in the world, the church. Theology lost the most important forum for the praise of God and thereby lost the means to apply the Bible's theological framework in the contemporary world. When it lost its church identity, theology also lost its accountability structures.[4] And as

4. The dilemma of heresy plagues modern evangelicalism and can be seen in the fact that two recent heresy trials in evangelicalism have occurred outside the context of the church—Ramsey Michaels at Gordon-Conwell Theological Seminary and Robert Gundry in the Evangelical Theological Society. Not surprisingly, these trials have been

theology became less accountable to the church, it lost sight of the boundaries of the praise of God.

The faithful proclamation of the church properly has both a positive and a negative side. The church is called to "preach the word . . . in season and out of season" (2 Tim. 4:2). She is commissioned with the responsibility of guarding the gospel and thereby retaining the standard of sound words (2 Tim. 1:13-14). She must serve as a faithful witness to the work of God and in this offer him endless praise. But she must also renounce the evil that opposes the work of God. She is to take up this negative task with no less fervor than she takes up the positive one. They are two sides of the same coin. These two tasks, the positive and negative aspects of the proclamation of God in praise and protection, are the hallmarks of a church theology. It is important to note that these tasks belong to the church and not to the abstract discipline of theology. Theology belongs to the church, and it is only to the extent that theology is grounded in the identity of the church that it will effectively own the tasks to which it has been called.

As things now stand, evangelicals have lost not only a church identity for their theology but also theological identity for their church. The church inevitably lost a taste for theology as theology lost a taste for the church. Evangelical churches are now enamored with the management of the people of God not by a theological vision but by a vision of success maximization. Evangelical churches have become skilled in the use of mass communication and mass marketing.

Even the proclamation of the gospel has been submitted to the techniques of effective mass marketing. A unique commodity (Jesus) is sold by very modern means. Like popular culture, evangelical churches have shown that they prefer the shallow repetition of slogans to sustained intellectual inquiry. As David Wells has noted,

> Evangelical theology . . . finds itself alienated from . . . the church whose habits of mind and interests now lie substantially elsewhere. . . . This is most unexpected, most grievous and most damaging. A Church which is neither interested in theology nor has the capacity to think theologically is a Church that will be rapidly submerged beneath the

very messy. For further comment on this problem, see John Meuther, "Contemporary Evangelicalism and the Triumph of the New School," *Westminster Theological Journal* 50 (1988): 339-47.

waves of modernity. It is a Church for whom Christian faith will rapidly lose its point and this is already well under way within evangelicalism. And a Church whose interests are thus adrift is one that no longer is an audience for whom theologians can think. They are on the point of becoming artists whose work no one bothers to view.[5]

How is theology to return to a church that no longer wants it? First, theologians will have to be convinced that it is good to return. This will not happen until they do a good deal more biblical/theological thinking about the identity and calling of the church and about the fact that the church is the primary context for their vocation.[6] They must also be more willing to speak from within the church and not merely to the church. As I have already suggested, rather than evangelical theologians, there must be Baptist theologians, Presbyterian theologians, Methodist theologians, and so on. One final suggestion: the professional theological community should stop trying to settle boundary questions for the community of faith. It is the churches that ought to be serving this function. The confessional character of the church cannot be determined at an interdenominational seminary or in the pages of a professional academic journal; these issues must be resolved in the church and for the church.

All of these suggestions will be useless unless and until the church itself regains an interest in theology. A modern evangelical theological vision will continue to be lifeless until it can be faithfully proclaimed and protected in the confines of the church. This will not happen in a church "submerged beneath the waves of modernity."

Theology and Popular Culture

The most prominent audience for any modern message is popular culture. It is the all-pervasive force that most strongly influences the minds of modern thinking. It is the fabric in which most people are conceptually clothed. Popular culture presumes to teach us not only what to think

5. Wells, "The Theologian's Craft," in *Doing Theology in Today's World: Essays in Honor of Kenneth S. Kantzer*, ed. Thomas E. McComiskey and John D. Woodbridge (Grand Rapids: Zondervan, 1991), pp. 193-94.
6. See Edmund Clowney's very fine article "The Biblical Theology of the Church," in *Biblical Interpretation and the Church: Text and Context*, ed. D. A. Carson (Exeter: Paternoster Press, 1984), pp. 13-87. Clowney points evangelical theology in the proper direction, toward a more fully orbed ecclesiology.

but how to think, not only what to do but how to live. Given the pervasiveness and strength of popular culture, modern theology must exercise great caution when it seeks to speak to it.

The architects of a modern theological vision must realize that they can neither escape from popular culture nor speak neutrally about it. It is not simply "out there" to be avoided at all costs. It is also "inside," and it inevitably influences the ways in which modern individuals perceive the entire world (including God).

In a helpful study, Bruce Nicholls has suggested that a prophetic stance toward modern culture includes three essential elements: a call to deculturalize distorting accretions to biblical faith in the believing community, a call to judge and condemn those elements of culture that are contrary to the Word of God in the larger culture, and a call to re-create and transform cultural elements that are consistent with God's revelation.[7]

Modern prophets can accomplish this threefold task only if they understand the nature of the popular culture surrounding them and accord it a significant theological treatment. Evangelical theology must neither ignore popular culture nor succumb to its subversive pressures. Although a determination of what constitutes an appropriate prophetic stance toward that culture will be extremely complex, it is absolutely necessary that evangelicals expend the effort to make the determination and then to adopt the stance.

In order to discuss this complicated task, it may be beneficial to isolate dominant patterns in popular culture that have a direct theological bearing on it. A fuller treatment of this concern would require much more than I can present here, but I hope that the beginnings of a paradigm may emerge from what follows.[8] Three fundamental values of modern popular culture will serve as the filters for the following discussion: cultural pluralism, confessional simplicity, and the cult of the self.

When we speak of cultural pluralism, we acknowledge that modern popular culture is actually a vast array of cultures. In a half-hour broad-

---

7. See Nicholls, "Towards a Theology of Gospel and Culture," in *Down to Earth: Studies in Christianity and Culture*, ed. Robert T. Coote and John Stott (Grand Rapids: William B. Eerdmans, 1980), pp. 49-62. Nicholls actually lists four points, but I take the fourth point to be an extension of the third.

8. For a much fuller treatment of popular culture, see Myers, *All God's Children and Blue Suede Shoes*. Myers's analysis is more profound than the title of his book might suggest.

cast of an evening news show, the modern viewer engages in conversation (admittedly one-sided) with figures as diverse as Yassir Arafat, Nelson Mandela, and Michael Jackson. This clash of cultures has become almost normal for the modern person.

Along with this modern melting pot has come a fascination with the pluralism of religions. Diversity has become a buzzword not only for advertisers and news anchors but also for theologians. And owing to the considerable depth of differences between the world's religions, many commentators presume that there is no way to settle the conceptual clashes among them. Popular culture reads that as an affirmation that all religions stand on an equal footing and on this basis elevates tolerance to the greatest of virtues.

The sociological fact of pluralism is thus transformed into a normative value. The fact that there are many diverse cultures and religions is taken to mean that this is the way things *ought* to be. In the process, the importance of truth is diminished, superseded by expedience and efficiency. Though most of the world's religions are monopolistic in their worldviews, popular culture challenges all such claims to exclusivity not by assessing their truth or falsity but by preemptively dismissing truth as a relevant category of assessment.[9]

The evangelical community has not been unstained in this regard. Although it has sounded the call for absolute truth with boldness, it has in more subtle ways succumbed to the pressures of this cultural pluralism. In many ways the movement has been culturally edited to give it the qualities of sociability and gentility. The civilizing process has involved deemphasizing the more offensive elements in evangelicalism — the concepts of inherent evil, sinful conduct, the wrath of God, hell, and so forth — and a corresponding accentuation of the positive. It has become the fashion among evangelicals to ask not what you can do for God but what God can do for you.

A second value that a modern evangelical theological vision must challenge is the confessional simplicity of popular culture. We have seen a similar sort of damaging oversimplification in recent political campaigns, in which it has been assumed that the prize will go to the candidate with the best sound bites. Issues of a great and complex nature are carved up and cooked down until they can be easily digested by a

---

9. See Leslie Newbigin, *Truth to Tell: The Gospel as Public Truth* (Grand Rapids: William B. Eerdmans, 1991).

mass audience. The slogan takes the place of the substance; it serves not as a distillation of a complex discussion but as a substitute for it.

In modern culture, the gospel is similarly rendered easily digestible. *The Fundamentals* cooked down the complexities of the gospel to a handful of essential doctrines in the early decades of this century. H. J. Cadbury noted that an early twentieth-century preacher gave voice to the reductionistic impulse in a different fashion by suggesting that "Jesus exemplifies all the principles of modern salesmanship. He was, of course, a good mixer; he made contacts easily and was quick to get *en rapport* with his 'prospect.' He appreciated the advertising value of news and so called his message 'good news.' His habit of early rising was indicative of the high pressure of the 'go-getter' so necessary for a successful career."[10] The evangelical presentation of the gospel too frequently reflects this modern penchant for packaging. Evangelicals have defended certain theological beliefs rather than a certain vision of theology, doubtless because individual beliefs are more easily packaged and better suited for mass consumption than is a complex theological vision. But the result is that evangelical theology no longer coheres like a well-crafted piece of clothing but has taken on the appearance of a patchwork quilt. There are no evident unifying themes, and what beliefs there are seem indiscriminately strung together. Theology, beyond the essentials, is often portrayed as peripheral and unimportant.

James Davison Hunter puts the issue this way:

> In the rationalized economy, mass production allows for widespread distribution and consumption while maintaining a high degree of quality control over the product. Likewise the reduction of the gospel to its distilled essence and the methodization of the conversion process make widespread distribution of the gospel possible, while maintaining a cognitive uniformity in substantive quality of the message and an experiential uniformity in functional quality of the process.[11]

Hunter goes on to suggest that while liberal Christianity dealt with the market competition of contrasting value systems by means of a passive

---

10. Cadbury, *The Peril of Modernizing Jesus* (London: SPCK, 1962), p. 11. Cadbury is referring to Bruce Barton, *The Man Nobody Knows* (Indianapolis: Bobbs-Merrill, 1925), pp. 195ff.

11. Hunter, *American Evangelicalism: Conservative Religion and the Quandary of Modernity* (New Brunswick, N.J.: Rutgers University Press, 1983), pp. 83-84.

ecumenism, evangelicalism has attempted to distill the message to an easily grasped package, to claim for it some uniqueness, and then to market it as superior in the marketplace of modernity. They have stressed evangelistic technique, which has led them to focus on compressing of the gospel message and to make use of innovative advertising techniques to determine what sorts of markets to target, what sort of people they should evangelize. Most modern church-growth manuals contain lengthy sections on demographics that suggest how to find the most likely prospects for conversion.

In the modern free market, truth does not always win out. The prize typically goes to whatever set of goods is packaged best. Ironically, the enigmatic mass marketing of *exclusive truth* has helped to push evangelicals further from their own theological heritage. It is not the exclusivity of the evangelical gospel that has gained for it wide recent approval in modern popular culture but rather the sophistication with which it has been packaged. Modern evangelical theologians would do well to go back and help the church reflect critically on this kind of evangelism strategy.

A final value worthy of our attention is the cult of the self in modern popular culture.[12] Peter Berger has argued that modern consciousness has involved a movement from fate to choice. The vast array of things that modern technology makes possible seems to suggest that an individual can do almost anything. Of particular significance is the change that the conception of the modern self has undergone. The modern person is not bound by the fates of history any longer. Berger illustrates this by looking at the modern concept of sexual lifestyles and the incredible increases of one's options in this area. The pluralism of sexual orientation is now an acceptable fact of society in large measure because of the recent discoveries in birth control technology. Freed of concerns about unwanted pregnancy and the like, the modern has shifted the focus to possibilities of maximizing human happiness. The self becomes all-important because the moderns suppose that they can now control their own destiny.[13]

Unfortunately similar attitudes are evident in the evangelical subculture as well. Beyond the obvious example of the health-and-wealth gospel,

---

12. On the cult of self, see Philip Rieff, *The Triumph of the Therapeutic* (New York: Harper & Row, 1966).

13. See Berger, *The Heretical Imperative* (Garden City, N.Y.: Doubleday-Anchor, 1979).

the degree to which evangelicals have become consumed with the self is evidenced by the predominance of self-help manuals on the shelves of every evangelical bookstore, the trend toward pop psychology and analyzing the "inner self" in evangelical radio programming, and, unfortunately, in the underlying framework of many evangelical ministries.[14] Simply put, evangelical subjectivism reflects the trend in modernity at large.

This fascination with the self gives rise to the new focus of theodicy for modern evangelicals — unhappiness. How can there be a God if we are not happy all the time? Evil has become a private emotion, and the new gospel is that God offers to heal us of that privatized evil. The church exists to make people feel comfortable and happy. This is simply hedonism baptized with Christian rhetoric. We have come a great distance from Edwards's vision of theology as reflecting the glory of God, a glory that is also the chief end of humankind.

Without calling for a return to the traditional asceticism of Protestantism, we ought nonetheless to think theologically about the living implications of the gospel. How are evangelicals to conceptualize their life in modern culture? How do cultural values influence the values of evangelicals? How are we to separate evangelical thinking from modern popular culture without isolating it from that culture? It is my contention that we cannot adequately answer any of these questions apart from a theological vision in which the past, present, and future are given meaning by their role in redemptive history. One cannot assume a prophetic stance in modern culture simply by opposing its dominant themes. It is true that part of the power of the prophetic voice lies in its distance from the mainstream values of the culture, and yet the underlying value of popular dissent in America soon transforms distant voices into mainstream voices,[15] and in becoming mainstream the voice inevitably loses its prophetic character. This is one of the paradoxical features of modernity.

---

14. Anecdotal evidence that confirmed this in my mind includes an experience of a church service I attended recently while traveling. The church was a growing evangelical congregation that prided itself on being relevant to the professional community in the surrounding area. The topic of the "talk" (thankfully it was no longer called a sermon) was codependency. The primary text was the manual of Alcoholics Anonymous. The primary goal of the talk was to help people feel good about themselves. Leaving the church, it occurred to me that if this is where evangelicalism is headed, I had to ask whether I was actually an evangelical.

15. See chap. 7 of Nathan Hatch's *The Democratization of American Christianity* (New Haven: Yale University Press, 1989).

A theological vision must carefully examine and appropriately challenge the conceptual foundations and underlying values of modern popular culture. It must not carelessly adopt and adapt the values of popular culture simply to ensure its own growth. It must maintain fidelity first of all to God rather than to its own success and growth. Evangelicals must learn to think theologically and be defined theologically.

Theology and the Academy

By the middle of the twentieth century it was fashionable to suppose that one could not properly be both an evangelical and a scholar. This view was popular among evangelicals as well as nonevangelicals. The spiritual decline of the modern university was widely trumpeted in evangelical circles. They maintained that rigorous academic reflection had an inherently un-Christian character. For their part, secular university faculties placed the evangelical coalition in the same category with their fundamentalist opponents as constitutionally opposed to reasoned argument and serious thinking. Scholarship was not possible for those who took religion too seriously. Religious dogmatism and free intellectual inquiry could not coexist.[16]

Undoubtedly there was an element of truth in these suppositions. Evangelical scholarship in this period had nothing of the depth or the quality of reflection characteristic of Augustine, Aquinas, Calvin, and Edwards or even of Warfield, Strong, and Kuyper. Evangelical theology in the early part of the twentieth century suffered from an inferiority complex that was in part justified. When its fundamental constituency become the popular subculture of mass media evangelism, it lost a vision for careful and critical reflection. It bypassed the university and thereby forfeited a forum that would have demanded a cogency and profundity of the evangelical theological vision that it sorely lacks today.

On the other hand, the secularization of the modern university is by now also well chronicled.[17] The fundamental religious values that

16. See Richard Hofstadter, *Anti-Intellectualism in American Life* (New York: Alfred A. Knopf, 1963), pp. 55-145.

17. See, e.g., Henry May, *The Enlightenment in America* (New York: Oxford University Press, 1976); Owen Chadwick, *The Secularization of the European Mind in the Nineteenth Century* (London: Cambridge University Press, 1975); Laurence Vesey, *The Emergence of the American University* (Chicago: University of Chicago Press, 1965); and Burton J. Bledstein, *The Culture of Professionalism: The Middle Class and the Development of Higher Education*

had brought many private and public universities into existence were largely abandoned by the mid-twentieth century. Departments of theology became departments of religion. The study of God was replaced with the study of the religious character of humankind. Even the study of religion lost its distinctive methodology and became parasitic on other disciplines in the university, notably the social sciences and historical criticism.

Theology (religion) in the university followed the larger culture in its compromise with the modern secularized spirit rather than being prophetic to it. Many spokesmen for the religion of modernity declared in the 1960s that liberal theology had become irrelevant because God had died, just as Friedrich Nietzsche had predicted at the end of the nineteenth century. The culture of the 1960s may have been uncomfortable with the notion that God had died but not with the notion that he had become irrelevant.

If these stereotypical assertions have an element of truth, they also serve to distort the picture just slightly. The evangelical community abandoned the university in America for a host of complicated reasons.[18] Not least among these was an evangelistic fervor relating to the frontier of American society. While moving west, evangelicalism unwittingly left behind the east, the university establishment. The movement was also motivated by the animosity of the social Darwinians who remained behind in the universities. The lack of an evangelical presence in the university can be attributed as much to evangelicals leaving that sphere of culture as to their having been kicked out of it.

How might an evangelical theological vision help us to understand our involvement in the marketplace of ideas again? How should present-day evangelical theologians seek to apply their own vision in the academy? A caution must be sounded in answering these questions. The quest for relevance (of an academic sort or otherwise) is inherently dangerous. The modern and theologically liberal intention to make the gospel more rele-

---

in America (New York: W. W. Norton, 1976). In developing my conceptual framework for understanding secularization in the academy, I am indebted to the insights of George Marsden in his forthcoming study of the secularization of the modern American university.

18. These reasons are traced by George Marsden in "The Collapse of American Evangelical Academia," in *Faith and Rationality: Reason and Belief in God,* ed. Alvin Plantinga and Nicholas Wolterstorff (Notre Dame, Ind.: University of Notre Dame Press, 1983), pp. 219-64.

vant to the modern person has ironically accomplished the exact opposite. Faith is a considerably less compelling option for the modern person than it used to be. To the extent that moderns think about religious faith at all, they tend to think of it in terms of the privacy of their own subjective closets, closets that are by necessity largely isolated from mainstream modern culture. One of the lessons to be learned is that the quest to return to the academy needs to be carefully tempered with a clear sense of the seductive potential of the modern university.

It must be clear from the outset that the evangelical abandonment of the universities was accompanied by a cultural compromise the like of which has rarely been experienced in Christendom.[19] Though the evangelical subculture has effectively resisted the naturalistic tendencies of the modern universities, it has succumbed to the pressures of popular culture, most noticeably in its fascination with the self and its marketing of the gospel. Like the broader culture, evangelicalism replaced the traditional sanctions of authority with the authority of the self. In modernity and in evangelicalism, social relationships are largely impersonal and arbitrary, and inevitably the focus has turned from the community to the individual and to the fulfillment of that individual through the internal resources of the self. Religious faith has been secularized and trivialized. Many have sought to harness the power of God for patently profane purposes, most notably securing the happiness of the individual.

In evangelical circles this is apparent in the way the Scriptures are used. While evangelicals on the whole agree that the Scriptures are authoritative, they demonstrate little agreement about how to interpret and apply them. Agreement about the source of theology (the Bible) has resulted in precious few other points of agreement. Part of the reason for this is the evangelical reliance on subjective intuitions as effective filters through which to appropriate the Scriptures. The Bible is read through the subjective leading of the Spirit rather than the hard work of redemptive/historical/grammatical exegesis. The authority of the text is grounded in personal experience with the text rather than in any objective quality or meaning the text possesses.[20] Evangelical fascination

19. For an extended argument to this effect, see David F. Wells, *No Place for Truth; or, Whatever Happened to Evangelical Theology* (Grand Rapids: William B. Eerdmans, 1993).

20. On this and related matters, see Scott Hafeman, "Seminary, Subjectivity and the Centrality of Scripture: Reflections on the Current Crisis in Evangelical Seminary Education," *Journal of the Evangelical Theological Society* 32 (1989): 129-43.

with self-fulfillment has also colored the use of the biblical text. Devotional reading of the Scriptures is divorced from sustained and serious study of the text, which in turn is severed from the use of the Bible in preaching. In these ways, evangelicals undermine the very authority of the Scriptures that they claim to defend.

As I suggested in Chapter 6, David Tracy and other postmodern theologians have spoken of the need for theology to be public.[21] They want theological reflection to take place in an open forum (i.e., the university) within an established framework of rationality. This framework would consist of a set of rules that would govern theological arguments, determining which are acceptable and which are not. In this vision of the academy, divergent theological views would be submitted to public scrutiny. Without this "public conversation," say its proponents, there is no hope of sustaining credible theological frameworks, and theology will inevitably be reduced to a set of private opinions. Tracy and the other postmodern theologians have argued that theology must be responsive to the contemporary marketplace of ideas. An often hidden assumption is that the marketplace of ideas is fair and neutral with regard to truth. This is a profound error. Nevertheless, the public arena does provide an important set of intellectual checks and balances without which religion will become so privatized as to lose all sense of truth.

A fundamental question remains for evangelicals: How can theology be responsive in the university without losing its distinctively normative status? Tracy and other postmoderns have argued that theology ought to be a public discipline addressed to all people and using criteria acceptable to everyone, on the analogy of modern science. "Theology," says Tracy, "by the very nature of the kind of fundamental existential questions it asks and because of the nature of the reality of God upon which theology reflects, must develop public, not private, criteria and discourse."[22] By public discourse, these theologians mean the willingness of theologians to make a theological argument by "giving reasons for which an account can be given"[23] and that may then appropriately be

---

21. See Tracy, *The Analogical Imagination: Christian Theology and the Culture of Pluralism* (New York: Crossroad, 1981); Robert Neville, *The Tao and the Daimon: Segments of Religious Inquiry* (Albany: State University of New York Press, 1982); and David Ray Griffin, *God and Religion in the Postmodern World: Essays in Postmodern Theology* (Albany: State University of New York Press, 1989).

22. Tracy, *The Analogical Imagination*, p. 4.

23. Neville, *The Tao and the Daimon*, p. 16.

judged by "those tests that are more or less explicitly applied to any account presented for public acceptance."[24]

A fundamental problem for this vision of the public character of theology is the methodological morass of the modern university in general and modern theology in particular. As with postmodernism, when theology is done "from below," it inevitably becomes parasitic on other anthropologically oriented disciplines. It has no set of distinctive normative guidelines and so dissolves into mere "conversation." Without distinctive norms, a theological vision can do no more than serve the felt needs of the community of interpreters.[25] And when these needs vary greatly, so will the competing theological visions. The standards of assessment will consist solely of the subjective adequacy of the vision, as judged by the community as a whole or relevant subsections. In the words of Tracy, "Community-wide arguments for the relative adequacy of any particular interpretation would be both encouraged and warranted. Conflict among various proposals may be our actuality, yet conversation is our hope."[26]

Quite obviously these are not standards of adequacy that the evangelical theological vision ought to seek to fulfill. The normative standard of the Scriptures ought to play the central role in the formation of this theological vision, and evangelicals ought not to apologize for this. In fact it could be argued that the approval of the academic community of interpreters would be a distinctly inauspicious goal at which to aim. In the modern university, the Scriptures are not one of the "approved norms," and it would be striking to suppose that an adequate area of agreement for the assessment of a theological framework could be assembled from fundamentally different assumptions.

However, it is still important for evangelicals to participate in the "conversation" with the rest of the academic community. They should participate not with the intent of gaining approval from the academic community but for the sake of gaining clarity and precision and profundity. The mere presence (and determination) of evangelicals in these

24. Griffin, *God and Religion in the Postmodern World,* p. xiv.

25. This is why "minority theologies" have become so prominent. When the entire community defines theology, the process will inevitably include groups that have previously been left out of the process.

26. Tracy, "Theological Method," in *Christian Theology: An Introduction to Its Traditions and Tasks,* 2d ed., ed. Peter C. Hodgson and Robert H. King (Philadelphia: Fortress Press, 1985), p. 55.

otherwise alien settings provides a necessary forum for the expression and application of their theological framework in carefully nuanced and subtle ways. It provides the opportunity to think about their theological vision with a depth of perception and a carefulness of expression. I am not advocating these goals as ends in themselves, but in an evangelical world where they are sorely lacking, the exposition and application of the evangelical theological framework and vision in the academic community can provide a significant corrective. Both the logical rigor and the profundity of the message have been lost in the populist-driven vision of the current evangelical subculture, and we will not regain them until we construct our theological framework *in part* with an eye on the current academic community.

In modern culture there is a great division between the public and private worlds of most individuals. Contemporary sociologists refer to this phenomenon as structural pluralism: the structures of our lives divide those lives into isolated and compartmentalized spheres.[27] One aspect of this is that religion in most modern societies is privatized. Its proper role is defined exclusively in terms of the satisfaction of personal or subjective needs. Symbols are internalized and are meaningful only in the private parts of a person's life. Evangelicalism is a thoroughly modern phenomenon in this regard. One important part of a strategy to overcome this privatization of the evangelical faith is a return to the university.

This is not a substantive proposal but a formal one. By itself it gives no indication of what the actual application of the evangelical theological vision will look like in this context. I am simply suggesting that unless the theological vision is in part appropriated in this context, it will continue to suffer from many of its current defects.

The evangelical message has possessed a kind of rigor in its contemporary exposition and application, but far too frequently this has taken the form of a functional rationality rather than a substantive rationality. Evangelicals are relatively clear on their own set of doctrinal red flags. They talk at length about the social boundaries as well. The function of these flags and boundaries is to separate "us" from "them," but it affords little sense of what makes "us" us. And rarely do the flags facilitate the integration of the diverse spheres of a person's life. There ought to be an infusion of controls through all spheres of human experience rather than simply in the orderly expression of the doctrinal

27. See Hunter, *American Evangelicalism*, pp. 13-15.

framework in which that experience is to be understood. Another problem is that the functional controls of modern evangelicalism undermine the supernatural providence of God. The proliferation of "how-to" manuals is evidence of this. The evangelical hunger for "four easy steps" is a sign of accommodation to the technological and functional rationality of our age. We see it in the methodical description of the conversion process by means of the four spiritual laws or other evangelistic techniques, for example. It is also evident in the systematization of the gospel into its "distilled essence." The result of all of this is a spiritual positivism.

How can evangelicals move away from spiritual positivism? They can take an important step in the right direction by returning to serious and sustained critical reflection, an art that has been all but lost in the contemporary evangelical community. As they turn to theology, their aim should be to produce not ease of understanding but rather depth of understanding. The endeavor to maintain fidelity to the entire counsel of God involves both painful and painstaking effort. It will not happen outside formal channels that are created with this explicit purpose in mind.

Part of the difficulty in creating these channels can be traced to the peculiar ways in which the evangelical subculture confronts the larger surrounding culture. Evangelicals have their own Christian college consortium, their own set of evangelical publishing houses, their own set of ministerial empires, and their own set of television programs. Evangelicals have created a culture so insulated from the secular community that they are at a loss to know what sustained intellectual inquiry is or what the outside community is up to in this regard. The evangelical cocoon that provides protection from the secular world also hinders careful reflection on that world. By opting out of the sorts of thinking that the larger culture engages in, we have made it that much easier to stop thinking altogether.

This fact is nowhere more evident than in the field of apologetics: for decades our apologetic efforts have been directed not at the secular world but at the Christian world! Is the problem that evangelicals are not really convinced of the truth themselves? How many evangelical authors engage the unconvinced rather than merely assuring the convinced? How many nonevangelicals read evangelical books? How often do nonevangelicals even enter Christian bookstores? Evangelical books literally preach to the converted and write off those who are not.

The impact of this trend on the evangelical theological vision is enormous. There is little impetus for strenuous and careful justification of the theological framework. Few see a need to get outside the cocoon of evangelical rhetoric. By returning to the university and carefully engaging that public sphere (with all of its flaws), evangelicals might manage to regain a sense of depth, genuine clarity, and profundity in their theological vision.[28]

---

28. "Whether we like or not," says Geerhardus Vos, "criticism can touch the essence of our religion, because religion has become incarnate, and for our sakes had to become incarnate and make itself vulnerable in historic form. As the Son of God while on earth had to expose Himself to the unbelief and scorn of men, so the work of the Gospel could not be what it is for us unless it were subject to the same humiliation" ("Christian Faith and the Truthfulness of Bible History," in *The Princeton Defense of Plenary Verbal Inspiration*, ed. Mark A. Noll [New York: Garland Publishing, 1988], p. 190).

Afterword

IT IS in the nature of this volume that I have presented only the skeleton of an argument. Many more volumes would be required to put flesh on the bones of these past three chapters. My work here is intentionally programmatic, a theological prolegomenon. Given that it is my goal to persuade evangelicals to think theologically and to live theologically, in many ways this book is actually a prolegomenon to prolegomena. I have to convince you that prolegomena are important before you will commit yourselves to constructing or engaging them.

Modern evangelicals need to think of their own redemptive history more carefully. Too often we think of our faith solely in private and individualistic terms. Too often modernity is subconsciously reflected in our life and worship. Too seldom do we open the doors to inhale the clean sea breezes of the past.

We live in a age that is fascinated with the self, a culture that has taken the subjective turn. Evangelicals have too often reflected the subjectivism of the age and thereby undermined the objective work of God in the world in history. The testimony of evangelicals centers too frequently on what Jesus means to them and what the Holy Spirit is doing in our lives. We speak too little about what Jesus has accomplished in his own life and death, too little about the ways in which the Holy Spirit is connected to Jesus and to the furthering of his kingdom. We emphasize the one who has the faith rather the one who is the object of faith.

And, sadly, as evangelicals have too frequently reflected the subjectivism of the age, our theology has too frequently been abstracted from our age. Our doctrine is too distant from life, and we offer nothing but the barest justification of our doctrinal thinking. We call on theologians only to settle theological questions — the kinds of questions that are interesting to no one but theologians. And too often the only theological questions we consider to be important are the boundary questions, the issues that separate "us" from "them." In this way we inadvertently define the evangelical identity negatively (describing what evangelicals are not) rather than positively (speaking of where evangelicals have come from and where we are going). When theology becomes abstract in this way, it is removed from the community of faith and ceases to be transformative.

In an age of microwaves, fax machines, and personal computers, life seems to move very fast. Ironically, these same phenomena condemn us to nothing but a fascination with the present moment. We cannot think beyond tomorrow or back past yesterday. We nurture the illusion that we control time when in fact time controls us. The pace of modern life is stressful to the point that it threatens our existence. Most people find it emotionally and psychologically impossible to slow down. Time has become so domineering that we do not dare to "waste" it.

It is my contention that theology must transform our sense of time. Theology must help us to connect the past, present, and future and thereby connect us with the God who created us, sustains us, and will redeem us. It is this connectedness of time that evangelicalism desperately needs. Evangelicals are fragmented and live fragmented lives because we have cut ourselves off from time and the one who created time.

We must allow theology to transform not only our particular beliefs but our entire orientation in the world. We must allow it to tell anew the story of our collective history and provide the framework in which it makes sense. We must allow it to serve as the anchor that keeps us from drifting on the sea of change called modernity. We must allow it to establish our identity by establishing our place in redemptive history. In knowing the past, present, and future we will know ourselves anew. We will be reacquainted with the God who holds the past, present, and future together. The hope of the gospel is that we will spend eternity basking in the glory of God, forever and ever and ever. May our theological vision prepare us for that.

Bibliography

Alston, William. *Concepts of Justification.* Unpublished manuscript.

Bainton, Roland H. *Here I Stand: A Life of Martin Luther.* Nashville: Abingdon Press, 1950.

Baker, David L. *Two Testaments: One Bible.* Downers Grove, Ill.: InterVarsity Press, 1977.

Balmer, Randall. *Mine Eyes Have Seen the Glory.* New York: Oxford University Press, 1989.

Barr, James. *The Bible in the Modern World.* New York: Harper & Row, 1973.
————. *Semantics of Biblical Language.* London: Oxford University Press, 1961.

Bauer, Walter. *Orthodoxy and Heresy in Earliest Christianity.* Edited by Robert A. Kraft and Gerhard Krodel. Philadelphia: Fortress Press, 1971.

Baum, Guilielmus, et al., eds. *Corpus Reformatum: Ioannis Calvini Opera quae supersunt omnia.* 59 vols. Braunschweig: C. A. Schwetschke, 1863-1900.

Baumer, Franklin. *The History of Modern European Thought.* New York: Macmillan, 1977.

Bavinck, Herman. *The Doctrine of God.* Translated by William Hendriksen. Grand Rapids: William B. Eerdmans, 1951.

Beale, G. K. "Did Jesus and His Followers Preach the Right Doctrine from the Wrong Text? An Examination of the Presuppositions of Jesus' and the Apostles' Exegetical Method." *Themelios* 14 (April 1989): 89-96.

Beardslee, John W., ed. and trans. *Reformed Dogmatics: Wollebius, Voetius, and Turretin.* London: Oxford University Press, 1965.

Bebbington, D. W. *Evangelicalism in Modern Britain: A History from the 1730s to the 1980s.* London: Unwin Hyman, 1989.

Bellah, Robert, et al. *Habits of the Heart: Individualism and Commitment in*

American Life. Berkeley and Los Angeles: University of California Press, 1985.

Berger, Peter. *The Heretical Imperative.* Garden City, N.Y.: Doubleday-Anchor, 1979.

——. *The Noise of Solemn Assemblies.* Garden City, N.Y.: Doubleday, 1961.

——. *A Rumor of Angels: Modern Society and the Rediscovery of the Supernatural.* Garden City, N.Y.: Doubleday, 1969.

——. *The Sacred Canopy: Elements of a Sociological Theory of Religion.* Garden City, N.Y.: Doubleday, 1967.

——, Brigitte Berger, and Hansfried Kellner. *The Homeless Mind: Modernization and Consciousness.* New York: Random House, 1974.

Berkhof, Louis. *Principles of Biblical Interpretation.* Grand Rapids: Baker Book House, 1950.

——. *Systematic Theology.* 2 vols. Grand Rapids: William B. Eerdmans, 1938.

Berkouwer, G. C. *The Second Vatican Council and the New Catholicism.* Translated by Lewis B. Smedes. Grand Rapids: William B. Eerdmans, 1965.

——. *Studies in Dogmatics.* 14 vols. Grand Rapids: William B. Eerdmans, 1952-1961.

Bledstein, Burton J. *The Culture of Professionalism: The Middle Class and the Development of Higher Education in America.* New York: W. W. Norton, 1976.

Blocher, Henri. *In The Beginning: The Opening Chapters of Genesis.* Translated by David G. Preston. Downers Grove, Ill.: InterVarsity Press, 1984.

Bloesch, Donald. *Essentials of Evangelical Theology.* San Francisco: Harper & Row, 1978.

Bloom, Allan. *The Closing of the American Mind: Education and the Crisis of Reason.* New York: Simon & Schuster, 1987.

Boff, Clodovis. *Theology and Praxis: Epistemological Foundations.* Maryknoll, N.Y.: Orbis Press, 1987.

Bonino, José Míguez. *Doing Theology in a Revolutionary Context.* Philadelphia: Westminster Press, 1975.

Boughton, Lynne Courter. "Supralapsarianism and the Role of Metaphysics in Sixteenth-Century Reformed Theology." *Westminster Theological Journal* 58 (Spring 1986): 63-96.

Bouwsma, William J. *John Calvin: A Sixteenth-Century Portrait.* New York: Oxford University Press, 1988.

——. "Renaissance and Reformation: An Essay in Their Affinities and Connections." In *Luther and the Dawn of the Modern Era: Papers for the*

Fourth International Congress for Luther Research, ed. Heiko A. Oberman, 127-49. Leiden: E. J. Brill, 1974.

Bray, Gerald. *Creeds, Councils and Christ.* Downers Grove, Ill.: InterVarsity Press, 1984.

————. "Theology in the Church: Unity and Diversity in Christian Theology." In *The Challenge of Evangelical Theology: Essays in Approach and Method.* Edited by Nigel M. de S. Cameron, 58-81. Edinburgh: Rutherford House, 1987.

Breen, Quirinus. "John Calvin and the Rhetorical Tradition." *Church History* 26 (1957): 3-21.

Brown, Colin. *Miracles and the Critical Mind.* Grand Rapids: William B. Eerdmans, 1984.

Bultmann, Rudolf. "Ursprung und Sinn der Typologie als hermeneutische Methode." *Theologische Literaturzeitung* 75 (1950): 206-11.

Cadbury, H. J. *The Peril of Modernizing Jesus.* London: SPCK, 1962.

Calvin, John. *Institutes of the Christian Religion.* Library of Christian Classics, vols. 20-21. Translated by Ford Lewis Battles. Edited by John T. McNeill. Philadelphia: Westminster Press, 1960.

————. *Second Defence of the Godly and Orthodox Faith concerning the Sacraments against the False Accusations of Joachim Westphal.*

Campbell, Alexander. *The Christian Baptist,* April 3, 1826.

Carpenter, Joel A. "Contending for the Faith Once Delivered: Primitivist Impulses in American Fundamentalism." In *The American Quest for the Primitive Church,* ed. Richard T. Hughes, 99-119. Urbana, Ill.: University of Illinois Press, 1988.

Carson, D. A. "Unity and Diversity in the New Testament: The Possibility of Systematic Theology." In *Scripture and Truth,* ed. D. A. Carson and John Woodbridge, 65-95. Grand Rapids: Zondervan, 1983.

Chadwick, Owen. *From Bossuet to Newman: The Idea of Doctrinal Development.* London: Cambridge University Press, 1957.

————. *The Reformation.* London: Pelican Books, 1972.

————. *The Secularization of the European Mind in the Nineteenth Century.* Cambridge: Cambridge University Press, 1975.

Childs, Brevard. *The New Testament as Canon: An Introduction.* Philadelphia: Fortress Press, 1985.

Chisholm, Roderick. *The Problem of the Criteria.* Milwaukee: Marquette University Press, 1974.

————. *Theory of Knowledge.* 2d ed. Englewood Cliffs, N.J.: Prentice Hall, 1973.

Clowney, Edmund. "The Biblical Theology of the Church." In *Biblical Interpretation and the Church: Text and Context*, ed. D. A. Carson, 13-87. Exeter: Paternoster Press, 1984.

————. *Preaching and Biblical Theology.* Grand Rapids: William B. Eerdmans, 1961.

————. *The Unfolding Mystery: Discovering Christ in the Old Testament.* Colorado Springs: Navpress, 1988.

Cobb, John B., Jr. *Christ in a Pluralistic Age.* Philadelphia: Westminster Press, 1975.

————. *Is It Too Late? A Theology of Ecology.* Milwaukee: Bruce Publications, 1971.

————, and David Ray Griffin, *Process Theology: An Introductory Treatment.* Philadelphia: Westminster Press, 1976.

Cone, James. *For My People: Black Theology and the Black Church.* Maryknoll, N.Y.: Orbis Books, 1984.

Copleston, Frederick J. *A History of Philosophy.* Vols. 4-6. Garden City, N.Y.: Doubleday, 1985.

Cox, Harvey. *Religion in the Secular City: Toward a Post-Modern Theology.* New York: Simon & Schuster, 1984.

————. *The Secular City: Secularization and Urbanization in Theological Perspective.* New York: Macmillan, 1965.

Cullmann, Oscar. *Salvation in History.* Translated by Sidney G. Sowers. New York: Harper & Row, 1967.

Cupitt, Don. *Taking Leave of God.* London: SCM Press, 1980.

Daly, Mary. *Beyond God the Father: Toward a Philosophy of Women's Liberation.* Boston: Beacon Press, 1973.

Davidson, Donald. "On the Very Idea of a Conceptual Scheme." *Proceedings of the American Philosophical Association* (1974): 5-20.

Davidson, Richard M. *Typology in Scripture: A Study of Hermeneutical 'Tupoß' Structures.* Andrews University Doctoral Dissertation Series, no. 2 (Berrien Springs, Mich.: Andrews University Press, 1981.

Davis, John Jefferson. *Foundations of Evangelical Theology.* Grand Rapids: Baker Book House, 1984.

Delattre, Roland Andre. "Beauty and Theology: A Reappraisal of Jonathan Edwards." *Soundings* 51 (Spring 1968): 60-79. Reprinted in *Critical Essays on Jonathan Edwards,* ed. William J. Scheick, 136-50. Boston: G. K. Hall, 1980.

Demarest, Bruce, and Gordon Lewis, *Integrative Theology.* Grand Rapids: Zondervan, 1987.

Dennison, James T. "A Bibliography of the Writings of Geerhardus Vos, 1862-1949." *Westminster Theological Journal* 38 (Spring 1976): 350-67.

Donnelly, John Patrick. "Italian Influences in the Development of Calvinist Scholasticism." *Sixteenth Century Journal* 7 (1976): 81-101.

Dorner, I. A. *History of Protestant Theology.* Translated by George Robson and Sophia Taylor. 1871. Reprint. New York: AMS Press, 1970.

Dwight, Sereno E. *The Life of President Edwards.* New York: N.p., 1830.

Dyrness, William. "How Does the Bible Function in the Christian Life?" In *The Use of the Bible in Theology: Evangelical Options,* ed. Robert K. Johnston, 159-74. Atlanta: John Knox Press, 1985.

Ebeling, Gerhard. *Introduction to a Theological Theory of Language.* London: Collins, 1963.

————. *Luther: An Introduction to His Thought.* Translated by R. A. Wilson. Philadelphia: Fortress Press, 1970.

Edwards, Jonathan. *God Glorified in the Work of Redemption, by the Greatness of Man's Dependence upon Him in the Whole of It.* Boston: S. Kneeland and T. Green, 1731.

————. *The Works of Jonathan Edwards.* Vol. 2, *Religious Affections,* ed. John E. Smith. New Haven: Yale University Press, 1959.

————. *The Works of Jonathan Edwards.* Vol. 4, *The Great Awakening,* ed. C. C. Goen. New Haven: Yale University Press, 1972.

————. *The Works of Jonathan Edwards.* Vol. 9, *A History of the Work of Redemption,* ed. John F. Wilson. New Haven: Yale University Press, 1989.

Ellis, E. Earle. *Prophecy and Hermeneutic in Early Christianity: New Testament Essays.* Grand Rapids: William B. Eerdmans, 1978.

Ellul, Jacques. *The Technological Society.* New York: Alfred A. Knopf, 1964.

Erickson, Millard. *Christian Theology.* 3 vols. Grand Rapids: Baker Book House, 1983-85.

Erikson, Erik. *Young Man Luther: A Study in Psychoanalysis and History.* New York: W. W. Norton, 1958.

Evans, Gillian R., Alister E. McGrath, and Allan D. Galloway. *The History of Christian Theology.* Vol. 1, *The Science of Theology,* ed. Paul Avis. Grand Rapids: William B. Eerdmans, 1986.

Fackre, Gabriel. *The Christian Story: A Pastoral Systematics.* 2 vols. Grand Rapids: William B. Eerdmans, 1984, 1987.

————. "Narrative Theology: An Overview." *Interpretation* 37 (Fall 1983): 340-52.

————. "The State of Systematics: Research and Commentary." Presidential address, American Theological Society, 12 April 1991. Reprinted in *Dialog* 31 (Winter 1992): 54-61.

————. "The Use of Scripture in My Work in Systematics." In *The Use of the Bible in Theology: Evangelical Options.* Edited by Robert K. Johnston, 200-226. Atlanta: John Knox Press, 1985.

Falwell, Jerry. *The Fundamentalist Phenomena: The Resurgence of Conservative Christianity.* Garden City, N.Y.: Doubleday, 1981.

Farley, Edward. *Ecclesial Reflection: An Anatomy of Theological Method.* Philadelphia: Fortress Press, 1982.

————. *The Fragility of Knowledge: Theological Education in the Church and the University.* Philadelphia: Fortress Press, 1988.

————, and Peter C. Hodgson. "Scripture and Tradition." In *Christian Theology: An Introduction to Its Traditions and Tasks.* 2d ed. Edited by Peter C. Hodgson and Robert H. King, 61-87. Philadelphia: Fortress Press, 1985.

Farley, Wendy. *Tragic Vision and Divine Compassion: A Contemporary Theodicy.* Louisville: John Knox/Westminster Press, 1990.

Faust, Clarence F., and Thomas H. Johnson, eds. *Jonathan Edwards: Representative Selections, with Introduction, Bibliography, and Notes.* Revised edition. New York: Hill & Wang, 1962.

Fee, Gordon, and Douglas Stuart. *How to Read the Bible for All Its Worth.* Grand Rapids: Zondervan, 1982.

Feinberg, John, ed. *Continuity and Discontinuity: Perspectives on the Relationship between the Old and New Testaments.* Westchester, Ill.: Crossway Publishers, 1988.

Feuerbach, Ludwig. *The Essence of Christianity.* 1841. Reprint. New York: Harper, 1957.

Feyerabend, Paul. *Against Method: Outline of an Anarchist Theory of Knowledge.* New York: Schocken Books, 1978.

Finger, Thomas. *Christian Theology: An Eschatological Approach.* Nashville: Thomas Nelson, 1985.

Finney, Charles Grandison. *Lectures on Revivals of Religion.* Cambridge: Harvard University Press, 1960.

————. *Memoirs of Rev. Charles G. Finney.* New York: A. S. Barnes, 1876.

Fiorenza, Elisabeth Schüssler. *In Memory of Her: A Feminist Theological Reconstruction of Christian Origins.* New York: Crossroad, 1983.

Foucault, Michel. *The Order of Things: An Archaeology of the Human Sciences.* New York: Vintage Books, 1973.

Foulkes, Francis. *The Acts of God: A Study of the Basis of Typology in the Old Testament.* London: Tyndale Press, 1940.

Frame, John. *The Doctrine of the Knowledge of God.* Phillipsburg, N.J.: Presbyterian & Reformed, 1987.

Frank, Douglas W. *Less Than Conquerors: How Evangelicals Entered the Twentieth Century.* Grand Rapids: William B. Eerdmans, 1986.

Frei, Hans. *The Eclipse of Biblical Narrative: A Study of Eighteenth and Nineteenth Century Hermeneutics.* New Haven: Yale University Press, 1974.

Fuller, Daniel. "Biblical Theology and the Analogy of Faith." In *Unity and Diversity in New Testament Theology: Essays in Honor of George E. Ladd,* ed. Robert Guelich, 195-213. Grand Rapids: William B. Eerdmans, 1978.

The Fundamentals: A Testimony to Truth. 12 vols. Chicago: Privately published, 1910-1915.

Gadamer, Hans-Georg. *Truth and Method.* New York: Crossroad, 1975.

Gaffin, Richard B., Jr. *The Centrality of the Resurrection: A Study in Paul's Soteriology.* Grand Rapids: Baker Book House, 1978.

————. "Geerhardus Vos and the Interpretation of Paul." In *Jerusalem and Athens: Critical Discussions on the Theology and Apologetics of Cornelius Van Til,* ed. E. R. Geehan, 228-37. Nutley, N.J.: Presbyterian & Reformed, 1971.

————. "Introductory Essay." In *Redemptive History and Biblical Interpretation: The Shorter Writings of Geerhardus Vos,* ed. Richard B. Gaffin, Jr., ix-xxiii. Philipsburg, Pa.: Presbyterian & Reformed, 1980.

————. "Systematic Theology and Biblical Theology." *Westminster Theological Journal* 38 (1975-1976): 284-99.

————. "Theonomy and Eschatology: Reflections on Postmillennialism." In *Theonomy: A Reformed Critique,* ed. William S. Barker and W. Robert Godfrey, 197-224. Grand Rapids: Zondervan, 1990.

Galileo. *The Assayer.* 1623.

Geisler, Norman. *Inerrancy.* Grand Rapids: Zondervan, 1979.

George, Timothy. *The Theology of the Reformers.* Nashville: Broadman Press, 1988.

Gerrish, Brian A. *Grace and Reason: A Study in the Theology of Luther.* Oxford: Oxford University Press, 1962.

————. "John Calvin on Luther." In *Interpreters of Luther: Essays in Honor of Wilhelm Pauck,* ed. Jaroslav Pelikan, 67-96. Philadelphia: Fortress Press, 1968.

————. *Tradition and the Modern World: Reformed Theology in the Nineteenth Century.* Chicago: University of Chicago Press, 1978.

Gilkey, Langdon. "Theology for a Time of Troubles." In *Theologians in Transition*, ed. James Wall. New York: Crossroad, 1981.

Goppelt, Leonhard. *Typos: The Typological Interpretation of the Old Testament in the New*. Translated by D. H. Madvig. Grand Rapids: William B. Eerdmans, 1982.

Gordon, T. David. "The Hidden Assumptions of Small Group Bible Study." Unpublished manuscript.

————. "Old and New School Christianity." Unpublished manuscript.

Griffin, David Ray. *God and Religion in the Postmodern World: Essays in Postmodern Theology*. Albany: State University of New York Press, 1989.

————. "Introduction: Varieties of Postmodern Theology." In *Varieties of Postmodern Theology*, ed. David Ray Griffin, William A. Beardslee, and Joe Holland, 1-7. Albany: State University of New York Press, 1989.

————. "Postmodern Theology and A/Theology: A Response to Mark C. Taylor." In *Varieties of Postmodern Theology*, ed. David Ray Griffin, William A. Beardslee, and Joe Holland, 29-61. Albany: State University of New York Press, 1989.

Grislis, E. "Calvin's Use of Cicero in the Institutes I:1-5: A Case Study in Theological Method." *Archiv für Reformationsgeschichte* 62 (1971): 5-37.

Guinness, Os. *The American Hour: A Time of Reckoning and the Once and Future Role of Faith*. New York: Free Press, 1993.

Gutiérrez, Gustavo. *A Theology of Liberation*. Maryknoll, N.Y.: Orbis Books, 1973.

Habermas, Jürgen. *Knowledge and Human Interests*. Boston: Beacon Press, 1968.

Hafeman, Scott. *Paul and Moses*. Tübingen: J. C. B. Mohr, forthcoming.

————. "Seminary, Subjectivity and the Centrality of Scripture: Reflections on the Current Crisis in Evangelical Seminary Education." *Journal of the Evangelical Theological Society* 32 (1989): 129-43.

Hall, Basil. "Calvin against the Calvinists." In *John Calvin*, ed. Gervase Duffield, 19-37. Grand Rapids: William B. Eerdmans, 1966.

Handy, Robert. *A Christian America*. New York: Oxford University Press, 1971.

Harrington, Daniel J. "The Reception of Walter Bauer's *Orthodoxy and Heresy in Earliest Christianity* during the Last Decade." *Harvard Theological Review* 77 (1980): 289-98.

Hatch, Nathan O. *The Democratization of American Christianity*. New Haven: Yale University Press, 1989.

————. "Evangelicalism as a Democratic Movement." In *Evangelicalism and Modern America*, ed. George Marsden, 71-82. Grand Rapids: William B. Eerdmans, 1984.

————. "Sola Scriptura and Novus Ordo Seclorum," in *The Bible in America,* ed. Nathan O. Hatch and Mark A. Noll, 59-78. New York: Oxford University Press, 1982.

————, Mark A. Noll, and George Marsden, *The Search for Christian America.* Westchester, Ill.: Crossway Books, 1983.

Hauerwas, Stanley, and L. Gregory Jones, eds. *Why Narrative? Readings in Narrative Theology.* Grand Rapids: William B. Eerdmans, 1989.

Hick, John. *God Has Many Names.* London: Macmillan, 1980.

————. "Jesus and the World's Religions." In *The Myth of God Incarnate,* ed. John Hick, 167-85. London: SCM Press, 1977.

————. "Pluralism and the Reality of the Transcendent." In *Theologians in Transition,* ed. James M. Wall, 60-66. New York: Crossroad, 1981.

————, ed. *The Myth of God Incarnate.* London: SCM Press, 1977.

Hodge, A. A. *The Life of Charles Hodge.* New York: Scribner's, 1880.

Hodge, Charles. *Systematic Theology.* Vol. 1. 1872. Reprint. Grand Rapids: William B. Eerdmans, 1946.

Hofstadter, Richard. *Anti-Intellectualism in American Life.* New York: Alfred A. Knopf, 1963.

Hooykaas, R. *Religion and the Rise of Modern Science.* Grand Rapids: William B. Eerdmans, 1972.

Hughes, Richard, ed. *The American Quest for the Primitive Church.* Chicago: University of Illinois Press, 1988.

Hunter, James Davison. *American Evangelicalism: Conservative Religion and the Quandary of Modernity.* New Brunswick, N.J.: Rutgers University Press, 1983.

————. *Cultural Wars.* New York: Basic Books, 1992.

————. "The New Class and the Young Evangelicals." *Review of Religious Research* 22 (December 1980): 155-69.

Jensen, Robert W. *America's Theologian: A Recommendation of Jonathan Edwards.* New York: Oxford University Press, 1988.

Johnson, Elliot. *Expository Hermeneutics.* Grand Rapids: Zondervan, 1990.

Johnston, Robert K., ed. *The Use of the Bible in Theology: Evangelical Options.* Atlanta: John Knox Press, 1985.

Kant, Immanuel. *Religion within the Limits of Reason Alone.* New York: Harper Torchbooks, 1960.

Kaufman, Gordon. *An Essay on Theological Method.* Missoula, Mont.: Scholars Press, 1979.

————. *The Theological Imagination: Constructing the Concept of God.* Philadelphia: Westminster Press, 1981.

Kelly, J. N. D. *Early Christian Creeds.* 3d ed. New York: D. McKay, 1972.

————. *Early Christian Doctrines.* New York: Harper & Row, 1978.

Kelsey, David. *To Understand God Truly: What's Theological about a Theological School.* Louisville: Westminster/John Knox, 1992.

————. *The Uses of Scripture in Recent Theology.* Philadelphia: Fortress Press, 1975.

Kennedy, James. *Evangelism Explosion.* Wheaton, Ill.: Tyndale House, 1977.

Kent, John S. *The End of the Line: The Development of Christian Theology in the Last Two Centuries.* Philadelphia: Fortress Press, 1982.

Kermode, Frank. *The Genesis of Secrecy.* Cambridge: Harvard University Press, 1979.

Kimnack, Wilson. "The Literary Techniques of Jonathan Edwards." Ph.D. diss., University of Pennsylvania, 1971.

King, Robert H. "The Task of Theology." In *Christian Theology: An Introduction to Its Traditions and Tasks,* 2d ed., ed. Peter C. Hodgson and Robert H. King, 1-27. Philadelphia: Fortress Press, 1985.

Kirk, Andrew. *Liberation Theology: An Evangelical View from the Third World.* Atlanta: John Knox Press, 1979.

Kline, Meredith G. *By Oath Consigned: A Reinterpretation of the Covenant Signs of Circumcision and Baptism.* Grand Rapids: William B. Eerdmans, 1968.

————. *Images of the Spirit.* Grand Rapids: Baker Book House, 1980.

————. *Kingdom Prologue.* South Hamilton, Mass.: Meredith G. Kline, 1988.

————. *The Structure of Biblical Authority.* Grand Rapids: William B. Eerdmans, 1975.

Koester, Helmut. "Gnomai Diaphorai: The Origin and Nature of Diversification in the History of Early Christianity." In *Trajectories through Early Christianity,* ed. James M. Robinson and Helmut Koester, 114-57. Philadelphia: Fortress Press, 1971.

Kraft, Charles. *Christianity in Culture: A Study in Dynamic Biblical Theologizing in Cross-Cultural Perspective.* Maryknoll, N.Y.: Orbis Books, 1979.

Kuhn, Thomas. *The Essential Tension.* Chicago: University of Chicago Press, 1977.

————. *The Structure of Scientific Revolutions.* Chicago: University of Chicago Press, 1962.

Kuklick, Bruce. *Churchmen and Philosophers: From Jonathan Edwards to John Dewey.* New Haven: Yale University Press, 1985.

Kuyper, Abraham. *Principles of Sacred Theology.* Translated by J. Hendrik DeVries. Grand Rapids: William B. Eerdmans, 1954.

Ladd, George E. *A Theology of the New Testament.* Grand Rapids: William B. Eerdmans, 1974.

Lakatos, Imre, and Alan Musgrave, eds. *Criticism and the Growth of Knowledge.* Cambridge: Cambridge University Press, 1970.

Lasch, Christopher. *The True and Only Heaven: Progress and Its Critics.* New York: W. W. Norton, 1991.

Lewis, C. S. *The Weight of Glory and Other Addresses.* Edited by Walter Hooper. New York: Macmillan, 1980.

Lindbeck, George A. "The Church's Mission to a Postmodern Culture." In *Postmodern Theology: Christian Faith in a Pluralist World,* ed. Frederic B. Burnham, 37-55. San Francisco: Harper & Row, 1989.

————. *The Nature of Doctrine: Religion and Theology in a Postliberal Age.* Philadelphia: Westminster Press, 1984.

————. "Scripture, Consensus, and Community." In *Biblical Interpretation in Crisis: The Ratzinger Conference on Bible and Church,* ed. Richard John Neuhaus, 74-101. Grand Rapids: William B. Eerdmans, 1989.

Lints, Richard. "Irresistibility, Epistemic Warrant and Religious Belief," *Religious Studies* 25 (December 1989): 425-33.

————. "Two Theologies or One? Warfield and Vos on the Nature of Theology." *Westminster Theological Journal* 54 (Fall 1992): 235-53.

————, ed. *Options in Evangelical Apologetics.* Grand Rapids: Zondervan, forthcoming.

Loewenich, Walther von. *Martin Luther: The Man and His Work.* Minneapolis: Augsburg, 1986.

Luther, Martin. *Luther's Works.* 55 vols. Edited by Jaroslav Pelikan, Helmut T. Lehmann, et al. St. Louis: Concordia and Philadelphia: Fortress Press, 1955- .

McComiskey, Thomas. *The Covenants of Promise.* Grand Rapids: Baker Book House, 1985.

McFague, Sallie. "An Epilogue: The Christian Paradigm." In *Christian Theology: An Introduction to Its Traditions and Tasks.* 2d ed., ed. Peter C. Hodgson and Robert H. King, 377-90. Philadelphia: Fortress Press, 1985.

McGiffert, A. C. *Protestant Thought before Kant.* New York: Harper Torchbooks, 1961.

McGrath, Alister E. *Reformation Thought: An Introduction.* Oxford: Basil Blackwell, 1988.

————. "Reformation to Enlightenment." In *The History of Christian Theology.* Vol. 1, *The Science of Theology,* ed. Paul Avis, 125-31. Grand Rapids: William B. Eerdmans, 1986.

Machen, J. Gresham. *Christianity and Liberalism.* New York: Macmillan, 1923.

Mackinnon, D. M. "Theology as a Discipline of the University." In *The Rules of the Game: Cross-Disciplinary Essays on Models in Scholarly Thought,* ed. Teodor Shanin, 162-74. London: Tavistock Publications, 1972.

McKnight, Edgar V. *The Postmodern Use of the Bible: The Emergence of Reader-Oriented Criticism.* Nashville: Abingdon Press, 1988.

McLoughlin, W. G. "Introduction." In *Lectures on Revivals of Religion,* by Charles Grandison Finney, vii-lii. Cambridge: Harvard University Press, 1960.

————. *Modern Revivalism: Charles Grandison Finney to Billy Graham.* New York: Ronald Press, 1959.

Maier, Gerhard. *The End of the Historical-Critical Method.* St. Louis: Concordia, 1974.

Marsden, George. "The Collapse of American Evangelical Academia." In *Faith and Rationality: Reason and Belief in God,* ed. Alvin Plantinga and Nicholas Wolterstorff, 219-64. Notre Dame, Ind.: University of Notre Dame Press, 1983.

————. "The Evangelical Denomination." In *Evangelicalism and Modern America,* ed. George Marsden, vii-xix. Grand Rapids: William B. Eerdmans, 1984.

————. *The Evangelical Mind and the New School Presbyterian Experience.* New Haven: Yale University Press, 1970.

————. "Evangelicalism in the Sociological Laboratory." *Reformed Journal,* June 1984, 20-24.

————. "Everyone One's Own Interpreter? The Bible, Science and Authority in Mid-Nineteenth-Century America." In *The Bible in America,* ed. Nathan O. Hatch and Mark A. Noll, 79-100. New York: Oxford University Press, 1984.

————. *Fundamentalism and American Culture: The Shaping of Twentieth-Century Evangelicalism, 1870-1925.* New York: Oxford University Press, 1980.

————. "Reformed and American." In *Reformed Theology in America: A History of Its Modern Development,* ed. David F. Wells, 1-14. Grand Rapids: William B. Eerdmans, 1985.

————. *Religion and American Culture.* New York: Harcourt Brace Jovanovich, 1989.

————, and Bradley Longfield, eds. *The Secularization of the Academy.* New York: Oxford University Press, 1992.

Marshall, I. Howard. "Orthodoxy and Heresy in Earlier Christianity." *Themelios* 2 (1976-1977): 5-14.

Marty, Martin E. "The Clergy." In *The Professions in American History,* ed. Nathan O. Hatch, 73-91. Notre Dame, Ind.: University of Notre Dame Press, 1988.

————. "Introduction: How Their Minds Have Changed." In *Theologians in Transition,* ed. James Wall, 1-18. New York: Crossroad, 1981.

————. "The Revival of Evangelicalism and Southern Religion." In *Varieties of Southern Evangelicalism,* ed. David Edwin Harrell, Jr. Macon: Mercer University Press, 1981.

May, Henry F. *The Enlightenment in America.* New York: Oxford University Press, 1976.

————. "Jonathan Edwards and America." In *Jonathan Edwards and the American Experience,* ed. Nathan O. Hatch and Harry S. Stout, 19-33. New York: Oxford University Press, 1988.

Meuther, John. "Contemporary Evangelicalism and the Triumph of the New School." *Westminster Theological Journal* 50 (1988): 339-47.

Miller, Perry. *Jonathan Edwards.* New York: W. Sloane, 1949.

Moeller, Bernd. "Piety in Germany around 1500." In *The Reformation in Medieval Perspective,* ed. Steven E. Ozment, 50-75. Chicago: University of Chicago Press, 1971.

Morris, Thomas V. *The Logic of God Incarnate.* Ithaca, N.Y.: Cornell University Press, 1986.

————. "Rationality and the Christian Revelation." In *Christian Faith and Practice in the Modern World,* ed. Mark A. Noll and David F. Wells, 119-38. Grand Rapids: William B. Eerdmans, 1988.

Muller, Richard. *Post-Reformation Reformed Dogmatics.* Vol. 1, *Theological Prolegomena.* Grand Rapids: Baker Book House, 1987.

————. "Scholasticism Protestant and Catholic: Francis Turretin on the Object and Principles of Theology." *Church History* 55 (June 1986): 193-205.

————. "Vera Philosophia cum sacra Theologia nusquam pugnat: Keckermann on Philosophy, Theology and the Problem of Double Truth." *Sixteenth Century Journal* 15 (1984): 343-65.

Murray, Iain. *Jonathan Edwards.* Edinburgh: Banner of Truth Trust, 1987.

Murray, John. "Systematic Theology." In *The Collected Writings of John Murray,* vol. 4, 1-21. Edinburgh: Banner of Truth Trust, 1982.

Myers, Ken. *All God's Children and Blue Suede Shoes: Christians and Popular Culture.* Westchester, Ill.: Crossway Books, 1989.

Neuhaus, Richard John. *The Naked Public Square: Religion and Democracy in America.* Grand Rapids: William B. Eerdmans, 1984.

Neville, Robert. *The Tao and the Daimon: Segments of Religious Inquiry.* Albany: State University of New York Press, 1982.

Newbigin, Leslie. *Foolishness to the Greeks: The Gospel and Western Culture.* Grand Rapids: William B. Eerdmans, 1986.

————. *Truth to Tell: The Gospel as Public Truth.* Grand Rapids: William B. Eerdmans, 1991.

Newman, John Henry. *An Essay on the Development of Christian Doctrine.* 1845.

Nicholls, Bruce. "Towards a Theology of Gospel and Culture." In *Down to Earth: Studies in Christianity and Culture,* ed. Robert T. Coote and John R. W. Stott, 49-62. Grand Rapids: William B. Eerdmans, 1980.

Nisbet, Robert. *The History of the Idea of Progress.* New York: Basic Books, 1980.

Noll, Mark A. *Between Faith and Criticism: Evangelicals, Scholarship and the Bible in America.* San Francisco: Harper & Row, 1986.

————. "Jonathan Edwards and Nineteenth-Century Theology." In *Jonathan Edwards and the American Experience,* ed. Nathan O. Hatch and Harry S. Stout, 260-87. New York: Oxford University Press, 1988.

————, ed. *The Princeton Theology, 1812-1921: Scripture, Science, and Theological Method from Archibald Alexander to Benjamin Warfield.* Grand Rapids: Baker Book House, 1983.

————, Nathan O. Hatch, and George Marsden. *The Search for Christian America.* Westchester, Ill.: Crossway Books, 1983.

Oden, Thomas. *After Modernity, What? Agenda for Theology.* Grand Rapids: Zondervan, 1990.

Ogden, Schubert M. *On Theology.* San Francisco: Harper & Row, 1986.

————. *The Reality of God, and Other Essays.* New York: Harper & Row, 1966.

Otto, Rudolf. *The Idea of the Holy.* New York: Oxford University Press, 1923.

Packer, J. I. "Biblical Authority, Hermeneutics, and Inerrancy." In *Jerusalem and Athens: Critical Discussions on the Theology and Apologetics of Cornelius Van Til,* ed. E. R. Geehan. Nutley, N.J.: Presbyterian & Reformed, 1971.

————. "Infallible Scripture and the Role of Hermeneutics." In *Scripture and Truth,* ed. D. A. Carson and John Woodbridge, 325-56. Grand Rapids: Zondervan, 1983.

Padilla, C. René. "Hermeneutics and Culture—A Theological Perspective." In *Down to Earth: Studies in Christianity and Culture,* ed. Robert T. Coote and John R. W. Stott, 63-78. Grand Rapids: William B. Eerdmans, 1980.

Paglia, Camille. *Sexual Personae: Art and Decadence from Nefertiti to Emily Dickinson.* New York: Random House, 1989.

Paley, William. *Lectures on Natural Theology.* 1802. Reprint. Houston: St. Thomas Press, 1972.

Parker, T. H. L. *The Oracles of God: An Introduction to the Preaching of John Calvin.* London: Lutterworth Press, 1947.

Pelikan, Jaroslav. *Historical Theology: Continuity and Change in Christian Doctrine.* New York: Corpus, 1971.

Pinnock, Clark. *Biblical Revelation.* Chicago: Moody Press, 1971.

—————. "How I Use the Bible in Doing Theology." In *The Use of the Bible in Theology: Evangelical Options,* ed. Robert K. Johnston, 18-34. Atlanta: John Knox Press, 1985.

—————. *Tracking the Maze: Finding Our Way through Modern Theology from an Evangelical Perspective.* New York: Harper & Row, 1990.

Piper, John. *Desiring God.* Portland: Multnomah Press, 1987.

Placher, W. C. *Unapologetic Theology: A Christian Voice in a Pluralistic Conversation.* Philadelphia: Westminster Press, 1989.

Plantinga, Alvin. "Advice to Christian Philosophers." *Faith and Philosophy* 1 (July 1984): 253-71.

—————. *Does God Have a Nature?* Milwaukee: Marquette University Press, 1978.

—————. "Reason and Belief in God." In *Faith and Rationality: Reason and Belief in God,* ed. Alvin Plantinga and Nicholas Wolterstorff, 16-93. Notre Dame, Ind.: University of Notre Dame Press, 1986.

—————, and J. Wesley Robbins. "On Christian Philosophy." *Journal of the American Academy of Religion* 57 (Fall 1989): 617-24.

Polanus, Amandus. *Syntagma theologiae christianae.* 1609.

Postman, Neil. *Amusing Ourselves to Death: Public Discourse in the Age of Show Business.* New York: Viking Press, 1985.

Pratt, Richard. *He Gave Us Stories.* Brentwood, Tenn.: Wolgemuth & Hyatt, 1990.

Preus, Robert D. *The Theology of Post-Reformation Lutheranism.* 2 vols. St. Louis: Concordia, 1970.

Quebedeaux, Richard. *The Young Evangelicals.* New York: Harper & Row, 1974.

Quine, Willard van Orman. "Two Dogmas of Empiricism." In *From a Logical Point of View: Nine Logico-Philosophical Essays,* 20-46. Cambridge: Harvard University Press, 1953.

—————, and Joseph S. Ullian. *The Web of Belief.* New York: Random House, 1970.

Ridderbos, Herman, and Richard B. Gaffin, Jr. *Redemptive History and the New Testament Scriptures.* Translated by H. De Jongste and Richard B. Gaffin, Jr. Phillipsburg, N.J.: Presbyterian & Reformed, 1988.

Rieff, Philip. *The Triumph of the Therapeutic: Uses of Faith after Freud.* New York: Harper & Row, 1966.

Robertson, O. Palmer. *The Christ of the Covenants.* Grand Rapids: Baker Book House, 1980.

————. "The Outlook for Biblical Theology." In *Toward a Theology for the Future,* ed. David F. Wells and Clark Pinnock, 65-91. Carol Stream, Ill.: Creation House, 1971.

Rogers, Jack, and Donald K. McKim, *The Authority and Interpretation of the Bible: An Historical Approach.* New York: Harper & Row, 1979.

Rogers, Jack, ed. *Biblical Authority.* Waco, Tex.: Word Books, 1978.

Rogerson, John, Christopher Rowland, and Barnabas Lindars. *The History of Christian Theology.* Vol. 2, *The Study and Use of the Bible,* ed. Paul Avis. Grand Rapids: William B. Eerdmans, 1988.

Rolston, Holmes III. *John Calvin versus the Westminster Confession.* Richmond: John Knox Press, 1972.

Rorty, Richard. *The Consequences of Pragmatism (Essays: 1972-1980).* Minneapolis: University of Minnesota Press, 1982.

————, ed. *The Linguistic Turn: Recent Essays in Philosophic Method.* Chicago: University of Chicago Press, 1967.

————. *Philosophy and the Mirror of Nature.* Princeton: Princeton University Press, 1979.

Ruether, Rosemary Radford. *New Woman — New Earth: Sexist Ideologies and Human Liberation.* New York: Crossroad, 1975.

————. *Sexism and God-Talk: Toward a Feminist Theology.* Boston: Beacon Press, 1983.

Sandeen, Ernest R. *The Origins of Fundamentalism: Toward a Historical Interpretation.* Philadelphia: Fortress Press, 1968.

————. *The Roots of Fundamentalism: British and American Millenarianism, 1800-1930.* Chicago: University of Chicago Press, 1970.

Sanders, E. P. *Paul and Palestinian Judaism.* London: SCM Press, 1977.

————. *Paul, the Law and the Jewish People.* Philadelphia: Fortress Press, 1982.

Scheick, William J. "The Grand Design: Jonathan Edwards' *History of the Work of Redemption.*" In *Critical Essays on Jonathan Edwards,* ed. William J. Scheick, 177-88. Boston: G. K. Hall, 1980.

Schneiders, Sandra M. "Does the Bible Have a Postmodern Message?" In

Postmodern Theology: Christian Faith in a Pluralist World, ed. Frederick Burnham, 56-73. New York: Harper & Row, 1989.

Schweitzer, Albert. *The Quest of the Historical Jesus.* London: A. & C. Black, 1910.

Sell, Alan P. F. *Theology in Turmoil: The Roots, Course and Significance of the Conservative Liberal Debate in Modern Theology.* Grand Rapids: Baker Book House, 1986.

Sellars, Wilfred. *Science, Perception and Reality.* London: Routledge & Kegan Paul, 1963.

Sizer, Sandra S. *Gospel Hymns and Social Religion: The Rhetoric of Nineteenth Century Revivalism.* Philadelphia: Temple University Press, 1978.

Sowell, Thomas. *A Conflict of Visions: Ideological Origins of Political Struggles.* New York: William Morrow, 1987.

Steinmetz, David. "The Superiority of Pre-critical Exegesis," *Theology Today* 37 (April 1980): 27-38.

Stonehouse, Ned B., Jr. *J. Gresham Machen: A Memoir.* Grand Rapids: William B. Eerdmans, 1954.

Stott, John R. W., and Robert Coote, eds. *Down to Earth: Studies in Christianity and Culture.* Grand Rapids: William B. Eerdmans, 1980.

Stout, Harry S. *The New England Soul: Preaching and Religious Culture in Colonial New England.* New York: Oxford University Press, 1986.

Stout, Jeffrey. *The Flight from Authority: Religion, Morality and the Quest for Autonomy.* Notre Dame, Ind.: University of Notre Dame Press, 1981.

Strong, Augustus Hopkins. *Systematic Theology: A Compendium and Commonplace-Book Designed for the Use of Theological Students.* Rochester, N.Y.: E. R. Andrews, 1886.

Stronstad, Roger. *The Charismatic Theology of St. Luke.* Peabody, Mass.: Hendrickson, 1984.

Sutphin, Stanley T. *Options in Contemporary Theology.* Lanham, Md.: University Press of America, 1987.

Sweet, Leonard. "The Evangelical Tradition in America." In *The Evangelical Tradition in America*, ed. Leonard Sweet, 1-86. Macon: Mercer University Press, 1984.

Sykes, Steven W. "Theological Study: The Nineteenth Century and After." In *The Philosophical Frontiers of Christian Theology*, ed. Brian Hebblewaite and Stewart Sutherland, 95-118. Cambridge: Cambridge University Press, 1982.

Tanner, Kathryn. "Theology and the Plain Sense." In *Scriptural Authority and Narrative Interpretation*, ed. Garret Gree, 59-78. Philadelphia: Fortress Press, 1987.

Taylor, Mark C. *Deconstructing Theology.* New York: Crossroad, 1982.

———. *Erring: A Postmodern A/Theology.* Chicago: University of Chicago Press, 1984.

Temple, Frederick. *The Relations between Religion and Science.* London: Macmillan, 1884.

Tolbert, Mary Ann. "Defining the Problem: The Bible and Feminist Hermeneutics." *Semeia* 28 (1983): 113-26.

Toon, Peter. *The Development of Doctrine in the Church.* Grand Rapids: William B. Eerdmans, 1979.

Tracy, David. *The Analogical Imagination: Christian Theology and the Culture of Pluralism.* New York: Crossroad, 1981.

———. *Blessed Rage for Order: The New Pluralism in Theology.* New York: Seabury Press, 1975.

———. "On Naming the Present." In *Concilium* 1 (1990): *On the Threshold of the Third Millennium,* ed. Philip Hillyer, 66-85. London: SCM Press, 1990.

———. "Theological Method." In *Christian Theology: An Introduction to Its Traditions and Tasks.* 2d ed., ed. Peter C. Hodgson and Robert H. King. Philadelphia: Fortress Press, 1985.

Tracy, Patricia. *Jonathan Edwards, Pastor.* New York: Hill & Wang, 1980.

Turner, James. *Without God, without Creed: The Origins of Unbelief in America.* Baltimore: The Johns Hopkins University Press, 1985.

Turretin, Francis. *Francis Turretin on Scripture.* Baker Book House, 1985.

Van Hoozer, Kevin. "The Semantics of Biblical Literature." In *Hermeneutics, Authority and Canon,* ed. D. A. Carson and John Woodbridge, 53-104. Grand Rapids: Zondervan, 1986.

Vesey, Laurence. *The Emergence of the American University.* Chicago: University of Chicago Press, 1965.

Vos, Geerhardus. *Biblical Theology.* Grand Rapids: William B. Eerdmans, 1948.

———. *The Mosaic Origin of the Pentateuchal Codes.* London: Longmans, 1886.

———. *The Pauline Eschatology.* 1930. Reprint. Grand Rapids: Baker Book House, 1979.

———. *Redemptive History and Biblical Interpretation: The Shorter Writings of Geerhardus Vos.* Edited by Richard B. Gaffin, Jr. Phillipsburg, N.J.: Presbyterian & Reformed, 1980.

Wacker, Grant. "Playing for Keeps: The Primitivist Impulse in Early Pentecostalism." In *The American Quest for the Primitive Church,* ed. Richard T. Hughes, 196-219. Urbana, Ill.: University of Illinois Press, 1988.

Wainwright, William. "Jonathan Edwards and the Sense of the Heart." *Faith and Philosophy* 7 (January 1990): 43-62.

Warfield, Benjamin B. *Calvin and Augustine*. Philadelphia: Presbyterian & Reformed, 1956.

—————. *Calvin and Calvinism*. New York: Oxford University Press, 1931.

—————. "Dr. Hodge as a Teacher of Exegesis." In *The Life of Charles Hodge*, by A. A. Hodge, 588-91. New York: Scribner's, 1880.

—————. "The Idea of Systematic Theology." In *Studies in Theology*, 49-87. New York: Oxford University Press, 1932.

—————. "The Resurrection of Christ: A Fundamental Doctrine." *Homiletic Review* 32 (1896): 291-98.

—————. "The Task and Method of Systematic Theology." In *Studies in Theology*, 91-105. New York: Oxford University Press, 1932.

Webber, Robert. *Common Roots: A Call to Evangelical Maturity*. Grand Rapids: Zondervan, 1978.

—————. *Evangelicals on the Canterbury Trail*. Waco, Tex.: Word Books, 1985.

Weber, Otto. *Foundations of Dogmatics*. 2 vols. Translated by Darrell L. Guder. Grand Rapids: William B. Eerdmans, 1981-1982.

Wells, David F. "An American Evangelical Theology: The Painful Transition from *Theoria* to *Praxis*." In *Evangelicalism and Modern America,* ed. George Marsden, 83-93. Grand Rapids: William B. Eerdmans, 1984.

—————. "Charles Hodge." In *Reformed Theology in America,* ed. David F. Wells, 36-59. Grand Rapids: William B. Eerdmans, 1986.

—————. "The Nature and Function of Theology." In *The Use of the Bible in Theology: Evangelical Options,* ed. Robert K. Johnston, 175-99. Atlanta: John Knox Press, 1985.

—————. *No Place for Truth; or, Whatever Happened to Evangelical Theology*. Grand Rapids: William B. Eerdmans, 1993.

—————. *Search for Salvation*. Downers Grove, Ill.: InterVarsity Press, 1978.

—————. "The Theologian's Craft." In *Doing Theology in Today's World: Essays in Honor of Kenneth S. Kantzer,* ed. Thomas E. McComiskey and John D. Woodbridge, 193-94. Grand Rapids: Zondervan, 1991.

—————. "Theology in Culture: The Fragmenting Vision." Unpublished manuscript.

—————. "Tradition: A Meeting Place for Catholic and Evangelical Theology?" *Christian Scholar's Review* 5 (1975): 50-61.

—————, ed. *Reformed Theology in America: A History of Its Modern Development*. Grand Rapids: William B. Eerdmans, 1985.

Wendel, François. *Calvin: The Origins and Development of His Religious Thought.*
    Translated by Philip Mairet. Durham, N.C.: Labyrinth Press, 1987.

White, Andrew D. *A History of the Warfare of Science and Theology in Christen-
    dom.* New York: D. Appleton, 1896.

Williams, Bernard. *Problems of the Self.* Cambridge: Cambridge University
    Press, 1973.

Williams, J. Rodman. *Renewal Theology.* 3 vols. Grand Rapids: Zondervan,
    1988-1992.

Wilmore, Gayraud, and James Cone. *Black Theology: A Documentary History.*
    Maryknoll, N.Y.: Orbis Books, 1979.

Wittgenstein, Ludwig. *Culture and Value.* Oxford: Basil Blackwell, 1980.

————. *Philosophical Investigations.* New York: Macmillan, 1953.

————. *Tractatus Logico-Philosophicus.* Translated by D. F. Pears and B. F.
    McGuinness. London: Routledge & Kegan Paul, 1974.

Wolterstorff, Nicholas. "Can Belief in God Be Rational If It Has No Foun-
    dations?" In *Faith and Rationality: Reason and Belief in God,* ed. Alvin
    Plantinga and Nicholas Wolterstorff, 135-86. Notre Dame, Ind.: Uni-
    versity of Notre Dame Press, 1986.

————. "The Migration of Theistic Arguments: From Natural Theology to
    Evidentialist Apologetics." In *Rationality, Religious Belief, and Moral Commit-
    ment: New Essays in the Philosophy of Religion,* ed. Robert Audi and William J.
    Wainwright, 38-81. Ithaca, N.Y.: Cornell University Press, 1986.

————. *Reason within the Bounds of Religion.* 2d ed. Grand Rapids: William B.
    Eerdmans, 1984.

————. "Thomas Reid on Rationality." In *Rationality in the Calvinian Tradi-
    tion,* ed. Hendrik Hart, Johan Van der Hoeven, and Nicholas Wolter-
    storff, 43-69. Washington: University Press of America, 1983.

Wood, A. Skevington. *Captive to the Word: Martin Luther, Doctor of Sacred
    Scripture.* Grand Rapids: William B. Eerdmans, 1969.

Wood, Charles M. *The Formation of Christian Understanding: An Essay in Theo-
    logical Hermeneutics.* Philadelphia: Westminster Press, 1981.

Woodbridge, John. *Biblical Authority: A Critique of the Rogers and McKim Proposal.*
    Grand Rapids: Zondervan, 1982.

Wuthnow, Robert. *The Struggle for America's Soul: Evangelicals, Liberals, and
    Secularism.* Grand Rapids: William B. Eerdmans, 1989.

Index

357